D0217112

ONONDAGA
COMMUNITY COLLEGE

Liberty on the Waterfront

EARLY AMERICAN STUDIES

Daniel K. Richter and Kathleen M. Brown, Series Editors

Exploring neglected aspects of our colonial, revolutionary, and early national history and culture, Early American Studies reinterprets familiar themes and events in fresh ways. Interdisciplinary in character, and with a special emphasis on the period from about 1600 to 1850, the series is published in partnership with the McNeil Center for Early American Studies.

A complete list of books in the series is available from the publisher.

Liberty on the Waterfront

American Maritime Culture in the Age of Revolution

Paul A. Gilje

UNIVERSITY OF PENNSYLVANIA PRESS
Philadelphia

Printed in the United States of America on acid-free paper

10 9 8 7 6 5 4 3 2 1

Published by
University of Pennsylvania Press
Philadelphia, Pennsylvania 19104-4011

Library of Congress Cataloging-in-Publication Data

Gilje, Paul A., 1951–
Liberty on the waterfront : American maritime culture in the Age of Revolution / Paul A. Gilje.
p. cm. — (Early American studies)
Includes bibliographical references (p.) and index.
ISBN 0-8122-3756-0 (alk. paper)
1. United States. Navy—History—18th century. 2. United States. Navy—History—19th century. 3. Sailors—United States—History—18th century. 4. Sailors—United States—History—19th century. 5. Seafaring life—United States—History—18th century. 6. Seafaring life—United States—History—19th century. 7. United States—History, Naval—18th century. 8. United States—History, Naval—19th century.
E182.G55 2003 2003062756
305.9'3875'097309033 22

To Ann

All that is told of the sea has a fabulous sound to an inhabitant of the land, and all its products have a certain fabulous quality, as if they belonged to another planet, from sea-weed to a sailor's yarn, or fish-story.

Henry David Thoreau, *Cape Cod*

We must come down from our heights, and leave our straight paths, for the byways and low places in life, if we would learn the truths by strong contrasts; and in hovels, in forecastles, and among our own outcasts in foreign lands, see what has been wrought upon our fellow-creatures by accident, hardship, or vice.

Richard Henry Dana, *Two Years Before the Mast*

Contents

Preface

Few words are more central to understanding the American past than "liberty." But few words have been more contested and ambiguous. Nonetheless, the Founding Fathers believed that the purpose of government was to ensure each man his liberty through protection of the individual and his property. In exchange, each individual had to concede a certain amount of his own liberty to government. Liberty could be endangered in two ways. First, if government amassed too much power, the people could lose their liberty. In 1776 revolutionary leaders argued that King George III and Parliament were guilty of this type of usurpation and that their rule threatened to lead to tyranny. But liberty could also be challenged from below through excess and licentiousness. Granting too much liberty could lead to a world where everyone pursued their own interests regardless of the rights of others, a situation which was akin to savagery. The leaders of the Revolution therefore sought a middle ground between tyranny and anarchy.

"Liberty" also came to epitomize the American cause. Slogans like "Sons of Liberty," "the Liberty Tree" or "give me liberty or give me death" have come down to us as the very essence of the American Revolution. During the years of the early republic the concept of liberty became deeply embedded in American culture, associated with the concepts of equality, civil rights, and the protection of property. Americans turned to their sacred documents of nationhood—the Declaration of Independence and the Constitution of the United States—and, conflating the two, proclaimed that they guaranteed American liberty.

We know a great deal about the ideology of the leaders of the American Revolution and how they sought to protect liberty. We also know that Americans have become transfixed by the word "liberty." But what did those further down in society—such as sailors—think about liberty? How did they apply this word to their everyday lives? And, how did they react to the reification of "liberty" in the years after independence as the phrase became so central to national identity?

This book examines the meaning of "liberty" to those who lived and worked in ports and aboard ships. The people of the waterfront themselves used the word "liberty" in several ways. Sometimes they referred to the higher ideals of the age, but often they referred to a more immediate and individual liberty that seemed to embrace the very "unlimited indulgence of appetite," as one revolutionary put it, that the Founding Fathers believed threatened to lead to anarchy. If liberty ashore allowed men to misbehave and pursue sensual bliss regardless of its impact on others, liberty at sea often released sailors from shoreside attachments and provided a geographical mobility unimagined by most of their landbound cousins. My aim has been to examine liberty—and its many costs—in all of its varied meanings for those who lived on the waterfront in the Age of Revolution. I acknowledge the concept of liberty as a moment of license as a self-evident truth for the waterfront world and as a foil against which we can measure the more rarified definitions of men like Thomas Jefferson. The Age of Revolution may have created a new society that cherished the word "liberty" and the ideal of equality, but the great democratic transformation affected those who lived and worked on the waterfront to a varying and usually lesser extent.

My starting point is the sailor's own understanding of liberty both ashore and afloat in an American maritime culture that remained largely the same from 1750 to 1850. Fine distinctions can be made between decades, between regions and ports, between types of shipboard labor, between work on ship and shore, between experiences of fishermen, whalemen, merchantmen, and men-of-war. My aim, however, particularly in Part I, has been to emphasize a larger unified American maritime culture, rather than focus on differences. After all, seamen sailed from ports around the United States and all over the world, and sailors shifted their berths among vessel types with uncommon ease. The same man might work on the waterfront one day only to ship out the next.

Despite the continuity of much of the maritime experience, the Age of Revolution was important to the people on the waterfront; the great revolutionary currents churning the Atlantic in the eighteenth and nineteenth centuries both had a profound impact upon, and in turn were affected by, the common folk of the maritime community. The people of the waterfront played a central role in the revolutionary conflict, first as the shock troops in the mobs of the resistance movement from 1765 to 1775, and then as combatants at sea. This participation infused the revolution with an egalitarianism it might otherwise not have had. Sailors could seize upon the rhetoric of the revolution to argue for their own rights. But they were also survivors in an age of great upheaval. Jack Tar's commitment to the American cause, in typical ambiguous sailor fashion, often owed less to ideological motivations than pragmatic personal interests.

The various meanings of liberty on the waterfront persisted into the years of the early republic. Throughout the 1790s and early 1800s, American trade expanded, creatiing increased opportunity for the people on the waterfront and placing many sailors in jeopardy from Barbary pirates, and the warring French and British. This development helped to identify the sailor's liberty with American liberty and Jack Tar became emblematic of our nationhood during this period. The War of 1812 was the consummation of this trend, as the maritime community thought that the war was fought to protect its rights.

After the war the waterfront still could not be fully incorporated into the American republic. Christian missionaries inspired by the Second Great Awakening sought to remake the waterfront in their own middle-class image, with limited success. In literature, Herman Melville, Richard Henry Dana, Jr., James Fenimore Cooper, and others portrayed the sailor as an embodiment of the democratic man. At the same time the efforts of living and breathing sailors to bring the benefits of the Age of Revolution home to the waterfront—in the form of organized labor—were largely frustrated.

Liberty on the waterfront appealed to me for many reasons. Rather than writing on brief dramatic episodes in the lives of the participants—as I did in my previous study of rioting, upon which this book builds—I wanted to focus on one group of laborers who had played a central role in popular disorder. Beyond the explosive moment of tumult, I wanted to follow real people into the workplace and into their everyday experience. Although the record contains mainly partial stories and anonymous characters, gradually I have pieced together enough material to portray maritime culture and tell stories about people who might otherwise be overlooked and almost invisible in our histories.

In contrast to the scenarios presented by other historians, maritime society as I see it during this period was not a proletariat ready to assert class consciousness. Nor could I identify a group of would-be embattled patriots responsible for founding a nation. Many sailors I encountered in diaries, letters, and memoirs often fit the stereotype of drinking, misbehaving, and living for the moment. Many others did not, and their perspectives are equally valid and valuable. Throughout I have tried to provide a balanced portrait of life at sea and ashore, and to recount the stories of men and women who survived events they could not fully understand.

Regardless of the attempted reform and the books on the common seamen, and even regardless of the articulation of revolutionary ideals coming from the waterfront itself, much of the maritime world continued relatively unchanged and seamen remained an exploited work force with little political voice. From the period before the first hail of the Sons of Neptune to the age of Melville, "liberty" retained many of its ambiguous and contested meanings on the waterfront.

PART I
ASHORE AND AFLOAT

1

The Sweets of Liberty

Horace Lane first went to sea when he was ten years old. By the time he was sixteen he had been pressed into the British Navy, escaped, traveled to the West Indies several times, and witnessed savage racial warfare on the island of Hispaniola. Although he experienced many of the perils of a sailor in the Age of Revolution, he avoided the wild debauchery of the stereotypical sailor ashore. In 1804, after a particularly dangerous voyage smuggling arms and ammunition to blacks in Haiti, his rough-and-tumble shipmates from the *Sampson* cruised the bars, taverns, and grog shops of the New York waterfront. One night a shipmate took him to the scene of the revelry. Lane remembered that "after turning a few corners, I found myself within the sound of cheerful music." As they approached the door, Lane hesitated. His companion shamed him into entering by declaring "What . . . You going to be a sailor, and afraid to go into a dance-house! Oh, you cowardly puke! Come along! What are you standing there for, grinning like a sick monkey on a lee backstay!" Lane could not handle the rebuke. Gathering himself, he mustered enough spunk to enter. No sooner had he crossed the threshold than he was met with "a thick fog of putrified gas, that had been thoroughly through the process of respiration, and seemed glad to make its escape." The room was packed with the humanity of both sexes and several races. In one corner loomed a huge black man "sweating and sawing away on a violin; his head, feet, and whole body, were in all sorts of motions at the same time." Next to him was a "tall swarthy female, who was rattling and flourishing a tamboarine with uncommon skill and dexterity." A half dozen other blacks occupied the middle of the floor, "jumping about, twisting and screwing their joints and ankles as if to scour the floor with their feet." Everywhere people shouted, "Hurrah for the *Sampson*!" Among the crowd some were swearing, "some fighting, some singing; some of the soft-hearted females were crying, and others reeling and staggering about the room, with their shoulders naked, and

1. While on liberty in a port, sailors spent money freely on liquor. Notice the woman in the window, probably a prostitute, and the black man in the background walking in front of the oyster and clam shop. "Sailors Ashore." From Hawser Martingdale, *Tales of the Ocean* . . . (Boston, 1840). New Bedford Whaling Museum.

their hair flying in all directions." Lane was horrified and beat a hasty retreat, proclaiming "Ah! . . . Is this the recreation of sailors? Let me rather tie a stone to my neck, and jump from the end of the wharf, than associate with such company as this!"[1]

A few more years, and many more adventures at sea, led to a change of heart. Lane recounts his conversion to hard living. He had agreed to deliver a letter to a young woman who worked at "French Johnny's," a notorious dance hall on George Street in New York. As he worked his way through the crowd outside, he approached the door blocked by a chain and a guard. After paying the cover charge, Lane stepped into "a spacious room, illuminated with glittering chandeliers hanging in the centre, and lamps all around." He was awestruck. "Never was there a greater invention contrived to captivate the mind of a young novice." Three musicians sat on their high seats and there were "about fourteen . . . damsels, tipped off in fine style, whose sycophantic glances and winning smiles were calculated only to attract attention from such as had little wit, and draw money from their pockets." Lane admitted that he "was just the man" and declared, "This was felicity indeed." Lane bought some hot punch, finding that after a while it tasted good. He summarized the rest of the experience in verse:

So I spent my money while it lasted,
Among this idle, gaudy train;
When fair Elysian hopes were blasted,
I shipp'd to sail the swelling main.[2]

Horace Lane offers us a wonderful view of liberty ashore. He allows us to follow him into the sailor's haunts by evoking a powerful sense of the sounds, sights, and even smells that enticed many young men into a particular mode of life. At first repulsed by the depths to which he sees his comrades of the *Sampson* have fallen, marked by the racial mixture of the waterfront dive, he is seduced by the light of chandeliers and damsels "tipped off in fine style" at French Johnny's. Lane's saga goes downhill from there, leading to a round of drunken debauchery and criminality, interspersed with adventures spread across the seven seas. Ultimately his is a tale of redemption that condemned the depravity that seemed to accompany liberty ashore.

Others viewed the sailor's liberty differently. Richard Henry Dana, Jr., and Herman Melville knew a great deal about the sea, both having served in the forecastle—where common seamen slept—in the nineteenth century. Dana wrote that "a sailor's liberty is but for a day; yet while it lasts it is perfect." The tar thus experienced an exuberance of liberty that was denied most others. Released from shipboard discipline, Dana asserted that he was "under no one's eye, and can do whatever, and go wherever, he pleases." Of his own initial "liberty" Dana exclaimed, "this day, for the first time, I may truly say, in my whole life, I felt the meaning of a term which I had often heard—the sweets of liberty."[3] Melville, in his own sardonic style, reiterated this point and captured the spirit of a world turned upside down when he declared that "all their lives lords may live in listless state; but give the commoners a holiday, and they out-lord the Commodore himself."[4]

Implicit in the views of both Dana and Melville is a political meaning of the word "liberty" that appears to belie the experience of Horace Lane. For Dana, the sailor's liberty gave him a sense of personal freedom, a release from restraints that bound his life at sea. Melville, whose work speaks more directly to the American democratic soul, has an understanding based on the collective experience of liberty. The sailor's holiday liberates not only the individual, but also the group, and enables the commoners to rule triumphant even if only momentarily. Lane, in contrast, bemoans the liberty ashore, viewing it as both a trap and a release that in many ways defined his very essence as a sailor. Lane sees this liberty as one component of the life of Jack Tar.

To understand the world of the waterfront, we must take a careful look at the sailor's liberty ashore, exploring the widely held image of the jolly tar. Sailors were not a proletariat in the making, nor were they a peculiar brand of patriot. They were real people who often struggled merely to survive. Sailors were a numerous and diverse body of people who shared a common identity. The great variety of men who comprised the waterfront and shipboard workforce, and the fact that many sailors did not fit the stereotype, will be the focus of this chapter.

At sea the sailor worked hard. His life was one of regulation from above and dangers all around. Ashore there was a sudden release. He could drink, curse, carouse, fight, spend money, and generally misbehave. For the sailor ashore there was no future, only the here and now. Although this image was not flattering, sailors were also often described as generous and tenderhearted. More important, the stereotypical sailor represented a culture and value system that challenged the dominant ideals of both the eighteenth and nineteenth centuries. Not only did the sailor ashore reject the traditional hierarchy of pre-revolutionary society, but his behavior represented the antithesis of the rising bourgeois values that became the hallmark of the Age of Revolution. Whether consciously or not, sailors played a role that had profound implications for the waterfront community and workers throughout society.

Drinking was a central part of the sailor's liberty ashore. Minister Andrew Brown's sermon in the 1790s on the dangers of the seafaring life focused as much on intemperance on land as on the perils of the deep. He cautioned that "the spirit of prodigality and wastefulness," terms he used synonymously with drinking to excess, "has long been regarded as one of the distinguishing characteristics of the seafaring life." He believed also that drinking "has been sanctioned by custom, and is now almost converted into a professional habit."[5] Forty years later, the members of the New-Bedford Port Society recognized "the exuberant joy" a sailor experienced once he came ashore and his eagerness for drinking whetted by the relative abstinence at sea. The New-Bedford Port Society also acknowledged the social pressures felt by a tar, admitting that he drinks "in token of cordiality and good will," and that "he treats his acquaintance in sign of generosity, or to escape the imputation of meanness."[6] After a long voyage, as other sailors busied themselves with calculations of "airy castles," one man honestly admitted that he would get drunk as soon as he got ashore, declaring, "it is the only pleasure he has in the world, and when he is pretty well in for it, he is as happy as any man in it."[7] The centrality of drinking to both the image and the reality of the sailor can be seen in popular depictions. Infused with a spirit of patriotism, and perhaps recognizing that sailors enjoyed the stage, creators of theatrical performances in the 1790s often included songs and portrayals of the American tar. In *Songs of the Purse* sailor Will Steady sings:

When seated with Sall, all my mesmates around,
Fal de ral de ral de ri do!
The glasses shall gingle, the joke shall go round;
With a bumper! then here's to ye boy,
Come lass a buss, my cargoe's joy.
Here Tom be merry, drink about,
If the sea was grog we'd see it out.[8]

Several songs and sea chanteys celebrated the sailor's drinking ashore.[9] In "Whiskey," the men proclaimed:

Oh, whiskey is the life of man.
Oh, whiskey, Johnny!

2. Jack Tar took great pride in his dress and his ability to dance and show off. This interior of a tavern has men drinking, a dancing sailor, a black man playing the fiddle, and several women with low-cut dresses in a scene similar to the ones described by Horace Lane. "Sailor's Sword Dance." From Hawser Martingdale, *Tales of the Ocean . . .* (Boston, 1840). New Bedford Whaling Museum.

It always was since time began,
Oh, whiskey for my Johnny!

The nineteenth-century chantey, sung while dragging ropes to hoist upper topsails, goes on to praise whiskey even though

Oh whiskey made me wear old clothes
And whiskey gave me a broken nose

Oh, whiskey caused me much abuse,
And whiskey put me in the calaboose.

The final stanza calls for a round of grog for every man, "And a bottle full for the chanteyman."[10] The self-mocking good cheer that underpins this chantey can also be seen in "The Drunken Sailor." The tars ask, "what shall we do with a drunken sailor?" only to answer, "Chuck him in the longboat till he gets sober."[11] As Samuel Leech, veteran of thirty years at sea put it, seamen viewed drinking as "the *acme* of sensual bliss."[12]

Along with excessive drinking, the sailor set himself apart by his language. The waterfront had its own peculiar argot. James Fenimore Cooper's sea novels depict the common seaman's idiom, but Cooper never could offer his reader the sailor's real language—curse, followed by curse, followed by curse.[13] Samuel Leech proclaimed that sailors "fancy swearing and drinking" were "necessary accomplishments of a genuine man-of-wars-man."[14] In a sermon offered especially for fishermen in Beverly, Massachusetts, before the spring run of 1804, Reverend Joseph Emerson urged them to trust in God, observe the Sabbath, and avoid swearing. As he stood before the weatherworn faces of the fishermen, he acknowledged that he understood how hard it was for sailors not to use strong oaths.[15] Common seamen prided themselves in swearing. Simeon Crowell admitted that as a young man about twenty in 1796 he took up bad language while in a fishing schooner off the Grand Banks. By the following year, his cursing had become so elaborate that he thought he might have shocked even some of the old salts with his "wicked conversation." He also had "learned many carnal songs with which" he "diverted the crew at times." Unfortunately, he did not copy any of these songs into his commonplace book. He did, however, offer a poem, "The Sailor's Folly," which he wrote in Charleston, South Carolina, on February 13, 1801:

When first the sailor comes on Board
He dams all hands at every word

He thinks to make himself a man
At Every word he gives a dam

But O how shameful must it be
To Sin at Such a great Degree
When he is out of Harbour gone
He swears by god from night to morn

But when the Heavy gale doth Blow
The Ship is tosled to and froe
He crys for Mercy Mercy Lord
Help me now O help me God

But when the storm is gone and past
He swears again in heavy Blast
And still goes on from Sin to Sin
Now owns the god that Rescued him[16]

Drinking and cursing ashore were a part of the general carousing that marked the sailor's life on the waterfront. One sailor looked back at his life and proudly pointed to his accomplishments at sea and ashore. Bill Mann had tremendous black whiskers and the "damn-my eyes" look of an old salt. Mann declared that he "had killed more whales, broken more girls' hearts, whipped more men, been drunk oftener, and pushed his way through more perils, frolics, pleasures, pains, and general vicissitudes of fortune than any man in the known world."[17] Such a sailor was supposedly hell-bent to live it up while ashore. According to J. Ross Browne, "a sailor let loose from a ship is no better than a wild man. He is free; he feels what it is to be free. For a little while, at least, he is no dog to be cursed and ordered about by a ruffianly master. It is like an escape from bondage."[18] George Jones described the experience of "liberty men" on an American warship in the Mediterranean in 1825: "They go; fall into all manner of dissipation; get drunk; are plundered; sell some of their clothes, for more drink; quarrel with the soldiers; come back with blackened eyes; cut all kinds of antics; become rude and noisy; are thrown into the brig; have the horrors, and then go about their work."[19]

Carousing frequently led to fighting. Often members of a crew, like Horace Lane's shipmates on the *Sampson*, bonded together, ready to take on all comers. Similarly in 1814, more than one hundred of Stephen Decatur's men from the frigate *President* were arrested after a fracas at a New York tavern. In this instance there were no serious injuries.[20] Other brawlers were not so lucky. In 1812 a group of drunken sailors attempted to gain entry into a New York dance hall but were excluded by the Portuguese owner, who claimed that he was having a private party. Insulted and outnumbered, the sailors left. On their way back to their waterfront boardinghouse, they met some shipmates. With that reinforcement they returned and tried to force their way in. The Portuguese came charging out, swinging their knives and killing one of the sailors. These conflicts occurred countless times in almost every port.[21]

One of the sailor's problems, leading to the drinking, carousing, and even some fighting, was that he often had money jingling in his pocket. After being paid off from a voyage a seamen might have a month's or as much as a year's wages at his fingertips. Even before the voyage, once he signed the articles of agreement, he was usually paid a month's wages. Most tars flouted mainstream values and asserted their liberty by spending that money—that chink—just as quickly as they could. Thomas Gerry, son of politician Elbridge Gerry, wrote home from aboard the frigate *Constellation* that money was "the *life* and *wife* of a sailor," but was "so scarce, that when we receive it the sum affords us no advantage and is offered to the God of *Pleasure* for want of a better berth."[22] Further down the social scale the attitude was much the same. On leave from a privateer in France in 1782, Ebenezer Fox spent money "with the improvidence characteristic of sailors."[23] Ned Myers declared, "As for money, my rule had come to be, to spend it as I got it, and go to sea for more."[24] Captured from an American privateer in 1776, cabin boy Christopher Hawkins found himself forced to serve aboard an English man-of-war for more than a year. Earning a full share of the prize money taken by the enemy of his country, Hawkins joined in the celebrating on a shore leave and quickly spent what he had earned. As Hawkins explained, the sailor's creed was "What I had I got, what I spent I saved, and what I kept I lost."[25] In a similar situation Joshua Penny, an American seaman pressed into the British navy, went on liberty in London sometime around 1800. Later he reminisced, "We went to London, with too much money not to loose a little. I had lived so long without the privilege of spending any thing, that I, too, was a gentleman while my money lasted." Penny concluded, "No man spends his money more to his own notion than a sailor."[26] Indeed, as they left port, superstitious old salts would toss coins they discovered in their pockets toward the dock to avoid bad luck.[27]

One positive trait of the spendthrift tar was his generosity. A sailor's song published in 1800 highlighted "honest Bill Bobstay," who sang like a mermaid and was "the forecastle's pride, the delight of the crew," but who remained as "poor as a beggar."

He went, tho' his fortune was kind without end.
For money, cried Bill, and them there sort of matters,
For money, cried Bill, and them there sort of matters,
What's the good on't, d'ye see, but to succoar a friend?

The song contrasted Bill with the purser named Nipcheese, known for his "grinding and squeezing" and plundering the crew.[28] Sailors often took pity on those less fortunate than themselves. Naval prisoners of war repeatedly raised collections for other mariners forced to serve the British during the Revolutionary War. Captain Charles Ridgley reported that after the survivors of the whaleship *Essex* arrived in Chile in 1821, having crossed thousands of miles of ocean in an open boat, the crew of the *Constellation* wanted to devote a month's salary to each of the survivors. Ridgely, however, knowing "that thoughtless liberality which is peculiar to seamen," limited the contribution of each man to one dollar.[29] Writing of his voyage to the Pacific on the American warship *Columbia* in the 1840s, Charles Nordhoff explained that "there is no more liberal-hearted fellow than a man-of-war's man. His greatest delight is to divide his little stock of worldly goods with some ill-furnished acquaintance." The sailor "would give away his last shirt and to an utter stranger, and feel happy as a king in doing so."[30] This generosity reflected many sailors' values. One marine serving with the navy in the opening decade of the nineteenth century, for instance, was repulsed by the acquisitive and self-aggrandizement values of Benjamin Franklin. After reading Franklin's autobiography, William Ray complained of "the parsimony of that lightening-tamer" in refusing to buy beer from his London landlady—a savings Franklin proudly highlights—because it disappointed "the woman in the trifling gains which she expected from him."[31]

Ray's criticism of Franklin suggests that, contrary to the experience of Horace Lane and closer to that of Dana and Melville, liberty ashore meant more than mere license. When sailors wore flamboyant clothes, drank, freely cursed, used their distinctive argot, bucked all authority, and engaged in brawls, they sent a message to the larger society. These seamen rejected two fundamental tenets of society, hierarchy in the eighteenth century and the acquisitive values of the middle class in the nineteenth century. The sailor on liberty ashore during the colonial and early national period was able to turn his back on the mainstream values and assert a type of freedom denied most landbound workers. The sailor's liberty represented a counterculture that had special attraction for the working class and for those on the margins of society; it included a strain of anti-authoritarianism that denied hierarchy ashore, and, in light of the emphasis on fraternity and brotherhood among shipmates, it contained a strong current of egalitarianism.[32]

The sailor's liberty enabled many seamen to avoid regular employment and encouraged disdain for the daily routine of land-based workers. Alfred Lorrain wrote that many sailors spoke with envy of farmers as they approached port, declaring that at least a farmer could be with his family in a storm. Resolves to stay on land and not "dip their feet in salt water" again, however, faded within weeks of coming ashore. Soon "the prettiest farm in the country could not hold them, as a general thing," and the call is "'Come boys—who's for blue water.'"[33] At one point in his maritime career Samuel Leech was apprenticed to a bootmaker in the hope of breaking from his "wicked mode of life." He dreaded "the confinement to the shoe-bench," however, which his "riotous fancy painted as being worse than a prison," and he rejoined his shipmates to engage in a life of "dissipation and folly."[34] John Elliott had a similar experience, finding "the shoemaker's seat did not furnish him that variety he had so long been accustomed to."[35] William Torrey "determined to abandon the seas" several times, only to find that on shore "time passed tediously."[36] Melville's Ishmael also had disdain for landsmen, who "of week days" were "pent up in lath and plaster—tied to counters, nailed to benches, clinched to desks."[37]

Locked into a world of authority and deference at sea, sailors enjoyed flaunting social barriers and relationships while at liberty on shore, where they could be "their own lords and masters, and at their own command." Sailors aped their social betters by playing at being gentlemen. Horse riding was "a favourite amusement with the son of Neptune," although few sailors displayed much horsemanship. As awkward as he might appear in the saddle, a seaman recognized that the horse had long been the prerogative of the rich and well born.[38] Many sailors also rented carriages as soon as they reached terra firma. To the landlubber the sight of a carriage reeling by with a couple of tars and a prostitute on either side may have appeared totally absurd; to the sailor it was the epitome of style.[39]

To assert a larger meaning for the sailor's acting the "gentleman" while ashore does not mean that the wild and excessive behavior reflected a specific consciousness. For most of the men on the waterfront their goals and gratification were more immediate and reflected simply a reaction to the world around them. And yet the sailor often consciously played up to his own stereotype. Boys learned the peculiar dockside values of the sailor from an early age. Ten-year-old Horace Lane and other young seamen on their first liberty in 1799 mimicked more seasoned sailors. Lane remembered that "monkey like, all that we heard or seen practiced by the sailors, we thought it becoming in us to say and do." Several of the older boys rented horses and a few carriages and took "each his fancy girl with him, to ride out and recreate at a tavern about three miles in the country." Seeing this, Lane went to the captain and asked him for some money. Then, with six dollars jingling in his pocket—more than a week's wage for an adult worker—he hired a horse and carriage and toured the countryside.[40] So ingrained were these values that sailors took liberty on the waterfront to be their right. As Philip Greggs recorded in 1788, once the brig *Eagle* touched the wharf in Philadelphia, he and the other crew members went ashore "agreeable to the Laws of Nations . . . in order to refresh themselves."[41]

Although the sailor's liberty allowed the sailor to enjoy excesses of personal freedom, seamen frequently lost their economic freedom. A sailor might enjoy a frolic, participate in rowdyism, and act the part of the jolly tar, yet he quickly spent the earnings from months and even years of labor. By using up his money the sailor left himself open to economic exploitation that curtailed his own freedom in the marketplace, and the freedom of all who lived and toiled on the waterfront. The fast and loose way of life pursued by many while on liberty led to difficulties in supporting a family and maintaining stable relationships. In all, life on the waterfront was often cruel and nasty.[42]

Despite a belief that he dictated the terms of his own labor, especially into the nineteenth century, the sailor often abdicated even this control over his life. Technically, and this process was stipulated by both British and American statutes, the sailor signed the articles of a ship of his own free will, agreeing to the conditions of employment and the rate of pay.[43] But the process of recruiting merchant sailors varied greatly throughout the revolutionary era, depending on circumstances, time, and location.

In the most basic manner of finding employment, the sailor, individually or as part of a group, had direct contact with the captain or shipowner and signed the ship's articles stipulating the conditions of employment. In 1762, Louis Pintard, New York merchant and owner of the *Catherine*, had the five-man crew sign the articles at his house. The men were recruited by either the second mate or one of Pintard's partners.[44] In 1809, William Peterson and several ex-shipmates in Philadelphia heard of a vessel in need of men. They went up to the captain and signed on together.[45] In this method, the sailor supposedly had the freedom to bargain for wages, although the labor market may already have set the basic wage. John Willcock walked along the New York docks in late 1783 or 1784 searching for a job. At one brig he was told that the captain wanted a hand, and while waiting for the captain, Willcock helped the crew to heave ballast. Work was scarce at the time, and when the captain appeared Willcock told him he would take whatever wages were offered. The captain assured him that he would not lose for not bargaining and allowed Willcock to join the crew.[46]

Recruiting could also be based on long-standing relationships. Around the turn of the nineteenth century in smaller ports, like Marblehead, Massachusetts, captains of fishing schooners recruited their crews locally from among men they knew and who knew each other.[47] In this situation relatives, friends, and neighbors formed tight-knit groups, relationships that occurred in merchant vessels as well. In 1762 the *Prosperous Polly,* out of Providence, Rhode Island, hired William Dunbar in Martinique. Dunbar, it turns out, was also from Providence and had known Captain Waterman for at least two years before he signed on. The crew list suggests that there were other connections on board. The carpenter's last name was also Waterman, and both the mate and the cabin boy shared the name Whipple. One sailor had been born in Ireland, had sailed out of Providence for at least two and a half years, and claimed to have know the captain for a somewhat longer period of time.[48] As a young man, Nicholas Isaacs fell in with a captain from Mystic, Connecticut, and relied on this gentleman for years afterward for employment.[49] In 1809, a friend of John Allen's family in Marblehead had an uncle in Portsmouth who needed a few more hands. Allen headed for the New Hampshire port, introduced himself to the captain, and signed on for the voyage.[50]

Parents and guardians sometimes made arrangements for a young man or boy. Simeon Crowell's stepfather insisted that the seventeen-year-old join a fishing schooner on the Grand Banks in 1795.[51] The mother of eleven-year-old Frederick Jordan signed him on the schooner *Mercy* in the Pocomoke River, Maryland, for a voyage to New York in 1774.[52] Earlier in the eighteenth century, John Fillmore chafed under his apprenticeship to a Boston carpenter. After many entreaties, his mother relented and allowed him to join a fishing vessel at age nineteen.[53] James Jenks's father signed him aboard the *Ocean* in the opening decade of the nineteenth century upon the promise that Captain Thomas Roach would rein in Jenks's wildness.[54] And in 1806 James Fenimore Cooper's friends and relatives interceded to make sure that his first voyage as a merchant seaman was relatively safe and under a good captain.[55]

3. This detail of a schooner near the Marblehead docks suggests the way the waterfront appeared in the second half of the eighteenth century. From Ashley Bowen Diary. Peabody Essex Museum.

Although these various forms of recruitment occurred between 1750 and 1850, personal connections may have been more important in the eighteenth than in the nineteenth century. Colonial American social relationships were based on deference and paternalism within a hierarchy. With the rising egalitarianism of the American Revolution, the concept of free labor spread. As commerce expanded and ports grew, the labor force became more anonymous. Since the employer-employee relationship did not depend on previous personal connections and would appear as strictly a business deal, the new labor context should have led to more independent contracts between the sailor and his employer. It did not. Instead, intermediaries like boardinghouse keepers became increasingly important in arranging work. Some boardinghouse keepers ran large establishments that could accommodate more than one hundred men, while others merely rented out space to two or three sailors from their sparse living quarters. Often they were ex-sailors themselves, or the wives of men at sea.[56]

During the eighteenth century these men and women loomed large in the lives of sailors both at sea and at port. In 1762, a Frenchman in Port-au-Prince wanting to maintain contact with his landlady gave a letter to a sailor going to New York to deliver to her.[57] Repeatedly, mariners who were suing for their wages in the 1770s and 1780s had innkeepers (the term "boarding-house keeper" does not appear frequently until after 1800) sign their bonds as surety in their court cases.[58] Assistance in wage disputes remained central to the boardinghouse keeper's relationship with sailors in the nineteenth century. Around 1800 young Nicholas Isaacs found himself stranded in New York, striving to get back wages. After a lawyer would not take the case, in stepped Mr. Spiliard, a boardinghouse keeper, who said he could get a settlement of $80 (Isaacs claimed he was owed $400). Spiliard was as good as his word, although he then presented Isaacs with a bill for $70.[59] Several years later, sailors from the ship *Union* gave Richard Jennings, who ran a New York boardinghouse, power of attorney to collect several hundred dollars in a court case involving an embargo violation.[60]

We know most about the boardinghouses during the nineteenth century, when they became the central clearinghouse for the hiring of seamen, and when they came under attack from reformers.[61] By the opening decade of the nineteenth century, boardinghouse keepers were very important to the waterfront in big ports like New York, Philadelphia, and Baltimore. The more sailors that were needed, the more central the boardinghouse became. Even in smaller, more specialized ports like Providence and New Bedford, the boardinghouse was crucial. In 1807, Captain Elijah Cobb visited sailor boardinghouses in Norfolk, Virginia, paid the advance to the landlords, and took their "obligations to see each sailor on board, at sun-rise."[62] The New-Bedford Port Society in 1831 reported that there were twenty-one boardinghouses in the whaling port, each serving between twenty and two hundred patrons. By 1845 there were at least thirty-seven boardinghouses serving hundreds of sailors.[63]

In the 1820s and 1830s reformers began to portray the boardinghouse keeper as a corrupting influence upon seamen. The relationship between the sailor and his landlord, however, was more complicated and subtle than the reformers thought. Some boardinghouse keepers were not exploitative and offered a sort of home away from home to the sailor. Nathaniel G. Robinson wrote his sister in 1843, describing his young widow boardinghouse keeper in sympathetic terms, proclaiming that she ran "a first rate boarding place" in New London. He made a point to tell his sister that the widow was a Methodist and lived with her mother and two young children.[64] Susan Gardner (Harose), who prided herself on the domestic and benign nature of her boardinghouse for American seamen in Le Havre, France, explained, "it is a great satisfaction to me to see all of these [sailors who had previously boarded with her] return the same as they would to a Mother's house."[65] The boardinghouse keeper passed on mail to friends and relatives.[66] Sometimes the landlord would act as a bank, holding onto money or possessions while the sailor went on a voyage. The boardinghouse keeper also might aid the tar, even if he had nothing in his pockets or if he fell sick. A shipwrecked Ned Myers hunted up his old Liverpool landlady, and as Myers reported, "the old woman helped me to some clothes, received me well, and seemed sorry for my misfortunes."[67] At the Providence Marine Hospital in 1840, one-fourth of all the sailors checked into the facility were brought there by one man, Jesse A. Healy, a boardinghouse keeper.[68]

Even the more unsavory landlords were providing, for a price, what seamen wanted. They greeted the sailor as he came ashore, took his baggage, and offered him lodgings, drink, and whatever other services he required. When the sailor's money ran out, they extended credit until they could arrange for the sailor to sign aboard his next voyage. When the sailor needed anything for his "kit," or sea chest, they provided it. When the sailor found himself in trouble with the law, they offered bail. While groggily getting his sea legs on his next voyage, many a sailor cursed his boardinghouse keeper as a landshark for taking him for all he was worth; but that sailor eagerly sought the same lodgings when he returned to port.[69]

Despite the large amount of money apparently passing through their hands, few boardinghouse keepers became very rich. George Gardner adamantly opposed his sister Susan's plan to open a boardinghouse after her sea captain husband died and she was stranded in Europe in 1825. Gardner wrote that it was "the last thing I should recommend" and argued that "it is a slavish business and very unprofitable." He also confided that he had stayed in many boardinghouses and had seen the "low discomforts" of the keepers, with many people leaving without paying their debts. From his perspective there were "Sundry Vexations incident to business."[70] With an advance from a friendly sea captain, Susan managed to succeed, even if she did not make a fortune. She wrote to her mother two years later that her establishment could accommodate about twenty men at a time. She had invested $2,000 in furniture, bedding, dishes, and other items, and paid $800 a year in rent. If the house were full she could clear four or five dollars a day over her expenses. With any luck she could earn $500 a year. The margin for error was slim. Most of her initial investment had been on credit. If forced to sell, she would be lucky to get half the value for the furniture and goods she bought and would be left with almost nothing.[71]

A sailor would probably stay with his own family if they lived nearby, but most sailors stopped in so many different ports, or had families at a great distance, that lodging in the boardinghouse became part of the identity of Jack Tar. Horace Lane proclaimed that to be a sailor in a port was to stay at a boardinghouse. Remaining in the cramped quarters of the forecastle was beneath a tar's sense of self-worth. Lane explained that as a young man, "I thought I was a sailor, and should disgrace myself if I did not do as the rest—viz. to go on shore to a boarding house as soon as a ship was made fast, and the sails furled."[72] This sense of identity with occupation and the boardinghouse led to distinctions between rank and race in some larger ports. John Remington Congdon, serving as second mate in 1840, went to a Liverpool boardinghouse that catered to men of similar rank. The men serving before the mast—common seamen—went to other boardinghouses, and the black cook went to yet another boardinghouse run by an interracial couple.[73] The boardinghouse and the landlord were thus prominent features of the waterfront community and crucial to the portrayal of the stereotypical Jack Tar.

Although boardinghouse keepers remained important in arranging work for sailors, by the 1830s and 1840s, specialized shipping agents opened offices in several cities and even sent runners into the countryside to recruit labor. These middlemen were particularly active in the whaling industry's search for cheap labor. In 1837 Jacob Hazen signed on with a shipping agent in Philadelphia, who sent him to an agent in New York, who in turn arranged for Hazen to join a whaler out of Sag Harbor on Long Island. The charges for the services, room, board, and outfitting came to more than $100.[74] Fourteen-year-old Eli P. Baker met the "runners of the ship *Mary*" in Albany in 1844. The agents brought him to New York and then sent him on to New Bedford and a two-year cruise without ever getting his father's permission.[75] J. Ross Browne believed he had been misled by the New York shipping agent who sent him to New Bedford. The agent had told him: "a whaler is a place of refuge for the distressed and persecuted, a school for the dissipated, an asylum for the needy! There's nothing like it. You can see the world; you can see something of life!"[76]

Recruitment into the navy or on privateers was similar to recruitment of merchant sailors. Occasionally American captains in dire need of men resorted to impressment, a policy generally limited to European powers. Navy recruiters usually set up a rendezvous house, supplied music and entertainment, as well as free drinks and a bonus, to any sailor willing to sign aboard.[77] Obviously this system was open to exploitation. William Ray admitted that "nothing but the insanity of Rum, violence, perfidy, artifice, or the most distressing penury, can draw men into a situation, where, instead, of meeting with promised smiles, approbation, reward and honour, they find nothing but frowns, chastisement, contempt, and disgrace."[78] The abuse could go both ways. Men might run away with the advance. Seven of the fifty-seven men Lieutenant William Henry Allen recruited for the *Chesapeake* in 1807 deserted before he shipped them off.[79] Boardinghouse keepers, especially in the nineteenth century, played an important role in the recruiting process. Charles Smith ran up $40.38 in charges with landlord William Fairgreve to be paid out of his advance upon signing with the navy. The detailed list of expenses included two weeks of room and board for $7.00, carting his kit for $0.25, sundry cigars for $1.81, cash loaned for $4.50, and a black silk neckerchief for $1.00; various clothes for his upcoming service in the navy made up most of the rest.[80] Recruiting was not always exploitative; men signed on with friends, relatives, and townsmen. Some captains went out of their way to reward men for enlisting or reenlisting. Captain Thomas Truxton of the *Constellation* offered a beaver hat, a black silk neckerchief, two months' advance pay, and two weeks' shore liberty to his crew in Baltimore to reenlist.[81]

Regardless of the type of vessel or the service he sailed for, the sailor went to sea to earn money. The laws of supply and demand had the greatest impact on what a sailor made. Between 1750 and 1850 monthly wages for common seamen varied from four dollars to fifty dollars. When demand was at its greatest, because of scarcity of labor or risks due to war, common seamen made their best money. If demand decreased, sailors' wages dropped and work became hard to find. A mariner's pay in New York declined by 50 percent in one year as the French and Indian War wound to a close. Wages were also high in Philadelphia during the 1750s and fell dramatically in the 1760s.[82] Toward the end of the Revolutionary War, John Brice signed aboard the ship *Nancy* as the first mate for £18 per month. As soon as the preliminary peace had been agreed to, the captain reduced the wages. Brice sued in court, only to discover that the judge agreed with the owners and ordered that Brice should be paid the higher wage until March 3, 1783, upon which he was to be paid "Customary Peace wages" for the completion of the voyage. The wages of an experienced seaman on the same voyage went from £5 to £3 a month (approximately $12.50 to $7.50).[83] After the Treaty of Paris of 1783, earnings were low, picking up again during the boom years of the 1790s.[84] Throughout the period, sailor wages generally stayed in the $8 to $17 range. Local conditions, too, made a difference. While a run from New York to Quebec that began in April 1761 brought seamen, who risked impressment,

110 shillings a month, a trip from Gloucester to Virginia eight months later paid only 45 shillings.[85] Horace Lane claimed that shortly before the War of 1812 he signed on to a vessel bound for Liverpool at Amelia Island, Florida, for $50 a month, when most American seamen made $12 a month. The captain paid this high wage because the vessel was sailing for Liverpool, where the risk of impressments was great. Skill level also mattered. On many voyages seamen were paid according to experience and ability. A greenhand might be paid half as much as as a seaman who truly knew the ropes, although the differential was usually only a few dollars a month.[86] Wages could even vary on the same voyage depending on conditions in the ports visited. Daniel Evans and Zebulon York signed aboard the *Aeolis* in Portsmouth in March 1804 for $16 and $13 respectively. After they ran from the ship in Charleston, South Carolina, two months later, their replacements cost $23 and $16 each.[87] The brig *Mary* had signed its crew in Providence in 1819 for wages that varied from $11 to $14 a month. When one of the poorer paid sailors jumped ship in Savannah, the captain had to offer $16 for his replacement.[88] Certain ports, like New Orleans, were notorious for higher pay differentials, and it was a lucky captain who did not lose most of his crew if local wages were more than in the port of origin.[89]

Often, the wage was only a part of the sailor's compensation. Private ventures—the ability to use some of the cargo space for their own purposes—frequently came into play. On both the voyage to Quebec from New York, and the poorer paid trip from Gloucester to Virginia in 1761, common seamen were granted their own "venture." Sometimes the articles signed by a sailor stipulated this right in detail; frequently it was merely assumed. Aboard the *Susanna and Ann* in 1762, which was running smuggled goods into New York, each sailor had ventures of two barrels of sugar worth £8 a barrel.[90] When a shipowner questioned one sailor about loading two casks of his own goods in Port-au-Prince in 1762, the sailor retorted that he "conceives every foremast man has a Right by Law to put on board" a private venture and that the shipowner would not have questioned the sailor's right to a venture in New York.[91] The contract for wages for a passage to the East Indies in 1831 included a quarter-ton privilege, which meant the sailor could ship five hundred pounds of goods as cargo.[92] In the early 1800s James Durand brought five hundred pounds of coffee to the United States for which he received $125.[93] Men like the Hammond brothers, who sailed in the 1820s and 1830s, constantly sent valued goods to their families to sell and for home consumption.[94]

As with everything else at sea, private ventures were based upon the vessel's hierarchy. Aboard the *Dolphin* in 1764 the master received 110 bushels, the mate 46 bushels, three men 36 bushels, and one man 27 bushels as their privilege.[95] Sometimes a ship's officers had the right to a portion of the cargo space and the crew would not.[96] This privilege could be so lucrative that although it was possible for the captain's monthly wage to be lower than the mate's and even the crew's, he could become wealthy and, if he were lucky and well connected, a merchant in his own right.[97] The greater the captain's investment of in the voyage, however, the greater was his responsibility for the commercial aspect of the voyage. Similarly, the private venture for the common seaman benefited both the merchant and sailor by cementing everyone's interest in the successful outcome of the enterprise.

The same principle of shared risk and shared profit underwrote most fishing and whaling voyages as well. Throughout this period fishermen were not paid a daily wage; instead they obtained a percentage of the catch. Fishermen in the 1790s in Marblehead, for example, signed written contracts binding them to a specific crew during the season. The owner of the vessel would be given two to two and a half shares. The captain would get only a little more than a full share. A shoreman who dried and processed the fish would get a full share, and the remainder of the eight shares would be divided among the crew based on the amount of fish caught by each individual. Apprentices in the five- to six-man crew might get a half share or nothing at all, except knowledge of the business for future voyages.[98]

Whaling articles also divided the haul into shares, only they were much more elaborate, with a wide range of shares given out based upon previous experience and job category. Each rank or rating would be given a different lay, or share of the money earned from the whales caught. Aboard the whaleship *Columbia* on a voyage from 1846 to 1850, the first mate signed for a 1/28 lay, second mate 1/40, third mate 1/60, two coopers for 1/70 each, two steersmen and an assistant cooper for 1/75 each, another steersmen for 1/80, the cook for 1/120, the steward for 1/130, two seamen for 1/140, another seaman for 1/150, and seven seamen for 1/160.[99] In the late eighteenth century, the lays for seamen would have been larger. The whaling industry changed between 1750 to 1850; voyages stretched from a few months to several years, and the pay and working conditions declined.[100]

Privateers operated similarly. In fact, the lucrative opportunities in times of war drew men into this service. Aboard the privateer sloop *Comet* during the Revolutionary War, the captain received five shares, the first lieutenant three shares, the second lieutenant, gunner, boatswain, and steward two shares each, the armorer one and one half shares, seventeen crew members one share each, and two boys one half share each. This could add up to significant money. One prize—a captured ship—could bring in £30,000. Half the money would go to the owners, the rest would be divided among the crew.[101] The *Yankee* privateer during the War of 1812 made seven successful voyages out of Bristol, Rhode Island. On the first, which lasted three months, each share paid $700, while the second voyage netted $338.40 a share.[102]

Naval vessels also offered prize money in addition to a basic wage that was often minimal. In the eighteenth century the British navy paid twenty-four shillings per month for an able seaman. The Continental navy did not offer much more during the Revolutionary War. By the nineteenth century, the American navy paid about two dollars a month less than the merchant service. The prize money, however, could add up to hundreds of additional dollars. During the Quasi War with France, Elijah Shaw, who served as a ship carpenter on the frigate *Constellation*, earned $320 in prize money in addition to $300 in wages.[103]

Shaw's earnings, at a time when a common laborer received a dollar a day, might seem like a small fortune. Somehow, few seamen ever seemed to get much ahead. A sailor had to work a month before he caught up with the advance paid on his signing the articles, and that money was usually quickly placed in the hands of a boardinghouse keeper. Expenses frequently ate away at earnings. After almost fourteen months at sea, Amos Towne was worse off than when he started the voyage. Between advances he received after he first signed on, and at various ports in Europe and the East Indies, as well as charges for clothes, tobacco, and board while ashore, Towne had to sign unto another vessel owned by John Carrington shortly after he returned to Providence in 1824 to erase the debt that he had accumulated while working on the ship *Franklin*.[104] Whalers and privateers too had previous commitments for the lays and shares. The typical earnings of the crew of the whaler *Gratitude* was $269.37 for a two-and-a-half-year voyage. Almost every man who earned this amount, however, was actually paid less than $100 because of advances and debts incurred before departure.[105] On some voyages the deductions stripped the sailor of almost all his earnings. Three years after exclaiming that he liked "whaling very well" and "the best of anything I have ever tried," James Webb reported to his mother that "I made nothing by the voyage—the owners claimed all when I got home."[106] Privateers might sell their shares, or a portion thereof, before they even left port.[107] Men in the navy also spent advances, incurred debts, or, like Shaw with his earnings, invested their small wealth poorly. On the positive side, payment of the sailor's wage had first priority if a shipowner went bankrupt and a few men managed to use their money to start life anew on shore.[108]

Not every sailor conformed to the stereotype by drinking, cursing, carousing, fighting, misbehaving, and spending to excess while on leave. Sailors with strong shoreside attachment were often more careful with their money. Some went to sea only to build up a bankroll that could be used to establish themselves in an occupation on shore. During wartime, men expected and sometimes achieved quick rewards through privateering. In peacetime the process took longer. Whaling offered an opportunity to accumulate capital. A successful whaling cruise in the nineteenth century might last two or three years, while the sailor's lay—his share in the profits—could amount to a small fortune of several hundred dollars. Even aboard regular merchant vessels, wages could add up if properly managed and saved. Amos Towne may have ended a fourteen-month cruise in debt to the shipowner, but others on the same voyage were paid seventy or eighty dollars in cash as they signed off.[109] Many men also hoped to make their careers at sea. Captains and other officers aboard ship came largely from the ranks of common sailors; at sea, knowledge and ability counted above all else.[110]

Who were the men who served as sailors and labored on the waterfront? Answering the questions is no easy task. During the period covered by this study there were many changes in English-speaking North America. A set of British colonies confined to trade with the West Indies and Europe, became an independent nation whose ships plied every ocean and whose seaman visited countless foreign ports. The dimensions of this huge workforce are staggering. Estimates of the number of colonial Americans working as seamen are hard to derive; English and American trade were so intertwined as to make distinctions almost impossible to detail. Thousands of seamen came in and out of colonial ports before the Revolutionary War. Naval warfare and privateers brought many more men to seek their fortunes at sea. Tens of thousands of men fought on the ocean waves from 1775 to 1783. In 1791 Thomas Jefferson estimated that there were also 20,000 men employed as merchant sailors or as fishermen.[111] That number increased dramatically in the expansion of trade that began in the 1790s. By 1818, a group of merchants and captains seeking to establish a mariners' church estimated that 15,000 to 16,000 seamen sailed through the port of New York each year.[112] The Board of Directors of the Boston Seamen's Friend Society reported 103,000 seamen in the United States in 1835.[113] By 1850 there may have been well over 100,000 American seamen and countless others laboring along the docks.

The first and perhaps the most important characteristic of this workforce was its diversity. Men of many nationalities could be found on the waterfront. Perhaps there was less variety before 1776 because of legal limitations on crew nationality dictated by the Navigation Acts. The seamen who offered depositions before His Majesty's Vice Admiralty Court in New York were born in England, Ireland, Scotland, the Channel Islands, Germany, and Scandinavia.[114] After independence, and as the American merchant marine expanded, the international mix became more pronounced. Many of the privateers and vessels commissioned during the War for Independence contained large numbers of men not born in America.[115] In a sampling of crew lists from 1803 to 1806 in Providence, Rhode Island, about 10 to 15 percent of crews were foreign born. These men came from many locations, including India, the West Indies, Italy, Portugal, as well as northern Europe.[116] Billy G. Smith found the same proportion of foreign seamen in Philadelphia in 1803. In 1807, as much as half of the men serving in the United States Navy in New York were foreigners.[117] Melville's New Bedford contained a hodgepodge of denizens from Mediterranean mariners jostling ladies to lascars (natives of India and Southeast Asia) and Malays, to "cannibals" and South Sea islanders like Ishmael's soulmate, Queequeg.[118] The New-Bedford Port Society, offering substance to Melville's literary portrait, reported in 1836 that one-third of all the sailors in the busy whaling port were foreigners.[119]

Blacks were an important component of the waterfront workforce. Horace Lane was struck, and perhaps intimidated, by the African American men and women at the dance hall he visited when he was sixteen. He should not have been surprised. Throughout the Age of Revolution blacks could be found in the dockside neighborhoods of almost every American port. During the colonial period most of these blacks would have been slaves; after 1776 more and more were free. These people worked in and sometimes owned grog shops, oyster stands, and other service-oriented businesses. Many were day laborers and stevedores. Blacks also worked as artisans in maritime trades like ship building, caulking, and sailmaking. A few, such as sailmaker James Forten of Philadelphia, managed to earn a modicum of wealth and respectability.[120] Most, including Frederick Douglass, a slave caulker in Baltimore before his escape from bondage and his career as an abolitionist, sought to carve out a niche for themselves through their skill and hard work along the waterfront.[121]

Douglass, disguised in sailor's garb, was able to travel undetected to the

North and his freedom because so many black men signed on as seamen in the merchant marine. The extent and character of the African American component of crews, however, varied over time. During the colonial period it was not unusual to find slaves serving aboard vessels. In some cases an entire crew might be made up of men in bondage. Free blacks also worked aboard ships. After the American Revolution, which created a large pool of free African Americans in both the North and the South, blacks became a significant element of almost every crew. At least one-fourth of Philadelphia's young black males shipped as sailors in the early nineteenth century.[122] In crew lists for several cities for the same period, the percentage of berths held by blacks usually hovered around 15 percent, while in some cities, like Providence, the total reached 30 percent. By the 1830s and 1840s, however, the number of African American seamen began to decline as several southern states passed laws discriminating against black seamen, and as racial prejudice intensified in both the North and the South. By the 1840s and 1850s many of the blacks still in the merchant marine were driven from the forecastle and worked as ship's cooks.[123]

Even among the American-born white seamen there were many differences in background and birthplace. The image of the chiseled New Englander as the embodiment of the American tar does not hold. True enough, many sailors hailed from New England, and in some areas of maritime industry, like the banks fishery that sailed from small ports like Marblehead and Gloucester, Massachusetts, many of the half dozen men crammed into the small schooners came from the same towns and knew each other all too well.[124] On long whaling voyages too, the crew might be taken from all over New England and include Native Americans as well as young farm boys eager to earn a stake to establish themselves on shore.[125] But the merchant sailing vessels, especially those that sailed from larger ports, contained men from up and down the seaboard. In the colonial New York Admiralty courts, only about half of the American-born men identified came from New York.[126] This proportion may have declined in large ports after the Revolutionary War. Less than 10 percent of the mariners in Philadelphia crews in 1803 were born in that city.[127] In smaller ports like Salem and Providence, the majority of sailors were locals.[128]

Many maritime workers traced seafaring roots back for generations. Others left the family farm to seek their fortunes abroad, knowing that they had a sparse patrimony if they stayed at home. A few seamen came from affluent backgrounds and hoped to learn the ropes in the forecastle before they moved to the quarterdeck. A variety of circumstances could lead a man to sign on with a ship. There were even some less ambitious souls—like Melville and Dana—whose education and temperament set them apart from their shipmates. Some sought respite and adventure. Samuel Smith's business plans went sour; he fell into debt and had nowhere else to turn.[129] One whaleman who taught school, farmed, and fished in the year before signing on a cruise, saw his stint at sea as yet another in a round of different employments. The forecastle included men from many different classes and backgrounds, as well as nationalities.[130]

Despite this diversity, sailors generally shared one characteristic: more than half were in their twenties. A ship might contain a boy of ten or twelve, like Horace Lane, who labored as a servant or cabin boy. A serious maritime career did not begin until the late teens. The average age of sailors was about twenty-five. Less than 20 percent of seamen were under twenty, most of these were eighteen or nineteen. By the time a man reached his thirties, he likely either moved on to a new occupation ashore, turned to fishing, labored on the docks, or was lost at sea. Approximately 20 percent continued to ship out into their thirties or forties, some as officers and some merely as "old salts." Surveys of American prisoners of war held during the Revolutionary War and the War of 1812 suggest that during hostilities, as job prospects dimmed on the waterfront and the lure of privateering offered the hope of quick rewards, the average age increased slightly.[131] Overall, compared to their white shipmates, black seamen were slightly older. In 1803 more than 80 percent of the white seamen and 70 percent of the blacks on crew lists in Providence were under the age of thirty.[132] Being a mariner was a young man's game.[133]

The waterfront workforce, however, included man at various ages. As reported in the reform publication the *Mariner's Church* in 1818 "there are many old Seamen, who are employed in fitting out vessels, many ship carpenters and others" who crowd the dockside neighborhoods.[134] "Old" Mr. Coats, the boatswain of the *Beaver*, gave up the sea after a China voyage in 1805–1806. He married and became a rigger in New York.[135] One master rigger who listed his employees in 1821 stated that they all had once followed the sea but now worked on shore.[136] Often these men turned to waterfront labor when shipboard life became too physically demanding for them, or when personal commitments, like providing for a family, convinced them to remain rooted in one community.

The range of shoreside labor was staggering. Many men who served at sea remained near the waterfront as stevedores, riggers, ship carpenters, sailmakers, blockmakers, and coopers. Others set up grog shops or boardinghouses.

4. This certificate includes five waterfront scenes: at top is a view of Salem harbor; one of the smaller pictures shows two men working a sugar press in a warehouse; the other three demonstrate various stages of preparing a vessel for sea. Salem Marine Society Certificate for John B. Knight, January 31, 1839. Peabody Essex Museum.

Some men turned to regular trades a few streets away from the docks as carpenters, shoemakers, and the like. Others went further inland. A few actually became farmers. Indeed, the boundaries between work ashore and work afloat remained fluid. Men who shipped out one month might stay ashore the next month. Many who labored at sea while in their twenties avoided service on the ocean in their thirties. Others shifted back and forth throughout their lives.

Sometimes it was a sense of wanderlust, or some mysterious unease like Melville's "growing grim about the mouth" and "damp, drizzly November" in his soul, that limited time on land.[137] At least twice during his teens Horace Lane attempted to wean himself from a sailor's life. Before his arms-running voyage in 1804 he spent two years ashore learning a trade, and in 1805 he tried blacksmithing for a while. Yet Lane complained that "There was a constant restless anxiety for something—I could not tell what." Intermittently thereafter he attempted to extend his stays on shore through labor as well as criminal activity.[138]

More often it was economic circumstances that compelled men to sign on for another voyage. To avoid going to sea, Samuel Leech worked on the docks loading and unloading ships. He found this "an uncertain employment," however, and reenlisted in the American navy.[139] In 1822 Joseph Oliver struggled to find work on the waterfront but could not. He had a sick wife and reported that he often went to bed at night without anything to eat. Confronted with this desperate situation, he thought that his only solution was to go to sea to earn some money.[140] Thomas Gregory was a junior officer on a privateer during the War of 1812. The end of that conflict found him stranded on the docks, without steady employment ashore. As he lacked basic navigational skills he signed as a common seaman, a step he philosophically dismissed by declaring that he will just have to "fart like a *Jack*."[141]

Many men thus passed easily from work on the waterfront to work aboard ships. French Canadian Joseph Baker arrived in New York City in 1799 and labored for a while making staves. After his partner ran off with his money, he went to Philadelphia, where he signed aboard an English vessel bound for Jamaica, hoping to make big wages as a ship carpenter there.[142] Nicholas Isaacs described how, after several years as a sailor during his teens, he sought work in New York City as a cooper making buckets. After about six months the other men complained that he was too young to be working as a journeyman, so he moved to another shop. Problems arose at this employer, and once again he went back to the sea.[143] Stephen Gray came from a family with strong maritime roots in Rhode Island; his mother's father was a ship captain and five maternal uncles died at sea. At age sixteen he "had a strong inclination to go to sea" and sailed to Cape Breton, but "had a rather unpleasant voyage." Gray tried seafaring two more times, with the same results, before apprenticing as a carpenter. Once he became a journeyman he signed aboard a vessel to New Orleans. From there he worked his way overland back to Rhode Island as a carpenter. The imprint of his years at sea was indelible; he continued to spice his diary with nautical terms and reported the comings and goings of local shipping for the rest of his life.[144]

Most seamen sought shorebound employment more toward the end, rather than the beginning or middle, of their careers. Ashley Bowen had worked intermittently ashore for more than twenty years as a seafarer before becoming a full-time rigger at age thirty-five.[145] Samuel Leech eventually broke away from the sea, and even the waterfront, and established himself as a shopkeeper in New England. Simeon Crowell started his sea career on fishing schooners on the Grand Banks, turned to sailing on coastal traders, and traveled at times to the West Indies. He became a mate and then a captain, and ended up settling in Barnstable and serving as inspector and deputy collector of the port.[146] The Hammond family of Rochester, Massachusetts, offers us further insight into how and why seamen sought shorebound employment. Bezeal Shaw, the oldest boy, had already gone to sea by 1818. He told his younger brother LeBaron not to follow him in his occupation. But LeBaron's options were not great—digging ditches with Irish laborers or going to sea. By 1830, four Hammonds were sailing out of the port of New York. Sometimes they served as mates; often they sailed as common seamen. LeBaron worked for a while on Mississippi steamboats, but by 1841 he had married and established a grocery in New York City. Two other brothers also gave up their maritime careers: Bezeal Shaw became a trader in New Orleans, Andrew a carpenter in New York. Like LeBaron they may have done so when they married and in an effort to settle down. If they needed a reminder of the dangers of continuing to serve as a seaman, they could think of their brother Timothy, who died of an illness contracted while at sea.[147]

Others remained more closely wedded to the sea all their lives while changing their nautical employment. Nicholas Isaacs filled many berths in his twenty years before the mast. He sailed in merchantmen throughout the Atlantic, fished the Grand Banks, fought aboard American privateers during the War of 1812, and had even been impressed into the British navy. About 1815 he moved to New York, got married, and thereafter worked the local fishing grounds and sold his catch to the city's markets.[148] After John Hoxse completed his apprenticeship at age twenty-one, he signed aboard a ship to serve as its carpenter. Within a few years he lost his arm in the battle between the *Constellation* and the French frigate *La Vengeance*. Thereafter he tried to earn a living running a grocery but failed. For two years he supplied wood locally to Newport, Rhode Island, before that work proved too physically taxing for him. Although he signed aboard a sealer for the South Atlantic, he was never paid any wages for his two-year voyage. Finally he settled in as a fisherman off the coast of Rhode Island.[149]

Some tars never left the forecastle. Crew lists throughout the period reveal men in their forties, and even a handful in their fifties. Luke Snow was forty when he served as a mariner aboard the *Halifax Packet* out of New York in 1760. In 1803 the *Charlotte* from Providence had a fifty-four-year-old on board. And in 1843 the *Rival of Calais*, also of Providence, had a fifty-year-old sailor.[150] Black sailors were more likely to continue as foremast men than

5. This sketch of a man in typical sailor garb on a dock was found in a journal, interspersed with handwriting exercises. Journal of William Alfred Allen (ca. 1840). New Bedford Whaling Museum.

white sailors. Many of the white men who stayed at sea became officers. According to Providence crew lists, almost every white man who remained a mariner moved up in rank.[151] The same was true of Salem seafarers in the eighteenth century.[152] Although this trend probably persisted throughout the Age of Revolution, in most locations some older whites served out their days in the forecastle. Moreover, as shown by the Hammond brothers, entry into the officer ranks was not necessarily permanent.

Seamen pursued a variety of options depending upon their opportunities—or lack of opportunities. Coming from a great many backgrounds, and heading in different directions with their lives, the men who populated the waterfront and labored before the mast defy any grand characterization. And yet, despite men who saved money, moved up the ranks, returned to a land-based life, the popular image of the hell-raising, spendthrift tar persists.

The expression of liberty that dominated the waterfront revolved around a freedom of action, in contrast to the property-bound definitions that preoccupied the age. While sailors worked to acquire money—an aim that would meet the approval of their landbound critics—the tar's concern with immediate gratification and rapid disposal of his wages implied a lack of respect for property that frightened those more concerned with the accumulation of wealth. For men who were disenfranchised and whose grasp on property was fleeting and tentative, the sailor's liberty ashore had a distinct appeal. The ideal of sailor liberty, however, fell somewhat short of reality. Excesses of liberty on shore led directly to the loss of economic and personal freedom.

2

The Maid I Left Behind Me

William Widger lay imprisoned by the enemies of his country. This sailor in the American Revolution had tried his luck as a privateer aboard the brig *Phoenix*. His luck ran short, and the British captured him and sent him to Old Mill Prison in England. Confined by walls and guards, he turned his thoughts to his home in Marblehead. He had a dream that reflected the concerns of many sailors far from home as they thought of the women in their lives. Widger's dream brought him to the Marblehead waterfront, where he quickly became frustrated by the inability of "his Giting home" since he stood on one "Side of the weay" and soldiers stood sentry on the other side. As in any dream, he somehow managed to proceed and met an acquaintance, "Georg Tucker," at the end of "Bowden's Lain." Tucker "Stouped and Shock hands with me and Said he Was Glad to See me." Then Tucker unloaded a bombshell and congratulated Widger on his wife just delivering a baby boy.

Startled, Widger asserted, "it was a dam'd Lye" and that "it was imposable for I had been Gone tow years and leatter." Again, dreamlike, Widger pushed on "in a Great pashan" toward Nickes Cove where he met the one woman he knew he could trust—his mother. The old woman (William Widger was thirty-two) asked the sailor if he was going home to see his wife. Widger responded that he "was dam'd if ever I desired to See hir a Gain." The maternal strings began to tug on Widger as his mother sought to ease his anger. She argued for the biologically impossible, asserting that "the Child was a honest begotten Child and it was Got before" Widger went to sea and that it was his. Widger was not to be moved, and repeated that it was impossible since he had been out to sea for two years and more. Widger continued "I was a dam'd foule to Coum home" and that he could leave in the brig he had arrived in. The debate went back and forth; the mother almost succeeded in convincing Widger to return home and see his wife and baby. Widger continued to remonstrate and swear, and, as he reports, "before I was don talking With hur a bout it I awaked."[1]

William Widger's dream highlights the contradictory meanings of liberty that shoreside attachments held for the sailor. Whether detained as a captive, or merely forced from home by his service at sea, the mariner could be both attracted to women ashore and repelled by them. Liberty on the waterfront allowed the sailor to engage in a variety of long- and short-term heterosexual relationships. Liberty at sea released the sailor, at least temporarily, from those relationships and compelled him to live in an all-male society where his imagination could run wild. He might long for absent loved ones, or he might relish the freedom of the fraternity of the forecastle. Most likely, he did both.

The many meanings of liberty for the sailor—personal independence, carousing, and freedom to choose where he worked among them—were intricately intertwined with his relationships with women and his fellow sailors and with his sense of masculinity. At sea (or as prisoners of war) men lived in a homosocial, not a homosexual, world. Life aboard ship presented challenges to male sexuality. Separation from women and close quarters in the forecastle created the potential for sexual activity with other men. Even the nature of the work could suggest a less masculine identity. Although the true mariner had to be prepared for the most arduous labor, he also often had to be proficient at tasks like mending and washing that could be considered feminine. Regardless of the possibilities, the image of Jack Tar was an idealized heterosexual man. Everyone aboard ship may not always have lived up to that ideal, but its persistence was fundamental to maritime culture and sailors' notion of liberty.

Widger's dream also suggests a conflicted understanding of women. On the one hand is the woman who gave him birth, a woman whom he trusted almost enough to believe that he was not cuckolded. Contrasted with this mother was the wife who could not be trusted. She was the temptress and betrayer, who while he was away had slept with another man, gotten pregnant, and delivered of a baby boy. These two images—which suggest the Madonna and Eve—represent extremes in the mind of the sailor. Yet somehow they became blended. After all, the mother stood in alliance with the wife, arguing with her son that he should still return to his family and claim the infant as his. Within the dream Widger is torn. On one level, he is still drawn to the fireside and his wife. On another, he continues to rant and assert a vague desire to return to the safety and camaraderie of the forecastle. Within the real world, there is no resolution. Rather than settling the debate, Widger, who corresponded with his wife while in Old Mill Prison, merely awakes.

Most sailors had an even more complex view of women including the sacred mother, beloved sister, innocent daughter, loyal sweetheart or wife, playful Mol, exploitive harlot, and exotic native. The boundaries between some of these remained vague and the categories often overlapped.

We should not confuse popular images of womanhood with reality. Women's experiences and their relationships with sailors were varied. Whether she was in an ephemeral or long-term relationship with a sailor, or whether she exploited or was exploited, Jack Tar's liberty exacted a high cost on a woman on the waterfront. These women's lives were therefore often hard. Women labored mainly as seamstresses, or in boardinghouses and taverns and in the commercial sex industry. Although they formed strong bonds with each other, theirs was not a separate sphere. Women interacted with men beyond their own family on a daily basis. Some of these women fulfilled the various fantasies of the sailor—including a sentimentalized domestic ideal—while he was ashore. Others did not.[2]

Personal relationships ashore could pull on or push upon Jack Tar affecting his notions of liberty. To better understand this aspect of the sailor's life, I will examine concepts of gender identity at sea, the many images of women for the male waterfront worker, and some details of the lives of the women on the waterfront.[3]

Any understanding of masculine identity on the waterfront must begin with how men viewed themselves. The forecastle created a peculiar environment that had the potential to threaten the heterosexual identity of sailors. Isolated from women for long periods of time, compelled to live and work in a confined space literally on top of each other, and at times forced to labor at work land based society deemed feminine, sailors could have created a more homoerotic identity. They did not. Instead, they developed a notion of manhood that reflected both working-class and youth culture that emphasized proficiency at skilled labor and heterosexual prowess.[4] For Richard Henry Dana, Jr., the ideal sailor fulfilled all the qualities of manliness. He complimented the mate on the *Pilgrim* by describing him as being every inch a man. Likewise, each crew member knew that "he must be a man, and show himself smart when at his duty." For Dana, "an overstrained sense of manliness is the characteristic of seafaring men." The manly sailor must confront the world with stoicism, ignore danger, minimize an injury, and avoid expression of feelings.[5] In 1836 "A Brother Cruiser" looked at a picture of "The Boatswain's Mate" and proclaimed, "such a picture as that, I love to look upon a real man-of-war's man—a hearty, able bodied, American seaman." His very look expressed "a love of enterprise, firmness of purpose, and a reckless daring." Such a sailor never forgot his birthright, "he is never a fawning, cringing, sycophantic creature, but *always a man*!" Yet this ideal sailor understood the military necessity of discipline and always tipped his hat to his superior officers.[6] From this perspective the manly sailor was independent and hardworking and knew both his duty and his place. There was something straightforward and honest in this portrait of the sailor that emphasized hard work and diligence rather than intelligence. J. Ross Browne, for instance, described one old salt, whom he greatly admired, as combining "all the noble generosity and daring of a real sailor—all those blunt, manly qualities which characterize the genuine son of Neptune—with the credulity and simplicity of a child."[7] Popular song reiterated these themes countless times. "Bonny Ben" in one song "was to each jolly messmate a brother." Perhaps even more important, "He was manly, and honest, good-natured and free."[8]

Ashore, all of these masculine characteristics became embodied in the manly sailor adorned in his best sailor garb, with a ready wit, generosity, and love of life. Understandably irresistible to any woman on the waterfront, the sailor possessed a strong libido that needed to be satisfied.

I took my love by the middle so small and gently lay'd her down
Those words to me she thus did say as we lay on the broom [heather]
Do what you will kind sir said she it's equal unto me
But little do my Mammy know I am in the broom with thee.[9]

At times the sailor could remain loyal to his sweetheart and he might eagerly promise to marry his love. Although such pledges of fidelity were sometimes serious, they often were expressions of the passion of the moment. A manly sailor could just as easily take or leave a woman.

If round the world poor sailors roam,
  And bravely do their duty,
When danger's past they find a home
  With each his fav'rite beauty
For Nan, and Sue, and Moll, and Bess
  And fifty more delight them,
And when their honied lips they press,
  Who says it don't requite them.[10]

If sailors objectified women and saw them largely as fit for serving the man's needs ashore—be they carnal or domestic—they saw themselves as users. Men came ashore, and whether it was to see a sweetheart or a harlot, they assumed that women would eagerly do their bidding. Only occasionally did sailors express any remorse over this attitude. The author of "The Husband's Complaint" declares that once he had a "loving Wife," but that he was not content and "led her an unhappy life." He came to appreciate her only after he lost her and soon remarried a woman who "turns out a drunken sot" and tells him, "I'll pay off your first wifes scores," constantly fighting and berating him.[11] In one version of "The Maid I Left Behind Me" the sailor goes off to sea after promising his love that he will return. Opportunity knocks elsewhere and he marries for money, forgetting the girl at home and his parents. The song ends with a lament as the sailor's past haunts his dreams.

My father is in his winding-sheet, my mother too appears,
The girl I love stands by their side to wipe away their tears;
They all died broken-hearted, and now it's too late, I find
That God has seen my cruelty to the girl I left behind.[12]

This attitude, although surfacing occasionally in popular song, is buried under a weight of evidence in which the sailor believes he has the right to take from the woman.

If the handsome sailor was the ideal ashore, and if that image had such a strong sexual component, what about the handsome sailor's sexuality at sea? Did the fact the sailors often cooked, sewed, and served—ostensibly female work—affect their sense of themselves as men?[13] Did the view of themselves as users transfer to sexual activity with other men at sea? Only a handful of comments about male sexual activity at sea exist in the many songs, diaries, reminiscences, ship's logs, court records, and other sources.

Herman Melville toyed with the sexual attractiveness of the ideal sailor for males. He described Billy Budd as "the Handsome Sailor," with both feminine and masculine characteristics. Thus Billy has a "smooth face all but feminine in purity of natural complexion." Melville characterized him as a "rustic beauty" competing with high-born dames. While asserting that "our Handsome Sailor had as much of masculine beauty as one can expect anywhere to see," Melville in the next instant compared him to "the beautiful woman in one of Hawthorne's minor tales."[14] He avoided more explicit discussion of homoerotic behavior with obscure references to "wooden-walled Gommorrahs of the deep." In *Moby Dick,* Ishmael shares a bed with Queequeg: "in our hearts' honeymoon, lay I and Queequeg—a cosy, loving pair."[15]

Such intimacy was no longer a private matter if authorities became aware of it. Buggery was one of the most frequent crimes punished with execution in the British navy from 1700 to 1861. It was less frequently punished in the American navy.[16] Inthe record of punishments aboard the *Congress* for 1845 to 1848, three cases may have represented homosexual activity. In December 1845 and again in February 1846, adult seamen and individuals rated as boys were punished for "scandalous conduct." The exact nature of that conduct is not delineated, yet given the host of other offenses listed, including insubordination, fighting, smuggling liquor, and drunkenness, the reader is left to suspect some sexual act.[17] Josiah Cobb provides a similar oblique reference to homosexual behavior in Dartmoor Prison during the War of 1812 when he says that the "unpardonable sin had been committed." Again, considering the litany of other crimes explicitly mentioned—fighting, gambling, drinking, stealing—the unmentioned crime was probably sodomy. Cobb comments further that "This [the 'unpardonable sin'—sodomy] was but seldom done;—howsoever depraved were the Rough Alleys [the criminal element among sailor prisoners of war held in Dartmoor] in other respects, there had been but two or three instances of this heinous sin being committed, on account of the serious penalty immediately following the conviction of the offender."[18]

A survey of more than one thousand whaleship logs in the nineteenth century turned up only three clear references to homosexual activity aboard ship. These cases all involved unwanted advances of one man upon another. In each, the reaction was much the same. The culprit was identified and removed from the ship. The captain often was matter of fact and responding to the wishes of his crew. Hiram Baily, for example, wrote to his owners explaining that the "green boys" (hands new to sailing) had complained that the steward had gone down to the forecastle in the night and "got into there berths when the lights were out and took there inexpressibles in to his mouth." While the green hands apparently objected, the captain did not take any action until three men had reported "that they waked up and found him in that Position," while another awoke and found the steward "fooling around him to do proberly the same thing." Baily intended to dismiss the steward in part as a result of these disclosures. His entire letter was written tongue in cheek and showed much good humor. He continued his description of the steward to the owners focusing not on his sodomy but on his incompetence as a steward. Moreover, Baily informed the owners that the steward had lied when he signed aboard the ship because he had incurred debts ashore that his advance could pay.[19] Although this case and others show general condemnation for unwanted homosexual activity, it leaves us wondering about acts between two consenting individuals out of sight—which was no easy task on any vessel—of the prying eyes of the crew.[20]

The one American source that comments extensively on sexual activity between males aboard ship is the diary of Philip C. Van Buskirk. According to B. R. Burg, when Van Buskirk joined the marines in 1846 as a drummer he entered a world peopled by working-class men who did not view this type of sexual activity as unusual, perverse, or even morally wrong. Mutual masturbation, riding the "chicken" with one another, and reveling in sodomy all fit into a continuum of the bisexual activity that occurred in brothels along the waterfront. Although most of Van Buskirk's love affairs went unconsummated, his descriptions are so explicit, and he is so consumed with the attractions of one boy after another, that he leaves the impression that it was almost impossible to walk across the crowded decks of an American warship without tripping over a pair of male lovers in each other's clasp. No doubt Van Buskirk participated in some homosexual activity; however, given his own penchant for exploring his mental universe to the exclusion of events and conditions surrounding him, he may have been a bit too preoccupied with his own particular sexual orientation.[21] Homosexuality existed at sea, as indicated by the buggery trials in the British navy, the "scandalous conduct" aboard the *Congress*, the "unpardonable sin" that occurred in Dartmoor, the few incidents noted on whaling ships, and even the homoerotic references in Melville—but it was not a rampant practice.[22]

The seafaring male's sense of masculinity revolved less around his bonds with men than around his relationships with women. While other sailors admired him because of his seamanship, stoicism, and hard work, the handsome sailor was handsome to women. It was as if the threat of the sea to unman the man —through separation from women, immersion in a homosocial if not homoerotic world, and the need to do some work that might be defined as feminine—created an overly developed sense of manhood. If maritime culture emphasized one type of manhood, it allowed for and indeed demanded many different types of womanhood.

Jack Tar's many images of women fulfilled some fantasy—domestic or sexual—for the sailor and reflected the peculiar nature of his liberty. In some instances attachments to women ashore could inhibit the sailor's liberty. In others men could take liberties with women ashore, or obtain liberty from women by going to sea. The sailors' images of women emphasizing domesticity reflected the attraction of home life to men whose work took them away from the family circle. Focusing on these images reminded them of what they

6. These sketches of matronly women with mopcaps found on the inside cover of the journal by William Henry Allen suggest the maternal images that many sailors took with them to sea. William Henry Allen, Journal of the *George Washington* (1800). Huntington Library.

lost when they abdicated control of their lives by going to sea. While too great a concern with the domestic sphere might bring ridicule, the manly sailor was expected to retain some sentimentality for the women who represented the homestead.

For most sailors the ideal of the sacred mother, symbolizing hearth and kin, was an important part of their view of women. Young men new to the sea often pined for their mothers and wished "themselfes to home with their mamys."[23] Midshipman William Henry Allen was so homesick on his first voyage that he drew two pictures of a matronly woman wearing a mopcap—probably his dead mother—in the front of his journal.[24] Even the most hardened sailor retained a tender place in his heart for his mother. Samuel Dalton, a salt who had spent years away from home in the navy and merchant marine and who was impressed in British service against his will, saw his mother as representing all that he had lost by his seafaring life. He wrote her in 1809 describing himself as "but a wanderer in the world." He lamented, "As the day comes it is spent in thoughts that Distract my soul to pieces & wishes for to once more behold my beloved Mother."[25] Joseph Valpey, captured by the British during the War of 1812, extended his sympathies to all older women while emphasizing their maternal role in household service. He wrote a poem extolling the virtues of elderly women—motherlike figures—who nursed the sick and were willing to do work that younger women would not.[26]

The relationship between the sailor and his mother became an important component of the sentimentalized nineteenth-century literature concerning seamen. The vision of the woman is not sexual, but domestic and maternal. The poem "The Sailor Boy's Mother" appeared in 1822 and recited the tragedy of a widow parting with her son and keeping him in her thoughts, even on a deathbed made more lonely by the sailor boy's absence. The lyrics focus on the mother resigning herself to God's will, laying in bed thinking of "her own darling son, Who wand'ring, had roamed far away on the billow." She felt great sorrow, "For she thought how her child all wrapped in his shroud, / Might sleep in the waves ere the dawn of to-morrow!" Her mind turned to the youth's happy childhood and how his activity comforted her "As she mourned for the husband who sunk in the ocean!" Then, after thinking of how the boy departed to go to sea,

Twas thus the poor widow then prayed for her child—
    Oh! may heaven preserve him far on the billow;
Then gently she sighed and most sweetly she smiled,
    As she thought of her orphan—and died on her pillow![27]

Recollections of other female relatives could also symbolize sentiments of domesticity—the loving sister and dependent daughter. The image of the sweet and absent sister evoked a domestic ideal of protective and almost maternal role. G. Bayley's poem in a letter to his sister Lavina, penned amid the scurrying of huge cockroaches on a prison ship in Jamaica and interrupted by an overgrown rat jumping onto the table where he was writing, highlights this relationship. "In every season of the varied year / Ive known a sister's love, a sister's care." Bayley continues with descriptions of peaceful rural scenes, emphasizing their bucolic nature and the presence of his beloved sister.

No birds now meet me with an early song
Lavina—was wont to share
A brother's pleasures and a brother's care

No more thy hand administers relief
Nor soothes my woes nor mitigates my grief.

Bayley sought strength and solace thinking of his sister "seated near some cool transparent brook," reading, gathering hazelnuts, or in simple conversation with "Her wit engaging and her heart sincere."[28]

In contrast, daughters appeared vulnerable and needing protection. One tale of shipwreck, a favorite form of literature among sailors, featured the two beautiful daughters of a ship captain. The daughters are both brave and helpless and are last seen seated with the father, waiting for the sinking ship to break up. Perhaps the father could have made it to safety, as several crew members manage to scamper to shore. Knowing that his daughters could not be saved, he did not even try. Instead, as one witness described it, he braced himself for the end, fighting back "the parental tear which then burst into his eye."[29] This sentimentalized portrait of a father unable to save his daughters was meant to pull on the heartstrings of a maritime readership fully aware of the power of nature and the limits of paternal protection for innocent daughters. It may have also subtly suggested the high cost such paternal care could entail.

When sailors turned their thoughts to their sweethearts or wives they combined both domestic and sexual fantasies. Jack Tar could idolize the woman of his dreams, envisaging a life of familial bliss, while recognizing that his absence created serious difficulties for his shoreside relationships. Although these reflections might be a source of anxiety and remind the sailor of the liberty he has lost by going to sea, they could also be a source of strength for men who not only had to battle the elements, but who also resided in an all-male culture for long periods of time. The temptations confronted by women appeared repeatedly in stories, songs, and stage productions of the loyal sweetheart awaiting her sailor love's return. Within this context the sweetheart was the true sexual object of the sailor threatened by others. This idealized vision of honest womanhood contrasted with William Widger's subconscious fears. Josiah Cobb reported that while sailor prisoners in Dartmoor during the War of 1812 passed hour after hour spinning yarns for each other, one of the favorite topics was the sweetheart left at home.[30] Joseph Valpey noted in his Dartmoor journal that he spent an "afternoon amongst My Friends in talking About the Salem Girls," and several of the poems he penned centered on his absent love.[31] The same concerns appeared in songs and chanteys.[32] One tune, found in the journal of Timothy Conner from his incarceration in Forton Prison during the Revolutionary War, highlighted the girlfriend's loyalty.

The song was in response to Polly's wish that the war be over. The sailor declares:

You true hearted women wherever you be
Pray take my advice and be arited [a righted] by me
Be true to your sweethearts and when they come home
Then you'll live as happy as Darby and Jone.[33]

Sailor songs from the 1790s and early 1800s repeated this theme several times. Henry goes off to sea and his beloved Sally patiently waits for him. Sometimes he returns and they are married. Sometimes he perishes at sea, and forlorn she looks out across the ocean, withers, and dies. Often, the sailor is sustained through all kinds of peril merely by thinking of his sweetheart waiting at home.[34] In Charles Dibden's "The Taken," Jack survives one ordeal after another, comforted by the tobacco box his Nancy provided him. Inside the box cover appear the words "If you loves I as I loves you, no pair so happy as we two." In the end he returns to his Nancy.[35] In the standard version of "The Maid I Left Behind," the singer remains loyal to his first love even though he travels the world over and sees exotic and rich women in several countries:

'Mongst all my many ramblings
　　My heart it still is pure,
The witchery of hundreds
　　It unchanging did endure;
For amidst the flash of foreign eyes
　　I never yet could find
One who could my affections wean
　　From her I left behind.[36]

Several of these songs were written for the stage and for a popular audience, including sailors.[37] Plays, too, often turned to the image of the female sweetheart remaining true to her absent sailor beau. In *The Purse; or Benevolent Tar* by J. C. Cross, the sailor's wife is pressured by a rich aristocrat, resists, and is rewarded when her husband returns to save her and her son from the clutches of the evil would-be suitor.[38] Isaac Bickerstaff's *Thomas and Sally: Or, The Sailor's Return* follows a similar outline, but also includes some revealing images of women. Sally is first seen sitting by a spinning wheel, representing domesticity and female industry. She and Thomas pledge mutual love to one another, then he is off to sea. Later, when Sally is again engaged in female industry (she is carrying a milk bucket), a rich squire offers her money, clothes, and promises if he can have his way with her. The squire is about to force himself on her when Thomas appears and rescues Sally.[39]

The resolution of such difficulties followed an idealized goal, especially in the nineteenth century, of domestic bliss. The happy couple in "The Dark-Eyed Sailor" marries after Mary passes a test of her faithfulness to her William in disguise. The song concludes:

In a cottage neat by the river side
It's William and Mary they do reside
So girls prove true while your lovers are away
For a cloudy morning oft brings a pleasant day.[40]

Similar images of domestic tranquility appear in the carvings of whalemen on scrimshaw. Typically the husband and wife gather around a comfortable chair, surrounded by children. In the background is a window with a ship in the harbor. Sometimes the carving portrayed a parting scene. Other times it represented an ideal of an ongoing domestic arrangement in which all relished one another's company. Such images may well have been simply the musings of a husband absent for years who wanted to present his wife with a token of his affection upon his return. They also reflect one aspect of women in the mind of the sailor.[41]

Seafarers could celebrate the virtues of married life, especially in contrast to more ephemeral liaisons. John Baker wrote a poem in his journal declaring, "I am Marry'd and happy with wonder." He chided "rovers and rakes . . . who laugh at the mention of conjugal bliss." Baker believed that only in marriage could "permanent pleasure be found," in contrast to "the joys of lawless connection" which were "fugitive and never secure." Such relationships were "Oft stolen in haste or snatched by surprise" and troubled by "doubts and fears." Men with a "mistress ye hire" were "misled by a false flattering fire" that threatens their destruction. Baker believed it was far better to be married, and he concluded his poem:

If ye ask me from whence my felicity flows
    My answer is short—from a wife
Who for cheerfulness sense and good nature I Chose
    Which are beauties that charm us for life

7. Scrimshaw often idealized the home and family and was likely intended as a present to a loved one when the sailor returned from his voyage. "Domestic Happiness." Kendall Whaling Museum.

To make home the mat of perpetual delight
Every hour each studies to seize
And we find ourselves happy from morning to night
By our mutual endeavours to please.[42]

Sentimental attachment to domesticity and praise for marital bliss formed only one small component of the sailor's portrayal of women. Jack Tar may have regretted the loss of relationships at home while aboard ship and extolled the virtues of mother, sister, daughter, and wife. But he also relished the liberty he gained by going to sea and the liberties he took with women along the waterfront. The braggadocio with which he expressed his heterosexuality became a crucial aspect of his manhood and gender identity. What emerges out of the various chanteys and sailor songs, as well as illustrations on scrimshaw and sea journals, is a vision of women that runs the gamut from the idealized sweetheart to the lusty maid eager for some fun to the harlot willing to sleep with Jack for a little quick change.

Some songs, like "When Seated with Sal," simply describe drinking and dancing with girlfriends and wives, having a grand time while briefly on liberty ashore. Prince Hoare's "The Sailor Boy" was written in this spirit. The sailor flirts with two girls, Poll and Nan, declaring, "Say shall we kiss and toy" while assuring them, "I goes to Sea no more." Yet his refrain seems to say the opposite: "O I'm the Sailor Boy, A Capering a shore."[43] This theme also appeared in sailor journals. The author of the logbook of the *General Wolfe* copied a bawdy poem in which the sailor attempted to seduce a young woman. The girl sees through the sailor, telling him, "You have a Longing Desire to insnare a maid, for when you have had your will with Me, than from me you shall go." The tar responded, "Don't you say so My Charming pretty Maid, for I will never leave thee, so never be afraid." The author knew such protests were untrue.[44] Frances Boardman copied a similar ditty in his journal in 1767 in which a ship carpenter seduces "Moley" with promises of marriage driven by "too lude desire." Not only does he not keep his pledge of fidelity, but before he goes to sea again he murders the young woman.[45] "Jack in His Element" emphasized the lack of fidelity on the part of the sailor and implies that women were objects of sexual gratification:

I have a spanking wife at Portsmouth gates,
A pigmy at Goree,
An orange tawney up the Straights,
A black at St. Lucie,
Thus whatever course we bend,
We lead a jovial life,
At every mess we find a friend,
At every port a wife.[46]

In a more bawdy vein, Timothy Conner copied several songs in his journal that focused on sexual gratification and mocked main stream morality.

When I was a prentice in my youth,
I pleased my mistress to the trouth;
I pleas'd my mistress every night,
And cuckold my master out of his sight.

Sailors no doubt enjoyed the idea of violating the marriage bed when some one else's wife was involved. They often assumed that every woman was a potential sexual target. In another song from Conner's journal, a young man arrives in town only to be met by two prostitutes, one of whom renders him her services. "The job being over he tips her the coin / She tips him the pox in the hight of his prime." The verse shows that sailors could laugh at themselves and the price of their sexual encounters. With complete aplomb, the young man decides

Now baby being pox't he solemnly swore
He'd pox the whole village in spite of that whore
For he knew that the women would coucle [cuckold] the Men
Now dam them I'll pox all if I can.[47]

Taking liberties with another man's wife could also lead to trouble, as one version of the chantey "A-Roving" makes clear. The sailor describes his advances on an Amsterdam maid:

And then I took her lily-white hand
In mine as we walked down the strand.

I put my hand around her waist
And snatched a kiss from her lips in haste.

Then a great big Dutchman rammed my bow,
And said, "Young man, dis bin mein frow."

Then take a warning, boys, from me,
With other men's wives don't get too free.[48]

Scrimshaw representations of this more sordid side of gender relationships are not as numerous. The Nantucket Historical Association has one piece that has a properly dressed woman on one side and a partially clad woman on a couch and in the arms of a man on the other. The woman in the more risqué engraving is succumbing to the man as the verse attached makes clear:

An easy yielding maid,
By trusting is undone;
Our sex is oft betrayed,
By granting love too soon.
If you desire to gain me,

Your sufferings to redress;
She said, o kiss me longer,
Before you shall possess.
But his kiss was so sweet, and so closely prest
That I languish'd and pin'd till I granted the rest.[49]

Seamen's journals sometimes contain interesting depictions of shore life, including dancing girls.[50] Alfred Terry decorated the front of his log with an alluring picture of a Mrs. N. H. Chamberlin, with "27 South Hudson Street" scrawled below the naked torso. Although the exact date and circumstances of the drawing are unknown, Terry was deeply smitten with her charms.[51] And throughout the period under study here, a few books contain Hogarthian scenes of women with ample breasts bulging from low-cut bodices in close proximity to Jack Tars.[52]

Sailors may have approached the subject of loose women with a certain degree of equanimity, but they could also view women as evil, out to take Jack for everything he was worth. Joseph G. Clark explained that the waterfront was rife with women seeking to lead a sailor astray for his money. "Degraded and unprincipled females, by feigned smiles and hypocritical and special graces" attracted the favor of a seaman, "extorting from him valuable presents, or otherwise making large draughts upon his funds." These women used men up, "relinquishing their victim only when the last dollar is transferred to their hands." At that point, they dumped the sailor "without even an apology or its equivalent."[53] This type of woman enticed young Horace Lane into a life of dissipation.

Although the image of the woman as exploiter appears in the eighteenth century, it may have become more poignant in the nineteenth century with greater urbanization and a perception that cities harbored many opportunities for sin. Stuart Frank, for example, argues that most eighteenth-century sailor ballads placed the seaman ashore in the midst of bucolic splendor courting a milkmaid or some other rural lass. In the nineteenth century, however, increasingly Jack Tar appeared in cities enticed by women aiming to take advantage of the sailor.[54]

The sailor's attitude toward his exploitation by women was mixed. Whaler Ezra Goodnough repeatedly described how at Mahe in the Indian Ocean he and his shipmates went "to see the ladies and it was a great time among the women." He referred to the prostitutes as "our sweethearts" and his own special girl as "my wife." His expectations of this relationship were pragmatic. He explained that he had to get his girl a new dress when he returned to Mahe

8. Alfred Terry must have been captivated by the charms of Mrs. N. H. Chamberlin when in New York. The opening page of Terry's journal kept in the South Pacific contains this drawing. Interestingly, there is almost a Polynesian look to the depiction of this New York woman. "Mrs. N. H. Chamberlin." Alfred Terry, Journal from the whaleship *Vesper*, 1842-1848. Mystic Seaport.

because "if I do not get her a new dress she will not remember me." Although the women in Mahe had to be paid to remember, "that is more than the girls at home do" since "they will not think of a poor Devil either for love or money." From this perspective Goodnough asserted, "there is plenty of girls i can get that are not particular wether they are married or not" and concluded "them are the ones for me[.] they are the comforts of life."[55] Goodnough was not alone in this approach to women. In the song "Sailor's Money" the tar willingly allows his landlady and her daughter to take his last penny—suggesting that the money was nowhere near as important to him as the pleasures it purchased.[56] Songs like "New York Girls" and "Charming Jane Louisa" are "played for laughs, with self-deprecating, first-person humor" in which the sailor mocks his own gullibility.[57] Horace Lane actually fell in love with one of the girls he met in French Johnny's. When he returned to port some time later, he discovered that "she learned to drink and swear and died wretched in Philadelphia."[58] In the song "Jack's Revenge" the sailor outsmarts the woman concerned only with profit. The sailor returns to his Kitty, pretending to be broke and down on his luck. Kitty tells him, "Begone from my sight, now you've spent all your money." The sailor, of course, shows her his bag full of money and leaves, despite her cries that she really loves him.[59]

The odd combination of images that may have played in the sailor's mind is suggested by the frequent reference to the madam of a bordello with the word "mother."[60] Of course this practice was not limited to the waterfront, and no doubt was in part based on the fact that such women were usually older than the employees rendering sexual favors. The irony was not lost upon waterfront customers. Moreover, the mobile maritime population sought out women who could provide services and fulfill some functions of being a mother, offering comfort and a bed, even if that included behavior not associated with more sentimental depictions of motherhood. The peculiar waterfront orientation of the mother label with houses of prostitution is suggested by the tongue-in-cheek reportage of an anti-prostitution riot in New York City in 1793. One newspaper proclaimed that the mob had attacked "Mother Carey's nest of CHICKENS" during the riot. Everyone in a port like New York would understand the joke; Mother Carey may have been the name of the keeper of this house of ill repute, but Mother Carey's chicken was also the common name of a sea petrel sighted on every cruise in the Atlantic.[61]

Although sailors could joke about their relationships with women ashore, there was also a dark side. A sailor could go to sea to escape from women who sought to control him. In this case going to sea meant liberty from tiresome shoreside attachments. The sailor sometimes viewed a wife as a tyrant who henpecked her husband, preventing him from enjoying himself. John Palmer copied a song into his Revolutionary War journal that claimed that a man who was married may as well be hanged because "His Wife at his Elbow Like an Emperor will Stand," ordering him about. A wife needed constant praise and presents. Moreover, women would not allow the sailor to spend his money and go to the tavern to drink with his shipmates. This ballad Palmer labeled a "true song" and concluded:

So a Bachelors Life I Do think is the Best
be him Drunk or be him Sober he may take his Rest
No Wife to Controle him Nor Children to Cry
O Happy is the man Who A Bachelor Dies.[62]

Going to sea also allowed a man to escape from a woman who would eventually betray him. Ultimately this view of women gave vent to expressions of misogyny. Charles Babcock wrote his brother Henry that his girlfriend was not to be trusted. Charles went on to exclaim that no woman could be trusted out of the man's sight for more than a week.[63] In a similar vein, Ebenezer Clinton copied the following lines on the inside cover of a journal:

Mankind from Adam have Been Woman's fools
Women from Eve have Been the Devil's tools
Heaven might have spar'd one torment when we fell
Not Left us Women or not threaten'd Hell.[64]

Nathaniel Ames had contempt for all women. He commented despairingly about the "Wapping landladies and sailor's wives" who came aboard ships in London. Such women were not to be trusted and were searched "in the most indecent manner" both upon coming aboard, for fear they were smuggling liquor, and upon leaving, for fear that they were stealing. Ames, who wrote his book to provide an unadulterated account of what it meant to be a sailor, also explained (wrongly) that most sailors do not marry because of the "proverbial infidelity of sailors' wives."[65]

Richard Henry Dana, Jr., offered a similar understanding of the seaman's view of women, focusing on the woman who married the sailor to obtain as much money as she could and, as soon as the tar set out on his next voyage, abandoned him. Dana described the despondency of "Chips," the carpenter, when the *Pilgrim* received a mail delivery and there was no letter from his wife, whom he had married just before leaving Boston. "Sails," the sailmaker, tried to comfort him by telling him he was "a bloody fool to give up his grub for any woman's daughter." Dana did not leave this negative portrait here; he went on to have Sails describe his own ill-conceived marriage. Sails had just been paid off with five hundred dollars from a Pacific voyage—a small fortune—rented a four-room apartment for his new wife—which was spacious beyond belief for a nineteenth-century working man—packed it full of furniture, and provided half pay in his absence for his next voyage. When he returned she was "'off, like Bob's horse, with nobody to pay the reckoning;' furniture gone,—flag-bottomed chairs and all;—and with it his 'long togs,' the half-pay, his beaver hat, white linen shirts, and everything else." Sails concluded with advice to Chips, telling him to "cheer up like a man, and take some hot grub! Don't be made a fool of by anything in petticoats! As for your wife, you'll never see her again; she was 'up keeleg and off' before you were outside of Cape Cod."[66]

The hazy boundary separating the various images of women in sailors' minds is suggested when Joshua Penny self-mockingly related how sailors go ashore and play the gentleman while their money lasted. Two such tars passed by a window where two "ladies" were sitting. One lady turned to the other and, in a voice intended to be overheard by the sailors, dismissively declared, "There goes two sailors, gentlemen for a week." Without missing a beat, one of the sailors turns to the other and says "Yes . . . and there sits two strumpets for life."[67] Perhaps the women mocked the pretensions of the seamen because they resented both the sailors' independence and their rejection of values that would have kept them closer to hearth, home, and female companionship. The sailors, not surprisingly for men who had been out at sea in a largely male fraternity, focused on the sexuality of the "strumpets." The women were not identified; they may have been prostitutes, or wives or sweethearts of men on the waterfront, or from a higher class. To Penny it almost did not matter. From Jack's cynical perspective, all women were captives to their sexuality and whatever relationships that entailed.

The interplay of these various images of women also appears in the sailor's approach to the exotic native. Here was the innocent child, trusting caretaker, carnal object, and sexual exploiter rolled up in one. The exotic female had long played a prominent role in travel and adventure literature. Captain John Smith, after having been rescued by other princesses, was saved by Pocahontas. Sailors had similar tales. In the Sumatran wilderness in 1780 escaped prisoner of war John Blatchford stumbled across a nearly naked girl who led him to safety.[68] The mulatto seaman Robert Adams reported sleeping with the wife of his Muslim master while held in Saharan Africa.[69] In a light-hearted song published in 1817, an unfaithfulship carpenter promised to be true to his wife, Sue, only to lay with an Indian woman as soon as he joined Perry on the Great Lakes.[70]

What really caught the maritime imagination was the South Pacific. After the first British and American vessels visiting the South Pacific reported naked women swimming out to vessels and having sex with any man who wanted it, and taking in payment the most trifling product of the industrialized world, sailors became enthralled with the notion that the South Sea islands were some sort of paradise. The story of the mutiny aboard the *Bounty* resonated for seamen throughout the first half of the nineteenth century in part because of the sexual encounters between the crew and Polynesian women.[71] Alfred Terry aboard the whaleship *Vesper* was struck by the looseness and cupidity of the women on Easter Island who boarded the vessel for the crew's sexual pleasure. His description of the women, while not exactly romantic, was certainly graphic. He wrote that the women were naked except for "a strip of bark around their wastes and a bunch of leaves in their crotch."[72] William Clarke thought the women on Tahiti were "salacious" and said that in order to obtain "luxuries they never dreamed of when in their natural state," the men "will prostitute their daughters and even their wives for a dollar."[73] The many portrayals of Polynesian women on scrimshaw depict a more attractive native than Terry and Clarke would have us think. The allure of the South Sea maiden also appeared in the Yankee ballad "The Lass of Mohee," in which the native girl invites the sailor into her hut and tries, unsuccessfully, to convince him to remain with her when his ship is ready to sail.[74] Herman Melville built his reputation as a writer by describing his experience on Typee in the Marquesas. The women not only were mostly naked, but they had a childish approach to the world that combined sexual curiosity with a desire to please. The girls who surrounded him when he first arrived were "unsophisticated young creatures" and "void of artificial restraint." They were "wonderfully polite and humane; fanning aside the insects that occasionally lighted on our brows; presenting us with food; and compassionately" regarded Melville in his afflictions. Their "prying inquisitiveness" unnerved Melville, who confessed that "in spite of all their blandishments, my feelings of propriety were exceedingly shocked, for I could not but consider them as having overstepped the due limits of female decorum." Melville was beside himself in describing the incredible natural beauty of his own personal favorite, the lovely Fayaway, who "for the most part clung to the primitive and summer garb of Eden." In the South Pacific native woman, the sailor found all that he imagined any female could be; a child to be taught and protected, a mother and sister to nurse him, a sweetheart to idealize, and a sexual object to gratify his desires.[75]

The reality behind the various images of women and the persona of the handsome sailor is complex and multifaceted. A sailor's liberty confronted women with difficult choices. Women left alone on shore sometimes sought solace in another man's arms. Men also turned to other women in some instances. Both males and females also engaged in more long-lasting relationships. Moreover, women learned to depend upon one another in a variety of ways. Finally, life on the waterfront sometimes reflected the sailor's gendered image of women and sometimes not. Users and takers could be men or women. There were also relationships based upon mutual love and appreciation.

The family remained important to many seamen.[76] The poignancy of William Widger's dream attests to his attachment to his family, despite his fears. Throughout his stay in Mill Prison, Widger wrote to his wife and received letters from her in turn. Others at Mill Prison had similar experiences. William Russell, held as a prisoner during the Revolutionary War, dreamed of his wife, declaring in November 1781 that "Would to God, I could in a Dream be sent into the arms of my beloved and adored Wife."[77] Jonathan Deakins wrote to his "Loving Wife" in 1782 to inform her he was still alive, but admitted that knowing her low circumstances back in Marblehead made him even more miserable. He signed the letter: "I remain your Loving husband Till Death."[78] John Mitchell, the American agent for prisoners of war in Halifax in 1814, received several letters from men captured by the British who petitioned for special permission to return home to take care of a sick or needy wife and family.[79]

Scrimshaw images reinforce the impression of how important the family was to men at sea. The whaler scrimshander, or carver, often portrayed domestic scenes. He also etched in the outlines of women based on the latest fashions from *Godey's Lady's Book*, a domesticated and refined ideal of womanhood that was often absent from his life. Perhaps more important, the scrimshander created a variety of implements to be used in the home, including elaborate pie crimpers and swifts used to hold yarn in the absence of the husband's helping hands. Similarly, scrimshanders decorated busks to be inserted into corsets, holding in the woman's waist and shaping her breasts, as an intimate gift to their loved ones. It was as if the whaleman who carved and crafted whalebone while absent for years at a time hoped to recapture a lost world of domesticity by creating an offering for the women in their lives to be used in female work, or even fashioning the female body.

Relationships between men and women could be sustained over long periods of time, in part through exchanges of letters.[80] Jacob Ball and Mary Timbrell started writing each other before they were married when he was a second mate. Their letters concerned mainly family and their daily activities. Jacob reported on his voyages, describing where he was to sail and under what circumstances. Once they were married Mary wrote of the purchases she made, money she obtained from the shipowner or the sale of items Jacob sent to her. She told him of the health of the children and other family news.[81] Similarly, the correspondence between Elizabeth Hodgdon and Nathan J. Coleman began before and continued after they were married. Coleman sailed out of Boston as a mate on relatively predictable Atlantic voyages. Their letters included expressions of love as well as pragmatic matters. Elizabeth lived in Rochester, New Hampshire, before and after marriage. She also ran a school to support herself when her husband was at sea, earning about $14 a month.[82] Cynthia Sprague and John Congdon each kept a journal to record

9. Whalers often traced their scrimshaw designs from magazines. These matching whale teeth depict two women in the latest finery, clothes that most women on the waterfront were not likely able to own. "Two women in finery." Kendall Whaling Museum.

10. Making whalebone busks, to be inserted into the front of a woman's dress to hold and form her breasts, was another type of scrimshaw. The relatively primitive illustrations on this busk show a woman sitting at a desk, no doubt writing to the absent sailor below. The ship is placed in between the two, symbolizing the reason for their separation. Scrimshaw from the Hinsdale Collection. New Bedford Whaling Museum.

their innermost thoughts, from his days as a second mate until she joined him on his voyages when he captained his own vessels.[83]

The intricate web of relationships between siblings and across generations often appears in this type of correspondence indicating that whatever transpired between a sailor and his romantic attachment ashore often fit into a larger complex of family relationships. Elizabeth Hodgdon wrote to her sister, Sarah, describing the death of a sailor who fell from the rigging at sea. The sailor had been an orphan raised in the Hodgdon household and may have been betrothed to Sarah since she wrote to Elizabeth shortly thereafter describing her despondency over the loss of her loved one, and expressing her hope that Elizabeth would never suffer a similar loss. In a less tragic vein, it is Elizabeth's job even before her wedding to write to Nathan's parents to inform them of his plans for his next voyage.[84] Elizabeth Hammond, like her sailor brothers, moved from the family farm to seek employment in New Bedford. There, she met and married a sailor. We are left to wonder at the circumstances of this romance, but she did write to her parents asking them, on three days notice, to drop everything and attend the wedding ceremony before her betrothed sailed on a new voyage.[85]

In other words, relationships between males and females were seldom in isolation from the world around them. In some instances, such as for officers and captains in the whaling industry of the mid nineteenth century, agents of the ship owners even came into play. Although shipping agents occasionally assisted foremast men and their families, their main concern was aiding the trusted officers who protected their investment. These businessmen therefore repeatedly paid advances to wives and even parents who needed economic assistance. One shipping agent, in an effort to convince a captain to extend a cruise, even promised to keep potential beaus away from the captain's fiancée. The U.S. Navy regularized the policy of allowing seamen to allot half their pay to their wives. This practice extended in some instances to the regular merchant marine if Dana's account of Chips is to be believed.[86]

Officers and captains, however, had many advantages in their ability to protect their wives and families. They had greater economic wherewithal and more job security, and starting in the late eighteenth century captains formed marine societies in most ports. These organizations assisted them if and when they became incapacitated and provided for their widows and families in the event that they should die. Captains thus consciously developed a larger sense of community to help insulate their families from economic disaster as they confronted the hazards of their trade.[87]

Further down in society, poor workers along the waterfront had fewer options. Yet here, too, contrary to stereotypes, men and women struggled to sustain relationships over long periods of time.[88] African Americans turned to the sea after the American Revolution to provide for their families and establish stable households. The pressures of the marketplace, and the poor wages earned by sailors, made this goal increasingly difficult to achieve. After 1830, most blacks with permanent families either sought to keep closer to shore through coasting (sailing on short voyages between various ports on the American seaboard), or obtained maritime-oriented employment on the waterfront.[89]

White sailors faced many of the same difficulties. The Reverend Thomas Tuckerman, a missionary to Boston's poor, kept a record of some of his visits to families in 1826. In brief vignettes, we can see husbands and wives working in and around the waterfront striving to make ends meet. Mr. and Mrs. Hutchings, both twenty-six years old, lived in a cellar in Friends Street. He supported his wife and two young children by digging mud from under the docks. The Grangers were in their thirties and had met two or three years earlier in Nantucket when he was a sailor. They moved to Boston, where he found work as a carpenter. Forty-year-old Mr. Hobson, a mackerel catcher who lived on Ann Street in Boston's North End, may have married a younger woman, for the couple had two children under the age of two. These couples appeared to be getting by. Others were not. James Cooke had been to sea for half of his twenty-eight years. After falling from a mast the previous spring and breaking his leg, he was unable to work. During his confinement his lungs started to go bad and he did not expect to live long. He and his wife had two children, a two-year-old and an infant. The future looked bleak for Mrs. Cooke. She might soon be confronted with supporting herself as did Mrs. Wilson on South Russel Street. Wilson's ropemaker husband had been "broken by intemperance." He entered the House of Industry—a kind of poorhouse—and she supported her large family by doing washing.[90]

Tuckerman detailed the occupation of the female only if she were the main breadwinner. In all likelihood, the wife in each of these families played a more significant economic role than Tuckerman's silence would indicate. Ashley Bowen, for example, worked as a fisherman, rigger, and seaman in Marblehead for several decades. Romance was not absent from his life; he had seen his future wife in a dream even before they met and could recognize her because she had five moles on her cheek. Regardless of her appearance, she was a worker. As Bowen labored away on the rigging of a fishing vessel, his wife Dorothy patiently sewed "colors" (flags) for his customers. When Dorothy died in August 1771, Bowen did not waste much time in finding a replacement. By November he had found himself a widow, had her property appraised, whitewashed his house, took his former wife's chest to his father's place, and moved the widow's goods to his house. On December 8 he was married, and then it was back to work for Bowen and, we assume, his new wife.[91]

The economic role of women can also be seen by their acting as deputy husband in the absence of their spouse.[92] Lydia Hill Almy lived independently during her husband's absence in the late 1790s, taking in boarders, settling accounts, and telling her father-in-law that it was none of his business how much money his son had left with her.[93] Several sailors in 1812 signed over future privateering gains to their wives.[94] Mary Ball worked hard to manage the family's affairs when her husband was at sea. Fisherman Richard

Pedrick gave his wife a power of attorney to collect dividends in 1810.[95] Two Marblehead women decided to split their sons' or husbands' prize money from two separate voyages.[96] Joseph Hart's fictional *Miriam Coffin* told of a woman who abused her role as a deputy husband.[97]

Most women, however, were often left to their own devices when their husbands or lovers went to sea. This experience was not so much the result of a separate sphere as it was a consequence of a separated sphere—the physical distance from the males of the family.[98] Many women along the waterfront earned their livings by washing, sewing, cooking, boarding, keeping a store, and even running houses of ill-repute. Some, especially those who were married to officers, retained a degree of independence. Many of these women did not live in opulence, and most had to work just to get by.[99] In East Greenwich, Rhode Island, Cynthia Sprague and her mother, who was a widow of a ship captain, worked as seamstresses. Often they had so much business that they could hardly keep up with the demand, and Cynthia turned down an offer to work in a factory.[100]

Others struggled. Ann Ludlow of Lombard Street in New York had not heard from her husband in over a year in 1805. She managed to eke out a living by taking in washing, sewing, and a few boarders (two sailors and a rigger, with two young women in the upper floor) in her small apartment. She even turned to her father in New Jersey for financial help.[101] Circumstances often compelled women into gray areas that left their neighbors wondering. A Mrs. Smith on Ann Street, whose husband was absent at sea, claimed to be making a living as a washerwoman. Others thought differently. George Leonard, a shoemaker who boarded next door, declared, "I have no doubt that it was a house of ill fame," and felt that since it was a quiet establishment, it "was one of the best sort." Seaman Jesse Casey, who boarded in the same house as Leonard, said that he visited Smith's three or four times a week when he was lonely. He did not believe it was a house of ill-repute, admitting that if it had been he might well have used her services. Having fallen behind in the rent, and under the accusation that she ran a house of prostitution, Smith was evicted.[102]

Many women faced hardship from a variety of causes, ranging from the difficulty making a living, the absence or loss of their spouse, or simply strains in their relationships. Thomas Gregory maintained contact with his wife while sailing for as long as fourteen months at a time. At one point his wife was ill, he got into debt, and he signed unto a voyage to Canton, China. His wife had to leave New York and stay with relatives in Norwalk, Connecticut. After he agreed to sail to the Orient four years later, Gregory explained that his wife "has anger herself quite sick" over the decision.[103] June Hammond went through three Marblehead husbands; the first two were lost at sea when she was relatively young.[104] Other circumstances could bring hardship to a family. The Eaton household in Brooklyn faced a crisis in 1840 because the father "drinks and wont work" and the mother "supports herself with one child and the 2 others live out."[105] Several women in Providence brought sick or disabled sailor husbands, sons, lovers, and boarders to the Marine Hospital.[106]

When confronted with adversity women often turned to one another for solace, comfort, and companionship.[107] Cynthia Sprague was disconsolate when John Congdon went to sea in 1841. Their exact relationship is unclear, although they had obviously discussed marriage. As soon as Congden left she reported in her journal that she was "too overwrought with emotion" and her eyes were full of tears. She cried for days. In this trying period immediately following separation, she found her greatest relief in talks with Susan Salisbury, whom Cynthia declared "feels for and sympathizes with me like an affectionate sister." Over the next year or so Cynthia and Susan visited each other almost daily, often staying at each other's houses and like sisters sharing the same bed. Cynthia also found support from the wife of one sailor who "knew how to sympathize with me" and told her the separation would be easier once she was married. A few months later Cynthia had the opportunity of reciprocating within the larger community of maritime women. She was asked to take her turn sitting up the night with a sick child. Although she was not feeling well, she joined the vigil, confiding, "but it is a Sailor's child, how could I say no." She shared her duties that night with a married woman, probably a sailor's wife, and even participated in preparing the child's body for a funeral when it died several days later.[108]

The same bonds of community also operated in larger ports. The Reverend Henry Chase visited families all along the New York waterfront in the 1820s. In this intricately bound community, many religious women interacted with each another. His visit at Mr. Smith's at 96 Henry Street provides some suggestion of the network of support shared by waterfront women. Upon his first visit, triggered in part by Mrs. Smith and a Mrs. Wood attending the Mariner's Church, he discovered Mr. Smith was at sea, and was expected home soon. Mrs. Wood, whose father and husband had been lost at sea was at the Smith residence which was down the block from her own house and across the street from her mother's. (Wood may have been there to help because Mrs. Smith's invalid mother lived with her.) The next visit was more dramatic. Unfavorable news had arrived from Smith's ship, and they feared he was lost. Consoling Mrs. Smith was a Mrs. Conner, from nearby Harmon Street, who also attended the Mariner's Church and whose husband had perished off Cape Cod the year before. Through Chase's diary we can see women striving to maintain connections with their loved ones, and, in the case of Mrs. Smith, turning to other women in similar situations to sustain themselves.[109]

Many of the women Chase visited were mothers as well as wives. After Chase offered his sympathies to Mrs. Smith, he crossed the street to find Mrs. Wood at her mother's. Apparently they were anxious, prompting Chase to commented in his diary: "Son of Mrs. Head [Wood's mother] just going to sea."[110] Several other women he visited had sons preparing for voyages. The main relationship that most seamen would have with a female before they went to sea was with their mothers. This close bond is evident in the fact that several young men on privateers signed over their share of future prize money to their mothers.[111] It was also not unusual for a sailor to recall his mother with fondness as he was about to die. Despite living what he described as a "profligate and dark life," Richard Sheel thought of the Methodism of his mother as he confronted death at the Marine Hospital in New York City in 1837.[112]

Mrs. Wood's concern for her brother, after she had lost a husband and a father, suggests a genuine attachment between a sister and a maritime brother, as expressed in the Bayley letter to his sister Lavina. That some sisters viewed their mariner brothers with maternal affection can be seen in a poem by William Alfred Allen's sister after he died at sea in 1849.

There perished my poor child
    Upon the ocean deep,
While moaning winds above him
    Their constant vigils keep.
Farewell, then, child of sorrow
    Thy grave is in the sea,
But long shall live thy virtues
    Enshrined in memory.

The poem is simply signed RA, and only the note attached to the document makes it clear that this is a sister's and not a mother's lament.[113]

The image of the helpless daughter at sea was mainly myth, for daughters, like most women, remained on shore. The real danger for young girls on the waterfront was from sexual exploitation. Lanah Sawyer, the daughter of a seaman, was seduced by a self-proclaimed gentleman who met her in the streets. He brought her to a house of ill-repute, Mother Carey's nest of Chickens, and spent the night with her. The defense lawyers not only brought Sawyer's morals into question, but also attacked all girls of her class. They argued that the only reason a well-dressed man would express interest in a sewing girl was for sex. Lanah's father was "well known amongst the seafaring People" and shortly after the jury acquitted the seducer, a riot broke out that led to the destruction of several houses of prostitution.[114]

Young women like Lanah Sawyer probably saw their behavior differently from the image portrayed by the defense lawyers in 1793. Yes, their station in life brought them out into the streets. And a young woman might even flirt with a man, whether he was a gentleman who deigned to pay her some attention, or a sailor with money in his pocket to buy a small favor or take her on a carriage ride. Like their male counterparts, many of these girls sought some liberty and autonomy in a world marked by dependence, especially female dependence, while also seeking some enjoyment and pleasure. Fifteen-year-old Margaret Graham was just such a girl in the summer of 1805. Her father, Archibald Graham, had knocked down a Portuguese sailor who had grabbed Margaret on the street. A few days later the Portuguese sailor sought revenge, stabbing and killing Archibald in a second brawl. The night of her father's murder, Margaret was in the company of other young women her age visiting waterfront houses with "fiddling and dancing."[115]

The boundary between this type of activity and prostitution was often vague. The playful Moll of popular song and the sailor's imagination may have been a Margaret Graham eager for some music and excitement. She might also be a young woman willing to exchange sexual favors ranging from a kiss to sexual intercourse for a treat. From the perspective of Archibald Graham, a rigger who knew all too well the dangers of the waterfront for a young girl, this was precisely what he feared. Ironically, his death may well have propelled Margaret in the very direction he had hoped to avoid. The greatest predictor of prostitution was the death of a parent, especially of the father.[116]

Unfortunately, the record betrays only brief glimpses of women like Margaret Graham. We do know that economic circumstances, women's work paid barely a living wage, convinced many women to take advantage of the market for commercial sex. The reformer's portrait of a prostitute as a young woman entrapped in a form of bondage brought to an early grave through dissipation and disease is not accurate. There were varying degrees of prostitution. Some was casual and viewed as an occasional supplement to meager wages. Some was more continual and professional. As such, it might lead to economic security, or a more sordid life, or it might be abandoned for marriage or another occupation.[117]

Sailors availed themselves of the prostitutes that worked the waterfront. New York's poorest and most competitive brothels sprang up along Water Street and Corlear's Hook.[118] Wherever the haunts of sailors, whether Fell's Point in Baltimore, or Ann Street on Boston's North End, there were sure to be houses of prostitution. There was an interracial component to much of this activity. As a young boy Horace Lane was taken aback by the black dancing girls of one New York waterfront dive.[119] In every port there was some mixture of races—black women sleeping with white men and black men sleeping with white women.[120] While waterfront workers were not the only clients of a city's prostitutes, wherever a sailor went, he sought out practitioners of the world's oldest profession. Richard Henry Dana, Jr., stated that Indian women, even married Indian women, served as prostitutes for sailors in California.[121] William McNally described how in the Mediterranean, in places like Port Mahon, Minorca, prostitutes were allowed aboard American warships.[122]

There is no easy characterization of waterfront women. Male liberty ashore and at sea placed serious constraints on women's lives. Some women no doubt sold their bodies, while others established stable relationships with men. Some sought the pleasures of the dance hall; others sought solace in religion. Many strove for survival in a tough, competitive world.

From the mid-1700s to the early nineteenth century, however harsh the reality and however varied the experience of women, the waterfront was not immune to the rise of the cult of domesticity. This ideal even reached whalemen who were out in the Pacific for years at a time. The scrimshander aboard a whaler that reeked of boiled blubber, opened the pages of *Godey's Lady's Book* and traced the outlines of a woman primmed in the latest middle-class fashions on a tooth wrenched from a sperm whale's mouth and polished with shark skin.[123] The image of the mother, like that of the sweetheart, gained greater force in the nineteenth century with rise of the sentimentality of the Romantic era. Although middle-class values did not permeate all of the laboring classes, they had some impact. Seafaring became sentimentalized and there was increased concern with the family.[124] Emiline Fish wrote her husband, Nathan, "with four Babys making known their several claims, and not less than two or three attacht to my elbow," but she invoked the saccharine ideal of domesticity when she urged him to return so that he could "feel sensibly 'there is no place like Home.'" He replied with even more sentimentality by wishing "myself at home where I could be employed about the Garden and rock the *cradle* and do some useful chores."[125] The concern with the com-

11. A sailor illustrated his Valentine poem to his love with a couple holding hands. The man's waistjacket, vest, and stance all indicate his maritime profession. The inscription reads: "When I'm far away and landsmen spread their wiley snares / Heed not what these flatterers say, but think on him whom the ocean bears / On one whom when the furious blast tears up and whitens o'er the sea/ High on the yard as quivering Mast, oft heaves a sigh and think on thee. / When gay trm'd sparks around thee swarm, like humming birds round some sweet flower / And praise with purtness evr'y Charm, and oft confess their witty power / Say wilt thou then forget, that youth who scorns all flattery / That youth who boils midst torrid heat, inspite of perils sighs for thee." "When I am far Away." Kendall Whaling Museum.

panionate marriage also became evident with the increase in the number of captains—especially those on long-distance voyages in whalers and clipper ships—who brought their wives aboard.[126]

Obviously, only a few couples enjoyed the privilege of going to sea together. There were also limits on how closely real life followed the domestic ideal. Cynthia Congdon felt the reach of these ideals even as she labored as a seamstress in her small seaport town in Rhode Island. In 1841 she tenderly confided to her journal, "last night I dreamed of my absent friend. He returned and I felt the soft kiss of love on my cheek. And heard his endearing voice. This was too much happiness for me to sleep and I awoke and found it was all a dream."[127] Like William Widger, Cynthia's understanding of gender roles could also be a source of anxiety. Cynthia was not concerned with infidelity. Instead, this proud and strong woman, who continued to work as a seamstress and be an intricate part of the East Greenwich maritime community, focused on her dependent status. In 1844, after her marriage to John Congdon, Cynthia wrote, "I dreamed that Mr. Wall called to see me and after walking around the room he says to me 'With the best information I can obtain your Husband is no more.' Oh said I Mr. Wall! don't tell me so and my great distress waked me with the tear dropping on my cheeks. It affected me so much that I slept no more that night. What shall I do without my Husband. God only knows."[128]

3

A Sailor Ever Loves to Be in Motion

John Ross Browne should never have gone to sea. He was, after all, a twenty-one-year-old gentleman with some education who had served as a reporter in Washington, D.C. In the summer of 1842 he wanted to see the world, sought to make his fortune, and had a penchant for romantic adventure. With smooth hands and fine clothes, he could not find a berth on a merchant vessel in New York. An advertisement for a landsmen caught his eye, and giving it hardly a thought, he signed with a shipping agent for a whaleship out of New Bedford. He was soon on his way to the southern oceans.

The first day at sea was a sobering introduction. Like most green hands, he quickly became seasick. The mate, however, insisted that everyone must work, and work hard, regardless of his condition. "After a day of horrors" the men were allowed to go below. Conditions did not improve. The forecastle, where sailors slept, "was black and slimy with filth, very small, and as hot as an oven." Its contents were none too attractive. "It was filled with a compound of foul air, smoke, sea-chests, soap-kegs, greasy pans, tainted meat, Portuguese ruffians, and sea-sick Americans." Still reeling from his first day on a ship, he found the Portuguese "were smoking, laughing, chattering, and cursing the green hands." "Groans on one side" contrasted with "yells, oaths, laughter and smoke on the other." Distressed, Browne thought that this was not "a very pleasant home for the next year or two," and was soon "sick and sorry enough," wishing heartily that he was ashore.[1]

The voyage only got worse. Browne had barely settled into his berth when a storm struck the vessel. With the bark "staggering along, creaking, groaning, and thumping its way through heavy seas," all hands were called on deck. Browne had no idea what to do and grabbed the first rope he saw, holding on for dear life. The mate came by screaming, "tumble up aloft, and lay out on the yards!" With the ship leaning at forty-five degrees Browne thought the idea preposterous. When the mate thundered "with the ferocity of a Bengal

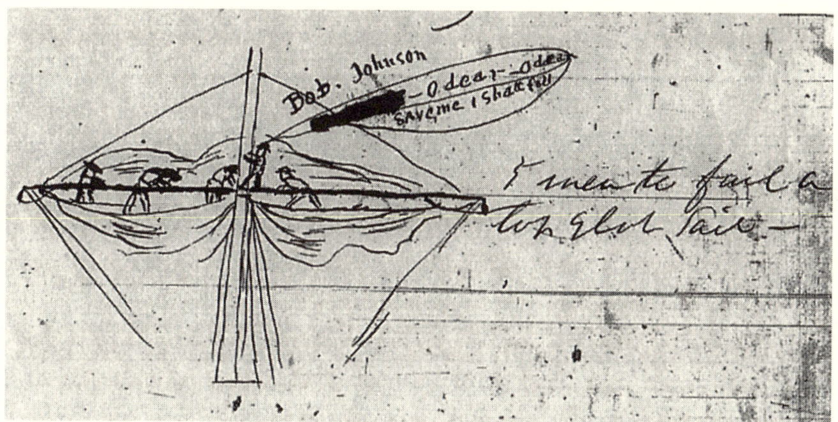

12. Intended to mock one green hand's fear of heights, this etching also shows seamen at work on a yard of a square-rigged vessel. "Etching of work in rigging." Francis Barrett, Log of the Ship *Edward*, 1849–1850. Nantucket Historical Association.

tiger," Browne started climbing delicately up the ratlines and found his way out onto the yardarm. There, with the guidance of a more practiced seaman, he hauled in a sail and secured it with a rope. Somehow he survived. But his romantic vision had been shattered. From that moment Browne saw existence aboard ship as a form of slavery with long, hard hours of work, intermittent boredom, and the lash as the ultimate form of coercion. Life, just as that first night, often hung by a thread.[2]

Browne's account offers us a nice antidote to a romantic portrayal of the sailor's life. Many seamen would agree: aboard ship the work was arduous and they were often miserable. Yet there was an attraction. Herman Melville begins *Moby Dick* with Ishmael on the waterfront, drawn to the sea as an escape. For Melville the sea attracted "crowds of water-gazers" who are "fixed in ocean reveries" and "must get just as nigh the water as they possibly can without falling in." He advised, "Take almost any path you please, and ten to one it carries you down in a dale, and leaves you there by a pool in the stream. There is magic in it." This magic cast its spell on landsmen, as well as the seasoned sailor like Melville. He believed that, like Narcissus, we see ourselves "in all rivers and oceans. It is the image of the ungraspable phantom of life; and this is the key to it all."[3]

Less metaphysical, yet with an equal appreciation for the attractions of the sea, Richard Henry Dana, Jr.'s description of his first days aboard a ship contrast with Browne's experience. (Browne may have written his book with a copy of Dana's *Two Years Before the Mast* close at hand.) After a long day of work, Dana took a moment to look over the expanse of ocean and proclaim, "I felt for the first time the perfect silence of the sea. . . . However much I was affected by the beauty of the sea, I could not but remember that I was separating myself from all the social and intellectual enjoyments of life. Yet, strange as it may seem, I did then and afterwards take pleasure in these reflections, hoping by them to prevent my becoming insensible to the value of what I was leaving."

Dana was shocked out of his daydreaming by orders from the mate and by the coming of a storm. While he, too, struggled up into the rigging for the first time, Dana did not dwell on the negative. He muddled through like Browne, but was up at dawn the next day and wrote "nothing will compare with the *early breaking of day* upon the wide ocean." Dana could be almost lyrical: "Notwithstanding all that has been said about the beauty of a ship under full sail, there are very few who have ever seen a ship, literally, under all her sail . . . light and heavy, and studding-sails, on each side, alow and aloft, she is the most glorious moving object in the world."[4]

The sea continued to lure more prosaic men as well as great literary talents like Melville and Dana. Some sailors rejected the limits and regularity of work ashore. Others were restless.[5] Often, beyond the thrill of the sailing vessel's bow cutting through the spray of salt water, men who went to sea sought a certain kind of freedom. On the waterfront a sailor might act out his fantasies and enjoy excesses of liberty; at sea he experienced a different freedom that came from the vast expanses of the ocean and the fact that he had the whole world to explore. Hugh Calhoun copied a poem in his journal on the "Traits of the Sailors Character." It opened with the following stanza:

> A Sailor ever loves to be in motion,
> Roaming about, he scarce knows where or why;
> He looks upon the dim and shadowy ocean
> As his home, abhors the land, even the sky;
> Boundless and beautiful, has naught to please,
> Except some clouds, which promise him a breeze.[6]

Another seaman, aboard a tension-ridden whaler with an abusive captain, admitted, "The life of a sailor in its best light is hard and unsocial," and then confessed that "The *Sea*, the dark blue sea, has its fascination, and its hails like the abandoned female is overlooked."[7] David Bryant noted "light and pleasant weather" in the logbook of the *Tartar* on February 7, 1816, and then commented that he was "just becoming habituated to the life [at sea] and suppose I could live a year without putting foot to land contentedly."[8] Benjamin Morrell, a seaman who worked his way up to captain, recalled how going to sea for the first time in 1812 excited him: "My soul seemed to have escaped from a prison cage . . . I could now breathe more freely."[9]

Life at sea was a study in contrasts—offering both unfettered liberty and a peculiar form of bondage. Set against the openness of the ocean and the exhilaration of seeing wind and sail driving a great vessel toward faraway places were the hard labor, the limits of board and plank, and the sailor's lack of control over the voyage. Despite the universal brotherhood of the sea and the male bonding that occurred between shipmates, petty conflicts and hatred built up between human beings forced to live on top of one other. Finally, the almighty power of the quarterdeck was tested by the many means of resistance and assertion of independence exerted from the forecastle. The sea simultaneously represented a passport to freedom and a life akin to slavery.

Being a common seaman was all about work. Ships were moving machines whose various parts needed constant adjustment, repair, and replacement as wind and water assaulted every inch of the vessel. The intensity of work surprised many a green hand. George Little had thought that "sailors must have a fine time, with nothing to do but eat, sleep, and look out." Before he even left port he was disabused of this notion, as the crew set to "rigging the head-pump, washing down the decks and sides of the ship, swabbing," and countless other tasks.[10] Once at sea the labor continued. Every rope had to be checked and repaired or replaced as needed. The masts and yardarms also had to be maintained, slushed with tar, adjusted, reset, and sometimes replaced. Sails, too, needed persistent tending. Rips and tears occurred in all weather. When a storm struck, if sails were not quickly furled, they could be in tatters or take down a spar or a mast. Even on the balmiest of days, a sail could wear out. The trick was to make repairs before that point. Decks needed to be cleaned. Sailors hauled equipment in and out, as well as up into the rigging and then down again. Leaks needed to be plugged, and pumps manned to disgorge the bilge water. The cargo had to be secured and checked. In short, on every day the entire vessel was expected to be ship shape. If there was no other work to do, the least skilled members of the crew were set to picking oakum. And before returning to port the work intensified as the captain wanted to enter the harbor and present the vessel in a condition that would make him look good. That end was to be obtained by bending the back of every seaman on board. In foreign ports the crew often had to land the cargo and overhaul the entire ship.[11]

The work depended on the kind of vessel a tar sailed on and his position. Many continued to sail in one capacity only, but sailors often did not remain in one type of service. Melville sailed in merchantmen, whalers, and a man-of-war.[12] Men along the waterfront sought opportunity wherever they could and at times had little choice in the matter. Ashley Bowen labored in the Marblehead fishing fleet, sailed to the West Indies and Europe in merchantmen, went whaling off the Carolina coast, and served in the British navy during the French and Indian War.[13] Simeon Crowell began his career in the 1790s in fishing, and later voyaged in small vessels that sailed along the coast and larger ships throughout the North Atlantic.[14] Gurdon L. Allyn went to sea in 1809 at age ten in fishing and coastal voyages out of Newport, worked on whalers and sealers, sailed three times around the world, fought in the Civil War as an officer in the navy, and returned to coasting and fishing as an old man.[15] James Fenimore Cooper's friend Ned Myers sailed on ships on most of the seven seas, went whaling, and even fought for the U.S. Navy on the Great Lakes.[16] Not every tar had such varied experiences, and many continued to sail in one capacity only, but it is a mistake to assume that the boundaries between different maritime occupations were any less fluid than the oceans Jack Tar crossed.[17]

Labor remained at a premium on American merchantmen, and each type of vessel had certain requirements. During the colonial period there was a drop in the average crew size in the eighteenth century as the threat of piracy lessened and vessels decreased their turnaround time in port. Depending on the voyage, the ratio of tons per man (the standard means of measuring ships) changed from about four to seven tons per man at the beginning of the eighteenth century to seven to ten tons per man to right before the Revolutionary War. These trends accelerated after American independence, in part because changes in design led to larger ships.[18] The relatively higher paying American ships gained a reputation in the nineteenth century for having smaller crews than European vessels of similar construction.[19] Shipowners drove down the ratio between tonnage and crew size, intensifying the amount of work for each crew member. Based on a sample taken from the Baltimore Customs records, the typical ship size in 1786 was about 192 tons with an average crew of just less than thirteen men. Twenty years later the average ship was 289 tons with a crew of eighteen men. This represented a change of about 15 tons per crew member to more than 18 tons per crew member.[20] In another thirty years, and with the introduction of many innovations in design and rigging that created the Baltimore Clipper, the average ship was almost 500 tons with a crew of less than sixteen, for a ratio of approximately 31 tons per crew member. Captains on these new vessels, with their sleek hull and vast spread of canvas, took pride in getting as much speed as possible out of every shift of breeze. In addition to the increased maintenance that came from the changes in tonnage-per-man ratio, crews repeatedly had to clamber into the rigging to take in or let out more sail. Changes in man-per-ton ratios appeared in almost all oceangoing vessels, including barks and two-masted brigs.[21]

We should not diminish the amount of work aboard earlier vessels, or aboard smaller craft. Coasting vessels, often sloops (one mast) and schooners (two masts) with fore and aft rigging, had fewer but larger sails than square-rigged vessels and were very good at tacking and therefore better able to sail into the wind and in coastal waters.[22] If the voyage were especially short, such as between Baltimore and Norfolk, these vessels could range from 10 to 40 tons, with crews of two to three men. With such a tiny crew, distinctions between captain and seaman were slight; everyone had to work nearly constantly.[23] The sloops and schooners that sailed between North American ports or to the West Indies ranged between 40 and 150 tons and had from three to eight men as crew. Small crews left little time for leisure. Like the full-rigged ship the ratio between crew and tonnage increased during the 1750 to 1850 period in these vessels as well.[24]

The watch system dictated labor rhythms at sea aboard all types of merchant vessels. Technically, sailors served four hours on and four hours off around the clock. A dogwatch in the evening, usually from four to eight, was divided in half with two hours for each watch to shift the time that each watch labored from day to day. In a crew of four, two men on watch saw to the ordinary immediate needs of the vessel. Even in a larger crew of ten, which included the captain, a mate, a cook, and possibly a steward, two or three seamen would be on duty at any given time. Obviously, if the vessel needed any serious alteration of sails, or if a storm struck, the captain called for all hands. The men not on watch duty would thus have their precious few hours of sleep disturbed by a burst of labor often sparked by a rush of adrenaline that came with every emergency.

The length of a voyage varied greatly, depending on the type of vessel and the nature of the trade. A coaster might be at sea for a few hours, or a couple of weeks. Transatlantic trips ran approximately thirty days going east and forty-five days going west.[25] Voyages to the West Indies might be shorter, but usually entailed several months away from port. As American commerce reached to South America, Africa, and the Pacific rim, vessels might be away from port for a year or more.

There was thus some predictability in many sailing trips, wind and weather permitting. A ship's papers were supposed to provide a full accounting of the crew signed aboard, and technically all crew members were to be brought back to the end point of the voyage. Likewise the articles of agreement signed by every seaman listed the projected ports of call. Deviation from that route was a violation of contract.[26] Sometimes a vessel would make regular runs to the same port or region. Between July 23, 1842, and April 18, 1843, the schooner *Gallant Mary* made eleven runs between Baltimore and the Caribbean.[27] In most instances, the crew would change on each voyage.

Despite efforts to maintain schedules, there was little predictability in a sailor's life. Weather often delayed a return trip. Other factors also came into play. Some captains altered course in search of better markets. If prices were too low in one port, the ship might try another. Even if there was no change in itinerary, if business was slow, turnaround time might increase from a few weeks to a few months or more. Mending damage might also hold up departure, especially if repairs were expensive and parts hard to come by. Changes in international politics, revolutions, wars, new trade restrictions, and pirates all affected voyages.

Sailors themselves, with their own notions of liberty, often cut their time short by leaving a ship. Nathaniel Ames remarked in 1832 that American sailors had no loyalty and signed off and on vessels wherever they might be. Tracing a Cape Cod man, he suggested, might "find him performing one voyage from Boston and the next from New Orleans; to-day carrying plaster from Passamaquoddy to New York and to-morrow in a French whaler off the Falkland Islands." Ames believed that it is as "impossible to calculate" a sailor's "movements as it would be to predict the direction and extent of the next skip of that most eccentric of all animals, a flea."[28] A seaman took his labor where he thought fit.

Jobs on ships required skilled labor. In responding to the advertisement for landsmen, John Ross Browne was applying for a specific position aboard ship. Sailors on larger vessels fell into three basic categories: able seamen, ordinary seamen, and boys (sometimes referred to as green hands or landsmen, but always, no matter the age, considered boys). On smaller vessels these ratings were less significant, although even on sloops and schooners of under 100 tons some distinctions were made. This hierarchy of skill appeared in crew lists from the eighteenth and early nineteenth centuries. Usually the sailor rated himself when he signed the articles of the vessel. An able seaman might sign on as an ordinary seaman if the captain was paying only those wages. A boy or ordinary seaman would almost never claim a higher status unless he was

13. Seamen needed to know how to handle a small boat as well as work on larger vessels. "Shore Party." New Bedford Whaling Museum.

capable of performing the work required. No one wanted to be at sea with a crew of eight, expecting that each watch would have at least one able seaman, only to discover that one of the supposed skilled sailors was incompetent. The whole crew would suffer.

Each category of seamanship had its skill level. Dana claimed that both able and ordinary seamen were expected to "hand, reef, and steer." These tasks entailed climbing into the rigging, furling and unfurling the sails, as well as commanding specialized knowledge of a variety of sails and ropes. An able seaman would be distinguished by his handiness with a marlin spike, neatly restoring and mending the rigging with "knots, splices, seizings, coverings, and turnings in." He must know how to "make a long and short splice in a large rope, fit a block-strap, pass seizings to lower rigging, and make the ordinary knots, in a fair, workmanlike manner." Ordinary seamen performed some of this work but had not quite mastered all of its elements. Landsmen and boys did the least pleasant and most mundane tasks, like slushing the masts and yards with tar, swabbing the deck, and coiling rope. They also had to go aloft and help in loosening and furling the sails in a subordinate capacity to the ordinary and able seamen.[29]

Every vessel's captain had total responsibility. The smaller the crew, the smaller the distinction between the captain and the rest of the men serving aboard a vessel. When the crew reached a total of four or five men there would also be a first mate. The captain and the first mate would each take charge of a watch. The first mate was usually responsible for keeping the ship's log, indicating date, conditions, and employment of the crew. Often mates did the most skilled work in the rigging and they had to be tough enough to make a hardened tar jump when they barked an order.[30] If the vessel was larger still, over 200 tons with a crew of ten, there was likely to be a first and second mate, each in charge of one watch. A second mate was frequently in an awkward position. He had to serve out orders, yet lacked the authority of his superiors. Too close to the common seamen, he was just beginning his career as an officer. One sailor commented that the second mate is "neither officer or man."[31] Larger vessels would have more elaborate hierarchies with a third mate and maybe a boatswain. In addition, specialized crew members might be hired like a ship carpenter and sailmaker. Most often, since knowledge aboard sailing vessels was acquired through experience, the captain and officers had worked their way from the forecastle to the quarterdeck, although personal connections helped one advance.[32]

Work on fishing vessels was organized somewhat differently. The distance between captain and crew, as it was on smaller merchantmen, was not as great. If there was fishing to be done, everyone sank their lines and hauled in the catch. Along the New England coast, a fishing boat usually also had a shoreman, whose job was to preserve and process the fish. Work was seasonal, in New England running from March to November. During this time a vessel might return to port three to four times to bring in the catch and refit. Labor came in spasms of intense activity, interspersed with slack moments during which the six- to eight-man crew entertained one another with story and song. Often they passed empty hours drinking.[33]

Conditions within the fishing industry of the New England coast experienced many gyrations, as Daniel Vickers explains. During the 1790s and early 1800s, fishing provided a degree of independence and profit for the fisherman. In the closing days of the colonial period and after the 1810s, however, the industry became more confining and under greater control of the merchants in port. Although the work force changed with these conditions, during the middle decades of the nineteenth century fishing became more of a

14. Whaleman John F. Martin drew this picture in his log depicting a crucial moment in capturing and killing a whale. "Whale boat attacking Whale." John F. Martin, Log of the Ship *Lucy Ann*, 1841–1844. Kendall Whaling Museum.

permanent occupation along the New England coast, and the essential outlines of the labor remained the same.[34]

Great changes occurred in the whaling industry. At the end of the colonial period, whaling voyages were just beginning to reach further into the Atlantic and last for several months. After a hiatus during the Revolutionary War, whalemen began extending their voyages. With the processing of the whales taking place aboard ship, vessels got larger and the time at sea longer. By the early nineteenth century, whalers had ventured into the Pacific. Eventually ships stayed at sea for three to four years as they scoured the globe for leviathans.

The hierarchy aboard ship became more rigid in whalers in the nineteenth century as the captain ruled over a crew of thirty to forty. Gradations in rank appeared with first, second, and third mates, as well as coopers, carpenters, sailmakers, harpooners, and a variety of seamen's ranks. Landsmen like Browne were at the bottom. Because of the size of the crew, the daily work on the vessel was easier than on a merchantman. Also, since speed was not of the essence and one spot on the whaling ground was as good as another, whalers seldom cracked much sail. Once a pod of whales was spotted, activity reached a fever pitch. Three to four boats were lowered, packed with four to six oarsmen, a boat steerer, and a harpoonist. If the men were lucky enough to fix on to a whale, and survive the ordeal by killing it, they had to drag the carcass back to the ship. The whale was then made fast to the vessel's side, and the blubber cut out and processed in the try works. The labor was messy and dangerous, and the stench was awful. It was not unusual in these circumstances for the crew to work twenty-four hours nonstop.[35] One whaleman reported that between hunting and cutting out whales, a crew had only five hours of sleep in fifty.[36]

Labor aboard a man-of-war differed from labor on a whaler or merchant ship. Despite the large crews (a frigate would have three to four hundred men), the officers saw to it that there was plenty to keep them busy. The structure of work remained the same whether the sailor served in the British or American navy. (American seamen also served in the French, Dutch, Danish, and other navies, but most were in the English-speaking services.) The daily maintenance work only increased as the aim was for total spit and polish. Dragging the holystone—a huge scrubbing stone—over sand and water on the decks every morning represented one aspect of this desire for cleanliness. Clothing, even the hammocks, were expected to be immaculate. Officers took pride in speed, so sails had to be constantly adjusted. Whether in peace or war, guns had to be worked, and the vessel made ready for battle. Impressment or recruitment into the British navy meant an undetermined sentence to this work. The American navy tended to have limited terms of service, in wartime for a specific voyage and in the nineteenth century for a set number of years.[37]

Privateers were less demanding in terms of work. Like a regular warship they would have large crews, as they had to be prepared to fight. A small schooner, for example, might have one hundred men. These vessels varied greatly in discipline. Some privateers were as spotless as a navy ship, but most fell short of that goal. Privateers had detailed duty lists, exercised their great guns, and called men to their battle stations regularly. Speed was also essential for a privateer, whether to chase down its prey or to escape the guns of a more heavily armed opponent. All privateersmen understood this and worked to make sure that the vessel could operate at its top speed.[38]

Living conditions aboard every type of vessel were cramped and without privacy. The forecastle of a merchantman might be twelve feet long, and almost as wide at its greatest breadth but tapered off toward the bow. A whaler's forecastle might be slightly larger to accommodate greater numbers. This confined space was the sailor's "dining and dressing room, bedchamber and parlor." The furniture was spartan. The beds were little more than

15. Although somewhat fanciful, this portrayal of a forecastle gives some sense of the crowded conditions and varied relationships aboard ship. "Life in the Forecastle." J. Ross Browne, *Etchings of a Whaling Cruise* (New York, 1846).

planked bunks with maybe a threadbare mattress, a blanket as cover, and a canvas bag stuffed with dunnage as a pillow. Sea chests made do as tables, and bunks served as chairs. Light came from a candle or old lamp. The toilet was in the "head" or the very front of the vessel. Warships had more space devoted to housing, owing to the number of men required by privateers and the navy. Sailors slept in hammocks swung tightly on the gun deck, next to and on top of one another. During the day, hammocks were folded and stowed along the ship's sides, providing added protection in a battle. The crew divided into messes of four to eight, prepared food and ate together (hence the term "messmate" to describe a relationship even closer than shipmate). Whether in a merchantman or a man-of-war, little if anything could be kept from the prying eyes of one's shipmates. Even journals were considered fair game for anyone who could read. Many a cruel joke was played on the green hand who strove to keep anything private from the rest of the crew.[39]

There was seldom enough food, and its quality often left something to be desired. The experienced tar tapped his hard biscuit before eating and watched the insects clamor to the surface to check on the disturbance. Meals consisted of salt beef or pork, duff, and lobscouse (a shipboard stew of meat, vegetables, and potatoes). Merchantmen had a cook who lived separately from the crew; in the nineteenth century African Americans increasingly held the position. This individual, despite the complaints of his fellow seamen, was expected to have some skill in handling the ship's stores if not in the culinary arts. His wage was often higher than the average seaman's. In the forecastle the men ate out of a common pot, called a kid, much to the chagrin of one green hand who described the forecastle's table manners as "hacking here and there, not unlike savages."[40] Sailors of all stripes sought to supplement their fare whenever they could through fishing or purchasing fresh vegetables and fruits while in port. The main beverage was water, provided in barrels on deck. Unless the vessel was put on short rations, sailors were welcome to use a dipper and quench their thirst whenever they felt the need. Coffee became increasingly important to sailors in the nineteenth century. Most sailors also made sure that they had their share of the daily grog.

The grog helped break the monotony of the routine. Long voyages or being becalmed could wear nerves thin. One log keeper commented, "there is such sameness & the same tegious [tedious] recurrence to Nautical observations that I am obliged to drive off the Hypocondriac, which hovers about me." Repeated cloudiness and rain could also be depressing. The same sailor wrote:

The darkened sky how thick it lowers
Troubled with storms & big with showers
No cheerful gleam of light appears
But nature pours forth all her tears.

He then added, "Long passage dark Gloomy weather very unpropitious, the *Blue Devils* hover round."[41] Shipboard existence could be tiresome and arduous. On a transatlantic voyage, one sailor complained, "slave like life this going to sea, completely imprisoned, [and] knocked about too and fro."[42] The humdrum of the trackless, endless sea and repetitive work plagued whalers when no whales were in sight. Browne reminded his readers that "every body who has ever read of the sea" was aware of the "monotony of a long passage." On the "clumsy barque," Browne explained, "time hung very heavily on our hands."[43]

Although familiar with tedium, a sailor knew that the sea was a dangerous place. Men died at sea. Dangling from the yardarm during his first storm, a green hand like Browne had better hang on for dear life. Even experienced seamen toppled from aloft in fair weather. Ebenezer Clinton described how twenty-nine-year-old John Nichols slipped off the yardarm a few weeks after leaving Boston. The crew made "Every Exertion to save him," to no avail.

"The poor soul Swam after the Ship a large time." Realizing his efforts were in vain, he lifted his hat and "twirled it over his head and threw it from him and gave up the ghost." Logbooks and journals report repeatedly of men taking such falls. Crashing onto the deck meant at the least serious injury. Sometimes sailors were lucky and the fall was cushioned by a wind-filled sail. Or they landed in the sea and could swim long enough to be saved, but many sailors could not swim a stroke. Even the deck and below held ample opportunity for accidents. Shifting cargo, broken equipment falling from aloft, a mishandled tool, back-breaking labor, an unexpected lurch of the sea, all held the potential for injury or death.[44]

A storm only intensified the danger, as the entire vessel could disappear without a trace. During one storm in September 1846, sixty-three men from the Marblehead fishing fleet drowned.[45] In 1815 the *Wasp* set sail into the Atlantic, never be heard from again.[46] Hurricanes left ships without masts, cast on their beam-ends, or at the bottom of the ocean. The schooner *Dispatch Packet* left Salem's Derby Wharf in September 1820 and arrived in Martinique twenty-eight days later. The voyage was uneventful, and after another month the *Dispatch Packet* headed back to New England. The ship never made it to Salem. For twenty-nine days "sea mountains" engulfed the schooner, throwing the vessel on its beam-ends, smashing its cabin, and sweeping away the masts. The men ran short of food, and had only rainwater to drink. After ninety-eight days at sea the schooner limped back to the West Indies and was condemned and sold as a wreck.[47] Anyone who braved Cape Horn knew that he put his life at risk in the stormy waters south of Tierra del Fuego. Tales about hair-raising experiences with wind and weather became staples for many sailors.[48]

The terrors of the sea went beyond drowning and sinking in a storm. Sailors left in a disabled vessel or who piled into a longboat after their ship went down sometimes faced harrowing ordeals. In 1765 the *Peggy* was sailing back to New York from the Azores when a storm left the ship a floating hulk. As the *Peggy* drifted for days, provisions ran out and the crew resorted to cannibalism before they were rescued.[49] The greatest saga of this kind was the story of the whaleship *Essex*. On November 20, 1820, an irate whale rammed the *Essex*, stove in her sides, and sent the ship to the bottom of the Pacific. Twenty men were left with three whaleboats. Having taken some provisions and water from the vessel, the crew embarked on a journey of epic proportions. Wrongly fearing cannibals on the nearest islands, the Marquesas about 800 miles to the windward, the whaleboats beat their way south and then east to reach the coast of South America—a trip of more than 4,500 miles. One boat and its crew were lost, three men voluntarily remained on a deserted island, and only six starved men were picked up at the end of their oddysey. To survive, these men had to eat the dead bodies of their shipmates. Worse, one boat crew drew lots to see who would be killed to provide sustenance for the others.[50] Even if a ship was not wrecked, lack of wind or contrary winds could also spell disaster. When a ship's water or provisions gave out, the crew faced an agonizing death. Short provisions might lead to scurvy or malnourishment, crippling a man for life, or cause accidents a healthy man might avoid.

Sickness and disease also created problems and could be fatal. The captain usually served as something of a doctor on all except naval vessels, which would usually have a doctor on board. He might have to pull a tooth, care for infection, or set a broken bone. Visiting a disease ridden-port could devastate a crew. The yellow fever epidemics that racked American ports in the 1790s and early 1800s came from ships from the West Indies. Mortality was especially high along the waterfront.[51] At sea the consequences of contagion could be catastrophic. With few extra hands on most ships, a disease like yellow fever or malaria, could leave a crew on a merchantman so short-handed that it might put the entire vessel in jeopardy. Yellow fever swept through one vessel in the West Indies, killing the captain and four others in August 1802.[52] A whale captain reported that he lost one man and had twelve others down on account of smallpox in 1839.[53] The close quarters aboard a warship spread disease rapidly. More than one hundred men fell ill after the frigate *Columbia* left China in 1839.[54] One reason that the British resorted to impressment so often in the West Indies was that the unhealthy climate so decimated the navy that captains desperately needed more manpower to sail and fight on their ships.

For many sailors the camaraderie at sea offered solace in the face of adversity. Special bonds developed between men who ate together, stood frozen watch together, reefed sail together, listened to one another's yarns, and lived within and opposed the same authoritarian structure. Each tar knew the dangers he confronted from the elements as well as from pirates and foreign predators.

Richard Henry Dana, Jr., relished the life of the forecastle and viewed it as a release from the supervision of the officers. He believed that "No man can be a sailor, or know what sailors are, unless he has lived in the forecastle with them—turned in and out with them, and eaten of their dish and drank of their cup."[55] The sense of community and shared experiences was very important to sailors and fostered equality before the mast. Although young Joseph Ward had been outraged by the eating habits of his shipmates, he quickly accommodated himself. Before the short voyage to Liverpool was over (they made soundings in seventeen days), he thoroughly identified with his fellow sailors. His constant complaints about the oppressive officers suggests that the sailors shared a resentment of those who commanded them.[56]

Other factors, however, also played an important role in bringing the forecastle together. Seasickness, experienced by nearly every green hand and by many an old sailor at the beginning of the voyage, served almost as a rite of passage for many. As both Dana and Browne could attest, seasickness did not elicit any sympathy, but it could form an odd bond between men who experienced this physical upheaval that marked the transition from landlubber to seaman.[57]

Work also molded a group identity. Sailors relied upon one another whether they hung precariously from a yardarm, labored on deck, or worked in the hold. The everyday experience aboard ship reminded every sailor of his dependence on his shipmates. Facing a crisis, whether storms or some unidentified warship on the horizon, the mutual dependence became even more apparent.

One daily symbol of the experience of group identity was the sea chantey. These songs reflected the group rhythms of work on a sailing ship to such a degree that specialized chanteys with particular beats were applied to different types of work. One man would sing the verse, following the general outlines of a well known chantey while fully capable of adding embellishments of his own, and the rest of the crew would chime in with the refrain. The hauling, tugging, or pushing would be tied to specific points in the chantey. There were chanteys for working the brake windless, capstan, halyards, sheets, and a wide variety of other tasks aboard ship.[58]

Whatever leisure time there was at sea obviously had to be spent with shipmates. On many vessels, Sunday was a day of slack work by common custom. Jack Tars would then take out their sea chests, rearrange their few possessions, mend and wash clothes, and spend time with each other without the immediate supervision of the officers. The dogwatch, too, was a period of relative ease. At these times tars shared stories or sang popular ballads. Men of the sea prized their ability to tell tales, holding their audience spellbound and stretching the truth past the point of credibility. Journals and books about the sea, especially in the nineteenth century, abound with examples of these yarns. Similarly, a sailor who could sing twenty or thirty verses of some well-known tune was held in high esteem. As Samuel Leech explained, sailors survived by singing songs, listening to "tough forecastle yarns," and telling jokes "with sufficient point to call out roars of laughter."[59] Such moments helped to cast the bonds that created the fraternity of the forecastle.

The forecastle, however, was not always united. In Herman Melville's fictionalized account of his first experience at sea, a mean-spirited sailor named Jackson bullied the entire crew.[60] John Larkin jumped ship from a whaler in the 1840s because of the ill treatment he received at the hands of the crew.[61] At times these hostilities could erupt into violence. Young Benjamin Seamans broke his leg in a scuffle with shipmate Levi Hall in 1798.[62] The second mate of the *Charlotte* who stepped between two fighting men was accidently stabbed.[63] Aboard the whaleship *Vesper*, the blacksmith's mate stole a knife from one sailor. The two men began to argue, throwing the ship into an uproar. The captain interceded and told the men to take off their shirts so they could fight it out; the captain would make sure they would have "fair play."[64] William Silver wrote in his journal in 1834 that "to day there was a recurrence of those broils which this voyage has been witness to too many of them for the benefit of those concerned or the credit of the officers."[65] Ship's carpenter Samuel Furgerson complained on a long Pacific voyage that "The People disputing on account of their stealing bread from each other." Furgerson later exclaimed, as he fretted over shortages on board, that there were "Dry times," since "warm weather and Short Allowance of water with Salt Beef makes bad Neighbors."[66] One sailor commented that, although fighting was forbidden on naval vessels, men regularly settled arguments with their fists.[67]

Tensions between different nationalities in a crew added to the misery of some sailors. Captain Samuel Tucker reported tension between the French and American crew members of the ship *Boston* in 1778.[68] Such animosities were not unusual for the multi-ethnic warships of the American navy. Similar problems occurred in merchantmen and whalers. On a voyage aboard the *Governor Thorp* from England to Boston, tension arose between the British seamen and American officers. After the captain manhandled one of the British sailors, the man complained, "that is the way you do in American ships." To which the captain replied, "Yes, you son of a bitch, I'll murder you." The captain then took the man into the cabin for a lashing.[69] While J. Ross Browne found much to admire in his American shipmates, he thought the foreigners were intolerable and objected to the idea of sharing living quarters with blacks. After he did not join a work stoppage protesting the captain's refusal to grant the men liberty in port, the Portuguese sailors wanted to drive him out of the forecastle. Isolated and hated by both captain and crew, Browne had to leave the ship.[70] Conflict occurred repeatedly between the

African American steward on the *Charles Phelps* and members of the crew. Silas Fitch, who noted these problems in his log, revealed his own bias by confessing that the steward was "the frowardest and sasyest darkey that I have ever saw."[71]

If relationships within the forecastle, running from amiable fraternity to armed hostility, were important to every sailor, cooperation between the forecastle and the quarterdeck—between the common seamen and the captain—was essential to the smooth functioning of the vessel. Technically the captain's power at sea was supreme. In signing the articles of a ship—the contract that established pay scale and regulations during the voyage—the sailor abdicated control over his person. The sailor not only agreed to work the ship but also consented to the discipline established by the captain and his officers. Nathaniel Ames described the captain as a "discretionary bashaw" who "enjoys the reality in its most exquisite form, the power of punishing, after which all 'having authority' so greedily aspire."[72] More than one observer compared the sailors' lot to that of black slaves.[73] Like the slave, sailors could be whipped as punishment. Discipline in the navy was most severe. In just six months the captain ordered men whipped almost ninety times aboard the frigate *Congress* in 1846.[74] Even on board merchantmen and whalers, captains used corporal punishment to keep sailors in line.[75] Captains also relied on physical force to terrorize a crew, beating, cursing, and threatening to kill the men if they so much as raised their arm in self-defense. Nathaniel Sexton Morgan reported numerous incidents of his captain pouncing upon seamen, especially the Kanaka (Hawaiian) natives and Portuguese, using "the worst and most profane language I have ever heard from mortal lips."[76] William McNally observed, "I know of no situation in which men can be placed where they can be rendered so completely miserable as on board of a ship, if the officers are disposed to make them so." If the captain did not want to redress grievances, the "vessel becomes a perfect hell, the law has left no alternative for the crew but to suffer his caprice, whims, and tyranny in silence for a long voyage, or else do a deed that will bring them to the scaffold, or haunt them to their grave."[77] As one old salt explained to a novice sailor, there was no ground between duty and mutiny. "All that you are ordered to do is duty," whether the captain was wrong or right, and "All that you refuse to do is mutiny."[78]

Life aboard ships was more complex than this simple dichotomy between mutiny and duty suggests. While in many instances the autocracy of the quarterdeck limited some aspects of the sailor's liberty aboard ship, the relationship between quarterdeck and forecastle was more often under constant negotiation.

16. Seamen aboard all types of vessels were subject to corporal punishment. "Flogging." Joseph Bogart, Log of the Bark *Samuel and Thomas*, August 16, 1847. Kendall Whaling Museum.

At sea there was supposed to be a clear hierarchy, with the captain on top, followed by his officers, followed in turn by the common seamen. The chain of command could breakdown at several points. In some instances aboard merchantmen a captain might find his authority undercut by the owners of the vessel. The seamen aboard the *Catherine* in 1762 could never quite figure out what position the mysterious Mr. Jerboe filled on the voyage. Sometimes he served as a seaman, sometimes as a master, sometimes as an owner, sometimes as a supercargo, sometimes as boatswain—making the sailors "look like Negroes, and as if they did not know their duty." He even meddled with the cooking. The crew did not appreciate this confusion. One called him "a sneaking sort of a fellow that an englishman would have nothing to do with." To confuse matters further, Jerboe took the starboard berth in the cabin, which was usually reserved for the captain, while the ship's master contented himself with the larboard or port berth.[79] Aboard the *Thomas Russell* on a voyage to the Pacific Northwest in 1798 and 1799, the presence of a supercargo and a well-connected clerk created ambiguous lines of authority. Perhaps knowing who paid the bills, the officers sided against the captain. No overt conflict erupted, but throughout the voyage the captain did not receive the accustomed level of respect and was often the butt of jokes and snide comments.[80]

As on the *Thomas Russell,* the captain sometimes found himself at odds with his officers. On a voyage from the Far East, Sargent S. Day thought that his first and second mates were inept and made "a damn'd humbug of everything" and could not wait to get rid of them. Day pleaded with the wind, "Blow my sweet breeze Blow & Deliver me from Two pieces of Trash not fit to take care of Hogs much more to have charge of a Ship Deck."[81] Whaling captain Charles G. Arthur apparently had continual problems with his officers aboard the *Zenas Coffin* on a voyage in the late 1840s. He reported to the owners that he had to discharge the third mate "for the benefit of all concerned." Arthur wrote a year and half later that he had discharged the first and second mate as well, declaring that he had done so "for the sake of having any kind of regularity and order on ship board." He explained further, "I have struggled all the voyage to make things as they should be but as I find out even before we left home there was as to say a combination entered into for them always to be right and I right if I agreed with them."[82] Another whaling captain confronted open disobedience by officers and crew, when, contrary to everybody's interest, they refused to lower the boats in pursuit of whales. In this situation the captain had to give ground.[83] Even John Paul Jones had tactical disagreements with his first lieutenant, Thomas Simpson, and repeated problems with Pierre Landais who, as a subordinate in command of the *Alliance* during the battle between the *Bon Homme Richard* and the *Serapis,* failed to come to Jones's assistance.[84]

Officers, too, sometimes wrangled with one another. As a mate, Sargent S. Day also found his subalterns incompetent. While the crew refitted the rigging at sea, Day remained on the deck and sent the second mate aloft to direct the men. From Day's point of view the whole job was bungled. He confided to his log that the mast was finally painted, although the second mate allowed the men to make "a long lumber job of it." There were other problems. Eventually everything got straightened out, "but a worse time I never see in getting up spars[.] No head aloft & nothing done right—for my part I am sick of such second mates & damn'd foolish work."[85] Samuel Chase complained that he had some "secret enemies" aboard the whaleship *Arab* and declared that there was "a traitorous wretch trying to black my character with the master of the ship."[86] Common seamen often paid for this type of backbiting. A mean-spirited first mate could easily take advantage of his authority by keeping the second mate and his watch on deck for longer than the usual four hours.[87]

The most crucial conflicts at sea, however, were between the forecastle and the quarterdeck. To prevent the captain from pushing the crew too hard, seamen ran away, organized work slow downs, and grumbled and showed disrespect. Occasionally, work stopped and blows exchanged. In extreme cases, the crew resorted to mutiny and piracy. The mere idea of these rare extreme violent acts affected shipboard behavior.[88]

Countless sailors jumped ship. Captains repeatedly complained about seamen absconding whenever they stopped in a port. Sometimes, a pet peeve convinced the tar to leave. Perhaps the captain and a particular sailor did not get along. Often a specific confrontation made the sailor exert his independence. Angered by a midshipman who had him flogged for not responding to his call, James Durand deserted the navy. He later wrote, "I considered myself my own man, as the term of my enlistment had been up these eight or nine months. Therefore I put on what clothing I could wear that belonged to me and quitted the ship."[89] Sometimes the decision to run away was a function of more general discontent. In 1781 almost everyone aboard the *South Carolina* was unhappy. During a stop in Bilbao, several seamen did not return from their liberty ashore.[90] Other times, the motivation was economic. A sailor might choose to leave one vessel simply because he would make a few dollars more a month on another.

Sailors relied upon a variety of subtle means to resist the will of the captain. Dana noted that "Jack is a slave aboard ship; but still he has many opportunities of thwarting and balking his master." After the crew of the *Pilgrim* was denied liberty in port on a Sunday and told to do work, they resorted to "*Sogering*." The men honed foot dragging to an art: "Send a man below to get a block, and he would capsize everything before finding it, then not bring it up till an officer had called him twice, and take as much time to put things in order again." Tools were not to be found and "knives wanted a prodigious deal of sharping, and, generally, three or four were waiting round the grindstone at a time." If a man was sent aloft, he would soon come slowly down again for something he had forgotten. "When the mate was out of sight, nothing was done. It was all up-hill work; and at eight o'clock, when we went to breakfast, things were nearly where they were when we began."[91]

Similarly, the ability to grumble, talk back, and swear also gave the sailors some powers and limited the captain's ability to command. One sailor even commented that grumbling was normal and was generally ignored by officers as long as the sailor then did his duty.[92] Captain John Manly, a noted Revolutionary War naval officer, complained in 1777 of the mutinous crew of the

Hancock, wanted to court-martial Philip Bass, Jr., for "abusing the commanding officer" with "ill language and seditious speeches," and singled out several other men "for treating the Officers with bad language."[93] Continental navy captain Gustavus Conyngham claimed that the crew of his privateer cutter *Revenge* had insisted, against his wishes, that they seize some neutral shipping because it carried English goods.[94]

Such resistance could flare into serious confrontations. On one voyage to China three members of the crew had "quite a row" with the second mate because they refused to clean out the roundhouse. In the fisticuffs that followed, the crew got the worse of it, and after the captain showed up "he scored the ringleader and gave him a double allowance of the mizzontop sail halyard."[95] The captain of the whaleship *Brooklyn*, Samuel Jeffrey, and cooper John Dunford argued over the use of an ax that Dunford did not want to lend to the captain. The captain claimed that Dunford pushed him, and as he was falling down he grabbed the cooper's beard, yanking out large chunks of it. Most of the crew quoted the captain as calling Dunford "a damned lying good for nothing son of a bitch" and then launching an assault, grabbing his beard and hitting him repeatedly. Dunford tackled the captain, hauling him down on top of him. The two wrangled on the deck before they were disengaged. Whichever story was true, it is clear that Dunford had challenged the captain's authority, standing up to him over the use of the cooper's tools, and then exchanged blows with him. Dunford lost the fight, his face was described as a terribly bruised and all bloody, but he suffered no further punishment. The captain apparently made his point, as had the cooper. Both men returned to work after the fight and Dunford obtained his discharge by mutual consent once the *Brooklyn* reached Maui.[96]

Despite the threat of punishment, the captain's authority could be challenged. Captain Sargent S. Day wanted a sailor named Boyeston to finish some work in the rigging before breakfast. Boyeston believed this demand unreasonable and "was making a long job of it to kill time." After completing half the assignment, he dropped some equipment overboard, climbed down from the rigging, and went to eat. Day stormed up to Boyeston and told him to finish the job. Boyeston said he would return to work after he ate. Reacting to this insolence, Day grabbed him. The sailor clinched onto the captain, and both tumbled over one another. The mate and the captain subdued Boyeston and put him in irons. The next day all hands were called to witness the flogging. Boyeston, however, apologized and promised to do his duty without question. Day had him cut down without a lash being served. The confrontation was hardly a triumph for Day—perhaps he had been too forgiving. Boyeston never completed the job, and his shipmates continued to challenge the authority of the captain.[97]

Physical abuse by officers or the captain did not squash resistance from the sailor. Grover W. Crosby, the mate of the ship *Edward Everett*, was a bully. He threatened, punched, and manhandled the crew. Crosby grabbed James Knowlton, a common sailor, by the neck and threw him on the deck for botching a cutting job, even though Crosby had partially caused the error by not letting the sailor sharpen his knife. In another incident, Knowlton accidentally dropped a tool. Crosby grabbed Knowlton by the hair, shook his fist in his face, and challenged Knowlton to a fight. The sailor declined; Crosby was not the kind of man anyone wanted to tangle with. When the ship reached port, the men complained to the captain, to no avail. As soon as the captain went ashore, Crosby threatened to toss several of the crew from the rigging into the sea. The men decided to stop all work. The captain did not tolerate this challenge to his authority and had the men brought ashore and put into jail. The next day the sailors agreed to go back to work and the abuse continued for the rest of the voyage.[98]

Few ships were as unhappy as the whaler *Israel* in 1841. A small confrontation off Madagascar, in St. Augustine's Bay, flared into mutiny. The captain ordered Wilbur Hodges to take some pumpkins away from the pigs on board. Hodges refused and the captain cuffed him on his ear. Hodges then clasped onto the captain, declaring that he was not to be struck, and insisting that if he were to be punished he must be put into irons. Several officers then joined in and beat Hodges and tied him into the rigging. All work stopped as only one man was then willing to do his duty. Two hours later the officers cut Hodges down and placed him in irons. After they released him the next day he ran to the forecastle, where his shipmates offered him sanctuary. Officers and crew exchanged rough words. One man called the captain "a damned old son of a bitch & whores pimp," shaking a fist in his face. It took a file of marines and the arrest of five ringleaders to restore order. Of the twenty-eight men who had sailed in the *Israel* at the beginning of the voyage, six deserted, five were sent home as mutineers, two were sent home sick, one drowned, and another died.[99]

Resistance from the "people" of a ship also occurred aboard regular navy ships in the early nineteenth century. Insubordination plagued the *Constitution* in mid-September 1812. Many of the crew were unhappy with the replacement of Isaac Hull with William Bainbridge as captain. Fresh from their victory over the *Guerrière,* the men remained personally attached to

Hull, while several sailors claimed that their previous experience with Bainbridge had been unpleasant. Two months later, off the coast of Brazil, "the men came on deck in a mutinous manner & complained to the Commd. that the allowance of bread & water" was not sufficient. After stern words and an explanation the men relented and went back to work.[100]

At times captains had to rely on strong-arm tactics. During an early China voyage to the Pacific Northwest, Richard Cleveland recruited a crew at Canton that he described as "a list of as accomplished villains as ever disgraced any country." The men became mutinous even before they left the coast of China. When they refused duty and armed themselves with axes and marlin spikes, Cleveland aimed two four-pounders at the men and gave each officer loaded pistols. He also stopped provisions for the crew. Faced with a stand-off, Cleveland allowed ten men to leave the ship for the inhospitable shores of mainland China. Finding an unwelcome reception there, the men pleaded to be permitted to return. Cleveland took four men back before heading across the Pacific.[101]

The shrewd captain recognized that there was a point beyond which he dare not push the crew. He might use brute strength—his own or others'—sweet words and promises, or curses and threats. The aim was always the same; maintenance of authority and the continued smooth functioning of the ship. Otherwise, a mutiny might succeed. During a voyage in the West Indies in January 1777, the crew of the *Tyrannicide* gathered outside their captain's door and demanded to know if he planned to return to Massachusetts. He ordered them away, and when they insulted him, he struck two of them. The crew returned to the forecastle and drew up a round-robin—a circular document traditionally used by sailors to pledge mutual loyalty during a mutiny—and refused duty. Properly cowed, the captain relented, ignored further "ill Language," and sailed for Boston.[102]

Even more important than the number of mutinies or near mutinies was the image of freedom cast by the most famous cases of shipboard rebellion. Almost every sailor had heard of the mutiny on the *Bounty*. Although some of the earliest published versions of the story stressed how eventually the law caught up with most of these mutineers, rumors persisted of the exotic life and complete freedom experienced by some. During George Little's visit to Hawaii in 1809, just as the Pacific was being opened to western shipping, it was whispered aboard ship that the English adviser to the ruler of the islands was one of the crew of the *Bounty*. Whether true or not, the point was that the men aboard Little's ship, and others, believed it and spoke of the man with reverence and awe as a result.[103]

Connected to the image of rebellion and mutiny, of course, was the issue of piracy. Popular literature then and now led to some misconceptions about piracy. Today the word "pirate" conjures images of Treasure Island or Blackbeard. The literature before 1850 may not have included Long John Silver, but it frequently mythologized piracy, or as it was often called, "going on account."[104] One self-proclaimed green hand even admitted that as a youth he played the pirate, especially Captain Kidd, "whose history in song I had made my study."[105] Technically piracy was any criminal activity on the high seas. Thus many real pirates were merely men who committed crimes at sea. Closer scrutiny of their activities presents an unflattering picture. Men like William Wood and John Holland in 1774 argued with their captain, killing and tossing him into the sea at night. The two pirates then broke into the captain's chest, taking both money and liquor. They promptly drank themselves nearly unconscious. When another schooner sent its mate aboard the next day, the two were beyond resistance. Holland stumbled about, fell overboard, and quickly drowned. Wood bragged about taking the captain's money but was easily secured and saved for the gallows.[106]

Life for men who turned piracy into a career was little better. Jean Lafitte has made it into American history textbooks because of his brief alliance with Andrew Jackson at the Battle of New Orleans. His pirate followers ultimately had to abandon their Louisiana base at Barataria and moved to Texas. There the forces of law and order caught up with them, killed many and arresting the rest. Piracy flourished in postwar periods in part because opportunity for legalized piracy in the navy or as privateers declined.[107] There was a brief flurry of West Indies piracy in the 1810s and 1820s, of which Lafitte's enterprise forms just one small part. These pirates were not necessarily attractive romantic figures such as appeared in James Fenimore Cooper's *Red Rover*.[108] Cuban Nicholas Fernandez, who joined a pirate crew in New Orleans in the 1820s, admitted just before his execution that the rough-and-tumble crew was often drunk. Alcohol numbed each man to incredible atrocities. Operating in the West Indies and off the coast of Brazil, the pirates burned vessels with passengers and crew aboard, serially raped women, and tortured captives.[109]

Most sailors rejected the brutality, illegality, and danger of piracy. Yet the counterculture represented by pirates held some attraction; pirates stood as symbols of men who freed themselves from authority and economic dependency.[110] Thus, the image of the pirate played upon the sailors' sympathies and lay deeply imbedded in their folklore. George Little reported that one Saturday night aboard the *Dromo*, a sailor sang more than twenty verses of the famous pirate song "My Name Is Captain Kid," much to the delight of the whole forecastle.[111] The odd combination of attraction and repulsion toward pirates appears in a story Hugh Calhoun copied into his journal in 1847. During a session of yarns and songs while the ship lay becalmed in the West Indies, one old salt told a tale from forty years before. During a heavy and tempestuous sea, two vessels smashed into one another. The larger vessel was almost unscathed, but the smaller vessel quickly sank and had only one survivor, who, with some danger to a boat's crew, was fished out of the sea and then taken to shore. There, the island's governor recognized him as a pirate who had twice escaped prison. The governor decided to hang him immediately, because, as the spinner of the yarn relates, "he was nothing better than a real Pirate whose murders were so numerous they couldn't be counted." If his actions were to be condemned, his plight evoked sympathy. The entire ship's crew was invited to watch the execution, in part as an object lesson. In the procession to the gallows, the pirate "looked pale and half dead when they brought him out[,] and for the soul of me I could not help pitying him." Surrounded by two rows of soldiers, "he stepped so firm and so willingly to meet his death." A chaplain spoke to him all the way, as he stared straight ahead; perhaps his mind was on "the fine vessel he had lost." The crew "saw the poor fellow swing off" and returned silently to the ship. There "was no laughing or joking, that day nor the next neither." The men all felt as if they "had some hand in it, and wished the poor man had been food for the sharks of the Sea rather than to have fall prey to the Land-Sharks." To remind all sailors entering port of the perils of piracy, officials took down the body and hung it in chains in the harbor. The storyteller reported that he saw the bones on the homeward passage "rattling in the Sea breeze and bleaching in the Sun," and ever since could not pass the place without thinking of that pirate.[112]

Although piracy and mutiny may have appealed to the sailor's anti-authoritarianism and sense of personal freedom at sea, and even led to some sympathy with the Jolly Roger, few seamen joined a mutiny and became pirates when the opportunity arose. William McNally quoted the dying words of mutineer Cornelius Wilhelms, that "the master treated them so badly" that the crew of the *Braganza* "were obliged" to murder the captain and mate as an object lesson for others. Yet McNally was fully aware that some of that crew refused to join in the crime. Likewise, during the vicious murder and mutiny aboard the whaleship *Globe* in 1824, many of the crew feared the mutiny leaders and abandoned them at the first opportunity to return to legitimate society.[113]

To help deal with the tensions and limitations aboard ship, captains

17. Although often romanticized, piracy could be gruesome and horrible to most sailors, as this illustration from an early nineteenth-century pirate story suggests. "Comstock Running Lambert Through the Body." William Lay and Cyrus M. Hussey, *A Narrative of the Mutiny on Board the Whaleship "Globe,"* introduction by Edouard A. Stackpole (New York, 1963; orig. pub. 1828). Kendall Whaling Museum.

granted sailors certain freedoms, suggesting that even officers recognized that their authority at sea had to be tempered by some liberty. Foremost of these was the grog ration—the dose of liquor that helped sailors through the hardships of the day. George Jones believed that nothing "would sooner stir up a mutiny in the ship, than a refusal to serve out grog."[114] William Clarke agreed, declaring that to "some old man of wars men" stopping grog was "the greatest punishment that can be inflicted on them," and they would rather "do without eating for two days than to have grog stopped."[115] In response to reformers' efforts to do away with alcohol aboard ships, Richard Henry Dana, Jr., echoed these sentiments. Dana confessed that although he did not particularly like rum, during his two years before the mast he took his ration eagerly and praised "The momentary warmth and glow from drinking it; the break and change which is made in a long, dreary watch by the mere calling all hands aft and serving of it out." Dana also believed that the value of drink lay in just "simply having some event to look forward to, and to talk about."[116] Henry Mercier admitted that "liquor is a sailor's idol," and that the grog ration was all-important to the average tar. He quoted the following lines:

For grog is our starboard, our larboard
Our mainmast, our mizen, our log—
At sea, or ashore, or when harbour'd,
The mariner's compass is grog.[117]

Aboard some ships an extra grog ration was issued on holidays or after some arduous task like reefing the topsails. Most war vessels served a helping as they prepared for action to inure the men to the bloody violence of combat at sea. In all of these cases the idea was to offer a taste of freedom—even though it was limited to a mere jolt of alcohol pumping through the veins—amidst the toil and confinement aboard ship.[118]

Other specific moments of license occurred occasionally aboard ships. A captured ship usually became completely chaotic between the time of surrender and the moment of occupation by the victorious enemy. Once the colors had been hauled down, sailors stopped obeying officers and quickly began to ransack their own ship. In a last bout of liberty before imprisonment, men broke into the liquor cabinets and drank themselves to oblivion. Others ran for the food chests and feasted on whatever they could stuff in their mouths, secreting leftovers that they hoped to hide from the occupying marines. Others stripped the ship of canvas and movable objects that they planned to trade once imprisoned. The victors behaved no better. Sometimes they would join the captives in the orgy of food and drink; other times, they simply robbed them. More than one captured merchantman was recaptured a few days later with a prize crew that was too drunk to manage the ship properly.[119]

At least two rituals also allowed for moments of misrule. On long voyages the captain would occasionally "pipe the men to mischief," for the men to dance, frolic, and enjoy a break from work. George Little, on a trading venture to the Spanish Pacific, reported that on February 18, 1809, the crew of the *Dromo* was piped to mischief and "the forecastle and main deck" were given up to the men to enact scenes which "were truly ludicrous." For a couple of hours "the crew were tripping away the merry dance to the sweet sounds of our ravishing band" while "The utmost good humor and harmony prevailed throughout."[120] Edward Cutbush, a medical doctor in the navy in the opening decade of the nineteenth century, believed that these amusements broke up the monotony of the voyage and cemented relations between the officers and the crew.[121]

The other ritual also occurred on long voyages and signaled the crossing of a major geographical line such as the equator. On these occasions there would be a visit from King Neptune—a sailor in disguise—who wore a "Fantastical

Rig." Anyone who had not crossed the line underwent ritual initiation. Often they would get "a good lathering with soap grease and shaving . . . with a barrel hoop." Sometimes the greenhorn's mouth would be filled with "lather." Each novice had to swear in good sailor fashion never to eat brown bread if he could eat white bread, never to walk if he could ride, and to always kiss the mistress instead of the maid—unless he liked the maid best. The "finishing touch" was "to souse them in a tub of salt water."[122] Despite the public humiliation, most sailors viewed the day as spent in "mirth and friendship."[123] Like piping to mischief, the ritual was intended to ease tension and boredom on a long voyage; and similar to rituals of misrule on land, the idea was to temporarily suspend the normal rules of behavior as a means of ensuring the traditional hierarchy the rest of the voyage. As a part of this carnival, sailors occasionally made pointed jabs at authority, asking questions of the initiates concerning their treatment at the hands of the officers and captain and the nature of their fare. On one voyage where relations were strained between the captain and the officers, "some queer questions were also asked respecting the Captains *former voyages*" which had been previously a topic of discussion and speculation. The captain had to promise an extra bottle or two of rum "to prevent more disagreeable questions being asked and the answers exacted." In the end the captain had gotten some broad hints to curse less, give more meat and grog, but no mischief or injury was done.[124]

Although life at sea confined the sailor, he was not as restricted as might at first appear. The physical setting, the psychological bonds and enmities, and the authority and resistance aboard ship all contributed to the sailor's appreciation for his peculiar brand of liberty. Wind and wave promised to release the sailor from any sense of permanent attachment on land; his shipmates confirmed and solidified the tar's identity; and a seaman could always proclaim himself his own man through acts of resistance ranging from a smattering of profanity to mutiny and piracy. Similarly, sight of shore promised a release from close quarters, an escape from despised crew members, and an end to the dictatorship of the quarterdeck.

PART II
REVOLUTION

4

The Sons of Neptune

John Blatchford told a fantastic story. He had signed aboard the Continental ship *Hancock* as a fifteen-year-old cabin boy in June 1777. He returned to his home on Cape Ann as a grown man sometime after the Treaty of Paris of 1783. In between he had served under six flags and had traveled half way around the world. During the American Revolution Blatchford paid a heavy price for his fighting for the revolutionary cause, sacrificing his freedom for years at a time. He also learned an important lesson: as a poor sailor buffeted about by capricious winds, sometimes it was best to accept one's fate, adjust one's loyalty, and work simply to survive. This was not a lesson Blatchford learned easily.

The *Hancock* turned out to be an unlucky ship. Despite sleek lines and great speed, she was captured off Nova Scotia on July 8, 1777. The British took the crew to Halifax as prisoners. At the time the British treated the American captives as pirates and traitors. Blatchford failed in an effort at escape, and then, like many young sailors taken by the British, he was put aboard one of His Majesty's ships. Blatchford bristled in his berth, repeatedly attempting to run away. Although his motive remains unclear—he could have been an ardent young patriot, or he could just have rejected the severity of British service—he landed in a Halifax jail charged with murdering a soldier. Sent to England for trial, Blatchford was somehow acquitted.[1] His freedom still eluded him. Along with more than eighty other Americans he was shipped on a vessel bound for the East Indies.

By this time Blatchford had begun to learn the importance of survival. When the captain of the ship told him that if he behaved well and did his duty as a sailor, he would receive "as good usage as any one on board," Blatchford felt encouraged. He admitted that "I now found my destiny was fixed—that whatever I could do, would not in the least alter my situation, and therefore was determined to do the best I could, and make myself contented as my unfortunate situation would admit."[2] He arrived in Sumatra in June 1780 only to find that he was condemned to serve as a soldier for five years. He sought in vain to continue to work as a sailor. Again, we cannot be sure of his motivation. Perhaps he believed that as a sailor he at least had some chance of escape when the vessel returned to Europe. Perhaps the thought of being stationed in Sumatra for five years was too much to bear for this now experienced seaman. Regardless, he and two other young New Englanders embarked on a dangerous course of resistance. Bolstering each other's spirits, the three men resolved to refuse to learn soldiering. The drill sergeant beat them daily, and finally they were put on short rations and were made to work in the "pepper gardens" under arduous conditions in the blistering heat all day. The three men then attempted an escape, killing a sepoy—a native guard—during their recapture. All three were sentenced to death. The British executed only the oldest boy, giving Blatchford and the other boy eight hundred lashes each.

Just as the two were completing their convalescence in the hospital they again sought to escape. This time they succeeded and wandered the wilderness for more than a month, at which point Blatchford's companion died. Blatchford continued for several more weeks, living off the country, in a state of near delirium. He even confronted a tiger at one point. Finally, he stumbled across a half-naked native girl, who he somehow persuaded to bring him to a nearby Dutch outpost.

The odyssey, however, was far from over. The Dutch took him to Sumatra's capital, Batavia. From there he signed aboard a Spanish ship heading for Spain. Near the Cape of Good Hope they ran into British cruisers. The Spanish ship fought the British off, but the damaged vessel was compelled to stop in Brazil. There the ship was condemned and Blatchford signed aboard a Portuguese vessel. He got to St. Helena, where he was stranded. If once he agreed to be a British sailor and not a soldier, now he knew he could not afford such scruples. He willingly served in the British garrison of this mid-Atlantic island.

There was no easy way home for Blatchford. Common seamen often found themselves constrained by circumstances in a world of revolution and upheaval. The best of few options for Jack Tar was to sail with the wind and see where chance might leave him. As Blatchford stood lonely guard on the desolate rock, he was amazed to see arrive the ship that had brought him to Sumatra (the vessel had made two trips from England to the East Indies in the meantime). The captain remembered Blatchford and, in dire need of seamen, signed him aboard as boatswain to help control a ship manned mainly by lascars.

Blatchford arrived in London about March 1, 1782. As a petty officer he was protected from the ubiquitous press-gangs that stripped nearly every incoming vessel of available men. Within two weeks Blatchford was at sea again, this time aboard a British storeship heading for the West Indies. Once in Antigua, he stole a small boat and made his way to the French in Montserrat. From there he shipped on a French vessel to Philadelphia. He was almost home. Off the Delaware Capes the British captured the vessel, and Blatchford found himself a prisoner of war aboard the *Jersey* prison hulk in Wallabout Bay near New York City. A bare two hundred miles from his native village, Blatchford had the good fortune to be exchanged within a week. As he had the bad fortune of sailing under the French flag when captured, he was taken to France in a cartel. In Brittany he signed aboard an American privateer from Beverly, Massachusetts, some of whose crew he knew from his youth. After a quick and successful voyage, he found himself stranded at the end of the war in France. He made his way to Lisbon and finally returned to Cape Ann.[3]

Blatchford was a survivor who does not quite fit our mold of either the embattled farmer of Concord Bridge or the wise Founding Fathers. Here was a young man who served under the American flag for less than two months in six years and who claimed to have made great sacrifices for the independence of the United States. And yet his story reminds us that the Age of Revolution, with all its upheavals, must be understood on the individual level.

Blatchford's story also suggests that liberty retained its many complex and contradictory meanings on the waterfront during the resistance movement and revolutionary war. Sometimes Jack Tar thought about an immediate liberty—both at sea and on shore; sometimes he thought about larger issues connected to the ideas of revolution; most times he had several ideas of liberty swirling through his head simultaneously. Whatever definitions of liberty appeared on the waterfront, the maritime world's understanding of liberty helped to shape the struggle for American independence.

The American Revolution began on the waterfront. Before there were any Sons of Liberty, the Sons of Neptune—as sailors called themselves—rioted in the streets in the name of the rights of Englishmen. The Sons of Neptune enforced the boycott against the Stamp Act in 1765 and 1766. The men and boys of the waterfront also were the driving force behind the disturbances that accompanied the opposition to the Townshend Duties of 1767. Many in the King Street mob of March 5, 1770 (the Boston Massacre) had experience at sea; two of the fatalities in the "Massacre" were sailors and a third was a ropemaker.[4] And, of course, the Boston Tea Party occurred in a harbor as well. Without this activity on the waterfront there would have been no American Revolution.

If many of the people on the waterfront took the lead in all of this disorder, others either remained in the background or actually supported imperial measures. John Blatchford's story reveals conflicting loyalties of the people of the waterfront. Customs informants, who became so inimical to the crowd, were often dockside workers or sailors searching for a reward. Throughout the anti-imperial agitation there were few loyalist mobs; ordinarily supporters of law and order did not feel a need to take to the streets. One striking instance where crowds offered to protect imperial officials occurred in Philadelphia in 1765–66. The White Oaks, a group of shipwrights and ship carpenters, defended stamp distributor John Hughes and his home and helped to negate the impact of the Anti-Stamp Act agitators.[5] More often, those who opposed the anti-imperial agitation remained quietly conflicted. Ashley Bowen, rigger and sometime seaman, was torn between king and country in the years leading to independence. His sentiments were well known, since he escaped imprisonment for loyalty to the king only by shipping out as a mate on a merchant vessel in 1778.[6]

Sailors in colonial seaports had a long history of participating in popular disorder, even if not every denizen of the waterfront joined in. Sailors' liberty ashore involed a great deal of waterfront rowdiness that ranged from mischief making to bruising battles between larger groups of men.[7] Occasionally, seamen might be used in a more organized fashion. In the bloody Philadelphia election riot of 1742, merchants relied upon men from the waterfront as shock troops to drive Quakers and Germans from the polls.[8] Similarly, in a move obviously organized by someone higher in society, seventy Philadelphians cut a vessel out from its moorings, towed it down the river, and unloaded smuggled goods in defiance of the collector of the port.[9] More often, however, waterfront workers acted on their own in colonial riots. Two types of disturbances stand out as important precursors to the popular disorder of the 1760s and 1770s: anti-impressment riots and Pope Day processions. Both were closely wedded to the waterfront.

Any time there was a British naval vessel in the vicinity, the men on the waterfront felt threatened. During war, His Majesty's thirst for men was insatiable. With higher wages on merchant vessels and the opportunity to make even more money on privateers, few British seamen were interested in the navy. To add insult to injury, British naval vessels lost countless men to desertion in colonial ports. In compensation for these difficulties in recruitment and retention, the British navy often searched ships entering and leaving ports and swept through the waterfront, forcing men into service. To protect their individual freedom, sailors in both Great Britain and the colonies rioted. There were at least twenty such occasions in North America during the colonial period.[10]

The most famous colonial anti-impressment disturbance, the Knowles riot, occurred in Boston in 1747. The behavior of this crowd reveals patterns that reemerged in the rioting of the 1760s and 1770s. Commodore Charles Knowles pressed men for his depleted fleet on the morning of November 17. This action distressed and enraged those on the waterfront. Sailors felt directly threatened, but shipowning merchants, too, were upset. Many of the men taken had been paid a month in advance, and without sufficient crews vessels could not sail. People became boisterous in the streets. Like the revolutionary mobs that later intimidated stamp distributors, and that took customs collectors and crown officials as hostages, a crowd seized a naval officer. Although they eventually surrendered the officer to Governor William Shirley, the crowd beat an undersheriff and, in an act of ritual humiliation typical of later disturbances, put him in stocks for ridicule. Revolutionary crowds would later break windows and threaten property; the anti-Knowles mob vandalized the townhouse where the assembly met. Finaliy, in another ritual that would reappear repeatedly in the 1760s and 1770s, Bostonians commandeered a longboat (in later riots the exact object might differ) and burned it in a huge bonfire.[11]

Pope Day celebrations were less directly connected to the waterfront. Starting before the 1740s in Boston, and then spreading to other ports like New York and Marblehead, the common people celebrated the Protestant succession in Great Britain by parading through town with effigies of the Pope, the Devil, and the Pretender (the Stuart claimant on the crown) on November 5, Guy Fawkes Day. Many of the participants in this activity were artisans, like shoemaker Ebenezer McIntosh, the leader of one of Boston's processions. The boundary between land-based trades and the waterfront remained vague. Often, these men would have some saltwater experience, and although we do not know the exact composition of the crowd, it is hard to imagine that in a place like Marblehead, which practiced this ritual in the 1760s, that the celebrants did not include denizens of the waterfront.[12]

The Pope Day processions have been examined by several historians for their intricate and sometimes conflicting messages—all of which speak to several meanings of liberty on the waterfront. On the most superficial level November 5 became an excuse for rowdy behavior. Artisans and waterfront workers could drink, shout, fight, and create discord in a moment of personal liberty. On another level the excuse for this misbehavior was in the name of patriotic support for the monarchy and the Protestant succession, which were seen as the guardians of traditional English liberty. Simultaneously, the symbolism of the celebration suggested a challenge to the social hierarchy that was often implicit in the sailor's liberty ashore. To pay for alcohol consumed on the holiday and the elaborate effigies, the crowds of street toughs exacted tribute from their more well-heeled neighbors. The effigies of the Pope and the Pretender were mistreated and then consumed in fire. While this activity asserted loyalty to the Hanoverian dynasty, the effigies' attire was aristocratic and their destruction was a subtle reminder of the liberty of the people to punish the king and the church if they abused power.[13]

The Pope Day ritual provided a model for many of the revolutionary mobs of the 1760s and 1770s. In New York City anti–Stamp Act rioters mimicked Pope Day behavior, marching through the streets with effigies of the Pope, the Pretender, and the lieutenant governor who threatened to enforce the unpopular tax. Many in the street during these disturbances on October 31 and November 1, 1765, had a maritime background. Robert R. Livingston, who struggled to restrain the mob, sought the assistance of privateering captains from the French and Indian War, believing that these men would have more influence over the seafaring community than any patrician or merchant. He also reported that a letter posted at the Coffee House threatened further disturbances and an attack on the local fort if the Stamp Act were enforced. The letter promised action on November 5 (Pope Day) and was signed "Sons of Neptune."[14]

Repeatedly in the years after 1765 the revolutionary movement depended upon the type of crowd action that appeared on the colonial waterfront. Mobs paraded with effigies, held great bonfires, demonstrated in front of potential victims, and intimidated individuals, compelling them to comply with popular wishes. Dockside crowds boarded ships in New York City and other ports to ensure that no stamps would be delivered. In Newport, the anti-Stamp Act mob was even led by a sailor.[15] After the passage of the Townshend Duties in 1767 the waterfront remained at center stage as mobs and customs officials faced off. In port after port mobs, heavily manned from the waterfront, sought to rescue confiscated goods or to punish customs officials. The dockside confrontation over the seizure of John Hancock's sloop *Liberty* in June 1768 helped to convince the British government to send troops to Boston. While British officials took possession of the vessel, a crowd manhandled the collector and, in an action reminiscent of the Knowles riot, towed his yacht to the Common and burned it in a bonfire.[16] This was only one of many incidents.

A Philadelphia waterfront crowd in April 1769 ordered constables off the wharves and pelted a customs official with stones and bottles when he hesitated to follow the police officers in their retreat. By the time the official returned with a stronger force, the suspected goods had been secreted away.[17] During the 1760s crowds paraded with effigies, intimidated victims, or had bonfires in almost every American port, including Falmouth (now Portland, Maine), Boston, Salem, Gloucester, Newburyport, Marblehead, Newport, Providence, New Haven, New London, New York, Philadelphia, Annapolis, Norfolk, Wilmington, New Bern, and Charleston.[18]

Refinements in mob tactics also came from the waterfront. Revolutionary crowds are best known for coating victims with tar and feathers as ritual humiliation. After a Salem dockside crowd tarred and feathered a minor custom's official on September 7, 1768, the practice became widespread. A year later a New York mob tarred and feathered "Two very obnoxious informers" because they had been responsible for the seizure of a small adventure of smuggled wine "the hard earnings of a worthy son of Neptune."[19] About the same time sailors in Philadelphia tarred and feathered a customs informer, paraded him through town, and then rowed him across the Delaware and left him on the Jersey shore.[20] Tar and feathers reflected some traditional crowd punishments, but the specific method had maritime roots. The measure had been used previously as a punishment by sailors, and one of the main ingredients—tar—was aboard every vessel, in addition to being a symbol for the common seaman.[21]

The close connection between the waterfront and revolutionary rioting can be seen in the tumult that led to the Boston Massacre. In the months before March 5, 1770, Boston's streets were often packed with crowds intimidating violators of nonimportation agreements and harassing customs collectors. The people of the waterfront played some, not a decisive, role in these disturbances. Tension also arose between the British soldiers and local laborers. Off-duty redcoats competed with waterfront workers for scarce jobs. The resulting animosity reached a fever pitch at a ropewalk, a trade connected to the waterfront, on March 2. A ropemaker offered a soldier some work. The redcoat balked upon discovering that the ropemakers only wanted him to clean their outhouse. This intentional slight led to a fight, which was soon joined by other Bostonians and soldiers. Brawls and minor frays broke out all over Boston during the next few days. By March 5 rumors were everywhere. Men on the waterfront in particular were eager for a fight. That evening brought more skirmishes. By nine o'clock a crowd on King Street pelted soldiers with snowballs and rocks. Amidst that confusion the soldiers began to fire, killing five and wounding several others.[22]

Why did so many people crowd King Street and harass armed soldiers? Why did sailors eagerly join the Stamp Act riots, customs disturbances, and anti-imperial demonstrations of the 1770s and 1760s? Each individual, no doubt, had many reasons for rioting. First, participating in a crowd was a form of entertainment for many in the eighteenth century. Second, immediate and personal economic interests were often involved. And third, larger ideological reasons were connected to but not derived from the intellectual currents so popular with the elite.[23]

People riot for specific reasons tied to grievances and larger social trends, but also because rioting can be fun. In moments of popular disorder society is turned upside down, and those trapped on the bottom of society briefly rule the streets. People can experience a personal sense of liberty; they can scream, shout obscenities with abandon, shatter windows, and stand entranced by the consuming flames of a bonfire. Both adrenaline and alcohol often add to the excitement. Rumors spread wildly, and an electric tension fills the air that can only be released, like a bolt of lightning with a great thunderclap, as the crowd goes into action. In colonial seaports the raw material for such social explosions could always be found on the waterfront. There, sailors with too little to do and a penchant for mischief were ready for fisticuffs.

In addition to enjoying the excitement of the moment, the maritime workers that filled the ranks of the pre-revolutionary mob had specific economic reasons for rioting. They were concerned with preserving the liberty to contract for their own labor. A decline in trade after the end of the French and Indian War meant that many who previously had had an easy time finding employment now struggled to get by. Sailors searched in vain for their next voyage. Stevedores and those tradesmen supplying ships also had difficulty finding regular work. Crowds could form easily in these years because so many men were idle. Any effort to restrict trade, or limit smuggling, directly threatened already strained livelihoods. Crown officials seeking to enforce these new imperial restrictions became ready scapegoats for these economic grievances. Similarly, in Boston and New York, the two ports with large garrisons in the late 1760s, the presence of redcoats competing for jobs to fill their off-duty hours led to repeated conflicts and rioting.

Impressment, too, remained an issue. The fear of being taken by a press-gang and placed in interminable service for little reward was a continual irritant throughout the imperial crisis. Years of opposing press-gangs had convinced many on the waterfront that the British government had no right to take their liberty (and here liberty means simply freedom from the physical restraints of the royal navy) from them. Many pre-revolutionary riots came in close proximity to anti-impressment disturbances. Both New York and Newport experienced anti-impressment disturbances about a year before their anti-Stamp Act riots, and much of the crowd opposition to the Townshend Duties in Boston occurred against a backdrop of threats of impressment.[24]

Revolutionary rioting also had an almost "constitutional" role as a way that the people could assert themselves in an effort to limit the power of government. If the leaders of the revolution believed that the more power the government had, the less liberty the people had, then the liberty of the people to demonstrate in the street was a crucial check on government. We can trace the development of this idea from the English radical tradition of the Real Whigs to the pamphlets and speeches of the leaders of the American Revolution. It would be presumptuous for us to think that those further down in society, without the high-flowing language and allusions to classical figures like Cato, did not understand their "constitutional" function as they clamored for liberty in the streets.[25]

Another popular idea about liberty had less tangible roots. Although colonial America was a hierarchical society, there remained a rough egalitarianism that some historians identify as class conflict. With roots in the English Revolution of the 1640s and before, this notion often expressed itself in eighteenth-century riots as a resentment of wealth and privilege. While appearing occasionally in disturbances before 1765, the imperial crisis created more opportunities for the people to assert themselves in the street, allowing this undercurrent of rough egalitarianism to come closer and closer to the surface. The republican ideology of the elite, which criticized a government rife with corruption, reinforced these tendencies. In turn, augmented by popular egalitarianism, that republican ideology shifted and, as best expressed in Tom Paine's *Common Sense*, became an attack on royalty and all hereditary privilege.[26]

The waterfront remained one of the places where this rough egalitarianism expressed itself the strongest. The "liberty" of the sailor, as he came reeling along the docks with money bulging in his pocket, expressed a freedom from restraint and hierarchy that stood out in this world. That the sailor might play the gentleman, renting a horse and carriage, served as a parody and challenge to traditional notions of deference. Embedded in this behavior, however unintended on the individual level, was a critique of social distinctions that was not lost on those who lived on the waterfront. Similarly, the willingness to jump into the fray, whether in the name of liberty or for the sheer joy of it, reflected a denial of normal constraints that oddly merged in one person the emotional, economic, and ideological reasons for participating in a riot before the American Revolution.

Maritime workers not only provided many of the shock troops for the mobs that underpinned the resistance movement of the 1760s and 1770s; they also helped propel the resistance movement toward greater social change and gave voice to a call for equality. As resistance moved toward revolution, and as mobs parading with effigies or tarring and feathering an opponent gave way to armed conflict, the American maritime worker continued to play an active part.

Histories of the American Revolutionary War do not dwell long on the combat experience of sailors. The main action, except for the French victory in the Battle of the Capes that cut Lord Cornwallis off at Yorktown, appears to have taken place on land. John Paul Jones receives a minor comment for the famous battle on the *Bon Homme Richard*. For the most part, we tend to focus on the land campaigns and assume that most American males who fought in the war served either in the Continental Army or the local militia. Such an assumption is misleading. At various points during the war some fifty-seven vessels served in the Continental navy. Add to this several dozen vessels in the various state navies, and an estimated 2,000–3,000 privateers and we have some idea of the American maritime effort. If each vessel averaged one hundred men, at least 200,000 men signed on voyages during the war.[27] Thousands if not tens of thousands of Americans sailed in the British navy or tried their luck on privateers flying the Union Jack. In addition, thousands of maritime craftsmen outfitted and supplied this armada. Sailing and fighting on the high seas was part of the war experience of many American males.[28]

Sea battles could be a gruesome business in the eighteenth century. Often the men were issued a double dose of grog to inure them to the blood that might follow. The noise could be deafening; Ebenezer Fox reported that he could not hear for almost a week after one engagement.[29] Smoke would blind most of the men. Discipline counted the most. During the *Bon Homme Richard*'s battle with the *Serapis*, the American officers had to go below repeatedly and compel men to return to their quarters.[30] Nathaniel Fanning described how the "mangled corpses" filled both ships, and declared, "To see the dead in heaps—to hear the groans of the wounded and dying—the entrails of the dead scattered promiscuously around, the blood (*American too*) *over one's shoes*, was enough to move pity from the most hardened and *callous breasts*."[31] Such battles with an exchange of broadsides and intense hand-to-hand combat with boarders were rare. Even rarer were fleet actions, which Americans would experience in the British or French navies.[32]

The aim of most naval action was to capture enemy merchantmen to disrupt commerce and earn prize money. From the American perspective, privateers were probably the most efficient means to this end. Some privateers were little more than whaleboats packed with men that could maneuver in shoals and around the shore. Christopher Vail and Thomas Painter both joined in this type of activity and even raided British-occupied Long Island.[33] Privateers such as the *Wasp* in 1782 stuck to coastal waters, like those between Maine and Nova Scotia. The *Wasp* captured and ransomed some fishermen, raided a loyalist settlement, and participated in a nasty local and personal struggle.[34] Many others ranged further into the Atlantic, seeking prizes in the West Indies and even in European waters. These vessels often had to run from bigger British warships, while plucking off merchantmen whenever they could. Some even sailed into a British convoy, if they were lucky enough to find one, cutting out as many merchantmen as they dared before the escort drove them off.[35]

As we have seen in the case of John Blatchford, American men fought on both sides in the war, and some easily serve in a variety of capacities; they might sail under several flags on warships, privateers, or on merchant vessels. Because of the harsh discipline and regulated life, most Americans detested service in the British navy. Even the king's own subjects in the British Isles avoided impressment as much as possible. Many Americans also found the American and state navies equally hateful. The issue for many a seaman was less which country he sailed for, and more how could he avoid being trapped far from home. Caleb Foot, after spending years in a British prison, was despondent over sailing in the *South Carolina* because he had been absent from his family for so long. He found all work "heart-breaking" and said that there was "nothing more destructive to the mind than to be cruising these seas [off the coast of Europe], beating from a lee shore." He wrote, "We endanger our lives, expose our health, and are very desirous of sailing for the Continent [America]." On New Year's Day in 1782 he prayed for deliverance from this slavery and declared that his service on the *South Carolina* was the "worst of hells."[36]

Why did men serve aboard American warships during the Revolution? At times some degree of coercion led a man to enlist, and like poor John Blatchford some men found themselves switching sides several times during the conflict. Their motivations and loyalty to the greater cause of liberty were therefore often ambiguous.

Crews aboard American warships during the Revolution varied in terms of their region, race, ethnicity, and even nationality. Sailors came from all over the new United States and included blacks as well as whites. James Forten, who later became an important black leader in Philadelphia, served as a powder boy aboard a privateer.[37] Many an "old country man"—someone born in England—sailed on American ships. Held as a prisoner aboard British ships off the coast of South Carolina, Francis Boardman escaped with a Mr. Penny, a ship's gunner in the British navy. Boardman and Penny traveled together until they reached Philadelphia, where Penny signed aboard an American vessel.[38] American warships also had great ethnic diversity.[39] Even a New England privateer largely recruited from one locality or colony might contain some foreign hands. Of the eighty-seven-member crew of the *Harlequin*, taken by the British in 1780, all but a handful came from Massachusetts. Yet the crew included six Europeans who had been on an English merchantman previously: three Germans, one Swede, one Dane, and one Portuguese.[40]

Vessels fitted out in Europe often had crews with higher proportions of non-Americans. Benjamin Franklin commissioned the notorious *Black Prince* in 1779. Almost the entire crew of this cutter came from Ireland. On its first voyage it had an American as a sham captain. The owners abandoned this pretense in the wake of its spectacular success.[41] When the British took the *Alexander*, a letter of marque carrying American papers, they found only three Americans on board. The rest of the men were chiefly from Spain, France, and the Netherlands.[42]

The polyglot makeup of American crews created problems. The frigate *Alliance*, under the command of French-born Pierre Landais, faced a crisis on a cruise from Boston to France when the seventy or eighty British members of the crew plotted to seize the vessel and carry it into an English port.[43] John Paul Jones confronted similar difficulties. On his renowned "mad cruise" that culminated with the battle with the *Serapis*, some of the British sailors on his ship slipped away and escaped to their homeland. In a calm off the Irish coast, a group of Irish sailors cut loose a barge towing the *Bon Homme Richard* and successfully reached shore. Another desertion occurred immediately after the battle off Flamborough Head. Eight or ten Englishmen stole a boat from the *Serapis* and sailed away with it, landing at Scarborough.[44]

The variety of nationalities aboard ships often led to ethnic conflict and mixed loyalties. Caleb Foot's *South Carolina* had Americans, Frenchmen, and others on its European cruise in 1781. On at least two occasions the rampant discontent aboard the vessel swelled into mutiny. In August 1781, Frenchmen and Englishmen threatened to take over the ship in a Dutch port. During the melee, one Frenchman had his arm badly cut and other seamen were wounded before the mutineers submitted to the officers. Off the coast of

Spain two months later, officers one night awakened the Americans in the crew, armed them, and told them to prepare for action, "for the Frenchmen were about to force them away from the ship." Again the mutiny was quelled.[45] The French sailors and marines aboard Captain Samuel Tucker's frigate *Boston* complained of ill usage while the vessel was in L'Orient, France, in June 1778. French officials interceded and asked the men if they wished to go ashore or "tarry aboard." Tucker then had to release forty-seven men who said they wanted to leave the ship.[46]

Although James Forten turned down the patronage of an English captain after his capture, and thereby guaranteed himself a berth in a prison ship, many other African Americans took a different tack. At Forton Prison in England in April 1778, whites accused two blacks of being informants for the British and inflicted three dozen lashes on one of the suspects. Racial tension, which otherwise went unnoticed by the British, must have increased thereafter because two days later all of the black prisoners were segregated into their own building.[47] Many other African Americans pursued their liberty by enlisting with the British. Moses Johnson ran away from his Virginia master after Lord Dunmore's proclamation offering freedom to all slaves who fought for the king. Unfortunately for Johnson, Americans captured him on a British privateer, took him to New Jersey, and sold him back into slavery.[48]

More than the varied and international composition of crews complicated the issue of loyalty; sailors felt strong attachments to shipmates and to hometowns. These bonds rarely interfered with the prosecution of the war; most of the time they merely preoccupied individual tars with personal loyalties that obscured the larger cause of American independence.

Conflicting personal allegiances plagued John Paul Jones. The crew of the *Ranger* objected to Jones's raid on the English coast in 1778 and expressed outrage when Jones arrested the *Ranger*'s first lieutenant, Thomas Simpson, after returning to France. These sons of New England had signed the sloop's articles largely on Simpson's account, "knowing him to be a Gentleman of honour, Worthey and capeable of his Officeships." They viewed Simpson as a "Faithfull, true and Fatherly Officer," and saw Jones as "ungratefull," "deceitfull," and "*Arbitrary*."[49] Personal attachment to another captain and crew lost John Paul Jones command of the *Alliance* only months after his triumph over the *Serapis*. The remnants of Jones's crew had been assigned to the *Alliance*, which came under Jones's direct command. Since the men from the *Bon Homme Richard* claimed that the *Alliance* had not aided them in the battle with the *Serapis*, and had actually raked the *Bon Homme Richard* with broadsides during the engagement, there was little love lost between the two crews.

Animosity intensified, fights broke out, and ultimately Pierre Landais, the *Alliance*'s previous commander and Jones's rival, stole the ship with the help of the original crew.[50]

Loyalty to a hometown was usually a man's primary allegiance, before even that to his country. As soon as a sailor first entered the yard at Mill Prison in England, fellow townsmen, eager for local news, quickly brought him under their protective wing. Visitors to prisons sought those men from their own local community and then treated them to beer and conversations of home.[51] Caleb Foot's letters from prison, full of personal lamentations to his wife, obviously penned them for a larger audience. Almost every letter included a list of Salem natives who wished to be remembered to their relations.[52] The margins and ends of letters from American prisoners were often crammed with the names of neighbors wishing their families well.[53] William Widger filled his diary with the names and birthplaces of recent arrivals in Mill Prison. He even copied a roster of Marblehead boys at Forton Prison. Widger also recorded a dream that transported him back to the waterfront of his beloved Marblehead.[54] Considering the varied nationality of sailors and their mix of allegiances, loyalty was a complicated issue, taking many twists and turns, including several layers of often contradictory obligations.

Part of the explanation for this confused loyalty among American sailors is that many were not particularly patriotic.[55] The war devastated shipping and fishing and curtailed opportunities in other occupations. Serving aboard a privateer, or even in the regular navy, offered the sailor and the landsman the chance to earn a living, and possibly to gain a small fortune.[56] Ebenezer Fox seemed to be largely pursuing the main chance in his naval service. Growing up poor in Roxbury, a stone's throw from the sea, he had been bound out at age seven to a local farmer. At age twelve, in 1775, he ran away to Providence and served as a cabin boy on two voyages. With four dollars in his pocket he returned home and apprenticed to a barber and wigmaker in Boston. In the spring of 1780, during a business slump caused by the war, he and his master agreed that he should try his luck on the Massachusetts ship *Protector*, with the two of them splitting the profits. After Fox returned from this adventure he completed his apprenticeship and set up his own shop.[57]

Self-aggrandizement led to complaints of the "Rapacity of the Crews in Stripping prizes of every Little thing they could lay their hands upon," including personal possessions that should have been off-limits.[58] Thomas Andros, who later became a minister, claimed in his memoirs in the 1830s that as a seventeen-year-old Connecticut boy he "had a full conviction at the time, that the Revolutionary cause was just." Such an assertion by an old man a half century later may or may not be trusted. More honest, surprising, and reflecting a sense of Calvinist self-deprivation, is Andros's confession that he was "among these deluded and infatuated youth" who, after the arrival of a rich prize in New London in the summer of 1781, "flocked on board our private armed ships, fancying the same success would attend their adventures."[59]

The concern with profit and earnings had a profound impact on the sailor's attitude toward his service. Fred Anderson has argued that the men who filled the ranks of the New England militia during the French and Indian War saw themselves more as contracted workers than as soldiers in a patriotic cause. They were willing to offer their labor as long as the employer upheld his end of the bargain in terms of length of enlistment, proper supplies, and appropriate compensation. If an official failed to fulfill any portion of the contract, the New England militia might mutiny or desert. A similar attitude among those who enlisted in the Continental Army helps to explain the large numbers of desertions and mutinies during the Revolutionary War.[60]

At sea the mind-set may have been intensified because a ship's articles were, in fact, a business contract. The result was that American captains struggled to maintain discipline, facing repeated desertions and mutinies. John Paul Jones often haggled with his crew over the division of prize money. Many of his discontented men simply left the ship. On October 14, 1779, twenty-five men deserted en masse from the recently captured *Serapis*. On October 30 the quartermaster deserted. On November 8 and 17 and December 13, 1779, the logs of the ships under Jones's command reported more deserters.[61] State navies struggled with desertion as well. On Connecticut's *Oliver Cromwell* from 1776 to 1777, 50 of 236 names are listed as having deserted.[62]

Perceived violation of contract was frequently the cause of these desertions. Similar motivation often led to mutiny. The crew of the *Washington* mutinied on November 29, 1775, because they had enlisted in the army and not as sailors. The "Free Company" belonging to the Pennsylvania armed boat *Ranger* refused duty in the same year because the provisions stipulated in the articles were not supplied. In 1778 the crew of the brigantine *Hazard* drew up a round-robin and demanded a return to port because their enlistment had expired and "that there would be the Devil to Pay among the People" if the voyage continued.[63]

Recruiters worked every angle to combine patriotism with other appeals. A poster early in the war addressed to the "JOLLY TARS who are fighting for the RIGHTS and LIBERTIES of AMERICA" urged sailors to "make your Fortunes now, my Lads, before its too late, Defend, defend, I say defend an Independent State."[64] Parading in the streets carrying a flag and attended by a band playing martial music, a later recruiter talked of the "zeal for the cause of liberty." He also sang a tune to attract apprentices by denigrating masters and offering adventure and opportunity:

All you that have bad masters
And cannot get your due;
Come, come, my brave boys,
And join our ship's crew.[65]

Andrew Sherburne reported that in Boston in 1781 a "jolly tar" was even more direct in promising monetary reward. The wily sailor accosted the fifteen-year-old Sherburne with "Ha shipmate, don't you wish to take a short cruise in a fine schooner and make your fortune?" Sherburne already had been to sea for two years and had signed aboard another privateer. Still, knowing that his own vessel would not be ready to sail for a few more months, he agreed to go with the "jolly tar," hoping to take part in the seizure of a few prizes and return before the other vessel was to put out to sea.[66]

Manpower was a key to success in naval warfare, and even small privateer sloops would pack up to a hundred men or more to swoop down, board, and overwhelm a merchantman. As recruiters always had difficulty obtaining a full crew, they used any method that might add a few men. Sherburne's captain, still shorthanded when he set sail, coasted down to Maine, stopping at each town and providing free food and drink to local men in the hope of signing intoxicated sailors.[67] Rendezvous houses—places where a ship would officially recruit men and have the sailors put their names or marks to a contract—were taverns. Recruiters offered drink and promised an advance to men who signed up for a cruise. Some men had little choice in the matter, having run up a debt to a bartender or boardinghouse keeper that could be squared only by signing the articles of a ship selected by the supposed patron. Men even sold their future shares of prizes before the cruise to obtain a larger advance. Officials also used more coercive measures like release from jail, and a few captains occasionally relied on impressment.[68]

The forces under the control of the Continental Congress, the state navies, and the privateers competed for men. Privateers' up to one-hundred-dollar advances gave them the edge. Both the army and the navy suffered losses. After completing two terms of enlistment in the army in 1776, John Palmer signed aboard a privateer, even though he had friends and relatives who had been "whipt almost to Death as well as starved too" while serving at sea.[69]

MANLY.

A FAVORITE NEW

SONG,

In the AMERICAN FLEET.

Moſt humbly Addreſſed to all the JOLLY TARS who are fighting for the RIGHTS and LIBERTIES of AMERICA.

By a SAILOR.—It may be ſung to the Tune of WASHINGTON.

BRAVE MANLY he is ſtout, and his Men have proved true,
By taking of thoſe Engliſh Ships, he makes their Jacks to rue;
To our Ports he ſends their Ships and Men, let's give a hearty Cheer
To Him and all thoſe valiant Souls who go in Privateers.
And a Privateering we will go, my Boys, my Boys,
And a Privateering we will go.
O all ye gallant Sailor Lads, do'nt never be diſmay'd,
Nor let your Foes in Battle ne'er think you are afraid,
Thoſe daſtard Sons ſhall tremble when our Cannon they do roar,
We'll take, or ſink, or burn them all, or them we'll drive on Shore.
And a Privateering we will go, &c.
Our Heroes they're not daunted when Cannon Balls do fly,
For we're reſolv'd to conquer, or bravely we will die;

18. This Revolutionary War broadside celebrated not only Captain John Manly, depicted in the illustration, but also the common seaman, as in the lyrics of the song. "Broadside of Manly, A Favorite New Song." New Bedford Whaling Museum.

Joshua Gott entered the army during the siege of Boston in 1775. Sent to New York in March 1776, he stayed with the Continental forces through several defeats, returning to New England in February 1777. For the rest of the war he signed aboard a variety of vessels, including the frigate *Boston* and a host of privateers and merchantmen. After one cruise he collected £231 in prize money.[70] As Benjamin Rush explained to Richard Henry Lee, "many of the Continental troops now in our service, pant for the expiration of their enlistments, in order that they may partake of the spoils of the West Indies." Others did not wait for the end of their enlistment. Repeatedly Continental officers searched privateers to reclaim deserters, and at times officials refused to allow privateers to sail until Continental ships were outfitted.[71]

Sailors in Europe, like John Blatchford in 1782, had few options other than signing aboard another warship. Many seamen found themselves returned to English prisons only months after having left their confines when recaptured from a new vessel. In later years these men explained their willingness to sign on with John Paul Jones or some privateer as an effort to seek revenge or even as an expression of their patriotism. The fact that they were penniless, in a foreign country, and unable to speak the language, and had no way of getting home probably best explains their choice.[72] Some sailors did not care what country they sailed for and eagerly signed aboard vessels of countries allied with the United States. Nathaniel Fanning even gave up his American citizenship so that he could become an officer on a French privateer.[73] A few American prisoners of war who escaped went to the nearest port and entered on British privateers. Joseph Myrick was born in Nantucket and had served in the *Black Prince*, the American privateer manned largely by Irishmen out of Dunkerque. In June 1780 he captained an American crew on a French privateer. Captured by the British in September 1780, he volunteered for His Majesty's navy a year later.[74]

Loyalty could be a clouded and confused issue not just for American seamen. British sailors joined American crews even though they could be executed for treason if they fell into the crown's hands. Englishman Charles White feared being hanged when he was captured aboard an American privateer. As soon as his captain ordered the colors lowered, White had his shipmates take a razor and mutilate his cheek to obscure the brand the British navy had earlier placed there for desertion. He passed as a wounded American and was later exchanged.[75]

Other sailors switched sides several times. Thomas Haley began the war in the service of Lord Dunmore, the royal governor of Virginia. Captured on a vessel owned by Dunmore and brought to Philadelphia, Haley incurred "several obligations"—probably debts to an innkeeper—and signed aboard the *Lexington.* When the British took the *Lexington,* he willingly sought to enlist in the royal navy.[76] William Lamb bounced in and out of the royal navy. Andrew Sherburne met him on the privateer *Ranger* in 1779 after the Americans took Lamb from a captured British ship and assigned him to duty. When the *Ranger* surrendered to a British warship, Lamb was pressed into the navy. Two years later, Sherburne met Lamb again in a holding vessel in England. By that time Lamb had run away and been reimpressed repeatedly.[77] The British captured Jonathan Deakens on an American vessel on July 26, 1782. Taken to London, he escaped only to sign aboard a British merchantman bound for the West Indies. A leak forced the vessel to put in to Ireland, where a press-gang snatched Deakens. After serving several months on board His Majesty's ships, and as the war was winding down, Deakens applied to the captain to become a prisoner of war and was sent to Mill Prison.[78] Christopher Vail spent more than eleven months as a prisoner of war in Antigua before he and about forty-five other Americans were put aboard British warships. Proclaiming themselves to be Americans, they at first refused to serve. The lash convinced them otherwise. Their objections, however, had one effect; they were later allowed to volunteer to sail in transport vessels heading to England. Once in Great Britain, Vail signed aboard a British privateer. He recorded the captain's interview with his shipmate, Foster. The captain wanted to know what country and port he came from. Foster replied he was an American from Boston. "Well," said the captain, "I suppose you are a Rebel." Foster answered no. "Are you willing to fight the French and Spaniards?" the captain asked. "Yes," Foster responded. The captain continued: "Are you willing to fight the Americans?" Faced with the possibility of prison or impressment, Foster said yes. "You will do then," and the captain moved on to the next recruit.[79]

Joseph Bartlett perhaps holds the record for being captured and recaptured repeatedly, often switching sides with amazing aplomb. As a seventeen-year-old he signed as a green hand aboard the *Grampus* out of Plymouth, Massachusetts, in 1778. They were captured by a British privateer. Kept aboard the prize to help work the ship, he was recaptured the next day by an American privateer, only to be taken again by the British the day after. Brought to New York, he was told he would be put on a prison ship. Left unguarded, he went to the next wharf and signed on a schooner heading for Halifax. No sooner were they at sea than they were captured by a ship from Beverly. He had been away from home for twenty days and had been captured four times. Bartlett may have been a slow learner, had few options for earning a living, or sought adventure, for he soon signed aboard another privateer. This time he was not captured. But the voyage was a disaster since it took part in the ill-fated Penobscot expedition in 1779 during which the British defeated an American flotilla off the coast of Maine. Intrepid as ever, Bartlett signed on to a Salem schooner in October 1779 and began another round of captures and recaptures. The British took the schooner. Again, he stayed with the prize, being promised his venture and his liberty if he commanded one of the watches (the prize crew was one officer and four "Negroes"). Just outside New York Harbor, however, they were taken by an American vessel and brought to Philadelphia. He signed aboard an American privateer only to desert off the Jersey shore because he and several shipmates decided that the captain was afraid to attack British shipping. In the spring of 1780 Bartlett signed aboard the *Aurora,* which fought a brutal battle with the British frigate *Iris*. Captured again, he was sent to New York and placed aboard a prison ship. He pretended to have smallpox so that he could be exchanged three months later. Bartlett still had not had enough of the high seas. He signed aboard a merchant vessel, only to desert because he didn't like the captain. He signed aboard another vessel, bound for Havana, and was captured for the eighth time and brought to the Bahamas. Despairing of being exchanged, he agreed to sail with a British privateer, which was captured by the *Columbia*, a letter of marque from Philadelphia. Bartlett joined the American crew and bragged how the fifty black sailors on the Bermuda privateer brought a hefty price in the Havana slave market. Five days after leaving Cuba, a British frigate took the *Columbia*. Placed in a Barbados prison, Bartlett and ten others escaped to a French island and made it back to North America by January 1782. Shipping out again to the West Indies, he was captured by a Bermudan privateer. Three weeks of isolation in the hold convinced him to work aboard this vessel. After this experience, he found shore employment in Bermuda, then shipped on a British merchant vessel to St. Thomas and from there managed to get passage to North Carolina. Sailing in a merchantman, Bartlett was captured one last time (for a total of twelve). As it was near the end of the war, he was exchanged and eventually made his way back to New England.[80]

As we have seen, the British imprisoned many American seamen.[81] Ten thousand men may have died aboard the prison ships in New York Harbor with many others living through that ordeal. The British held about three thousand at one time or another in England, and kept scattered hundreds throughout the Atlantic world from Canada to the West Indies and sent a handful to Africa and the East Indies.[82] Conditions on the prison ships in

19. Conditions on prison ships were deplorable and often led to starvation, illness, and death. "Jersey Prisoners." Collection of Howard B. Rock.

North America, especially in New York, were appalling. Although the sailors were farther from home, the English prisons were better. All of the prisons tested the beliefs, loyalty, and life of Jack Tar.

Of the several prison hulks used in New York during the war, in later years American sailors focused their collective memory on the most notorious vessel—the *Jersey*. Descriptions of this prison ship that came to encapsulate their sacrifice and experience as prisoners of war were frightful. The nauseating and foul air assaulted Thomas Dring as he approached the *Jersey*. Sent aboard at night, he was soon separated from his shipmates. He was forced to lie among a mass of humanity, clutching his few possessions, fearing that he would be robbed by a desperate sailor. Dring noted the contrast between men "who had breathed the pure breezes of the ocean" and "the pent-up air of a crowded prison-ship, pregnant with putrid fever, foul with deadly contagion." They had been left "to linger out the tedious and weary day, the disturbed and anxious night" in "wearying and degrading captivity, unvaried but by new scenes of painful suffering, and new inflictions of remorseless cruelty." Disease was rampant. To prevent a fatal case of smallpox, Dring inoculated himself soon after he arrived, while he still had some strength. He found someone with a pox full of pus and took a pin and "scarified the skin" of his hand "between the

20. This early nineteenth-century wood engraving suggests the foreboding image of the prison ships during the Revolutionary War. The wood structure in the middle of the vessel, which was probably used as a hoist, appears more like a gallows. "Jersey Prison Ship." From Ebenezer Fox, *The Adventures of Ebenezer Fox* . . . (Boston, 1838). Collection of Rita Broyles.

thumb and fore-finger," applied the matter, and bound up his hand. The next day he was ill with a mild case of the disease.[83] Many did not survive the smallpox, yellow fever, and other diseases that swept through the prisoners. While Christopher Vail was in the *Jersey,* seven or eight men died a night. Locked below decks each evening, with more than one thousand other men, those with dysentery would come to the foot of the steps, but were not "permitted to go on deck, and was obliged to ease themselves on the spot, and the next morning for 12 feet round the hatches was nothing but excrement."[84] This living—and dying—nightmare was seared into the memory of many on the waterfront.

Conditions were less onerous in Great Britain, where American captives were usually sent to either Forton or Old Mill (sometimes just referred to as Mill) prisons. As on the prison ships, food was of poor quality and amounted to two-thirds the rations provided in the British navy. Although this meager fare left men hungry, the living conditions were not as crowded and disease not as prevalent as on the *Jersey*. The death rate in English prisons was much lower than in the prison ships, and was even lower than in the regular British navy. After investigating complaints about conditions in Mill Prison in June 1781, the Commissioners of Sick and Hurt Seamen proclaimed, "no people ever enjoyed more perfect health than they [the American prisoners] have done since their Confinement." This statement may have been an exaggeration; but of 631 men confined in Mill Prison from May 1777 through June 1781, only eighteen had died.[85] A year later, the total had risen to fifty-five, still only about a 5 percent mortality rate. Prisoner William Russell wrote to his wife in 1781 that "The Usage we receive, (if I am a judge) is very good." Russell no doubt sought to ease his wife's concerns for his well being, but the fact was that they were "allowed the liberty of the yard all day" for exercise, had an "open Market at the gate" to buy additional provisions and to sell handicrafts, and had relatively "comfortable lodgings," especially compared to the cramped quarters at sea or in a prison hulk.[86] Life was not easy in the prisons, however. Smallpox epidemics threatened, and the isolation and helplessness was enough to drive a person to distraction.[87] Whether brought to England or New York, or any place the British held prisoners of war, the sailor faced a rough road.

The well-documented experience in the prisons in England offers insight into the loyalties of sailors during the American Revolution. Three key areas—desertion to the enemy, escape, and prisoner self-organization—help us to understand the ambiguous loyalty and liberty of Jack Tar.[88]

Desertion—the willingness to defect to the enemy—is central to our understanding of the mentality of the common sailor. John Blatchford was coerced to defect, resisted, paid a heavy price, and eventually became willing to serve any master as long as he could survive and get home. To some extent all Americans captured during the Revolutionary War faced a similar dilemma. The failure of more sailors to come to the same conclusion as poor Blatchford suggests that American tars were committed to the cause of liberty, but this argument is not as conclusive as it first appears.[89]

One out of eight prisoners in England at one time or another petitioned for a royal pardon to enter either His Majesty's navy or serve the king in some other capacity. Almost all of these petitions were granted. Were these men disloyal to the American cause? Were they mostly "old countrymen"—born in the British Isles—as some prisoners suggested? Were these sailors merely "citizens of the world" ready to sail under any flag?

The answer in each case is, perhaps. These American sailors were not always disloyal to the United States. A few tars had little choice in the matter. Some men volunteered, or so they claimed, with the intention of getting a better opportunity to escape. Samuel Knapp of Salem entered the royal navy in 1780 after a year and a half in prison, only to run from his ship and escape to France.[90] Ebenezer Fox, held aboard the *Jersey* prison ship, said that he enlisted in the British army with the promise that he would be stationed in the West Indies away from the fighting with American troops, and in the hope that he could make good his escape.[91] Although sailors' later statements about their rationale for serving the king cannot be entirely trusted, their desertion to the enemy cannot easily be labeled disloyalty—or loyalty.

We know the nationality of only about one-third, or 130, of the men who joined the British service from prisons in England. Of that number, 70 percent were American born, while slightly more than one-quarter of the "volunteers" were from the British Isles. These percentages differ from the overall proportions within the prison population: 90 percent of the prisoners were Americans.[92] This difference is not enough to substantiate claims that most, or even half, of the volunteers were "old countrymen." Birthplace also does not dictate commitment to one side or another. Some loyalists in North America traced their lineage to the earliest settlements in Virginia and Massachusetts. There were "old countrymen," like Tom Paine, who spoke virulently for revolution and independence.[93]

Many "volunteers" were neither loyalists nor patriots hoping to escape. Their reasons for defecting to the British had little to do with questions of allegiance and more to do with an attitude toward the world. Not every seaman conformed to a pattern that emphasized survival over ideology. A sailor's life was often confined and under regulation whether crowded into a forecastle of a merchantman or restricted to the narrow limits of his hammock on a warship's teeming gundeck, or bound by the walls of Forton or Mill Prison. The British navy provided an alternative. A sailor anxious for some movement and bored with his daily grind might sign on in the hope that the royal navy offered a marginally better life and maybe a change of scenery.

If the loyalty of those who "volunteered" to join the British remains ambiguous, the commitment and allegiance of those who stayed behind was equally unclear. After a group of volunteers left Mill Prison for the British navy in December 1778, a petition asserting loyalty to Congress and opposition to enlisting with the British gathered less than half the signatures of the remaining prisoners.[94] Even for those not proclaiming their patriotism, there were good reasons not to enter the royal navy. A British official reported that harsh treatment from fellow prisoners prevented men from entering the king's service.[95] Sailors did not need discouragement from their comrades, as every tar knew that living conditions aboard His Majesty's ships could be abysmal. The food in British service, while greater in quantity than the prisoner's fare, was often little better in quality. Overcrowding and strict discipline made life difficult aboard His Majesty's ships. A sailor had a little control over his life on a royal warship as he had as a prisoner of war. At the whim of the admiralty, he might be whisked off to the frigid waters and storms of the North Atlantic or the pestilence and sweltering conditions of the West Indies or Africa.[96] Anglo-Americans on both sides of the Atlantic shared a long tradition of avoiding navy service that included anti-impressment riots. Sailors therefore shunned the royal navy, especially if there was another way out.[97]

For the common sailor that hope lay in an exchange of prisoners. Although the Continental government organized few regular cartels (agreements to allow prisoner exchange) in North America, local and state arrangements occurred intermittently.[98] In Europe negotiations dragged on for years. Rumors of exchange constantly passed through the prisons, and despite delays, the chance for an exchange kept many tars from petitioning the king to join his navy. A rumor of a cartel heard aboard a British warship convinced Caleb Foot, who apparently was serving as a British sailor, to change his status to a prisoner of war. So optimistic was Foot that he ecstatically proclaimed that leaving the warship and entering Forton Prison "was like coming out of Hell and going into Paradise." Although Foot tended toward hyperbole, his hopes for exchange echoed other prison commentators. Unfortunately for them, cartels did not become regular in England until the war was almost over.[99]

Another way out of the prisons was escape. In North America escape was difficult. Some men managed to break out of the prison ships in New York Harbor, and there were escapes from Halifax, Charleston, the West Indies, and elsewhere.[100] These efforts pale in comparison to the experience of the men in England. Year after year, hundreds of sailors slipped over, under, and through the walls of Mill and Forton prisons. British officials were beside themselves with their inability to control this epidemic of breakouts. During some periods, escapes from Forton Prison occurred almost every other day. The diaries, reminiscences, and even the British records are so often punctuated with reports of tunneling, massive breakouts, and persistent and sometimes spectacular deceptions, that it is easy to suppose that the escapes are a testament to Yankee ingenuity and of the commitment to the cause of independence.[101] As in the case of desertion, however, this issue is complicated and the sailors' motives perplexing.

The idea of escape was neither new nor novel to sailors. Throughout the eighteenth and nineteenth centuries seamen jumped ship—as well as abandoned wives and lovers—for a variety of reasons often connected to their own understanding of liberty. Sailors ran away to enjoy the attractions of a brief stay ashore, to find higher wages elsewhere, or to escape a harsh captain or miserable conditions aboard ship. It mattered little to Jack if he were leaving a warship, a merchantman, a whaler, or a fishing vessel. Sailors also ran away to sea, for reasons ranging from the unfaithfulness of a wife to wander lust.[102]

Nor were American prisoners of war the only escapees. British soldiers and sailors escaped from their American captors in droves to return to the British lines or to fight in the Continental Army. Others settled in the countryside, whereas some signed aboard American or British privateers. The French were also great escape artists. During their protracted contests with Great Britain from 1754 to 1815, tens of thousands of Frenchmen were captured. They, like the Americans, tunneled, broke out en masse, and had some fantastic escapes.[103]

Despite these similarities, American sailor prisoners of war confronted some unusual circumstances. Exchanges were delayed as the English charged American seamen taken to Great Britain with treason and piracy. In the eighteenth century belligerents ordinarily drew up an agreement quickly to facilitate exchange. When France, Spain, and Holland joined the United States in its war for independence, each government had its own agreement for cartels and thousands of captured men were shuttled among the warring parties. With the expectation of speedy return to his own country, a French, Spanish, or Dutch sailor had little cause to put himself at risk by running away from prison. That some men did so suggests that prisons were poorly guarded.[104] Americans, on the other hand, had every reason to try to escape when the chances for a cartel looked bleak.

The treatment of American and allied officers also helps to explain the many American escapes. Rules of war usually dictated a parole for any officer who pledged his honor to remain within a district specified in his enemy's territory and swore not to take up arms until exchanged according to convention rules. The British, however, considered American officers pirates and traitors and threw them into prison. Initially they even shared quarters with common seamen. Officers vehemently objected and successfully petitioned for separate facilities with their own fireplace, locked doors at night to protect their possessions, and privies.[105]

Successful escape was largely for and by officers. Nathaniel Fanning proudly proclaimed that of the 367 officers held in Forton Prison the year that he was there, 138 made their escape to France.[106] Timothy Connor records almost as many officers as enlisted men among the escapees recounted in his journal.[107] Although the numbers in the roster of prisoners of war held in England compiled in the twentieth century differ from these calculations, the message was similar. Over half of the men identified as captains, more than a third of the subaltern officers, and approximately a fifth of the petty officers successfully escaped. Only a little less than 5 percent of the common seamen managed to do so.[108]

The inegalitarian nature of prison escape was noticed at the time. Caleb Foot wrote to his wife in August 1780: "But what can I say or what can I do to get my liberty? It is impossible for one without the help of some friend. It is almost impossible for a man to make his escape from this [place] without the help of money."[109] Charles Herbert knew from hard experience that Foot was right. Herbert had escaped with more than one hundred others through a tunnel on a cold December night and wandered around the wintry countryside only to be quickly recaptured. Herbert lamented, "Our officers that have made their escape so many times lately, may thank good friends and their money for getting off; but a poor foremast hand, with no friends, and no money in his pocket, would stand but a poor chance to get off, if he was without the walls."[110] The English recognized the need for money to escape as well. One anonymous letter to the admiralty complained of the frequent escapes from Forton Prison and declared, "you may Depend that those who can get money will not long remain Prisoners."[111] The cost for escaping varied and was generally out of the reach of the common sailor. Samuel Cutler, who had been a clerk aboard a privateer, spent more than £38 to escape and to obtain passage to America.[112] Nathaniel Harrington, Jr., a ship's surgeon, paid only half a guinea (about ten shillings) to escape Forton in 1780. It cost him at least another five guineas (about £5) to get to France, where he had to borrow another £5 before signing aboard a new vessel.[113]

Both officers and common seamen had many reasons for risking the punishment of being placed in isolation for trying to escape. Loyalty and patriotism did play some role in the minds of many escapees, especially the officers. Sailors probably also had a strong desire to get back to business—not only of fighting the war, but also of making money in the war. Somehow the financial loss of being captured and the expense of the escape had to be recovered. Most escapees signed aboard privateers and warships soon after reaching France.[114]

For many sailors the reason for escape was even less lofty and long term. A number of escapees, men who scratched away to dig tunnels for weeks or who merely arranged things with a corrupt official, breaking out meant only a brief bout of liberty. Like sailors on shore leave, they would get drunk, have sex, and then be back a day or two later to their berths in prison. Carpenter John Long saw Drury Lathing, an American prisoner, in a bar outside Forton's walls "with a young Woman drinking together" in September 1781. He does not describe the entire transaction between the two, although we can well guess what was intended.[115] This type of liaison occurred repeatedly. One prisoner, Thomas Kinsey, escaped Forton at least sixteen times. No sooner would he be returned to close confinement in the infamous black hole reserved for recaptured escapees, than he would break out again. Either he was very unlucky, or he was in close collusion with his keepers. British bureaucrats, who paid a small fortune as a reward for his recaptures, seemed to think he was getting help.[116]

Shrewd tars and prison officials profited from the special conditions of imprisoned Americans, who were committed to prison for the capital offenses of treason and piracy. Parliament and the admiralty thus set a reward of £5 for the recapture of any escapee (the reward for other prisoners of war was ten shillings).[117] The lower-level bureaucrats, especially those at Forton, appear to have been very corrupt. One British officer complained that the clerk at Forton Prison "lives like a Gentleman and keeps his horse" on a meager salary that was obviously augmented by illicit means.[118] When Long the carpenter interfered with the clerk's arrangement with the young woman and the prisoner Drury Lathing, the irate clerk promised that Long would soon find himself aboard a British warship. The next day a press-gang arrived at the construction site where Long was working to drag him off to a fate many viewed worse than prison. The army guard at the prison rescued Long, but the constant escaping and recapturing continued until officials reduced the £5 reward to normal levels.[119]

We do not know how many of the prisoners were "five-pounders" who escaped merely to split the reward, and how many had other motives. By 1780 and 1781, British officials believed that the majority of escapes fit the five-pounder category. The quick capture and return of most escapees suggests that a large number of "foremast hands" who did not have enough money to buy their way out of England seized the opportunity for a spree.[120] Other sailors, however, like Israel Potter immortalized by Herman Melville, escaped only to melt into the English population.[121] A few signed aboard English merchantmen or British privateers. Press-gangs picked up less fortunate tars who were either on their way out of the country or in a tavern. Others bought passage or stole boats to get across the Channel.[122]

The coordination necessary for many of the escape attempts, at least those by others than the "five-pounders," focuses our attention on the third key area of the prisoner-of-war experience—prisoner self-government. Like desertion and escaping, the organizational efforts of American prisoners also needs to be placed in a larger context. British soldiers and sailors held in America petitioned for a redress of grievances several times, and on at least one occasion drew up a pact vowing to abide by a mutual parole.[123] Even more disciplined were the French prisoners of the 1790s and early 1800s. These men established their own courts of law, and, despite republican principles, set up an elaborate caste system differentiating groups of prisoners.[124]

Little is known about the exact nature of the American self-government in the prisons during the Revolutionary War. Aboard ships like the *Jersey* officers took a leading role in some form of organization. In the rules drawn up by the prisoners late in the war, the oldest officer was judge in ad hoc courts to try those who violated regulations.[125] Prisoners at both Mill and Forton prisons organized not only to escape, but also to petition authorities and to regulate behavior among themselves. Just as aboard the *Jersey*, prisoner self-government may not have been as egalitarian and infused with democratic principles as has been suggested.[126] Although separated in their sleeping arrangements after January 14, 1778, officers and seamen in England met on a daily basis in the exercise yard. Officers therefore had plenty of opportunity to continue to influence men they previously commanded.[127] Officers acted as intermediaries when John Thornton, an agent for the American Commissioners in France, visited the prisons, and they supervised the relief money raised by subscription from sympathizers in England.[128] A few months after the officers gained separate quarters, Thomas Wren described his efforts to aid the prisoners in a letter to Benjamin Franklin. Wren added that he "communicated the intelligence of yours [concerning a potential exchange] on the 21st to the Officers at Forton, and they to the people, which gave the whole body of them great pleasure and contentment."[129] Three officers acted as spokesmen in a letter the prisoners in Forton wrote to Franklin in the fall of 1778 pleading for exchange. After the celebration of the victory at Yorktown almost turned into a riot, the American officers stepped in to quiet their countrymen.[130] It appears that the prison walls did not wholly diminish the authority of the quarterdeck.

The role of officers in drawing up the various petitions sent to British and American officials is less clear. According to Timothy Connor, in March 1778 the officers petitioned the king for an exchange.[131] Many major petitions listed no names and were signed generically with labels like "Petition of upwards of two hundred American Prisoners at present confined at Mill Prison."[132] Common seamen demonstrated the capability of sending individual petitions, even if they could not sign their names. Yet if a series of names appeared on a petition, an officer's name might well come first.[133] The content of the petitions provides few clues into the sailors' mindset. Ordinarily the petitions addressed specific conditions and perceived abuses. The language stressed the humility of the petitioners and the power of the petitioned, conforming to the legalistic standard of the day. It is impossible to tell whether the petitions came from organizations of common seamen or organizations controlled by officers.[134]

The officers' influence on the articles of regulation in the prisons is not certain. The articles limited drinking, brawling, and gambling—common practices among sailors that the officer corps opposed. Although seamen had a voice in the regulations, the control of officers was not precluded. Aboard the *Jersey,* officers were active in meting out punishments, while in Mill Prison one provision, which would be tough for many sailors to accept, outlawed "blackguarding" (cursing) and forbade "any improper language to any officer or soldier" (notice who is listed first) "who are now, or may hereafter be, appointed to preside over us." Some men opposed these provisions and created a great "uproar" by refusing to be "conformable to the rules and articles." These malcontents tore down the articles at night. The prisoners supporting the regulations beat three of the most vehement opponents the next day. Men continued to sell their clothes to obtain money for drink, they continued to gamble, and they continued to brawl. These regulations may have represented a democracy of the lower decks in action, or an attempted assertion of power by officers and the more respectable of the common seamen.[135]

If many sailors were not entirely driven by the spirit of '76 and an ideology of egalitarianism developed from below, ideas about liberty, patriotism, and loyalty to the American cause were not entirely absent. Some sailors seized upon the symbols of the Revolution and made them, even if only temporarily, their own in slogans, songs, and celebration. Cabin boy Christopher Hawkins proudly sported pewter buttons on his jacket with "Liberty and property" emblazoned upon them. On the night a crew of one hundred privateersmen were first captured and crammed into a crowded cable tier of a British warship, the men taunted their enemies by singing patriotic songs with refrains like "For America and all her sons forever will shine."[136] Timothy Connor included at least three patriotic American songs in the notebook he kept at Forton Prison.[137] On July 4, 1778, the walls of Mill Prison pulsated with excited noise as the men formed thirteen divisions, gave three cheers, and joined in a great huzzah at the end.[138] The sailors hoisted the American flag upon their hats along with the words "Independence" and "Liberty or Death." In 1781 William Russell sold some clothing "to raise a 'Little Money' to keep *Independent Day.*"[139] Prisoners also celebrated American victories. After the news of Cornwallis' surrender reached Mill Prison, the prisoners wore American cockades and they taunted the guards to shoot.[140] (French and British prisoners also celebrated national holidays.) Amid all the hardship, short rations, and daily grind, Charles Herbert was able to buy Tom Paine's *American Crisis* while in prison.[141] Andrew Sherburne described a mutiny over short rations aboard a cartel ship as a "revolution" and called the United States the "land of liberty."[142] For many of these men, patriotic symbols and survival in the prisons helped to mold their national identity. In the years after independence, the prisoner-of-war experience, especially the suffering on the *Jersey*, came to represent the waterfront's commitment to the new nation of the United States.

Jack Tar was pushed and pulled in many directions, and his values, consciousness, and understanding of liberty were peculiarly his own. The ramifications of these special circumstances began to appear in the prerevolutionary mob. Men from the waterfront participated in the popular disorder of the 1760s and 1770s for mundane as well as high-minded reasons. Whatever brought the individual sailor into the streets, he democratized the resistance movement and drove the revolution in a more egalitarian direction. Once the war broke out, the heterogenous mix of men who served aboard American ships reacted to the ideals of liberty in a variety of ways. Some may have taken the concept of liberty at face value and may have used it to challenge the authority of the quarterdeck. Others clung to the idea of liberty as it had long appeared on the waterfront.

The concept of "liberty," while crucial to the rhetoric of the revolution and an important signpost for American patriotism, ordinarily had a very specific meaning for common seamen. On a day-to-day basis, which was the way many sailors lived, these men cared little for abstraction. When Caleb Foot told a British official in Quebec that he had no regard for His Majesty or the locks on his doors, he proclaimed that "What I was after was *my* liberty" (emphasis added). He wanted to end his imprisonment and was not referring to a larger sense of American liberty.[143] William Widger similarly celebrated the news of Yorktown because it raised expectations among the prisoners that they would thereby "obtain our Liberties" and leave Mill and Forton prisons.[144] Young Joseph Adkins wrote Samuel Cutler that he had "obtained his liberty" after his release from service aboard a British man-of-war.[145] In none of these references was there any suggestion of a larger meaning—instead "liberty" meant individual freedom right then and there.

For many tars, especially those who remained in the forecastle, life was a continual round of abdicating liberty—usually aboard ship—and reckless

21. The British viewed the Scottish-born John Paul Jones as a rogue. In this illustration Jones is portrayed shooting a sailor for trying to haul down the colors on the *Bon Homme Richard*. There is no contemporary evidence for this incident. "Capt. Paul Jones Shooting a Sailor." Printed for R. Sayer and J. Bennett (London, 1780). Philadelphia Maritime Museum.

behavior while ashore. Repeatedly sailors aboard a defeated or outmanned ship that was about to surrender broke into the ship's locker and, in a last binge—one last fling at liberty—guzzled as much liquor as they could.[146] In this sense even the "five-pounders" who escaped to gain their liberty, if only for a few hours, and the prisoners who opposed the articles of regulation in Mill Prison and continued to drink, gamble, fight, and curse, were asserting their liberty.

This mentality, emphasizing immediate liberty without regard for the long-term future or without regard to revolutionary principles, helps to explain the complex reactions of sailors concerning loyalty and patriotism. At times sailors overcame their own concerns, at other times they did not. Many sailors remained trapped and were denied liberty whether confined by prison walls or by life aboard ship: Caleb Foot described his experiences serving on British warships, enduring over a year and a half in Forton Prison, and spending time in the *South Carolina* as hellish.[147] Under these conditions commitments to nation and family might seem distant and the only attainable goal was some immediate liberty.

The contradictions of the loyalties of the common sailor may best be seen in the story of Joshua Davis. Excited about turning twenty-one, the day he became "free," Davis lay chained by his feet to seven other American sailors on the deck of a British holding vessel in Spithead before being transferred to Mill Prison. With the aid of a sympathetic English sailor, Davis obtained a bottle of gin. Naturally he passed it round to his companions. After the bottle was empty, Davis, "feeling pretty merry," sang a tune that began

Vain Britain, boast no longer proud indignity—
By land your conq'ring legions, your matchless strength by sea;
Since we have your braver sons incens'd, our swords have girded *on*,
Huzza, huzza, huzza, huzza, for *war* and *Washington*.

Two months later, Davis—no longer a prisoner—was serving in His Majesty's navy.[148]

5

Brave Republicans of the Ocean

James Durand almost mutinied. He believed that there was a contradiction between a "government which boasts of liberty" and the autocracy of the quarterdeck. He complained bitterly of the midshipmen, no more than mere boys, who ordered grown men around with verbal abuse. And he declared that "no monarch in the world is more absolute than the Captain of a Man-of War." He believed that flogging was an outrage "on human nature," especially because a man might be punished "for a crime no more serious than spitting on the quarter deck."[1] When an injustice took place on the frigate *Constitution* in the Mediterranean in 1807, he was ready for action.

The drama began after Lieutenant William Burrows, in command with Captain Hugh Campbell ashore at Catania, Sicily, confronted a sailor on deck in front of hundreds of the crew. The man had been out of earshot when the lieutenant had called him. Now Burrows wanted him flogged for insubordination, even though, like many of his shipmates, his term of service had expired. These seamen clung to the same contractual notions that had appeared among sailors and soldiers in the late eighteenth century. In the minds of the "people of the ship," to punish unfairly a man who was not technically in the navy was too much to bear. Burrows ordered the man to take off his shirt. He refused. Burrows then grabbed a hand spike and swung it at him with all his might. The nimble tar ducked and Burrows missed. The crew supported their shipmate: the boatswain would not flog the man, and many seamen declared that there should be no punishment. Faced with disobedience, Burrows ordered the marines to fire on the crew. They sympathized with the sailors and did not obey him. All of the officers then armed themselves and ordered the crew below. That command was obeyed and peace was preserved. Upon his return to the ship, the captain sought to avert a full mutiny. He spoke to the men whose enlistment had expired and listened to their grievances, which centered around being flogged after their time had expired and not yet returning home. The captain compromised, asking them to do their duty while promising to head for the United States as soon as he had finished his business at several Mediterranean ports. Campbell also pledged that "from now on, no man shall be published unless he deserves it." Three sailors—the boatswain, the man who was to be flogged, and another man who spoke out during the confrontation—were placed in irons and kept there until the return to Boston.[2]

This little-known episode of American naval history represents only a small portion of James Durand's experiences. Born in Connecticut in 1786, Durand first went to sea at age fourteen. His earliest voyages were to the West Indies, where he personally saw some of the bloodiest results of the Age of Revolution in St. Domingue. He even visited the site of one mass grave said to contain the bodies of 120 whites massacred by blacks during their revolt against slavery. At times he reaped large profits from wages and from his private ventures; he also survived shipwreck and the loss of all his worldly possessions. He served in the United States Navy in the Mediterranean, fighting the Barbary pirates.[3]

After the near mutiny and his return to the United States, Durand had had enough of the navy. Although he was a petty officer, he jumped ship before the final paying off after a young midshipman had him flogged for some imagined offense. This action appears irrational, since Durand lost money by it. But with his enlistment up, he was going to assert his liberty despite the cost.[4] Durand turned to the merchant marine, sailing to France. At Nantes he claimed to have seen Napoleon Bonaparte, although he was singularly unimpressed. After leaving port the British captured the vessel. Kept as a prisoner for months, he was released after the ship was condemned as a blockade runner. Penniless again, he signed aboard a Swedish vessel. In March 1809 he signed aboard an English merchantman, but before it could sail a press-gang came aboard and seized him along with twelve other Americans. His protection—an official document stating that he was an American citizen—was of little help. Despondent, he ate nothing for twelve days, until fear of a flogging convinced him to do as he was told.

Like so many other sailors, James Durand was a survivor. He quietly fell into the routine of the ship, demonstrating a willingness and ability to fight against the French, and was wounded twice in battle. He also joined the captain's band, learning to play the clarinet. For at least three years he was denied the right to go ashore. When finally given shore liberty, he admits to "enjoying every kind of diversion I thought proper." Treatment degenerated once the United States and Great Britain went to war and Durand complained of being lashed several times so that the British "could vent their damnable fury on us." Unlike thousands of other impressed American tars, Durand never surrendered himself as a prisoner of war. In 1814, however, in a cruise off the coast of New England he refused to do his duty and was placed in irons. He received his discharge September 21, 1815, well after the war was over, and, fearing another press-gang, quickly signed aboard a vessel bound for New York and returned home after an absence of thirteen years.[5]

Bundled into the life of this Jack Tar are many of the various strands that made up the experiences of American sailors after the Revolutionary War. The years of the early republic brought opportunities for sailors to earn money. Shipping expanded rapidly in the 1790s and early 1800s because the United States could be a neutral trader in a world immersed in the French Revolutionary and Napoleonic Wars. If money could be made from trade to the West Indies, or crossing the Atlantic to bring goods to one or another of the belligerents, there was also great risk. Barbary pirates threatened to capture and enslave American seamen; France and Great Britain each sought to limit American trade with the other; and press-gangs searched for manpower in ports and on the high seas. James Durand's experience touched each of these issues. While much of his life stands as a simple testament to the fortitude of so many sailors, it also suggests that amid this effort to survive, some ideas of the Age of Revolution had seeped into the forecastle.

In the years after American independence the sailor experienced a tension between his efforts to survive from day to day and his role as an agent of the ideas of revolution. This experience needs to be placed in the larger context of the Age of Revolution. Durand's visits to the island of Hispaniola and his comment on Napoleon suggests that the sailor could bear witness to several of the great changes agitating the Atlantic. The sailor responded to these changes, but the exact nature of that response is hard to detail. Unmentioned in Durand's reminiscences, the waterfront also retained a role in American politics after the Revolutionary War. This role was not easily predicted: sometimes a sailor pursued his own interest and sometimes he advocated revolutionary ideals. Often Jack Tar's political role was limited by his mobility and by the sailor's penchant for misbehavior and his own notions of liberty. Because sailors faced unusual hazards in this period, connected as Durand's story suggests in part to the upheaval that came with the Age of Revolution, Jack Tar also emerged as a symbol of liberty for the new nation. Whatever the individual concerns of the sailor, Americans from many levels of society began to rally around him as the United States entered the War of 1812.

The American Revolution unleashed forces beyond anyone's control. What began in the streets and alleys of the port towns of colonial America in the 1760s soon engulfed most of the Atlantic world. Driven to the edge of bankruptcy by its repeated wars of empire, France erupted into revolution. Once the Bastille fell on July 14, 1789, the French pushed the limits of revolution further, calling for not only liberty but also equality and fraternity. Extremists came to power, inaugurating a reign of terror that included the execution of tens of thousands who supported the old guard; among the casualties were Louis XVI and his family in 1793. The French also sought to export their revolution throughout Europe and across the Atlantic. To nearly everyone's surprise, black slaves in the West Indies responded to the ideas of the Age of Revolution. A great uprising of slaves in the French colony of St. Domingue in August 1791 began a struggle that lasted more than a decade. This conflict included a bloody and confusing civil war, intervention by the Spanish and the British, and several French invasions. The ultimate result of all of the bloodshed was the creation of a novel experiment—the free republic of Haiti comprised largely of ex-slaves. Great Britain itself, which after 1793 stood as the main opponent of the French Revolution and the Napoleonic Empire that followed it, was not immune to the egalitarian currents swirling through the Atlantic. Authorities had to smash an indigenous reform movement during the great conflict. More germane to our purposes was what happened on the waterfront and at sea. The British navy experienced massive mutinies at Spithead and the Nore in 1797 that reflected the ideals of the age. Even more distressing to the forces of order and reaction was the single ship mutiny of the *Hermione* in the Caribbean during the same year. Each of these three events—the French Revolution, the Haitian Revolution and the great British mutinies—had a profound, if difficult to define, impact on the American waterfront.[6]

Although Durand was unimpressed with Napoleon, and another sailor found Robespierre more concerned with business than revolution, many Americans on the waterfront were attracted to the ideals of the French Revolution.[7] For example, while Boston's elite celebrated George Washington's birthday in 1793, mariners, laborers, and mechanics held their own street celebration commemorating the president's birth and the French Revolution. This combination would not have pleased the father of the country.[8] In April and May of that year, support for the French Revolution reached a feverish pitch in several ports as news of war between France and Great Britain arrived, and as Citizen Edmond Genet, the French republic's new ambassador to the United States, traveled overland from Charleston to Philadelphia. When Genet landed in Charleston he had been greeted by crowds and officials. He quickly went to work trying to persuade the United States to fulfill its 1778 treaty obligations by commissioning four privateers. Arming and recruiting these vessels set the Charleston waterfront abuzz; every sailor knew the opportunity that a privateering commission presented. Self-interest and ideology seemed to be joined for the common sailor. The French frigate *L'Embuscade* preceded Genet to Philadelphia and helped to prepare his reception by displaying huge banners streaming from its mastheads proclaiming the revolutionary message: "Enemies of equality, reform or tremble!" "Freemen, behold we are your friends and brothers!" and "We are armed for the defense of the rights of man!" As the French sailors disembarked and filled the various taverns and grog shops, they became the talk of the waterfront. The idea of fighting for liberty and making prize money—the French frigate had captured several vessels as it had crossed the Atlantic—appealed to the denizens of the waterfront.[9]

Support for the ideals of the French Revolution sometimes spontaneously erupted on the waterfront. After *L'Embuscade* appeared in New York in the summer of 1793, a dockside crowd eagerly greeted its crew. Carrying a liberty cap, the French sailors joined with Americans and paraded from Peck Slip through the city to Bowling Green, where they demolished the remnants of the statue of George III that had been torn down in 1776. Many in the crowd wore the French tricolor as they sang the carmagnole—the tune to a lively dance popular among French revolutionaries.[10] During *L'Embuscade*'s fight with the British ship *Boston* in New York Harbor, after a challenge had been issued at the Tontine coffeehouse, New Yorkers watched the two ships pound each other with broadsides for two hours. Although some in the crowd supported the British, the loyalties of the waterfront lay mainly with the French. Thousands cheered *L'Embuscade* as it returned to New York the next day escorted by a fleet of fifteen French warships that had just arrived from St. Domingue.[11]

Some waterfront residents even turned French victories and holidays into their own. In January 1793, Bostonians had celebrated the French victory at Valmy at Oliver's Dock, renaming it Liberty Square and erecting a liberty pole. Waterfront Boston made the connection between the French and American revolutions explicit during a public festivity a month later by offering a toast that declared: "May the citizens of the spot which in 1765 witnessed the destruction of an infamous Stamp Office, be ever famous for celebrating events propitious to the Equal Liberty of all Mankind." Oliver's

Dock, as every Bostonian knew, was the site of an anti–Stamp Act riot on August 14, 1765, in which a mob tore down a building owned by stamp distributor Andrew Oliver.[12] Another celebration of French events occurred after news of the French recapture of Toulon arrived in New York City on March 7, 1794. Throughout the day "cannon fired, and bells rung," and in the evening Americans and Frenchmen danced the carmagnole at the Tontine coffeehouse around their two national flags. Three days later some eight hundred American citizens and Frenchmen paraded through the streets behind French and American flags and a liberty cap, singing French patriotic tunes.[13] The liberty cap and tricolor cockade became important symbols in several port cities during the 1790s, and Bastille Day became a major holiday for many.[14]

If the waterfront seemed to be teeming with the ideals of the French Revolution during the 1790s, not that many of its denizens joined in the struggle itself. The French Consul's office in Philadelphia printed out a broadside entitled "They Steer to Liberty's Shores" in August 1793. The handbill called upon "all able bodied seamen who are willing to engage in the cause of Liberty" to join in the fight for the republic. Such volunteers would be acting just like "the heroes from France in the American revolution" and would be "a glory to themselves and an honour to the country which gave them birth."[15] We know that some American seamen joined French privateers and the French navy during this period. We also know that this recruitment was frowned upon by the United States government and that some men were arrested for signing on with the French.[16] In any case, there was an easier way to earn a living. Sailors could make money in the expanding merchant marine without directly engaging in warfare. In 1799 and 1800, when popular opinion had turned away from the French, a notorious court case suggested that the price for striking a blow for liberty, equality, and fraternity could be high. Three sailors murdered the supercargo, the mate, and one crew member of the schooner *Eliza*, claiming that they had acted in the interests of France and intended to take their prize across the Atlantic to the French Republic. The court saw their action as piracy and all three were hanged.[17]

The reaction to the rebellion in St. Domingue on the waterfront was also not clear cut. The French fleet that arrived in New York in August 1793 was packed with mutinous sailors who may have retained enthusiasm for their revolution, but they had also just left the nightmare of St. Dominigue. The stories of horror and woe that they told along the waterfront must have had a chilling effect.[18] Throughout the 1790s and into the early 1800s waves of refugees swept into America's port cities—as many as 10,000 arrived in 1793 alone. Some of these were royalists distraught by the revolution in France and the rebellion in Haiti. Others, like the French sailors in 1793, may have believed in the revolution, but shuddered at the bloodshed and loss of life in the disease-infested West Indies. Whatever their politics, they spread the word of slave rebellion and racial warfare.[19]

Like James Durand, American sailors could see St. Domingue for themselves. Although white sailors did not appear to support the revolution or emancipation, they were curious to view a world turned upside-down. Midshipman John Roche, Jr., visited Haiti in 1800 aboard the *Constitution*. He found it "melanchollly to see the devastation that has been made in this fine Island since the reign of the blacks." And he commented directly that "it is diverting to see how the world is revers'd in those parts."[20] These views were not limited to a would-be officer. Durand's own curiosity to see the carnage suggests a certain detachment from the conflict. Similarly, Horace Lane made several trips to the island in his youth. He denounced both blacks and whites, declaring that each party "were at that time perpetrating the most horrid acts of barbarous murder and massacre." Sometimes Lane's ship was engaged in bringing arms and ammunition to the black government. Lest this suggest a higher mission and commitment to the slave rebellion, on the same voyage the ship would also smuggle white passengers off the island. Lane takes pains to describe the crews on these trips as being particularly unruly both aboard ship and in port. Gun-running was a dangerous activity and called upon a sailor's cutthroat tendencies.[21]

Black sailors had a different view of the situation in St. Domingue, according to a few strands of suggestive evidence. Julius Scott has unearthed the story of Newport Bowers, a black sailor and laborer. Born a free man in Massachusetts, Bowers lived and worked on the Baltimore waterfront in 1793. As French refugees swarmed into American port cites, Bowers decided to see what was happening in St. Domingue. In the West Indies Bowers became a middleman or agent between the blacks on the island and the American vessels seeking trade. Combining ideology and pursuit of the main chance, Bowers remained in St. Domingue for six months before leaving the island with the profits he earned, and in the company of ex-slaves who had won their freedom from the French.[22]

Black waterfront workers, even if they did not travel to the West Indies, heard the same stories as their white counterparts. Moreover, many of the refugees who arrived in the American ports were blacks who would be most at ease communicating with those of their own race. On several occasions crowds of French Negroes—including men who served as mariners—took to

22. This document from an important waterfront trade association has pictures highlighting republican ideology, benevolence, and scenes of waterfront labor. "Certificate: Society of Master Sailmakers of the City of New York, 1795." New-York Historical Society.

the streets inspired by the Haitian Revolution. As many as 250 French Negroes and other blacks in New York City rioted in front of Madame Volunbrun's house on August 10, 1801 in opposition to her planned attempt to export her slaves to Virginia and prevent their manumission in New York. On July 5, 1805, a group of Philadelphia blacks terrorized whites they encountered, "damning the whites and saying they would shew them St. Domingo."[23] Jeff Bolster estimates that thousands of African American sailors visited St. Domingue during the 1790s and early 1800s. Many of them seized the opportunity to run from their ships and claim protection of the local authorities. On at least two occasions black crew members mutinied in the West Indies and sought asylum in St. Domingue. Other African American tars simply took pride in the fact that people of their race had created an independent nation that white captains, as well as the U.S. government, had to treat with some degree of respect.[24]

Perhaps most threatening to white Americans was the hope for freedom that many slaves gained by the example of the Haitian Revolution. Denmark Vesey, a free black who lived in Charleston, South Carolina, and who had

☞ *Stop Runaway !—*

DESERTED from on board the ſhip ELIZA, ELKANAH HAMBLIN, Maſter, lying in this port, on the evening of the 19th inſt. a black Sailor, by name JESSE CARPENTER, about five feet eight inches in height—a ſtout, well proportioned fellow—carries in his countenance a ſurly, impudent look—and is remarkably talkative and ſaucy.—Had on when he went away, a blue ſailor's jacket, the ſeams covered with white canvaſs, and a pair of new blue cloth trouſers in ſhape much larger at bottom than uſual.——Whoever will take up ſaid Deſerter, and return him to the ſubſcriber, or confine him in any goal, ſo that he may be brot to juſtice, ſhall receive TEN DOLLARS reward, and all neceſſary charges paid, by

ALLEN SHEPHERD.

Newbedford, 6 Mo. 23d, 1796.

23. Signing a ship's articles bound a sailor to the terms of employment. This advertisement for a ship deserter used a stamp for a runaway slave, suggesting some similarity between the condition of a sailor and a slave. *Medley,* June 23, 1796. New Bedford Whaling Museum.

been a slave in St. Domingue in the 1780s, watched Haitian developments avidly. Organizing a slave conspiracy in 1822, Vesey promised his followers that Haitians would aid their cause once they struck a blow for freedom. During the first decade of the nineteenth century several states had tightened their controls on the free black population in the South with one eye on St. Domingue. After the uncovering of Vesey's planned rebellion, South Carolina took even more drastic action. In a vain attempt to cut off the channels of communication with the West Indies, South Carolina passed the Negro Seaman's Act of 1822 to prevent free black sailors from wandering the wharves, spreading tales of a nation of men who had overthrown slavery and expelled whites.[25]

The great British mutinies of 1797 also had an effect in the United States. As every American seaman knew, conditions in the British navy were awful. Pay had not been increased since the seventeenth century and food and treatment were dreadful. Confronted with these realities, and in part inspired by the Age of Revolution and examples of successful English collective action, British sailors organized at least three separate mutinies. The first of the great mutinies occurred on April 16 at Spithead on the southern coast and involved the Channel fleet. The seamen petitioned for a redress of grievances and asserted a continued loyalty to the king and to their admiral, Lord Richard Howe. Placated by having some of their demands met, and granted a royal pardon, they abandoned their work stoppage on May 14 and returned to duty.

More threatening to the state, and reflecting a greater radicalism, was the mutiny at the Nore, at the mouth of the Medway on the southeastern coast of England. Hoping to copy the success of the seamen at Spithead, and influenced by the works of Tom Paine, the men on the ships at the Nore refused duty on May 12. Here the seamen drew up a Revolutionary Constitution, asserting control over ships through committees and, when officials appeared intransigent, threatened to blockade London and even join the French. The mutiny disintegrated over time, and by June 16 authorities reasserted control. Several courts-martial ensued leading to the execution of thirty-six men, including Richard Parker, the president of the delegates of the fleet.

The third major mutiny, aboard the *Hermione,* involved just one ship and was in reaction to the severity of one man, Captain Pigot. Given the events that had occurred at Spithead and the Nore, larger principles emphasizing the rights of man could not have been entirely absent. The action of the *Hermione* crew took place in September in the West Indies and was more desperate than the other mutinies. After a series of cruel punishments, members of the crew burst into Pigot's cabin, slashed him with cutlasses and axes, and then pitched the still breathing captain overboard. Several other officers were also killed. Once in control, the mutineers sailed to a South American port and surrendered the ship to Spain. The crew scattered, knowing that they were marked men.[26]

Americans were involved in all three mutinies. Hundreds of Americans were in the fleets at Spithead and the Nore, and at least four Americans were on the *Hermione* during the mutiny.[27] Men who were at Spithead and the Nore also subsequently served on American ships, and several tars from the *Hermione* joined the American merchant marine and navy after the mutiny. We have little evidence of what they thought and can only imagine the yarns spun along the waterfront or in American forecastles and gundecks by these mutineers. One Boston publisher even printed the transcripts of the trial of the Nore mutineers.[28] Newspapers, too, reported these events.[29] Americans may well have empathized with the aims of the sailors, especially considering the growing opposition to British impressment. Congressman John Marshall observed that "the act of impressing an American is an act of lawless violence," and that keeping an American on board a British warship "is a continuation of the violence, and an added outrage." Any impressed American aboard the *Hermione* would have been simply "liberating himself by homicide" and therefore justified in his actions. But there were limits to such sentiments. As Marshall explained, "A pirate"—and the British subjects among the *Hermione* mutineers were considered pirates—"under the law of nations, is an enemy of the human race."[30] The success of the *Hermione* mutiny threatened all quarterdeck authority. Even though Captain Pigot had a reputation for cruelty and had stopped several American vessels and impressed some of their seamen, American officials could not countenance the rebellion on the part of the British sailors. The British spared no expense in tracking down the *Hermione* mutineers. When their agents identified *Hermione* crew who were British subjects on American vessels, even on Durand's *Constitution*, the United States surrendered the men to the British and the gallows. Their American counterparts, however, were protected by the United States government.[31]

We may never know if some *Hermione* veteran told a wild tale of murder and bloodshed aboard the *Constitution* to Durand and his shipmates. Nor can we trace a direct line from Spithead and the Nore to Durand's concern with the autocracy of the quarterdeck. Nor can we be sure what images American sailors took from their experience with the French and Haitian revolutions. All we can say for sure is that the ideas of the Age of Revolution were familiar on the American waterfront, and that on a few occasions, such as on

Durand's Mediterranean cruise in 1807, those ideas came churning to the fore.

As important as all of this revolutionary tumult was to the American waterfront, dockside workers cared most about their own American Revolution. Sailors knew they had played a vital role in the mobs of the resistance movement, and they held their sacrifices aboard the prison ships like the *Jersey* in reverence. Given this collective memory, what happened to the "Sons of Neptune" in the years after the resistance movement? And, given their exposure to a world in upheaval, did Jack Tar build on his experience in the 1760s and 1770s to become an agent of revolution? The waterfront crowd experience of the 1780s, 1790s, and early 1800s may give us some clues. On the one hand, the people of the waterfront remained active in the crowd—as in their support of French. On the other hand, the meaning and context of mob behavior was changing. Revolutionary leaders had needed the mob shouting in the streets threatening and at times perpetrating acts of violence to provide the muscle behind the resistance movement. Success meant that the mob was no longer needed. Now, theoretically, the government represented the people, and crowd politics imperiled the new order. The implications of this change took decades to work themselves out, but for sailors it meant a diminished role in politics. Waterfront crowds continued to appear in the politics of the early republic and repeatedly followed patterns of protest, parading, and rioting developed during the 1760s and 1770s. However, the people in the street were no longer a driving force for a revolution. At times they helped guide and sustain the movement toward democracy. At times, too, those on the waterfront supported Federalist policies. Emphasis on voting left a transient and impoverished section of society on the political periphery and the mob increasingly lost its legitimacy.[32]

In the best of all possible worlds, at least from the perspective of the nation's leaders, sailors would still march if called upon and help to solidify public opinion in support of the republic. Thus Federalists repeatedly used a scaled-down ship on wheels as the centerpiece of their parades to celebrate the ratification of the U.S. Constitution. Representing both the ship of state and the promise of trade and prosperity, these vessels identified the waterfront with the new form of government. In Philadelphia the ship was called the *Union* and was manned by "a proper crew of Officers and Seamen."[33] In the New York parade, organizers christened the frigate the *Hamilton*, after the state's leading Federalist, manned it with a crew of twenty "jolly tars," and fired a thirteen-gun salute at the climax of the celebration. In both cases the participation of waterfront workers as well as the city's tradesmen was carefully staged and limited. The score or so sailors aboard each vessel, if they were real sailors, represented just a small proportion of the seamen in both ports.[34]

If the people on the waterfront could sometimes be guided, most of the time the maritime community retained a mind of its own. As the politics of the 1790s and early 1800s intensified in the split between the Federalists and Jeffersonian Republicans it was not always a forgone conclusion which way they would turn. More often than not, the egalitarian nature of the Jeffersonians retained an attraction for people on the waterfront. But by no means did the waterfront remain united, and conditions could vary from port to port. Sometimes, such as when Jefferson's policies hurt trade and threatened jobs, many sailors followed their personal interests and turned to Federalism.

In 1794 and 1795, as war threatened with Great Britain over trade restrictions, waterfront crowds expressed their Republican sympathies in several actions reminiscent of revolutionary mobs of the 1760s and 1770s. In the spring of 1794 Philadelphians dismantled a schooner that had been hired to carry five British officers home on parole. In Baltimore, a mob from the maritime neighborhood of Fell's Point tarred and feathered a British captain and his apprentice for flying a flag at half mast at the expiration of the embargo of 1794. Several incidents erupted in Norfolk, where crowds demonstrated sympathy for the French, unrigged a pilot boat suspected of informing on a French convoy leaving the port, and tarred and feathered a man who spoke disrespectfully of the French. Fisher Ames, a Federalist, thought this violence "worthy of Mohawks" and believed "the multitude in these towns but half civilized" and feared that the country would be "mobbed" into a war.[35]

The pro-British Jay's Treaty only intensified all of this activity. Sailors were distressed by British seizures of American shipping and irate over the treaty's failure to protect against impressment and to fully open the British West Indies to American trade. In June 1795 men on the Boston waterfront dismantled a vessel believed to be a Bermudian privateer that had captured American shipping. After arms were found in the hold, the crowd burned it to the water. Like earlier mobs, this one demonstrated a certain degree of discrimination by towing the vessel into the harbor when the conflagration threatened other ships.[36] Throughout the summer, after the full details of Jay's Treaty were revealed, crowds formed in Boston and elsewhere and, in actions borrowed directly from earlier Stamp Act disturbances, burned John Jay in effigy. Philadelphia ship carpenters and sailors led a similar disturbance on July 4. As many as five hundred paraded through the city streets, solemnly escorting a cart with "a transparent painting of *Mr. Jay*" that portrayed him presenting the treaty to an admiring senate. Jay had the treaty in his left hand, while in his right hand he held up a pair of scales that had "*Virtue, Liberty, and Independence*" outweighed by "British Gold." The display also included the inscription "*Come up to my price, and I will sell you my country.*" Armed with clubs and stones, they fought with a party of light horse. Although the crowd did not burn the effigy in front of Vice President John Adams's residence, as called for in the original plan, they set fire to it upon returning to their own neighborhood of Kensington, following ritual well established during the 1760s and 1770s.[37] Riots in New York, Baltimore, Portsmouth, Charleston, Savannah, and other seaports, while including a wide spectrum of urban residents, contained many sailors angered over Jay's Treaty.[38]

The ideal of equality and the principles of Jeffersonian Republicans may have had a certain appeal to those on the waterfront, but other issues could also redirect public opinion. After the Jay's Treaty hoopla settled down, a new threat to American shipping emerged. The French government was not pleased with the change in American foreign policy represented by Jay's Treaty, which essentially repudiated the alliance between the United States and France and gave the British favored trading status. French warships and privateers began seizing American vessels, leading to the Quasi War. With their livelihood at stake, many on the waterfront became less concerned with the ideals of the revolution. Hostility to the French increased and the Federalists gained in popularity. In the fall of 1796 repeated confrontations occurred between the crew of the French privateer *La Bellona* and the citizens of Wilmington, North Carolina. Residents believed the *La Bellona* planned to raid American shipping after leaving port. These brawls culminated in a riot in which one American seaman was killed, and an angry crowd tossed the privateer's guns overboard and trampled the French tricolor.[39] A similar disturbance broke out in Savannah in August 1798 against a Spanish privateer.[40]

Although the Federalists had decried the mobs that had opposed Jay's Treaty and disparaged every Republican crowd, they seemed to look the other way when disturbances did not protest their policies. And Federalist policies were good for the waterfront in a number of ways. In preparation for war, Federalists began to expand the American navy. This meant employment in shipyards to finish construction on frigates like the *Constellation* and *Constitution*. It also meant recruitment of thousands of sailors. These men now swaggered along the waterfront, singing pro-Federalist and patriotic songs, and brawling with anyone expressing Republican or pro-French sympathies.[41] Although some individuals still expressed those sympathies, and there was even one incident of a fight between a gang of tough sailors and a recruiting party from the *Constitution* in Portsmouth, the anti-French policies of the Federalists were genuinely popular on the waterfront.[42] Whatever the innate appeal of the ideal of equality, sailors recognized their self-interest. No one wanted to be aboard an American vessel captured and sold as a prize by the French. Not only did the seizure take away the merchant's property, but it also negated the seaman's contract, leaving him broke in some distant port. Thus a common seaman might eagerly join with his naval counterpart in praising the Federalists. In July 1800 the crew of the *Ann and Hope* took great pride in outsailing a French privateer. They also made "Cockades & Other preparations for the blessed day that may Once more [bring] them to their friends & Country" as they approached Providence after a cruise of more than a year.[43]

Patriotic songs that appeared at the time and trumpeted sailors and American commerce also favored the Federalists. Many songs, adapted from British tunes during the 1790s and early 1800s, were popularized on the stage and published in collections like *The Festival of Mirth and American Tar's Delight* and *The Sailor's Medley*. Typical of this genre was "Fly ye traitors," a Federalist attack on Jeffersonians, Jacobins, Talleyrand, and the French.[44] Among the other sailor tunes that Charles Clinton copied on his voyage to the Pacific that began in 1802 was "Adams and Liberty," which heralded the second president's role as a defender of trade and the common seaman:

In a Clime where rich vales feed the marts of the world
Whose Shores are unshaken by Europe's Commotion
The Trident of Commerce Should Never be hurled
To incense the Legitimate Powers of the Ocean
But should pirates [the French] invade
Though in thunder arrayed
Let your Cannon Declare a free charter of Trade.

The song ended with a pledge to defend the sailor: "That never shall the Sons of Columbia Be Slaves, While the Earth bears a plant or the sea roles its waves."[45] Following the instinct of self-interest and survival, many on the waterfront had switched sides.

The end of the Quasi War crisis with France and the defeat of the Federalists in the election of 1800 brought most of the waterfront, although not Charles Clinton, back into the Republican fold. During the opening decade of the nineteenth century, Great Britain loomed as the greatest threat to sailors, and waterfront crowds demonstrated their opposition to impressment and restrictions on trade. Suddenly ideals and interests coincided. British

24. Alexander Anderson was a prominent engraver in the 1790s and early 1800s. "Detail of Ship Caulkers." Alexander Anderson, Scrapbook. New York Public Library.

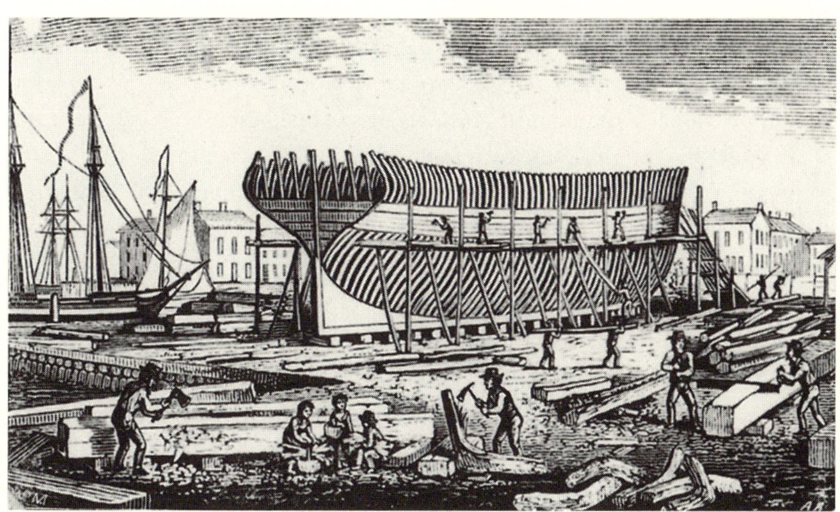

25. Many ship carpenters had experience at sea. Notice the similarity in the dress of the workers in the front of the picture to the dress of sailors in other illustrations in this volume. "Detail of Ship Builders." Alexander Anderson, Scrapbook. New York Public Library.

audacity reached new heights in 1806 when squadrons stationed off American ports searched vessels for deserters or British seamen who could be pressed into His Majesty's service. In late April the HMS *Leander* fired upon an American vessel just off of New York harbor, killing sailor John Pierce. A crowd of "our republican fellow-citizens" quickly formed in New York City, seized ten cartloads of beef destined for the British fleet, and "in triumph, and amid shouts of thousands, conveyed it to the Alms House." Crowds also desecrated a Union Jack, threatened the British consul's house, and compelled any British officer ashore to go into hiding.[46]

Similar revolutionary-like crowd action broke out in several seaports in reaction to the British navy attacking the USS *Chesapeake* and killing three men and seizing four British deserters on June 22, 1807. A mob in Norfolk, Virginia, almost within sight of the outrage, destroyed two hundred casks of water destined for the British fleet. In Philadelphia, another crowd unshipped a rudder of a British supply vessel, and in Charleston a crowd abused a young man who mocked the public mourning for the American seamen killed aboard the *Chesapeake*. These actions resembled the limited and focused destruction of property typical of seaport crowds opposing British imperial regulations in the 1760s and 1770s. During the *Chesapeake* crisis this parallel was even more stark as residents in the Norfolk area organized a Committee of Correspondence to oversee defense in the face of a supposed British invasion.[47]

The Embargo, which Jefferson offered to avoid war in the wake of the *Chesapeake* affair, pulled waterfront workers in contrary directions. In an effort to compel Great Britain and France to allow the United States to have free trade while they were at war with each other, and to force the British to stop impressing American seamen, the Embargo of December 1807 prohibited exports from leaving the United States. Jefferson believed that republican Americans did not need trade with Europe, and that corrupt Europeans depended on American imports and commerce. He miscalculated. The Embargo had a devastating impact on the American economy and on the waterfront. Jack Tar may have sympathized with Jeffersonian notions of equality, but suddenly he found himself without employment. Yet revolutionary ideals remained a force among sailors, while self-interest led to public calls for assistance fueled by the fires of popular disorder. Republican leaders sought to sustain waterfront commitment to revolutionary ideals through moments of public display in key Republican seaports. In New York, Jeffersonian politicians took this opportunity to celebrate the contributions of American seamen to the American Revolution and demanded a public ritual to provide a proper burial for the men who had died in the *Jersey* prison ship in Wallabout Bay. During the war the British had simply deposited the remains in shallow graves in nearby mudflats. The ebb and flow of the tide exposed the rotting bones, which were afterward collected by Nicholas Romaine, who owned the gravesite. Confronted with an Embargo that would be unpopular on the waterfront, Republican politicians organized a huge parade and ceremony to inter the bones of the prison ship martyrs in a safe resting place and to demonstrate their continued support for the maritime community. The centerpiece of the procession was the "Grand National Pedestal," which included these messages on its panels in all capital letters: "Youth of my country! Martyrdom prefer to slavery" and "Sires of Columbia! Transmit to posterity the cruelties practiced on board British prison ships." Three hundred sailors—"brave Republicans of the Ocean"—escorted the pedestal, taking precedence over leading politicians.[48]

Baltimore Republicans took a different tack, staging a large procession to celebrate electoral victories in the fall of 1808. The demonstration included thousands of Baltimoreans, who in good Jeffersonian style placed symbols representing the yeoman farmer and the honest tar in close proximity. In the middle of the parade came one politician, carrying a poplar branch, under a banner emblazoned with the words "God Speed the Plow." Three hundred sailors marched with a banner proclaiming "A Proof that all American seamen are not gone to Halifax" (to gain employment during the Embargo). Next another local politician was drawn in a car, surrounded with "boughs of poplar and evergreen, as emblems of rural life, and civic triumph" and holding a plow. Another flag declared "Commerce and Agriculture united." Following this display came "The elegant schooner 'Democratic Republican,'" reminiscent of the ships used in the celebrations of the Constitution in 1788, "commanded by Captain Stiles and other seamen, boatswain, etc." The assembled host marched from Fell's Point "traversed the various streets" of the city before returning to the waterfront neighborhood where the procession began. That night the crowd gathered around a huge bonfire on Hampstead Hill, the flames of which were fed by British gin captured from a would-be smuggler.[49]

Such efforts, however, did not entirely placate the waterfront. As one Federalist epigram put it:

Embargo read backward, O-grab-me appears,
A scary sound ever for big children's ears.
The syllables transformed, Go bar 'em comes next
A mandate to keep ye from harm, says my text.

Analyze Miss Embargo, her letters, I'll wage,
If not removed shortly, will make mob-rage.[50]

"Mob-rage" might reflect waterfront interests in two ways. First, unemployed sailors of whatever politics might be unruly and even criminal. Second, following patterns of the disorder of the 1760s and 1770s, sailors might join in massive resistance to government measures that opposed their personal interests.

Public officials saw loyal Republican seamen seeking to organize demonstrations to appeal for public assistance as a threat to order. Reports of a planned meeting in New York sent the mayor, Marinus Willet, into a panic; he ordered newspapers to publish advertisements discouraging the assembly and drew up a plan to deal with the disorder should the sailors meet. Ignoring the mayor's pleas, people from the waterfront held their rally on January 9, 1808. Although the meeting was peaceful, they passed resolutions that contained a veiled threat if the city government did not provide some relief.[51] A few days later penniless sailors in Philadelphia marched to the City Hall under the banner of the Stars and Stripes. They asked Mayor Robert Wharton what they should do, as the Embargo prevented them from obtaining work. The mayor responded with soothing words and offered a vague promise of assistance. The crowd peacefully dispersed.[52] The next month, Baltimore waterfront workers demonstrated. Marching from Fell's Point, these sailors handed the mayor a petition which stated, "by reason of the EMBARGO, they are reduced to the necessity of applying to your honor for relief. Many of us are now in arrears to our Landlords, and our prospects are bad, as we are incapable of gaining a support by any other way than by our profession as Seamen." In this Republican town the mayor expressed great sympathy for the sailor's' plight, and like his counterparts in Philadelphia and New York, promised to try to find some way of helping them.[53] Good words and some relief efforts kept sailors in these seaports in line. They remained committed to Republican ideals despite their own interests.

The same did not hold for all seamen, especially in strongly Federalist New England. In several ports, crowds, following patterns of behavior inherited from the American Revolution, acted to evade and nullify the restrictions on trade imposed by the Embargo in part out of principle and in part in pursuit of personal interest. In August 1808, for instance, a Newburyport, Massachusetts, mob threatened to rescue a sloop seized by a revenue cutter for violating the Embargo. Only the last-minute intervention of some Federalist politicians saved the government vessel from destruction.[54] A crowd of two to three hundred in Providence took possession of another seized vessel in January 1809, cut a passage through the ice, shipped its rudder, and sent the sloop to sea.[55] Similar incidents, including the burning of one captured sloop to prevent the collection of prize money, occurred in New Haven and Gloucester.[56] A more violent outbreak occurred in Castine, Maine, where the schooner *Peggy* from Nova Scotia, manned mainly by Americans, attempted to force the release of 150 barrels of flour. Customs officials stepped in and the smugglers fired shots, killing at least one man before the officials retook the *Peggy* and arrested some of the smugglers. Later a mob of twenty to thirty local men in disguise rescued the prisoners.[57] The men in these disturbances were repeating history; forty years earlier their fathers and grandfathers had used similar techniques to avoid customs regulations imposed by Parliament and to demonstrate opposition to imperial regulation. Although the government and the cause were now different, once again the wharves resounded to the pulse of rowdy waterfront crowds.

As the waterfront continued to harbor mobs reminiscent of the revolutionary rioting, sailors also were brought into play in electoral politics. Once again ideals seemed to take a back seat to interests. The resulting voting irregularities, however, were generally condemned as old-fashioned and reflecting undue influence. During voting in New York in 1800, marines from the *John Adams*, "were marched to your polls, with drums beating and colours flying, to overawe the freedom of election" from the perspective of one Republican editor. The mayor and other officials disrupted a similar effort in 1806.[58] Philadelphia Federalists used strong-arm tactics in a State House Yard meeting against the Embargo in January 1809. Republicans claimed that the Federalist leadership, including naval officers like Thomas Truxton and Richard Dale, hired sailors to keep a Republican procession away and to intimidate any would-be opponents of Federalist resolutions.[59] Republicans, however, were capable of the same devices. During the 1808 elections in New York, inspired by the ritual interment of prison ship victims, two thousand sailors and workers marched to the polls "huzzing" for Republicans and declaring, "No Jersey prison ships—no war—no TORIES—No FEDERALISTS—our country *forever*."[60] In a New Bern, North Carolina, election in 1814, Federalists charged that Republicans imported sailors to coerce voters, cast illegal ballots, and beat off any opponents.[61]

By the opening decade of the nineteenth century, both Federalists and Republicans readily denounced mob action by their political opponents. Thomas Jefferson, after all, had warned against the mobs of great cites and viewed them as cancers ready to eat out the heart of a republic.[62] James Madison believed sailors to be dependent creatures, too easily swayed by those in authority, and hence potentially disruptive to republican government. Madison wrote that the sailor's "virtue, at no time aided, is occasionally exposed to every scene that can poison it."[63] If these Republican leaders expressed qualms concerning sailors and urban crowds, Federalists were often vitriolic in discussing the mob. William Plummer looked at the crowds in the street and saw "a vast pile of cumbustibles, and a spark may produce a flame that will end in mobs and spread blood and destruction through the streets."[64] Fisher Ames more eloquently likened "mob-government" to "a West-India hurricane" that "instantly strews the fruitful earth with promiscuous ruins, and turns the sky yellow with pestilence."[65]

Political mobs were bad enough, and provided ample reason to minimize the political impact of sailors. The waterfront also continued to provide the "cumbustibles" for a whole gamut of seaport disturbances on both sides of the Atlantic. Whenever a riot broke out, and sailors were nearby, they were sure to join in. Jack Tar thus played a role in the largest urban disorders of the day, like the New York's doctors' riot of 1788 and the bawdy house riots of the 1790s, as well as the series of disturbances that shattered Baltimore in the summer of 1812.[66] Beyond these big riots, countless sailor frays that broke out near the dockside were a constant reminder of the volatile nature of the waterfront. Typical was a Baltimore riot on August 19, 1799, in which "a large banditti of those sailors" from the American warship *Maryland* gutted a grocer's shop on Argyle Street in Fell's Point, beat the grocer, and drove the neighbors out of their houses. The men then went to the Market House, where authorities intervened and saved a black man from being severely handled.[67] In September 1804 a riot broke out in Philadelphia after some Spanish sailors stabbed William Barry, an American seaman. His shipmates then launched an attack on a house owned by a Spaniard and "tore it to pieces."[68] Similar disturbances occurred repeatedly, with or without an ethnic motive.[69] Americans even rioted in other countries. Sometimes they did so as an assertion of national identity, and sometimes in the spirit of rowdyness. Young Joseph Ward of the ship *President Adams* joined a Liverpool anti-impressment riot in late June 1809, declaring that he had a "right" to participate since one member of his ship's crew had been pressed. A few days later, on the Fourth of July, he was in a crowd of American sailors fighting an anti-American mob of carpenters, riggers, and others—many of whom no doubt rioted with Americans against impressment the week before. Yet Ward reports these disturbances in his journal as one big adventure, without much grand purpose.[70]

The legacy of all of the waterfront crowd activities was mixed. The "Sons of Neptune" shouting in the street take a back seat in the written history of this period. Many did not vote, or were prevented from doing so by mobility and property qualifications. Sailors' role in the party politics therefore has often been missed. No doubt many clung to ideologically consistent ideas, whether equality (Republican) or a concern for commerce and order (Federalist). A waterfront crowd was as likely to demonstrate in support of one set of policies or another, depending on circumstances and location. Jack Tar's penchant for pursuing his own interests and ideas evades the the standard ideological boxes historians like to use.

If the political significance of the waterfront crowd is often missed during the early republic, the sailor as an individual emerged as a central political symbol for the new United States. In large part this symbolic significance grew out of the importance of commerce to the American economy and the recognition that sailors, in particular, took risks to sustain that commerce.[71] Prior to the War of 1812 the American Jack Tar faced special hazards: conflicts with the Barbary pirates, the complex diplomatic web spun by the competition between France and Great Britain, and impressment into the British navy.

Although a handful of seamen were captured by Barbary corsairs before 1793, it was only in that year, when Algierian pirates extended their depredations into the Atlantic, that the plight of the enslaved American seaman received national attention. News that Americans, especially white Americans, were held by dark-skinned North Africans galvanized public opinion. Mathew Carey and others published historical accounts and geographical descriptions of Algeria. Plays and novels appeared that contrasted virtuous, liberty-loving Americans with corrupt and autocratic Algerians.[72] Supporting this contrast were the reports of the prisoners' treatment. The men had their heads shaved, were given the coarsest of clothes, and were led to work in chains. They received sparse food and were kept in dungeons. One commentator sought to remind readers that "the people of the United States" rely upon trade and the sailors who conduct that trade "to preserve their liberty at home." Americans, therefore, "cannot be unconcerned at knowing the fate of those countrymen, who, by being exposed to the severe and perilous duties of the sea" have to endure "the hard condition of slaves, to the most ferocious enemies to humanity."[73] The eventual return of the tars imprisoned by Algiers was a triumphant moment for Americans. The surviving hostages entered Philadelphia on February 8, 1797, "escorted by many hundred of their fellow citizens" and were taken to the Indian Queen tavern, where the streets were thronged with people.[74]

John Foss's account of his capture and the conditions of his slavery gives us some clue as to how the enslaved sailors reacted to their situation. The Algerians captured Foss and his shipmates, robbed them of almost all of their personal belongings, and compelled them to work their own ship. After arriving in North Africa, the Algerians put the Americans to work on the waterfront, rigging ships and preparing them for sea. Foss said it was the hardest work he had ever done. Finally, after almost three years, he was released. Up to that point Foss had focused on survival; now he could assert his ideological commitment for a receptive American audience. Told of their imminent "Liberty" Foss declared that "this filled our hearts with joy, and we imagined ourselves the happiest people in [the] world. For a long period we had been suffering the most inhuman slavery; loaded with an insupportable weight of chains, and now expecting to enjoy Liberty; the greatest blessing human beings ever possessed."[75]

In another instance, four hundred American seamen of the *Philadelphia* found themselves hostages and treated as slaves when the frigate ran aground in Tripoli harbor in 1803. Like Foss, they adapted to their circumstances, enduring almost two years of hard work for the bashaw (governor) of Tripoli. The bashaw took advantage of any special skill the men had, using carpenters, blacksmiths, and coopers in their trades. The rest of the men had to do manual labor. Six men sought the easiest path to survival, abandoned their upbringing and "turned Turk" by converting to Islam and earning a degree of freedom. Those who remained in prison survived on meager rations. Always showing their pragmatic streak, they soon learned to trade loaves of bread for vegetables and other foods.[76]

Notwithstanding these harsh conditions, sailors sought relief where they could. On several occasions groups of prisoners illicitly obtained alcohol and got drunk, even though they might be beaten as punishment by their captors afterward. On a lighter note was the New Year's celebration for 1805. The Danish consul, who had often come to the American prisoner's' aid, provided some wine to the men of the *Philadelphia* to bring in the new year. The first group of men sent to pick up the wine tapped into the barrels before they left and got too drunk to carry the load. More sailors were sent. They, too, got drunk, but managed to bring the wine back to the prison.[77]

The "people" of the *Philadelphia* not only demonstrated their survival skills in captivity; they also expressed democratic ideas and revealed that they continued to have a mind of their own. They repeatedly petitioned the bashaw and American officers concerning their conditions. The tars even conducted a work stoppage after the bashaw cut off their food in the hope it would compel the American forces besieging the city to relent.[78] Likewise, they saw themselves as making great sacrifices for American liberty. During a celebration of Christmas, for instance, they joined in a song that highlighted these concerns.

Columbia! While the Sons of fame
Thy freedom through the world proclaim
And hell-born tyrants dread the name
    That wills all nations free;
Remote, on Barb'ry's pirate coast,
By foes enslav'd, a miscreant host,
No more the rights of man we boast;
    Adieu, blest Liberty![79]

One captive, marine William Ray, wrote a book intended to play upon the popular sympathy for the American tar captured in Tripoli, offering his story to "readers whose patriotic bosoms glow with the consecrated fire of American liberty." Ray, however, seized the opportunity to make a larger point about the treatment of seamen in the U.S. Navy. Ray resented the American officer corps, and, like Durand, decried the denial of rights and the use of the lash against seamen aboard ship. He saw his treatment aboard American naval vessels and in a Tripoli dungeon as similar—both came from autocrats who had little respect for the common man. Ray declared, "petty despotism is not confined alone to Barbary's execrated and piratical shores." He believed "that base and oppressive treatment may be experienced from officers of the American, as well as the British and other navies." From his perspective, many American officers "can act the insolent tyrant, inflict tortures for petty offenses, and often for no offenses at all, and with contemptible pride and brutal ferocity, that would disgrace the character of a savage despot."[80]

Despite Ray's complaints, the sacrifice of the crew of the *Philadelphia* was recognized and rewarded. After a peace was signed, the prisoners became heroes and martyrs in the cause of liberty and were sent back to the United States. In the capital they were feted and were received by President Thomas Jefferson. The navy also provided each man with a suit of clothes worth sixty dollars, and paid wages for the full nineteen months of captivity plus seven dollars a month for rations. These freed sailors were also identified with American liberty and the triumph of American naval might. Raynor Taylor's published song "The American Captives Emancipation" thus lauded the heroics of Stephen Decatur and Edward Prebble, representing the quarterdeck, as well as the sacrifice of the common seaman. The second verse identifies the liberated "people" of the *Philadelphia* with American liberty.

Strike, strike barb'rous Moor, now strike off our chains
For Peace has return'd, and tis Freedom that reigns;
Hail Captives no more!—You were born to be free!
And hail lovely Peace, with divine Liberty!

The third verse highlights a different kind of liberty for the Sons of Neptune.

Come, Come honest Ship-Mates, and be of good cheer,
Drink deep of the bowl, and drown every care,
From the dark dungeon freed, let us now jocund be,
Sons of Neptune, lets drink—the brave lads of the sea.[81]

Even in identifying Jack Tar with America the more immediate notion of a sailor's liberty was not forgotten.[82]

The encounters with the Barbary pirates helped to bring the common seamen literally and figuratively to the center stage of American nationalism. In 1802 the play *The Tripolitan Prize, or, American Tars on an English Shore* was performed to sell-out crowds in New York City. At one point a leading character asked the audience, "What! an American Tar desert his duty?" The theatergoers responded, "Impossible! American tars forever! True blue will never stain!" Such enthusiasm was built upon the identity between the American seamen who confronted the Barbary pirates with those who fought in the American Revolution. After the victory at Tripoli, theater bills included reenactments of both the Battle of Bunker Hill and the action against the Barbary pirates. Francis Scott Key, years before he penned "The Star Spangled Banner," wrote an ode to the heroes of Tripoli. Similar to what became the national anthem in rhyme and even the music it was set to, the poem was a paean to American sailors, proclaiming, "Our fathers who stand on the summit of fame," the Revolutionary heroes,

Shall exultingly hear, of their sons, the proud story,
How their young bosoms glow'd with the patriot flame,
How they fought, how they fell, in the midst of their glory,
How triumphant they rode, o'er the wandering flood
And stain'd the blue waters with infidel blood;

How mixt with the olive, the laurel did wave,
And form a bright wreath for the brow of the brave.[83]

It took more than the capture of a few hundred seamen on the distant Barbary Coast and a handful of naval victories in the Mediterranean to elevate Jack Tar as a symbol for the United States. The work of sailors on merchant ships that fostered American prosperity and their service on warships in the defense of the republic in a complicated world at war also fostered this emblematic seaman.

The experiences of John Foss after he was released from Algiers testifies to just how complicated that world was, and how vulnerable a sailor could be. The twists and turns of his journey home, and the number of times the vessels he was on were searched or seized would almost be comic, except for the fact that Foss had already spent years as a slave and on several occasions was robbed of what little he had earned. From Algiers he sailed to Marseilles, where he spent eighty days in quarantine because others on the ship had come down with the plague. Surviving that ordeal, and not contracting the deadly disease, Foss signed on as first mate of the *Fortune* of Philadelphia. This vessel, which had brought the freed captives to France, had been leased by Joel Barlow from Jewish merchants in Algiers. The owners also obtained questionable American papers in Marseilles to avoid being seized by some Italian states at war with Algiers. The ruse was too clever by half. In February 1797 the British captured the vessel off Marseilles, after it had sailed to North Africa and returned with what must have been a contraband cargo. The British took Foss's clothes and money, pressed one man from the ship, and left Foss stranded. Somehow he made it to Leghorn in Italy, where he signed on a Ragusan ship for Philadelphia. Before leaving the Mediterranean the vessel was stopped and searched by a French privateer, a British ship, and two Spanish privateers. Once past the Straits of Gibraltar it was boarded two more times: first by another Spanish privateer, whose crew robbed the sailors' clothes and personal belongings; and then by a British warship that politely let them go. Having run this gauntlet, the vessel eventually made it to the United States.[84]

Under these circumstances, a sailor considered himself lucky to ever get home. John Hoxse's ship, carrying what he admits was largely an illegal cargo, was captured by a British privateer, probably in 1795. Fortunately for him, the prize crew got drunk, and the Americans retook the vessel, bringing it safely to port. On his next voyage, to the West Indies, things did not go as well. The

French seized and condemned his vessel. Left penniless, he worked his way to Baltimore where he arrived without clothes or money.[85] Even if the shipowner managed to salvage some profit in these situations, the seaman was bound to lose. After the French seizure of John Crowinshield's *Margaret* off Tunis a decade later, the American consul at Naples arranged for Crowinshield to split the cargo with the privateer and retain his ship. Crowinshield lost $35,000 on the deal. He at least obtained some of his money from the initial investment. Common sailors were left with nothing. Years later in 1837, when France settled claims resulting from wartime seizures, Crowinshield even got more of his money back. But a sailor who threatened to sue for his small share was unsuccessful.[86]

Confronted with the confused state of international politics, even as Jack Tar emerged as a symbol for the new nation, many sailors remained more concerned with survival than anything else. Americans, however, took note of this vulnerability and recognized the crucial role of sailors to the nation's economy. Although Madison viewed sailors with some suspicion as a dependent group of workers, he recognized their centrality to the nation and called them an "important class of citizens, whose occupations give the proper value to those every other class."[87] While he was secretary of state, John Marshall referred to sailors as "this valuable class of men."[88] The Republican mayor of Baltimore explained in 1808 that "the sailors were a highly useful class of citizens" and deserved assistance in times of adversity.[89] Simultaneously, songs about the everyday travails of sailors—including the hard work, the threat of storms and shipwreck, as well as the deprivations of pirates or navies of other nations—gained in popularity.[90]

International crises, especially the Quasi War with France, brought the sailor to the fore. Not only was he important as a victim of seizure, but, even more significantly, he became a symbol of sacrifice for American liberty. One song published in a collection entitled *Patriotic Medley* directly linked the sailor in drinking toasts to the defense of "America, Commerce, and Freedom."[91] Most important was the success of the American navy against the French. In particular, Thomas Truxton's capture of the French *L'Insurgente* represented a victory not only for the captain, but for American seamen and American shipbuilding in which the people of the waterfront defended the rest of the nation. While the song "Come all ye Yankee Sailors" gave some credit to "a bold commander," the reckoning for the French who were attacking American commerce and trade "should be paid by brave yankee Boys."[92] Jack Tar's role as the defender of the nation appeared in the "True American":

26. Americans took great pride in their success in the Quasi War with France 1798-1800. "Merchant Ship *Planter* Beating off a French Privateer, July 10, 1799." Published by John Fairburn (London, 1800). Philadelphia Maritime Museum.

When our enemies rise and defiance proclaim,
Undaunted to battle we fly;
Forget the soft ties that enervate the frame,
And fight 'till we conquor or die;
Our sweethearts we leave, nay our children and wives,
And brave all the dangers of wars,
We fight that the rest may live peaceable lives,
And stand till the last in their cause.[93]

Impressment became the most important issue faced by Jack Tar in this period, making the seaman both a survivor and a symbol for American liberty. As many as ten thousand Americans were impressed by the British between 1793 and 1815. More than four thousand seamen applied to the Secretary of State to be released from impressment.[94] In the War of 1812 alone, a total of 1,421 men who had been impressed were transferred to prisoner-of-war status in England; 151 did so in the West Indies or Nova Scotia; and 219 remained in the Royal Navy until the end of the war.[95] These men, and countless others like James Durand, demonstrated their ability to adapt to even the most oppressive conditions. Simultaneously, their cause became a rallying point for all Americans in the defense of the rights of man.[96]

The uproar surrounding the issue of impressment helped to convince many American sailors that they were central to American nationhood. A violation of Jack Tar's liberty by impressment became a violation of American liberty. The experience of impressment varied greatly, often making sailors feel helpless in a capricious world. Some sailors were able to escape the clutches of a press-gang, and some were forced to serve in the British navy for a decade or more.

Not every sailor who fell into the hands of the British was impressed. Protections often worked, leading to a discharge. In 1793 Joshua Penny was released several times in Liverpool after he showed a protection.[97] It was even possible to obtain your freedom with a special appeal long after impressment. John Bateman had been taken out of the brig *Ulysses* sometime around January 1807. Ten months later he was aboard HMS *Jason* in New York harbor writing to the collector of the port, David Gelston, for assistance. He urged Gelston to "lose no time in getting me my liberty." Bateman had a "helpless family" which included a wife and several children, and he was "afraid they may be in much want." Gelston contacted the British captain, explained Bateman's situation, and the fact that he had sailed out of New York for twenty years, and thereby obtained his release.[98] The U.S. government worked to obtain the discharge of thousands of men through official protests, with mixed results. Before the beginning of 1804 the State Department filed more than two thousand protests; almost half of these men were discharged by the British navy. The success rate declined thereafter. Of 903 applications of pressed sailors between October 7, 1807, and March 31, 1809, only 287 were discharged. For the rest, the British refused the applications, never responded to the specific case, or dismissed the request for a variety of reasons.[99]

Americans complained that the British were often high-handed. One British officer told an American merchant captain that he had impressed two of his sailors in part because the American threatened legal action against the British captain, a move he considered "*Foolish Pretensions.*"[100] On its return voyage from Morant Bay, Jamaica, in November 1805 the brig *Susanna* spotted the British ship *Dianah.* The brig sought to escape a search by the British, but when the warship fired a shot, the *Susanna* had to heave to. The British officer who came on board told the Americans that they had greatly displeased his captain by sailing to the leeward to avoid him. As punishment he pressed the mate, who as an officer was ordinarily immune to seizure, and another man. The American captain lowered a boat to visit the *Dianah* and plead for his men. The British captain told him he would release the mate if the American surrendered an Englishman. The American replied that he had no Englishmen on board. The British captain told him to go back to his own vessel and that he would keep the mate "to be Evidence" against the captain "for disobedience to his orders." Further negotiations convinced the British to surrender the mate, although only after the Americans had given up two more seamen.[101] Eliphalet Ladd, the second mate on the Philadelphia ship *Thomas and Sarah*, tried to stop a press-gang from seizing one of his men, John Eddes, while they were preparing cargo on shore in Kingston, Jamaica. When Ladd attempted to show the certificate of protection to the British officers, one of them called him a "damned rascal" and struck him with a cutlass. Ladd, too, was forced onto the British warship, where he found that Eddes had already been whipped with a rope end. Somehow Ladd managed to get released. Eddes, however, disappeared into the British navy.[102]

Stripping a crew of even a few men at sea could leave a vessel in a precarious position. After the British pressed the first mate and a sailor from the brig *Drake* on August 12, 1803, the remaining men were "too weak" to work the vessel, and it had to put into Antigua, the nearest port "to the great loss of the adventure."[103] A crew was particularly vulnerable to impressment if a vessel was seized and condemned for violation of trade regulations. A British frigate searched the ship *Prudent* in the Indian Ocean in 1805, and pressed "three free born sons of liberty." The next day the British boarded again, taking two more men. After the captain protested that they might as well seize the ship and all of his men, the British captain ordered a prize crew to impound the vessel and sail it to Ceylon, where it was condemned in a Court of Admiralty.[104]

The issue of impressment was not as clear-cut as American diplomats and sailors claimed. Some of the men who sought release from the British navy through applications to the State Department were born in Britain or had deserted from His Majesty's navy. British captains believed they had a right to these men. Protections were notoriously easy to obtain, either through purchase or merely a falsified affidavit. Repeatedly the British denied applications for seamen from the State Department because the man did not fit the description on the protection. Americans also voluntarily joined the British navy, although they might later seek escape by claiming they were impressed. In one case, the supposed pressed man (an African American) had been the slave of an American captain and had sought his freedom in a British warship. In another, Jesse Emmons had been so badly treated by Captain Ben-

THE IMPRESSMENT OF AN

American Sailor Boy,

SUNG ON BOARD THE BRITISH PRISON SHIP CROWN PRINCE, THE FOURTH OF JULY, 1814 BY A NUMBER OF THE AMERICAN PRISONERS.

THE youthful sailor mounts the bark,
And bids each weeping friend adieu:
Fair blows the gale, the canvass swells:
Slow sinks the uplands from his view.

Three mornings, from his ocean bed,
Resplendent beams the God of day:
The fourth, high looming in the mist,
A war-ship's floating banners play.

Her yawl is launch'd; light o'er the deep,
Too kind, she wafts a ruffian band:
Her blue track lengthens to the bark,
[illegible] soon on deck the [illegible]iscreants stand.

Around they throw the baleful glance:
Suspense holds mute the anxious crew—
Who is their prey? poor sailor boy!
The baleful glance is fix'd on you.

Nay, why that useless scrip unfold?
They damn'd the "lying yankee scrawl,"
Torn from thine hand, it strews the wave—
They force thee trembling to the yawl.

Sick was thine heart as from the deck,
The hand of friendship wav'd farewell;
Mad was thy brain, as far behind,
In the grey mist thy vessel fell.

One hope, yet, to thy bosom clung,
The captain mercy might impart;
Vain was that hope, which bade thee look,
For mercy in a Pirate's heart.

What woes can man on man inflict,
When malice joins with uncheck'd power;
Such woes, unpitied and unknown,
For many a month the sailor bore!

Oft gem'd his eye the bursting tear,
As mem'ry linger'd on past joy;
As oft they flung the cruel jeer,
And damn'd the "chicken liver'd boy."

When sick at heart, with "hope deferr'd."
Kind sleep his wasting form embrac'd,
Some ready minion ply'd the lash,
And the lov'd dream of freedom chas'd.

Fast to an end his miseries drew:
The deadly hectic flush'd his cheek:
On his pale brow the cold dew hung,
He sigh'd, and sunk upon the deck!

The sailor's woes drew forth no sigh;
No hand would close the sailor's eye:
Remorseless, his pale corse they gave,
Unshrouded to the friendly wave.

And as he sunk beneath the tide,
A hellish shout arose;
Exult[illegible]ly the demons cried,
"So f[illegible]re all Albion's Rebel Foes!"

27. The waterfront rallied to the idea that the rest of the country identified with their plight as victims of impressment. "The Impressment of an American Sailor Boy." Broadside, 1814. New-York Historical Society.

ners on an American merchantman that he voluntarily entered the British navy as soon as the vessel reached Cowes. Having escaped the torment of Captain Benners, he sought release from the British navy. Since Benners kept the sailor's protection, and the British viewed him as a legitimate recruit, he was not discharged.[105]

Often British captains felt they had little choice and held onto pressed Americans tenaciously. A captain on the Grenada station in 1805 declared that "he did not regard American protections" and was determined to press forty more men to complete the complement of his ship. In the same year, another British officer said he would cruise off Bermuda until he pressed all 110 men he needed for his vessel.[106] As another captain explained to four Americans he had just seized in the West Indies, "men I will not look at your protections—my ship is in distress, and I will have men to carry me to England."[107] Under such circumstances, there was little the individual tar could do but bend his will to fate and struggle to make the best of a bad situation.

Whatever the British rationale, impressment became a major irritant in Anglo-American relations. Politicians decried the practice, for it challenged American sovereignty. Most important, impressment posed a threat to every American who went to sea, proving a trial for those who fell into the hands of the British navy.

The story of James M'Lean reveals how difficult the ordeal of impressment could be for the seaman. Born in New England, he was impressed three times by the British. He was first taken in Grenada, sometime around 1798. Protesting his forced recruitment and showing the British captain his protection signed by a notary in New York made little difference. The officer accurately replied, "I could get one, if I was in America for a half a crown as good as that." The captain then continued, no doubt taking note of the name, "it is no use for you to pretend that you are an American, for you were born in Scotland." A lieutenant then stepped forward in support of his captain's assertion and declared "yes, that he [M'Lean] was [born in Scotland] for I knew his friends at Greenock." This lie sealed M'Lean's fate, and any further complaints were greeted with the threat of punishment. After serving for more than a year, and fighting in the Battle of Nile, M'Lean managed to run away from a watering party. He signed aboard an American vessel in England, but before he could depart, in January 1801, he was pressed again. As in the past, the officers ignored his protection. One officer declared that "he had plenty, like me on board, and that he did not believe I was ever in any part of the U.[nited] States; you are either Scotch or Irish." Just as in his previous experience, any effort to resist was met with the threat of punishment. Another officer told M'Lean, "Me noble scotch Yankee, I'll find means to make ye" obey. M'Lean escaped the British navy in 1805. For awhile he managed to keep his freedom, serving on an English merchantman, an American schooner, and then a French merchantman turned privateer. On this last voyage he had the misfortune to be captured, robbed of his belongings, and thrown into irons. Although he declared himself an American, by this time he had lost his protection. He found himself once again in His Majesty's navy, serving until 1813, when he deserted for a third time and made his way to the American shore.[108]

It should come as no surprise that M'Lean published his account during the War of 1812. For years the plight of the impressed sailor had been trumpeted as a vital issue to national interests. War with Britain only highlighted Jack Tar's significance as a symbol of the United States. Typical of this development was a poem Joshua Penny added to the end of his book on his travail as an impressed sailor. Originally the poem appeared in the *New York Public Advertiser* and was entitled "The Kidnapped Seaman." It begins with this call:

Sons of FREEDOM break your slumbers,
Hear a brother's piercing cries.
From amid your foe's deep thunders,
Hear his bitter griefs arise.[109]

Even though their day-to-day political role had been diminished, most Jack Tars, armed with this recognition of their significance to the republic, believed that the United States went to war with Great Britain in 1812 to protect their liberty. Regardless of personal behavior and excesses of liberty that many Americans found distressing, and regardless of the difficulty in detailing the impact of the Age of Revolution, the people of the waterfront viewed themselves as at the center of the republican stage in the great drama to defend American liberty.

6

Free Trade and Sailors' Rights

Samuel Leech knew the horror of naval warfare. When he was fourteen years old he served as a powder boy attached to the fifth gun of the main deck of the HMS *Macedonian.* On October 25, 1812, his sleek frigate was pounded by the American frigate *United States* in the mid-Atlantic Ocean. Although the ships were rated similarly, it was not an even match; the *United States* broadside contained 786 pounds of metal to 546 pounds for the *Macedonian*; the *United States* had 478 men aboard, the *Macedonian* had 301. In the ninety-minute contest more than one-third of the British crew were killed (forty-three men) or wounded (sixty men). The Americans suffered only seven killed and five wounded. Although the *United States* was damaged in the battle, the *Macedonian* "lost her mizzenmast, fore & maintopmasts and mainyard & was much cut up in her hull." Somehow the Americans were able to bring this shell of a ship back to the United States as a prize.[1]

Leech went beyond these statistics in his memoir, providing a vivid account of what it was like to survive this battle. The crew was both excited and anxious when the American frigate first appeared on the horizon. As the ships closed the captain ordered the *Macedonian* cleared for action, and "the whole dread paraphernalia of battle was produced." The crew, after a few minutes of confusion, stood at the ready to do its "best service" for the country. It was difficult to see anything from Leech's post. As the ships neared each other, three of the *Macedonian*'s cannon went off. The captain ordered the men to hold their fire. The "motionless suspense" was broken by the dull thud of cannon from the American vessel. "A strange noise" that "sounded like the tearing of sails" whizzed over their heads. It was the wind of the enemy's shot. Soon both ships roared with cannon fire, "trembling" the ship. Metal shot struck the sides of the *Macedonian,* and "the whole scene grew indescribably confused and horrible." Leech compared it to "some awfully tremendous thunderstorm, whose deafening roar is attended by incessant streaks of lightening,

28. Samuel Leech vividly described the hell aboard the *Macedonian* during the battle with the *United States*. "*United States* capturing the *Macedonian*." Painted by T. Birch, engraved by S. Seymour (Philadelphia, 1815). Philadelphia Maritime Museum.

carrying death in every flash, and strewing the ground with the victims of its wrath." It "was rendered more horrible than that, by the presence of torrents of blood which dyed our decks." The men shouted with excitement and feverishly worked their guns.

As Leech ran back and forth with his powder, he witnessed a scene that became seared into his memory. Suddenly he saw blood "fly from the arm of a man stationed at our gun," although he saw nothing strike him. The cries of the wounded filled the gundecks. The two boys of the gun next to him fell almost at the same time. One "was struck in the leg by a large shot; he had to suffer amputation above the wound. The other had a grape or canister shot sent through his ancle" and had to lose his foot. Another boy's powder caught fire and the flame burned away most of his face. As the boy stood there in agony with both hands lifted, a passing shot instantly cut him into two. The wounded were carried down to the surgeon with his dreaded saw and bloodied operating table. The dead were quickly tossed overboard. Leech noted one man with his hand cut off by shot "and almost at the same moment he received another shot, which tore open his bowels in a terrible manner. As he fell, two or three men caught him in their arms, and, as he could not live, threw him overboard." Leech "distinctly heard the large blood-drops fall pat, pat, pat, on the deck" as a wounded man was carried past him. The American fire was devastating. "The large shot came against the ship's side like iron hail, shaking her to the very keel, or passing through her timbers, and scattering terrific splinters, which did a more appalling work than even their own death-giving blows." Amidst the chaos "the work of death went on in a manner which must have been satisfactory even to the King of Terrors himself."[2]

What did this fourteen-year-old boy think about the hell he was living through? In his memoirs Leech recalled, "I felt pretty much as I suppose every one does at such a time." To run was impossible. Officers were stationed below with orders to shoot any man who abandoned his post. "To give way to gloom, or to show fear, would do no good, and might brand us with the name of cowards, and ensure defeat." Leech concluded, "Our only true philosophy, therefore, was to make the best of our situation, by fighting bravely and cheerfully." Regardless of appearances, each man took his situation seriously. Standing "amid the dying and the dead," Leech turned his thoughts to God, recognizing that at any moment he might meet his maker.[3]

After the firing finally stopped, the *United States* shot out ahead of the *Macedonian*, made some quick repairs, and prepared to continue the conflict. The British frigate was crippled and hardly able to maneuver. In such a condition, the Americans could have raked the *Macedonian* fore and aft, with little chance for the British to respond. The British captain decided to haul down his colors.

Leech now found himself a prisoner of war. Men abandoned their battle stations, piled on clothing, broke into the ships stores. Several men stuffed themselves with food and drank as much alcohol as they could before the American boarding party arrived. Leech, too, left his post. He raided the officers' stores and then headed for the steerage, where the wounded had collected. The sight was, if anything, worse than the carnage he had seen during the battle. Men were groaning and crying. "The surgeon and his mate were smeared with blood from head to foot: they looked more like butchers than doctors." He found a few of his messmates, and together they looked for the other men they had shared their meals with. Two were wounded. Leech and some of his other messmates had to hold one of these while the doctor cut off his leg above the knee. "The task was most painful to behold, the surgeon using his knife and saw on human flesh and bones, as freely as the butcher at the shambles does on the carcass of the beast!"[4] As he was a boy, he remained aboard the *Macedonian* to help with the wounded and clean the vessel. He stayed on the captured frigate on its voyage to the United States. Imprisonment was relatively lenient. The fourteen-year-old made friends among the American prize crew, and was even allowed to mess with them. Once they reached the North American coast, and after a brief stay at Newport, the *Macedonian* and the *United States* sailed to New York, where the Americans were treated like triumphant heroes.

Although the officials wanted to exchange the crew of the *Macedonian* in a cartel, many British sailors slipped off the vessel and melted into the American population. Indeed, a great many signed on to the American army and navy. Leech also determined to run away. To be exchanged meant being sent to sea again aboard a British naval vessel. The United States held out unlimited possibilities. On Christmas day 1812 Leech escaped from the *Macedonian* to the streets of New York. For a few weeks he lived off of some money he had earned showing American visitors the *Macedonian*. Then he signed on as an apprentice to a bootmaker. A chance meeting with a cousin sent him to Salem, Massachusetts. From there he signed aboard an American warship, the *Syren*.[5]

Leech's experience reveals just how easy it was to shed one's nationality along the waterfront. He had fought with spirit, joining in the shouting of the *Macedonian* crew. Now, he posed as an American, as had many of his countrymen, and volunteered to sail under his enemy's flag. Aware that capture might well mean being strung up from the yardarm, Leech grew his hair long and wore it hanging loosely around his neck in ringlets, instead of the accustomed queue of British seamen. He also donned typical American clothes, leaving the top buttons of his shirt open and displaying his collar in the American style. These precautions paid off when the *Syren* was captured by the British off the coast of Africa on July 12, 1814.[6]

Although Leech looked like an American on the outside, we will never know for sure how long it took him to become an American on the inside—in the way he thought and the way he approached the world. Leech wrote his memoirs thirty years after his capture, and after he had spent more than twenty-five years living in the United States. By the time he wrote *A Voice from the Maindeck*, his identity was American. In explaining the defeat of the *Macedonian*, he mentioned not only the disparity between the vessels, but also a difference in the attitude of the crew. He seemed to forget the commitment of the *Macedonian* crew to the battle that he so vividly described. On the one hand, he noted that the British tars fought lustily regardless of the carnage about them, and that some of the men wanted to continue the battle after the captain had surrendered. On the other hand, he declared that many of the men on the British ship, including Americans, had been impressed and "were in service against their will," whereas the Americans were fighting to maintain "free trade and sailors' rights." In fact, Leech seized the opportunity to justify the American cause in the war, as would any patriotic American in 1843, by asserting that Great Britain "had impressed American seamen" and "had violated the American flag by insolently searching their vessels for her runaway seamen."[7]

As a young deserter from the British navy, Leech knew that the process of becoming American was more complicated than growing his hair long and changing the cut of his clothes. He jokingly related the story of an Irishman who pretended to be an American before the war. When his vessel was searched by a British cruiser, his true identity was impossible to hide. A British officer asked the man what part of the United States he came from. The Irishman replied, "I used to belong to Philamadelph, but now I belong to Philama York." The officer detected the man's brogue, and impressed him into His Majesty's navy.[8] Leech also jokingly related his first ill-fated effort to pass as an American. Fortunately for him he was being questioned by an American officer shortly after his escape from the *Macedonian* in New York. He, too, claimed to be from Philadelphia. He had even rehearsed that he had lived on Pine Street. The officer, however, seeing through the ruse, had some fun with poor Leech by quizzing him on the various side streets that crossed Pine. Leech, despite his best efforts, soon became befuddled. He had almost salvaged the situation when the officer saw that one of his concealed buttons had British insignia. The officer asked if Leech had gotten the buttons in Philadelphia. Leech admitted, "This was a shot which raked me fore and aft. I hauled down my colors and stood silent. The officers laughed heartily as one of them said, 'Go below, my lad; you will make a pretty good Yankee.'"[9]

By the time Leech joined the American navy a year later, not only had he altered his exterior appearance and grown physically, but he had become committed to the ideal of equality. Service aboard the *Syren* seemed to fit his new approach to the world. Leech claimed that his American officers treated him better that had the British officers. After a midshipman attempted to order him to wash clothes for him, Leech simply refused this "sprig of American aristocracy" and never heard any more about it. Such impertinence would have earned him a flogging on the *Macedonian*. When physically threatened by a noncommissioned officer, Leech reported the incident to the first lieutenant, who then reprimanded the man. Leech was never again troubled by any other "would-be tyrants."[10]

Leech shared his democratic ideals with the rest of the *Syren*'s crew. After they were captured and brought to Cape Town, the enlisted men were separated from the officers. As Leech put it, "we had lost the natural exactors of discipline among seamen." Like prisoners during the Revolutionary War and those held elsewhere during the War of 1812, "to remedy this deficiency, our first step was to adopt a set of regulations in respect to order, cleanliness, &c., and to appoint certain of our number to enforce them."[11] American sailors during the War of 1812 also resorted to collective action to assert notions about their proper treatment even as prisoners of war. Finding some of the sergeants in charge of their guard manifesting "a surly, tyrannical temper, annoying us in many little things," the prisoners returned "their abuse in a rather provoking kind of coin." Whenever the guard was under the command of one of these noncommissioned officers, the sailors compelled the entire guard to stay on duty longer by delaying the prisoner roll call at the end of the shift. If the sergeant on duty treated the Americans fairly, the wily tars promptly formed for the head count. The soldiers soon got the message and the bullying ceased. Similarly, the prisoners organized a successful protest against the poor quality of bread provided.[12]

The Americans held in Cape Town, like their compatriots in other compounds during the war, could push resistance to extremes. A crisis erupted after an English doctor, offended because two sailors had hung their wash in the walkway to his office, threw the laundry into the mud. The two prisoners responded with "a volley of sailors' oaths." These "wrathful ebullitions" angered the doctor, who ordered the two men into solitary confinement. The rest of the prisoners saw this as "a manifest case of injustice," and they resolved "not to submit to it." When the sergeant came for the two men, they "all turned out in a body," declaring that they would be punished together or no one would be punished at all. The whole guard was called out and ordered to load and fire. The prisoners maintained their defiance, shouting "Fire away! You will have but one fire, and then it will be our turn." Outnumbered and aware that a bloodbath might ensue, the sergeant backed down and the issue was dropped.[13]

By the time Leech returned to New York after the war, he was an American. For a few years he lived like many sailors. He had picked up the vice of gambling in prison, and to that he added drinking and all the other sins seamen committed while on liberty ashore. He ran through his one hundred dollars pay from the voyage on the *Syren* and soon joined the navy again. This time he found his situation less to his liking; he complained of the floggings and his treatment in the democratic language of his adopted country. Eventually he deserted, headed for New England, established himself as a storekeeper, and experienced a religious conversion.[14] A part of him always remained a sailor. In the 1840s, he so impressed Richard Henry Dana, Jr., with his storytelling, especially in relating the terror of warfare at sea, that the author of *Two Years Before the Mast* encouraged Leech to write his own memoirs. Perhaps even more revealing was what happened when Leech visited the *Macedonian*, by then in the service of the United States. Years after he left the sea he called the crew shipmates and entertained them with tales about that frightful day in October 1812.[15]

Although Leech was born in England, his story conveys in large part what it was like to be an American seaman during the War of 1812. Embedded in his *A Voice from the Main Deck* is a vivid portrait of the sailor's life in an exchange of broadsides in battle. Whether aboard the *Macedonian* or the *Syren*, Leech, like every sailor who put to sea, risked life and limb. Similarly, reasons for joining the war at sea were often mixed. Although Leech fully understood the patriotic explanation of the war as an old man, he was less clear about his motivation for signing aboard the *Syren* in 1814. Apparently he needed to find employment after living at his cousin's in Salem for about a year. The cousin wanted Leech to learn sailmaking. Leech merely asserted that "by this time I had quite a desire to go to sea again." No doubt the three-month advance he received upon joining the navy, which enabled him to buy clothes and pay his board, contributed to this desire.[16] Most American sailors' motivation combined pragmatism and patriotism. Leech's experience aboard the *Syren* and as a prisoner of war in Cape Town also demonstrated how at sea and ashore American sailors often practiced a rough egalitarianism and expressed a spirit of liberty that reflected national values and a long maritime tradition of rowdyism. American tars exhibited their odd notions of liberty even when held captive. Tragically, not every British officer reacted as did the Cape Town sergeant. On April 6, 1815—months after a peace was agreed upon—British soldiers fired on an unruly crowd of American prisoners in Dartmoor prison in western England. This "massacre" of American seamen became embedded in the collective memory of the waterfront, and, like the *Jersey* prison ship of the Revolutionary War, came to stand for the sailor's sacrifice for American liberty.

During the War of 1812, sailors recognized that they remained an important symbol of the United States, while simultaneously struggling to survive the tempests that swirled around them. The people of the waterfront believed that the war was fought in large part to protect seamen from impressment. Politicians spoke directly to this issue. In his message asking for a declaration of war against Great Britain, James Madison highlighted the plight of the seaman by decrying the "thousands of American citizens" who should have been protected by their flag, had "been torn from their country . . . to be exiled to the most distant and deadly climes, to risk their lives in the battles of their oppressors, and to be the melancholy instruments of taking away those of their own brethren."[17] Madison reiterated this point in his second inaugural address by stating "that the cruel sufferings" of American seamen "have found their way to every bosom not dead to the sympathies of human nature."[18]

Once hostilities began, common seamen shared in the limelight of naval victories that became the pride of the nation. Within six months of the start of the war, Americans won five single-ship actions, including the frigate battles by the *Constitution* over the *Guerrière* and the *Java*, and the *United States* over the *Macedonian*. Although Britain's losses did not put a dent in its overall naval superiority, they were humiliating nonetheless and thus a source of pride to Americans.[19] The naval war did not always go so well for the Americans. For most of 1813 and 1814, the American navy remained bottled up in protected harbors, unable to get past the British blockade. After the defeats of 1812, and recognizing that the American frigates outsized the smaller British frigates, the British admiralty ordered its captains to avoid single ship actions. However, one such action took place on June 1, 1813, just off Cape Cod. In this short battle a well-trained British crew on HMS *Shannon* pulverized the unlucky *Chesapeake*. The American frigate had proclaimed its support for the war's ideals by flying a banner with "Free Trade and Sailors' Rights" emblazoned on it as it left Boston harbor. The untrained crew experienced fifteen minutes of the same kind of hell that Leech and the *Macedonian* crew had suffered for over an hour; 48 Americans were killed and 98 were wounded out of a crew of 379.[20]

While relishing the victories and suffering defeats, seamen could still also pursue their own interests and goals. The *Chesapeake* lost its battle with the *Shannon* in part because much of its crew were untrained raw recruits. Many of the veterans had refused to reenlist in a dispute over prize money. Similarly, aboard the *Constitution* the change of command after taking the *Guerrière* left many men unsatisfied. Isaac Hull had been popular among the men, and the new captain, William Bainbridge, was seen as something of a Jonah—among other things, it was he who had lost the *Philadelphia* off Tripoli. Before the *Constitution* left Boston for a cruise to the South Atlantic there was a great deal of muttering, and only a few weeks before the crucial battle with the *Java*

Bainbridge had to quell a near-mutiny as the men complained about short rations.[21] When HMS *Pelican* captured the USS *Argus*, some of the American crew may have been suffering the aftereffects of having drunk too much wine from a prize captured the night before.[22]

The experience of Ned Myers offers a window into the seaman's mind during the war. Out of work at the beginning of the conflict, Myers and a shipmate signed aboard a gunboat in New York. Like other sailors they hated these small vessels that Thomas Jefferson had hoped would be able to protect the American coast. Offered the opportunity to serve on the Great Lakes, Myers and "every man and boy volunteered." After a brief liberty, the men headed for Albany and Oswego. Their journey was more frolic than orderly progression. Myers explained: "we went through the country, cracking our jokes, laughing, and noting all oddities that crossed our course."[23] Once on Lake Ontario, Myers was assigned to several vessels and took part in sea and land battles. His concerns, however, were often immediate and mundane; he and his shipmates sought plunder and liquor before anything else. One exploit that netted a few gallons of whiskey "seemed to us to be a scrape, and that was a sufficient excuse for disobeying orders, and for committing a crime." The booty itself was not the main aim. Myers confessed that he "was influenced more by the love of mischief, and a weak desire to have it said" that he "was foremost in such an exploit, than from any mercenary motive."[24]

Capricious winds and fickle fate had a dramatic impact on this sailor. He was aboard the schooner *Scourge* in the early morning hours of August 8, 1813, when a sudden squall overwhelmed the vessel and sent it to the bottom of Lake Ontario in a matter of minutes. Though he did not know how to swim, he survived in part because he was sleeping on the deck and some raindrops awoke him just before the storm hit. Rescued by the *Julia*, he was captured a few days later, in a battle with the British. After a British officer wounded him for being saucy upon capture, Myers went below for a bandage. He found his remaining shipmates and some British sailors breaking into the ship's whiskey and bread bags. Both the British and Americans "without distinction of country, sat down to enjoy themselves" and even began to sing "for good-fellowship." The "jollification" did not last long before a British officer broke it up.[25]

Then began Myers's experience as a prisoner of war in which he was shipped across Canada to Halifax and then to Bermuda, and back to Halifax. Throughout his twenty months of captivity, Myers drew some odd distinctions. He agreed twice to work as a sailor aboard British transports to earn better treatment, more food, and some money. He spent time in a prison ship in Bermuda, and later on Melville Island near Halifax, and attempted to escape several times. On one of these occasions in Nova Scotia, he and two others made their way to a small port and signed aboard a British privateer, hoping, Myers claimed, to find their way back to the United States. At the rendezvous house they pocketed the £4 advance and then spent a day drinking, awaiting the return of the vessel to port. The next twenty-four hours, Myers confessed, "was pretty much a blank with us all." The following day a British patrol seized them and sent them back to prison.[26] Despite his willingness to serve on a privateer and aboard transports, Myers resisted efforts to force him into the British navy. At one point Myers and some other prisoners were put aboard a British warship and ordered to work, with the intention "to swallow us all in the enormous maw of the British navy." They refused and for the greater part of two weeks were "playing green, with our tin pots slung around our necks." Myers amplified on the comic scene, recounting that the British sailors "began to laugh at us, as real Johnny Raws, though the old salts knew better."[27] However much he might adapt to his circumstances, Myers would not bow to the pressure of the British navy. Although born in Canada, Myers saw himself as an American. He told James Fenimore Cooper, "I was determined not to yield" to any entreaties or arguments to enter His Majesty's navy. "I did not like England, and I did like America. My birth in Quebec was a thing I could not help; but having chosen to serve under the American flag, and having done so now for years, I did not choose to go over to the enemy."[28]

An odd combination of American nationalism, democratic principles, contractual obligations, and a concern with their own interests created a different kind of navy. Conditions aboard American naval vessels were not nearly as autocratic as William Ray and James Durand would have us think. For example, when Samuel Leech's captain on the brig *Syren* died during the 1814 cruise, the first lieutenant asked the crew if they wanted to continue the voyage, a request to which the crew heartily agreed. Such an appeal to democracy was unthinkable in the British navy. There is some evidence to suggest that Leech's comment about his lenient treatment on the *Syren* was not merely the reflection of the peculiar conditions on that vessel. Shortly before the outbreak of war, Moses Smith related a story of how one tar avoided a flogging appealing to an officer's national sensibilities. When the man was tied up ready for the lash, he turned to the lieutenant and declared, "I thought it was a free country; but I was mistaken. My father was American born, and my mother too. I expected to be treated as an American myself; but I find I'm not." Whether in earnest or merely using a clever ploy, the plea worked. The lieutenant had him cut down and placed him in irons instead.[29] The independent spirit of the American sailor can also be seen in some of Smith's own experiences. As the warship *Adams* was preparing to get to sea several crew members broke into the provisions and helped themselves to food and drink. Naturally they got drunk, but the officer who caught them simply disregarded this dereliction of duty. Shortly thereafter Smith was promised a quartermaster's berth if he agreed to sign aboard a gunboat. Against his better judgment Smith accepted this promotion. As Smith explained, "there was so much clearing away, and dressing up, and walking about, and making signals, that I sighed for the unrestrained station I had just left" aboard the *Adams*. When the lieutenant discovered Smith's dissatisfaction he was "mortified" and "even went so far as to threaten to stop" Smith's grog and then flog him if he asked for a transfer. Smith retaliated and wrote, "In revenge for this, my plan was to intoxicate myself that I might be broken on purpose." Unfortunately for Smith, as he explains, "they overlooked this folly in me, and I returned to my duty again."[30]

These tendencies were accentuated aboard the privateers that far outweighed the American navy in numbers and in impact on the British. Although the U.S. Navy during the War of 1812 numbered 23 vessels and captured 254 enemy craft, at least 517 authorized privateers captured 1,345 British prizes worth $45.5 million.[31] Service aboard privateers also differed from the regular navy. Speed and stealth were the main trademarks of a privateer. Battle, even with an equal foe, was to be avoided. Instead, these vessels, often schooners that could sail like the wind, played cat-and-mouse games. The aptly named *Young Teazer* during a two-week span in May 1813 either chased or was chased almost every day. It eluded capture and obtained two prizes during this part of the cruise.[32] Although privateersmen gambled with their lives, the payoff could be quite handsome. In 1813 the schooner *Thomas* took two prizes which sold for a total of $214,531. After fees, customs duties, and the owner's share, $92,246.35 was split into 891½ shares. The captain got nine shares. The least a crewman received was about $800.[33]

The men who wrought this devastation on British shipping came to their trade for a variety of reasons. Josiah Cobb admitted that he did not sign aboard a privateer in 1814 out of patriotism. Instead, it reflected this eighteen-year-old's infatuation with the idea of going to sea. Many of his shipmates had even more base motives; they were in it for the money. Cobb's shipmates were Irish, English, French, Spanish, Dutch, and, of course, American. Many of the men "could hail from no quarter of the globe, but whose destination required no conjuring to ascertain." Cobb was surprised to find that some in the crew had left regular occupations on shore, including a forty-

29. American privateers during the War of 1812 were usually swift schooners like this vessel, which had closed with HMS *Pylades,* mistaking it for a merchantman. Relying on their speed, the Americans added insult to injury by flying a pennant proclaiming "Catch Me Who Can." "HMS *Pylades.*" Peabody Essex Museum.

year-old carpenter with a wife and children. These men were dissatisfied with "not making money fast enough." As one man put it, he would "cruise for dollars, where they were to be found in greater plenty than in the place of his birth." Cobb and his shipmates were unlucky, and all they got for their efforts was six or seven days of intense seasickness before being captured by the British.[34]

George Little served aboard at least two privateers during the war and had a very low opinion of both crews. On one vessel, sailing out of Baltimore, the captain wanted to use Cartegenian (Colombian) papers to raid the shipping of several nations. Little saw this as piracy. The crew was all for it. They were "composed of all nations; they appeared to have been scraped together from the lowest dens of wretchedness and vice, and only wanted a leader to induce them to any acts of daring and desperation." Little left that vessel in the Caribbean, but later joined another privateer. The men were no better than on his first privateer. They were "selected from the very elite and respectable portions of the lowest sinks located in the 'Five Points,' 'Hook,' and other places of like celebrity in New York." They were "a motley crew of loafers, highbinders, butcher boys, &c. &c."[35]

The behavior of many privateersmen reflected this rough makeup and an emphasis on personal interest over lofty ideas. It was not unusual for privateersmen to be drunk and riotous during the capture of a merchantman. Petty thievery was rampant, as privateer boarders stole from crew and even passengers.[36] While American privateers did not capture neutral shipping, they stopped and searched such vessels, helping themselves to small items like fruit and wine. Divisions in the crew and among the officers broke out. One prizemaster decided to take a prize from the *Herald* to Spain "in hope's of Making his fortune."[37] In another instance a lieutenant and a captain had a falling out, with the lieutenant refusing duty and being put ashore at the first opportunity. Similarly crews and captains could disagree. On one schooner the men conducted a work stoppage for two days because the captain had limited them to one gill of New England rum a day when they expected twice that. For two days "never one of them so much as lifted a spun-yarn." The captain could hold out as long as the weather was pleasant. After it began to turn foul, "Our captain found that his government was democratical . . . he conceded to the large and fearful majority; and the New England spirit carried the day."[38]

"New England spirit" and "democratical" government were odd ways of describing relationships aboard armed ships. Several crosscurrents seemed to have brought the American Jack Tar to a peculiar understanding of himself. The nation may no longer have depended on his presence in the street. However, he had been held up as a symbol for the new republic for more than twenty years. Sailors recognized the image of themselves in that symbol and obtained a sense of meaning and direction from it. Like any reflection off the surface of the ocean, where wind and wave were constantly in motion, the likeness was imperfect and incomplete. Men fought in the war for many reasons—sometimes they were patriotic and sometimes they were mercenary. Often they were both. And, regardless of the larger issues at play, as in the street so also on the planks of a ship—sailors continued to pursue their own varied agendas.

A strange mixture of patriotism, democracy, pursuit of the main chance, and rowdiness all appeared most graphically in the experiences of prisoners of war. As the war dragged on, the British tightened their blockade of the United States and swept more and more American vessels from the sea.

Thousands of men were captured. The British collected these prisoners in depots in the West Indies, Cape Town, Nova Scotia, and England. A few lucky individuals were exchanged. Most prisoners, however, ended up at Dartmoor.[39]

Patriotism could emerge in the most unlikely places. Cobb's mercenary crew members showed their true colors once his brig surrendered and behaved the same way many of the crew of the *Macedonian* had when captured. All work on the vessel stopped and every man had license to do what he wanted. Several broke open the hold, stealing food and liquor. Many got drunk. Cobb grabbed some coffee and food for himself. Others stripped the vessel of canvas and rope. By the time a boarding party arrived, delayed through the night because of high seas, the brig's rigging was a mess. And yet the night after they were thrown into the cable tier of the capturing British frigate, the sailors joined in song proclaiming American victories over the British. They did so in part to taunt their captors, but it also expressed national pride in men who Cobb claimed had more sordid motives.[40]

Patriotic songs and poems appear in some of the journals kept by prisoners of war. Alden White copied several such tunes in a prison ship in Halifax, including "Major Andre," "Decatur's Victory," and an untitled work that celebrated John Paul Jones's famous battle in the *Bon Homme Richard*.[41] Joseph Valpey wrote patriotic poems in his journal. One was entitled the "American Tar" and highlighted the role of the "sons of Columbia[,] the American tar" in the war. It included the following stanza:

On the salt briney ocean our Eagle is a hovering
Directed by Neptune Assisted by Mars
Our Brave Constitution with fix't Ressolution
Commenced all the rights of American tars.[42]

Robert Stevenson Coffin addressed a similar theme in a song he wrote as a prisoner aboard HMS *Vestal* in Barbados in 1814.

The time is not distant, when our Eagle shall soar,
Unmolested and free, to roam earth's farthest shore,—
When Brittania shall yield, and candidly own,
That in vain she clam'd Neptune's Trident and throne;—
For our tars *will* be free
To traverse the sea
Though between every billow rise bulwarks of stone![43]

Prisoners also celebrated national holidays. The six hundred Americans in Dartmoor on the Fourth of July in 1813 raised two standards over the prison. British officials ordered soldiers to cut them down, and the redcoats managed to capture one flag. The prisoners successfully defended the other, even though the British fired into the crowd, wounding two.[44] The prisoners in Halifax celebrated the anniversary of independence in 1814 by decorating their prison with a huge painting suspended from the ceiling, displaying American naval victories, over which "was the Emblem of Liberty, standing on the Lion with a spier in her hand in the act of percing it through the Lions head." Completing the scene was "the American Stand of Arms—handsomely drawn."[45] American prisoners aboard the *Crown Prince* raised their national flag "as high as the top of our railings," had a fife and drum play "Yankee Doodle," cheered prisoners on other vessels, and heard an "inflammatory" oration from a man who had been impressed by the British and had surrendered himself as a prisoner of war once the hostilities broke out. One prisoner, thrilled with the experience, wrote, "we felt the spirit of freedom glow within us; and we anticipated the day when we should celebrate our anniversary in that dear land of liberty, which we longed to see, and panted after, as the thirsty hart pants after the water brooks."[46] In the same year the number of men held at Dartmoor had increased dramatically, and the prisoners made elaborate plans to celebrate national independence. They obtained two hogsheads of porter with the keeper's permission and several gallons of rum without his permission. They greeted the day by raising a banner with "All Canada or Dartmoor prison for life" emblazoned across it. The men collected in the yard and, just as if they were back in the United States, listened to an oration trumpeting American naval victories. The sailor speaking also detailed the causes of the war, emphasizing Britain's violation of neutral rights and practice of impressment. He contrasted the tyrannical government of England with "the happiness our countrymen enjoyed under so mild a government." They then sat down to a dinner of beef and soup, the best that could be had under the circumstances, and spoke of the president and congress, "for whom we sailors have the greatest respect."[47]

Democratic and egalitarian ideals surfaced in prison. The British often lodged officers and men together, much to the discomfort of those accustomed to the quarterdeck. Placed aboard the prison ship *Nassau* with 750 American prisoners, Captain Jeduthan Upton and eleven other officers put up a screen "to keep a little separate from the ship's company." The cramped quarters, however, were not conducive to such distinctions, and Upton reported that "our situation is very disagreeable on account of sailors who think they are equal to any of us and take advantage."[48] Benjamin Waterhouse commented that "Liberty is the parent of eloquence," and was struck by the aplomb with which an American approached his officers. "When an American speaks to an officer set over him, he utters all that he has to say, in a ready and fearless manner." He also explained that the United States was "a country of laws; and their very sailors are full of 'rights' and 'wrongs;' of 'justice and injustice;' and of defining crimes, and ascertaining 'the butts and bounds' of national and individual rights."[49]

How deeply these men had imbibed of the ideals of their republic can be seen in their efforts to set up self-governing organizations in prison after prison. Like Leech and the Americans at Cape Town, prisoners repeatedly organized themselves into small self-regulating republics.[50] The effectiveness of the prisoner self-government varied. The men placed aboard prison ships in Jamaica in 1812 and 1813 created some sort of committee system, although they had difficulties enforcing provisions against theft.[51] Halifax prisoners, with officers taking a leading role, not only had their committee system to try infractions of agreed-upon regulations, but the committee also kept a count of all prisoners, noting when they were sent to the hospital and when they were returned.[52] Aboard the prison ship *Jason* the officers, "knowing much depended upon the regulation of the prisoners, suggested" that the sailors "form a government to control prisoners in their every day activities."[53] Committees also negotiated for better treatment of prisoners, and on the *Nassau* in April 1813, "the people drew up a resolve" against prisoners volunteering for service in British ships. Aboard the prison ships in Bermuda the president of the committee negotiated issues like the quality of the food served and the type of work the prisoners could be expected to do.[54] The committees on prison ships in England "made laws and regulations respecting personal behavior, and personal cleanliness," especially because there were "a good many lazy and shiftless men who were willing to live like hogs and to wallow in dirt and filth." Serving on a committee could be hazardous. In Bermuda, several convicted criminals assaulted the president of the committee the day after a trial led to corporal punishment. After no one came to the president's aid the rest of the committee resigned, forcing an election and replacement by new committee members. At least one prisoner confessed in his account of his incarceration that he avoided serving as a judge in prison for fear of retribution.[55]

The most elaborate committee system emerged in Dartmoor Prison. As the numbers of prisoners increased in 1813, lack of self-organization created deplorable conditions, including men stealing from one another. As Charles

Andrews put it, "Honesty and integrity are but mere chimeras in dire necessity." Their situation "resembled more a state of nature than a civilized society." To remedy this deficit "we appointed a legislative body, to form a code of laws." To enforce the regulations the sailors also created a tribunal "to try and convict all criminals according to law and evidence."[56] More and more seamen were poured into the prison in 1814. The defeat of Napoleon led to the release of the French held at Dartmoor, and Americans replaced them in the other prison yards. All except one prison compound developed a committee system, normally with twelve members, that tried cases of theft and imposed regulations pertaining "to the cleanliness of the interior of the buildings, and defining each one's rights."[57]

The one area of Dartmoor that did not follow this system was Prison Number Four. When Americans arrived in Dartmoor they were all put in Number Four with Frenchmen who were considered too dangerous or criminal for the other prison yards. After a fight between the French and American prisoners in July 1813, the British separated the two groups, leaving most of Number Four to the Americans. In February 1814, at the request of the white American prisoners, the blacks were relegated to the upper floors in Number Four. Finally, in September 1814, after most French prisoners had been released and several other prisons opened to Americans, only blacks and the most derelict whites remained in Number Four.[58] At this point, the government of this building became autocratic under the leadership of an immense—one report stated he was seven feet tall—African American named Richard Craftus.[59] King Dick, as he was called in the prison, ruled with an iron hand and wielded a huge club to enforce his authority. If any of his men were "dirty, drunken, or grossly negligent," he threatened "them with a beating; and if they are saucy, they" were "sure to receive one."[60] White commentators believed that these strong-arm tactics reflected the lack of democratic principles among the prison blacks. Jeff Bolster has suggested that the rule of King Dick had antecedents in African American culture in New England and New York in which blacks parodied Yankee democracy by holding mock elections parallel to the regular elections and selecting their own governor or king. Bolster believes that this "king" fulfilled an important function for New England blacks as a community leader and that the emergence of King Dick in Dartmoor was an extension of this practice. From this perspective King Dick and his followers also represented a form of self-rule.[61]

If American prisoners could act in concert with one another in creating little republics in the prisons, they also expressed a strident individualism in the pursuit of the main chance. Some men concentrated on personal improvement, studying in schools, learning to read and write. It was even possible to learn navigation in an effort to advance from the forecastle to the quarterdeck. Perez Drinkwater kept a journal in Dartmoor in which he worked out a series of navigational problems, wrote notes on the kinds of records a captain needs to make, rehearsed bookkeeping procedures, and detailed business practices at a customs house for selling a cargo. Drinkwater noted a poem that denied the sailor values of generosity and asserted what would become middle-class notions of thrift.

I had both money and a *Friend* and took his word therefore
I asked my money of my *Friend* for see him I would not
if I had my money and my *Friend* and take his word no more

I lent my money to my *Friend* of whom I got great store
I loos my money and my *Friend* and naught but worse I got
I'll keep my money and my *Friend* and I had once before.[62]

Others sought to make a profit in business. Although the French controlled most employment and enterprise in Dartmoor when the Americans arrived, Yankees eagerly took their place in 1814 as the French prisoners started to be released. Americans set up shops selling tobacco, potatoes, butter, and a host of other specialized items. There were also "grocery-shops" that "sold glasses of rum, pipes, ha' penny-worths of tobacco, butter, snuff, tea, coffee, trickle, &c." Americans also produced items for sale, like model ships, hats, wooden shoes, gloves, and clothing. Some Americans opened a beer house, while others started a school to teach reading, writing, and arithmetic for sixpence a month. These businesses provided as, Charles Andrews suggested, a new meaning to the phrase "free trade and sailors' rights."[63] Often several prisoners would bind together, almost like "joint stock companies." Josiah Cobb and his messmates ran a soup business until one day two of his partners drank up all of their capital in a Sunday spree instead of buying the week's supplies. With all of these "shops and stalls where every little article could be obtained" it was possible for a "man with some money in his pocket" to "live pretty well through the day in Dartmoor Prison."[64]

The most prominent business, however, was gambling, which occurred in almost every prison.[65] After the failure of the soup enterprise, Cobb went into a partnership on a wheel of fortune. He estimated that the game favored the banker by about 25 percent.[66] Nathaniel Pierce and his partners set up a "Bread Wheel," probably a game of chance whereby the winner received a loaf

30. While in Dartmoor Prison, sailors would use the bones from their food to make elaborate ship models like this one of an English frigate. New Bedford Whaling Museum.

of bread, by which he was able to live "very well."[67] One of the favorite games was Keno, a type of bingo. The advantage of this form of gambling was that it was drawn out and did not cost very much, enabling the prisoner to occupy an hour or two.[68] Prison committees occasionally attempted to stop gambling because some men would sell their clothes in order to back a wager and it often led to quarrels.[69]

One of the most prominent areas of gambling and entrepreneurial activity in Dartmoor was Prison Number Four. If many white prisoners looked askance at the form of government in the African American prison, they did not shun it as some untouchable ghetto. Quite the contrary. Prison Number Four was the very center of social and cultural life among the Americans at Dartmoor. Joseph Valpey admitted that he went to Prison Number Four "to see the Fashions and pass the time," while Nathaniel Pierce confessed that "I have spent considerable of my time" in the "Black's Prison," declaring that the activity there "is very diverting to a young Person, indeed their is more amusement in this Prison than all the rest of them."[70] Simon, one of King Dick's lieutenants, declared himself a minister to the gospel. His religious services attracted whites and blacks from all over the prison. While questioning the depth of Simon's Christianity, Benjamin Waterhouse had to admit that "his performances have an imposing cast; and are often listened to with seriousness." More significantly, it was in this prison that the pursuit of the main chance took its most obvious form. Black entrepreneurs engaged in a wide variety of occupations. A visitor to Prison Number Four saw a "strange assemblege of antics." There were schools for boxing, fencing, and dancing. Some blacks drew pictures with coal and charcoal. There were raffles "and tricks of slight-of-hand." One's "sense of hearing" would "be regaled with the sound of clarionets, flutes, violins, flagelets, fifes, tamborines, together with the whopping and singing of the negroes." Twice a week the blacks of Number Four even performed theatrical plays.[71]

All of this activity depended upon cash circulating in the prison. Money came from a variety of sources. At times the American government paid a small sum to each prisoner. Larger infusions of cash came from prize money. Some of these funds were earned aboard American ships, but much of it came from the British navy. More than one thousand impressed Americans were sent to Dartmoor, claiming prisoner-of-war status, and carried in their pockets money gained from their years in His Majesty's service. Relatives, too, might send money. One sailor wrote to his affluent father to have a correspondent in England pay him two hundred dollars to ease his life.[72]

Pursuit of the main chance among sailors involved more than economic activity. Many sailors followed their own course, regardless of larger ideological issues. Just as in the Revolutionary War, although in smaller numbers (only about 220 men in Dartmoor), some men sought their way out of prison by joining the British navy. These sailors "justified themselves on the plea of self preservation; that there was a possibility of escaping and saving their lives; and if detected by their country, their death was distant, but here [Dartmoor] it was speedy and certain." Whatever their plea, if their fellow prisoners discovered their intention they were in for some rough treatment.[73] Others, like Ned Myers, simply agreed to work on British transports to get out of prison.[74] Still others pretended to have another nationality. At various times the British allowed Swedish, Dutch, and Prussian nationals captured on American vessels to leave prison. When French prisoners left Dartmoor well over one hundred Americans who knew some French managed to join in their release. As

Charles Andrews explained, "Yankees were citizens of all nations whose language they knew."[75]

Prisoners, regardless of the committees that supposedly policed them, still engaged in criminal activity. Often they stole from one another and misbehaved. One prisoner lamented that young men who fought for their country and for "free trade and sailors' rights" were placed "amid vice and roguery." These activities varied from prison to prison and from group to group. Conditions differed markedly on two British prison ships in England where American captives were held earlier in the war. Whereas the committee managed to keep good order aboard the *Crown Prince*, aboard the *Bahama* the men cared little about cleanliness and did not obey "good and wholesome regulations."[76] Men on prison ships in Bermuda and in Jamaica were also often difficult to control. In Dartmoor there was even a criminal gang, the Rough Allies, who declared themselves outside the normal bounds of the committee system. These men were "riotous, disorderly, filthy, thievishly inclined, or in anywise guilty of rowdyism." Another prisoner described the Rough Allies "as rascally a set of devils as ever escaped drowning." They bullied other prisoners and created as much of a ruckus as they could. Even among the regular prisoners there were men who would get drunk and fight with one another.[77]

This misbehavior contributed to an undercurrent of rowdiness that periodically disrupted the prison, at times in good-natured fun but at other times in a threat of greater violence. The Rough Allies, and other prisoners, would occasionally shout "Keeno! Keeno!" as a signal to make a rush at some person and knock him over. They even played this prank on the British sentries.[78] Sometimes the prisoners would join together and flout the authority of their British keepers. A few days after a man accidentally fell overboard from a prison ship in Jamaica and the guards fired upon him, prisoners tossed a hat over the side to watch the guards fire on it.[79] Prisoners in Dartmoor played a similar trick, lowering a jacket over the wall at night to see the guards' reaction.[80] The men aboard the *Crown Prince* had little respect for the British officer in charge of the vessel. After word got around that he had been caught in having a sheep commandeered from a local farmer, and had to pay compensation, the prisoners had great fun at his expense by shouting "Baa! Baa!" when he and his family came aboard the ship. American prisoners also contested their inadequate provisions by refusing to eat them and even tossing them overboard. They stopped work if they thought that they were not being treated fairly. They hustled would-be British recruiters, and on several occasions fought with their guards.[81] In this context the confrontation over dirty laundry described by Leech was not unusual behavior for American prisoners of war. One British official in Barbados confided to an American prisoner that his countrymen had "such a wild, reckless, daring, enterprizing character, that it would puzzle the d——l to keep them in good order."[82] Benjamin Waterhouse admitted that the sailors' behavior in prison was often "provoking," but believed that it was "never malignant, much less, bloody." He traced it to a "spirit of *fun* and frolic, which our people indulge in beyond all others in the world." Waterhouse saw this behavior "as one of the luxurient shoots of our *tree* of *liberty*," showing "the strength depth, and extent of its roots, and the richness of the soil."[83] Yet its ultimate outcome was to have tragic consequences.

In the months after diplomats agreed to the Treaty of Ghent (December 24, 1814), ending the war, American prisoners at Dartmoor were caught in a world in limbo. Peace promised to bring their release. Neither the British nor the American government seemed eager or able to deal with six thousand unruly sailors. These men could care less about delays caused by the niceties of treaty ratification. Left to languish through another austere winter, they grew ever more resentful of the walls and guards that bound them to their desolate fate. With liberty on the horizon, but still out of reach, Jack Tar took rowdyism to a new level and pushed his keepers to the edge and then beyond.

Trouble began soon after word of the treaty reached Dartmoor on December 28, 1814. That day passed in boisterous celebration with banners flying from all the prisons. One standard had the words "FREE TRADE AND SAILORS' RIGHTS" emblazoned on it, because the sailors were convinced that this ideal formed the "groundwork of the treaty." Captain Thomas G. Shortland, commandant of the prison, persuaded the Americans to take down these banners only after he agreed to fly both the British and American flags at his house.[84] Two days later, more impressed Americans arrived from the British navy. These men, however, were tainted by the fact that they had declared their citizenship only after hearing of the treaty and as a means of escaping His Majesty's service. Sixteen had even served in HMS *Pelican* when it took the *Argus*. After they bragged of this fact, Shortland had to intercede and remove "these traitorous villains" from the prison. Even more galling was the appearance of two men who the previous winter had volunteered in prison to serve in the British navy. The American prisoners determined to punish these men. Some wanted to kill them; others were for giving them the lash. Finally, "it was unanimously concluded to put upon them a mark, which would be a lasting stigma." Patriotic tars seized them "upon a table, and tattooed with U.S. on one cheek, and a T on the other, for United States Traitor."[85]

Tension remained high during the next month. Sometime in January Shortland provoked another confrontation with the Americans. He insisted on counting the prisoners in the cold and wet air of the yard. After submitting to this hardship for a few days, the Americans in a body refused to stand in the yard to be counted. Shortland stopped the market and ordered the guard to drive the Americans to their assigned prisons. The obstinate tars held their ground and told the militia guard that if they charged with their bayonets they would disarm them. Recognizing that he did not have enough men to force the issue, Shortland backed down.[86]

The prisoners no doubt were emboldened by the fact that they knew the war was over and their status more ambiguous. As they waited in anticipation of their release that winter, escapes, which had occurred only rarely before, now increased as the guards eased their vigilance. Still the prisoners suffered, and in early February smallpox broke out.

Amid growing discontent another incident further increased the tension at Dartmoor. Four American prisoners had been held permanently in solitary confinement for attempting to blow up their vessel before it could become a British prize. One of these men escaped from the cachet—black hole—and ran into a mass of prisoners standing in the yard. His countrymen, believing that his crime was an act of patriotism, protected him. Shortland closed down the markets and denied every privilege to compel the prisoners to surrender the man. When that did not work he marched into the yard with two hundred soldiers. "The prisoners were ready for this, and standing united, surrounded the soldiers and told the officers they were prepared to defend themselves and the man." Faced with such defiance, Shortland ordered the soldiers to retire. The standoff lasted six more days before Shortland abandoned all hope of retrieving the man and reopened the markets.[87]

American prisoners had intermittently challenged British authority before. With peace in the offing, they were now developing defiance into an art form. Another month went by and news of the ratification of peace arrived. Some prisoners now obtained their release through friends, or by signing on with an American captain. The British did not seem to mind escapes since the men were likely to be pressed as soon as they appeared in a port.

Prisoners increasingly relied on traditional forms of collective action. On March 17, Shortland told the prisoners that they would be released as soon as the American agent, Reuben Beasley, was ready to receive them. On the same day a letter arrived from Beasley insisting that the men would not be sent back to the United States until the sailors who had not had smallpox were inoculated. The coldness of the letter annoyed the prisoners. Believing that Beasley had often ignored them, the prisoners had a long list of grievances against him. Now, he seemed to stand between them and their return to America. On March 25 the prisoners determined to punish Beasley by resorting to a crowd ritual developed during the resistance movement against Great Britain in the 1760s and 1770s. They paraded with an effigy of Beasley and held a mock trial. They accused Beasley "of depriving many hundreds of your countrymen of their lives, by the most wanton and most cruel deaths, by nakedness, starvation, and exposure to pestilence." An "impartial and judicious jury" of his countrymen convicted him of this crime "upon the testimony of five thousand seven hundred witnesses." His sentence, read to the effigy, was to "be hanged by the neck on the top of prison No. 7, until you are dead; your body is then to be taken down and fastened to a stake, and burned to ashes, which are to be distributed to the winds, that your name may be forgotten, and your crimes no longer disgrace our nation." Before the prisoners carried out this sentence on the effigy in front of the guards and British officers, they read a stylized confession in which Beasley admitted his many faults and his long history of neglect of the prisoners. As one observer put it, this action was not "the conduct of an infuriate mob; but it was begun and carried through by some of the stediest men within the walls of Dartmoor Prison."[88]

It is not clear what Shortland thought of this spectacle. Perhaps he was glad that the prisoners were focusing their wrath on Beasley instead of the British. Whatever his thoughts, he would soon come to realize that this crowd behavior was going too far. Everyone expected the prisoners to begin leaving Dartmoor soon. In anticipation of their release the various prison shops broke up on April 2. Probably for the same reason the contractor who supplied the prison with bread decided to unload his store of hard bread on the prisoners on April 4. (The contractor was obliged to serve soft bread on a daily basis, keeping a store of hard bread in case of emergency. If the prisoners left Dartmoor before he could use the bread it would probably be a total loss.) On the fourth Captain Shortland went to Plymouth, and the perfect opportunity to get rid of the damaged stock appeared. Many of the prisoners had had similar experiences in other compounds. In January 1814, the prisoners aboard the *Crown Prince* had refused to eat for two days when they were served hard bread instead of soft bread. Although one sailor reported that this "embargo on our bowels" was "a pretty tough piece of self-denial," the Americans held out for two days before the British relented and the prisoners "established the Yankee character for inflexibility, beyond all doubt or controversy."[89] Now that peace had been agreed upon and liberty close at hand, American Jack Tars would only be more obstinate in their rights and again refused to eat the hard bread. As the day wore on, tensions increased, as did the hunger pangs in the pit of every prisoner's stomach. By evening the Americans had determined to "die by the sword than the famine." When the time came for them to return to the prison houses, as usual in the evening, they charged the gate and broke it open, sending the soldiers stationed there in hasty retreat. Alarms bells sounded, drums rolled, and the entire garrison was called to arms. Word spread through the countryside and militia bands began to march to Dartmoor. The prisoners stood in front of the storehouse, confronted by soldiers with fixed bayonets. Undaunted, the Americans persisted in their demands, declaring that the soldiers did not have orders to fire and that if they did "they must abide by any consequences." They also threatened to level the storehouse, and every prisoner would march out of Dartmoor unless bread were served out immediately. The contractor realized his mistake and promised to serve the soft bread if the men returned to prison. The Americans withdrew, taking a clerk as hostage. That night, as they ate their soft bread, the Americans knew they had won the day.[90]

Shortland, who arrived on April 5 with two hundred extra soldiers, must have known it too. He also must have resolved that he could no longer allow an American mob to rule Dartmoor. That decision would earn him infamy among American sailors.

On April 6 American prisoners were playing ball in the prison yard. These men were "ready dogs and ripe for fun." They repeatedly threw the ball over the wall. An obliging guard retrieved it for awhile, although he soon grew tired of this game telling the men that the next time they should go fetch it themselves. The men were willing to push the joke further, and began digging a hole in the stone wall in front of the guard. A huge crowd collected and shouted encouragement to the men, who worked away at the stone. Two men even used metal bars, until they had a hole big enough for a man to crawl through. The sentry told them to stop their digging; he received only insults and taunts for his efforts. He was even told to go ahead and fire his musket if he dared.[91] At the same time, in another part of the prison, some sailors had gained permission to lay on the grass between a railing and the walls, an area usually off-limits to the prisoners. A privilege for a few became a right for the many, and the area filled with Americans. The crowding led to some jostling, and then scuffling. The Americans threw pieces of turf and even old shoes at one another "principally in play" and with "considerable noise."[92]

American prisoners later claimed that there was no serious threat, and that both incidents reflected spirited play by bored men waiting to be released. Given the context of recent events, the disturbance and the possibility of escape seemed real enough to Shortland and the British guard. As it was approaching seven in the evening, the regular time for the American sailors to return to their prison buildings, Shortland alerted the garrison and ordered the alarm rung. Confused and curious, hundreds of prisoners ran to the main gate between the market yard and the prison yards to see what all the fuss was about. The press of humanity, or the mischievousness of a few tars, forced the gate open, further creating the impression that the Americans were going to break out of Dartmoor. As prisoners piled into the market yard some were shouting "Keeno! Keeno!"—the prison phrase for a free-for-all.[93] Shortland appeared with a file of soldiers. Other soldiers lined the walls. Amid the noise and commotion, Shortland determined to control the prison, and ordered his men to lower their bayonets to the charge position and force the crowd back. The mass of prisoners stood so close to the soldiers that the order was difficult to execute. Gradually the British pushed the prisoners out of the market square toward the prison buildings. Several Americans were not ready to beat a retreat, and dallied in the passage between the square and prison yards. Perhaps emboldened by past experience, they were "making a noise, hallowing, insulting, and provoking, and daring the military to fire."[94] Some of the soldiers claimed the prisoners hurled stones as well as epitaphs. One reported he had his cap knocked off.[95] In these strained circumstances a shot rang out. The prisoners later swore that Shortland had ordered the firing out of hatred and spite.[96] No matter who was responsible, shot after shot ensued. The initial round seemed to have no real effect since several soldiers raised their weapons and fired over the crowd. A few prisoners brazenly shouted more insults, crying out, "Fire you buggers, you have no shot in your pieces or guns."[97] British soldiers, angered by the repeated taunting and loss of face two days before, leveled their guns into the mob, and once their weapons were empty thrust their bayonets in every direction. Some prisoners scurried back to the buildings, crowding the doors in an effort to escape the bloodshed. Others paused to throw more stones at their attackers. The Americans later claimed atrocities were committed. Several witnesses described one wounded man turning to his attackers to beg for mercy; Shortland, so the prisoners reported, had a party of soldiers riddle the sailor with bullets.[98] The British officers said that they strove to control their men, who continued the massacre out of "individual irritation and exasperation."[99] A few soldiers fired into the prison buildings after the sailors withdrew inside. While Americans viewed this action as wanton savagery and proof of British brutality, the soldiers

31. Reminiscent of Paul Revere's famous engraving of the Boston Massacre, this portrayal of the Dartmoor Massacre appeared at the top of a broadsheet decrying the British action of April 6, 1812. Detail of "Horrid Massacre at Dartmoor Prison, England" (1815). Nantucket Historical Association.

argued that the prisoners had thrown stones at them from the doorways and from inside the buildings. One American, confessing that he was a little groggy that evening because he had been drinking, admitted that he dared the soldiers to "fire and be damned" and tossed a stone out of his prison at the guard.[100] The shooting lasted about twenty minutes. After the ruckus quieted down at last, seven Americans lay dead; scores more were injured. Several had to suffer amputation as a result of the wounds. And the Dartmoor Massacre became etched in the mind of American tars as the ultimate example of British perfidy.[101]

A somber and vengeful mood descended upon the American prisoners in the days after the incident. The Dartmoor prisoners' committee put together its own report of the massacre, fearing that official channels would not properly represent the "brutal" massacre. They took depositions from prisoners who all accused Shortland of a "predetermined act of atrocious murder." From their perspective, Shortland, who they also said was drunk at the time, planned the entire incident.[102] The American sailors expressed their anger as they began leaving Dartmoor a few days after the massacre. Flags escorted the men to the coast, proclaiming Shortland a murderer and depicting scenes to

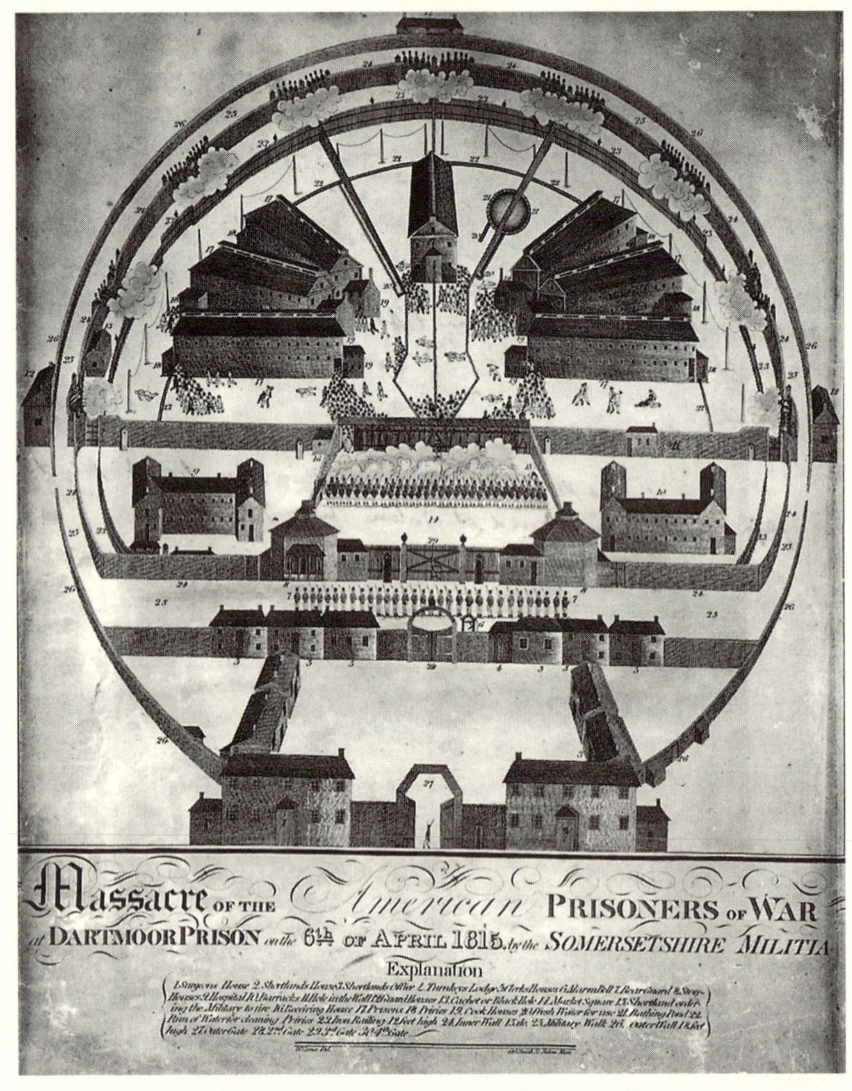

32. In 1815 several sketches of the circular-shaped Dartmoor Prison appeared to dramatize the massacre. In this plan the Americans scramble back to their prison houses as the British fire from all directions. On the right side of the wall that runs across the middle of the prison, just below three sailors each holding a fallen comrade, was where the American ball players had dug a hole. Between the inner ring of fences and the wall was where Americans had thrown grass and dirt at one another. The massacre began in the inner court yard where the shooting file of soldiers appears. "Dartmoor Massacre." W. Carnes (Salem, [1815]). Peabody Essex Museum.

remind each sailor of the terrible event.[103] One banner had "the representation of a tomb, with the Goddess of Liberty leaning on it, and a murdered sailor lying by its side." The inscription proclaimed "Columbia weeps, and we remember."[104] Upon their return to the United States, newspapers filled with stories of the Dartmoor Massacre.[105] Handbills appeared depicting the "HORRID MASSACRE" showing how "the unarmed American Prisoners of War were wantonly fired upon by the guard" and describing Shortland as "blood thirsty." An enraged citizenry joined in the outcry. Within a few months, however, the anger waned and the story disappeared.[106]

The official reaction was more measured. Shortly after the event a British court ruled the shooting justifiable homicide. A joint Anglo-American commission, American Charles King and Briton Seymour Larpent, investigated the massacre, drawing up a report by April 26, 1815. They interviewed guards and prisoners and were confronted by a maze of contradictory evidence. Ultimately they provided a balanced narrative that exonerated Shortland and shifted blame to the militia guard and the American prisoners. The incarcerated sailors viewed the King-Larpent report as a whitewash, and declared that it was concluded without hearing all of the depositions collected by the Dartmoor prisoners' committee. Diplomats on both sides wanted to put the issue behind them. The British Prince Regent expressed his regrets over the incident and offered to compensate the families of the killed. American diplomats quibbled over the responsibility of Shortland but decided not to dwell on the loss of a few sailors.[107]

Dartmoor would remain in the popular consciousness of the waterfront for a long time. However the sailors may have behaved, whether they had pursued the main chance in prison, or had espoused the ideas of the Age of Revolution, the massacre was seen as the ultimate price Jack Tar paid for American liberty. In the wake of the War of 1812, at the dawn of the Era of Good Feelings and in the shadow of Andrew Jackson, Dartmoor carried little lasting resonance with the rest of the American public. As the nation turned inward to exploit a continent, many a sailor must have begun to wonder if anyone away from the waterfront cared for Jack Tar.

PART III
LEGACY

7

Proper Objects of Christian Compassion

The Reverend Henry Chase cared about sailors. He began his missionary work on New York's waterfront in 1820, serving the newly opened Mariner's Church on Roosevelt Street. He also labored up and down the rough-hewn streets of the Fourth and Seventh Wards, visiting families, holding prayer meetings, talking to sailors. Chase's was a personal crusade. He felt "gratified and animated" in his efforts. He reported that "The solicitude of sailors and their families to be visited—their eagerness to receive tracts—to be instructed—to be prayed with—and the inquiry 'What shall I do to be saved'" rendered these visits "peculiarly pleasing."[1] At times he lost his voice and was overwhelmed by the effort. Yet he persisted, marrying couples, baptizing children, distributing tracts and Bibles, and preaching the gospel.

His efforts were prodigious. During one winter month Chase visited almost sixty homes, working his way in the cold along Banker Street, over to Henry Street, down Pike and Division Streets, and into the side streets. At each residence he sought the state of religion in the family, and often found out much more. On January 7, 1823, he stopped at Mr. Blandford's on Pike Street. This ex-seaman now worked along the shore, had a large family, and was ill at the time Chase visited him. Blandford told Chase that he was glad to see him, but admitted that he was negligent about religion, despite getting a religious education as a youth. Blandford was anxious about his soul, confessing that "death was awful to him." He said that he frequently started at night with terror from his pillow, and strove to pray for mercy. Mrs. Blandford, too, had "a very interesting state of mind." Chase prayed with them, leaving them in tears. He also gave them two religious tracts. The next day he stopped at Mr. Wood's on Ludlow Street. The Woods had two sons at sea, and it had been more than a year since they had heard from one of them. They were very concerned for his safety. Staying with them was a nineteen-year-old sailor, Joseph Weeks, who had been shipwrecked off Cape Hatteras and lost everything. Mr. Wood may have known Weeks's father, who also had been a seaman. Although Wood could barely support his own family, they were nursing Weeks, who was so ill at times that he was as helpless as a child. Chase promised to try to find some assistance for Weeks, prayed with the family, and left two tracts. Mrs. Morgan on Henry Street was home alone when Chase stopped by. She complained that her husband got drunk every night and that she "had trouble enough with him." He left two tracts with her, one on drunkenness. He found Mr. Hyer on Oak Street preparing to go to sea, even though his wife was sick with consumption. Chase, however, reported that she was ready for death, quoting her as saying, "Glory be to God, I shall soon be with Jesus." Chase prayed with the family before continuing on his visits. At another Pike Street address, Chase stopped to see Mr. Turner, an elderly rigger. He had been sick for three weeks and presumably out of work. But he had been to the Mariner's Church and liked it, even if he had not gone often. He also had several religious books and a Bible. Living with him as a boarder was a young sailor named David Redman, "a man of steady habits" who attended church regularly. Redman had been in Dartmoor Prison for two years during the war and showed Chase a testament he had gotten while a prisoner. Chase gave him some tracts and a report of the Marine Bible Society.[2]

Out of these efforts Chase came to know and understand the waterfront. Chase saw it all. Husbands lost at sea. Wives abandoned for months and years at a time. Children left without education. Sickness and poverty were everywhere. His job was to bring religion to these people and open their hearts to Christ. It could be a daunting, yet fulfilling task. He was devoted to his calling. When yellow fever struck the city in August 1822, and anyone who could afford to leave headed for the country, Chase remained on the waterfront because the sailors wanted the Mariner's Church to stay open.[3]

Chase seemed to enjoy the prayer meetings the most. These were held in the Mariner's Church on Sunday and Wednesday evenings, and at homes and boarding houses on other nights.[4] Chase reported that "the addresses and prayers of sailors, broken and artless indeed, but fervent and sincere, have often struck landsmen with astonishment, and moved them even to tears."[5] On the evening of January 2, 1823, Mrs. Mansfield hosted a prayer meeting at her Pike Street home. The meeting began with a sailor reading a psalm from the Bible. He then prayed and followed with remarks exhorting parents to talk to their children about God and to pray with them. Then a Norwegian sailor stood up, declaring that they should approach God with "Sincerity and solemnity" since "God is a consuming fire." He described his former wickedness when he followed the sea, and said that he "frequently prayed to God to

33. Waterfront families worshiped at New York's Mariner's Church during the 1820s, 1830s, and 1840s. *Sailors Magazine* (Sept. 1835). Kendall Whaling Museum.

send the ship, cargo, captain, and the crew all to the Devil." Only the prayers of well-meaning friends on shore saved him. Another sailor then spoke a few words and offered a prayer with "humility and sincerity." Chase had been an observer up to this point. He now added a few remarks and, of course, a prayer. As the meeting was closing another sailor said that he would like to sing. Then in a "clear shrill musical voice" he offered a hymn extolling the power of the almighty and love over hate. As Chase headed home, Peter Smith, a sailor, accompanied him, pouring out his heart to the minister.

While Smith was on a voyage the previous winter, his thoughts turned to religion after two men fell overboard, one with an oath on his lips as he met "a watery grave." After Smith returned home he discovered that his wife had begun to attend the Mariner's Church and had become anxious for her soul. Between going to church and participating in prayer meetings he at last had found peace, "having previously seen himself to be a wretched and undone sinner, justly exposed to hell and deserving to be cast out forever." Now Smith saw "Jesus Christ as the only savior, to whom he has been able to flee for refuge." Has any missionary ever had a more fulfilling evening? Chase had been in a room full of men and women who had seen the bottom. These people knew sin firsthand, and now they turned to him for guidance and to religion for deliverance.[6]

This work was both exhausting and exhilarating. Another minister was hired, John Truair, to help with the visits, prayer meetings, and services. The Mariner's Church struggled under its mortgage, and the Society for Promoting the Gospel Among Seamen in the Port of New York (SPGAS) had difficulty raising money. Hopes that sailors flush with cash from their voyages abroad would fill the society's coffers proved unavailing; those who attended the weekly services often had barely enough for themselves and had little left over for charity. The merchants and sea captains who sat on the board of directors did what they could. Truair toured the countryside, preaching and raising hundreds of dollars, but it was not enough. By July 1823 the society was $6,000 in debt. Although the SPGAS could not always pay his salary, and even let him go for awhile, Chase remained on the waterfront for decades ministering to sailors, dockside workers, and their families.[7]

Chase's efforts were part of a larger movement in the nineteenth century born out of the Second Great Awakening. Religious revival and the Age of Revolution were intimately intertwined as the United States moved toward increased democratization in the first half of the nineteenth century. The evangelical call for a special relationship between the individual and God became a clarion for equality. It also asserted a new morality that demanded a certain mode of behavior and insisted that the individual claim responsibility for his own actions. Evangelical religion took the ideals of revolution and incorporated them into a middle-class mentality that offered its own definition of liberty—a liberty to open one's heart to God, pursue one's own economic interest through hard work, and exert personal discipline.[8]

Evangelical reformers turned their attention in many directions in this period. But sailors had a particular attraction because so many sailors had an understanding of liberty that was antithetical to evangelical notions. The

Reverend Edward Dorr Griffin explained this appeal succinctly, telling his New York congregation that "As ruined and immortal beings, seamen are certainly the proper objects of Christian compassion."[9] The evangelical rationale for converting the waterfront went much deeper. This reform proceeded by a variety of specific measures, culminating in movements against flogging and the grog ration. Some sailors welcomed religion and reform and began to espouse middle-class ideas on liberty. Many others rejected these efforts to alter the sailor's concept of liberty and to change his world from the top down.

The reform effort to reach the waterfront was only one province in the larger benevolent empire that emerged in nineteenth-century America. In substance and form it appeared much like other provinces: it traced its roots to British antecedents; reflected an evangelical fervor born out of the Second Great Awakening; and found its greatest support among the emerging middle class.[10] The men who began to think about helping the sailor after the War of 1812 acknowledged their intellectual debt to the British. In recounting their history they turned first to the activities of Englishman John Thornton to aid British sailors and soldiers in the 1770s and 1780s. After Thornton's death little was done for the sailor until the British organized the Naval and Military Bible Society during the opening decade of the nineteenth century. The British then began to form Bethel Societies, which held prayer meetings under a Bethel flag raised on ships in port.[11] Although there may have been some prayer meetings held on the New York waterfront and some organizing for reform in Boston before the War of 1812, it was only after that conflict that the movement gained momentum.[12]

The Reverend Ward Stafford was the driving force behind the change. Stafford had been hired by the Female Society for the Poor of the City of New-York and Its Vicinity. As part of his report to that organization in 1817 he identified sailors on the waterfront as an appropriate missionary target. Packed along the waterfront were men and women who needed both charity and guidance. In March 1817 he helped start the first New York organization to aid seamen—the Marine Bible Society of New-York. Other endeavors soon followed: the SPGAS in 1818 and the New-York Bethel Union in 1821. Stafford seemed to enjoy fund-raising and toured New England and elsewhere, leaving in his wake a host of local marine Bible societies. Back in New York Stafford also arranged for the multidenominational support for the Mariner's Church on Roosevelt Street, which opened June 4, 1820, with Stafford as its first minister. Stafford, however, was too busy for the day-to-day cares of such a dispersed congregation and quickly turned the pulpit over to Chase.[13]

Stafford, Truair, and even Chase were the foot soldiers in a larger army of reformers recruited from an emerging middle class. During the nineteenth century, the United States came to be dominated by acquisitive capitalists and men on the make who claimed as their revolutionary legacy a set of values emphasizing hard work and delayed gratification. Personal discipline became a hallmark of this middle class. Oddly, despite a hard-nosed approach to business, they sentimentalized family relations and held up the sanctity of the home as a refuge from work. The middle class was also susceptible to the evangelicalism of the Second Great Awakening and came to believe in the perfectibility of mankind. Religion and reform thus went hand in hand, with members of the middle class often footing the bill.[14] Stafford found financial support among the merchants and ship captains belonging to New York's middle class. Ten of the thirty managers of the New-York Bethel Union in 1821 were ship captains, and at least nine were merchants or businessmen of some kind.[15] Reform roots ran deep with the men who first supported the crusade to change the waterfront and bring Christianity to seamen. Divie Bethune, the first president of the New-York Bethel Union, was a prominent merchant in New York. He was also an ardent Presbyterian and the son-in-law of Isabella Graham, who spearheaded the first female reform organization in New York in the 1790s, the Society for the Relief of Poor Widows with Small Children.[16]

The appeal to reform seamen reached beyond New York to the middle class of other ports as well. Both Stafford and Truair went on the road to collect money and garner support. Their efforts quickly reaped results. In July 1817 the people of New Haven formed a Marine Bible Society.[17] Community after community followed suit, organizing Bible societies or Bethels, and even building other mariner's churches. Boston reformers began holding seamen's meetings by 1818, and in 1822 evangelicals in South Carolina formed the Charleston Bethel Society. Similar activities appeared in New London, Providence, Baltimore, and other ports. Prayer meetings were held in a Philadelphia sail loft, leading to a Bethel organization, and the laying of a cornerstone of a church devoted to seamen in 1824.[18] Once the work had begun, it seemed to spread like wildfire, eventually reaching inland to the Great Lakes and even along the nation's canals.[19]

Like other reform activities, the many local associations eventually sought some sort of national cohesion. An abortive effort occurred in 1825 and 1826 with the formation of the short-lived National Seamen's Friend Society. A more permanent organization appeared on May 5, 1828, when a group of merchants and sea captains organized the American Seamen's Friend Society (ASFS), dedicated to "improve the social and moral condition of seamen uniting the efforts of the wise and the good in their behalf." It also provided a clearinghouse for reform information by publishing the *Sailors' Magazine and Naval Journal,* a new journal based on an English precedent, and offered a national umbrella for the local societies that had appeared in almost every port. Throughout the 1830s and 1840s and beyond, the ASFS played a leading role in bringing the gospel to the waterfront and seeking to reform the lives of its denizens.[20]

Why were sailors such "objects of Christian compassion"? The ministers, of course, pointed to the Bible. They repeatedly cited Psalm 107 as indicating that men of the sea had a special relationship to God: "That they that go down to the sea in ships, that do business in great waters; these see the work of the Lord, and his wonders of the deep." Pastors like the Reverend Abiel Abbot, preaching to Beverly fishermen before they headed to the Grand Banks for the March run in 1804, also highlighted the fact that Jesus Christ recruited many of his disciples among the fishermen in the Sea of Galilee.[21] These religious connections were reinforced by a belief that "there is no place in the world, where a man feels his own insignificance and dependence upon the almighty God more than at sea, and no where his goodness and mercy more evident."[22] The danger of the occupation, where a man's life depended upon his balance aloft, meant that every lurch of the sea could bring death and a meeting with his Maker.[23] The sailor was "exposed to the storm and the tempest" and "how often is his frail bark destroyed, and all of his property scattered by the winds of heaven?" Worse, "many who left their friends and their native land . . . have been suddenly and unexpectedly summoned into the world of spirits."[24] This image evoked a certain sympathy from a middle class that devoured the literature of Romanticism emphasizing the awesomeness of God and the unpredictability of nature.[25]

Reformers believed that Jack Tar also had some special attributes that made him particularly well suited as an object of missionary zeal. While decrying some aspects of the sailor's behavior, the middle class often had an overromanticized notion of the sailor. "Rough and weather-beaten as the poor mariners commonly are," reformers believed that "it sometime happens that an exquisitely tender heart lies under this rugged exterior."[26] One contributor to the *Sailor's Magazine* queried, "Who does not love the sailor? Who is not willing to acknowledge that, taking them as a class, there breathes not a more noble, generous, and self-sacrificing set of men?"[27] This sentimental image could be taken to extremes. The 1832 report of the New-York Bible Society extolled these virtues of the seaman by declaring that "the sailor converted, is a *sailor still*—the creature of feeling—moved by impulses from the *heart* rather than the *head*—strong and ardent in his attachments—generous to a fault." The report even wistfully expressed envy for some values that the middle class had rejected. "Unschooled in the cold, selfish principles and practices of the civilized, and we regret to say, *christianized* society, he deals out his favors with no miserly or reluctant hand—his last shilling he cannot refuse to a suffering comrade; and in the accomplishment of his purposes, no difficulties can discourage—no dangers intimidate him." Such charity and energy, it was hoped, could be turned to evangelical purposes.[28] As another reformer explained, sailors were a wholehearted class of people. "If they are engaged in the pursuit of sinful pleasure, they go into it with a whole heart. And just so if they engage in the cause of religion. They do nothing by the halves."[29]

What sailors did with their liberty ashore was also important. The repentant seaman's sins almost brought him closer to God: "When the Savior subdues their rebellion and impenitence, their expressions of gratitude to God and the instruments of their conversion, are more affecting than those of almost any other class of converts."[30] Jack Tar was such a good sinner that he seemed the perfect candidate for reform. His list of sins included "habits of intemperate drinking," gambling, swearing, and "intimately interwoven with intoxication and profaneness, is the sin of lewdness."[31] Christian sailors eagerly confessed their evil ways. One seaman stood up at a prayer meeting and declared that he had spent twenty-two years in sin and had "profaned the name of God without any remorse of conscience; grog shops and places of dissipation were my only places of resort; I considered intemperance no crime." Another admitted that the "company of the gambler, cardplayer, and tipler was his delight" before he found peace with God.[32] In a way, it was the very things that made the stereotypical sailor a man of the sea that made him an object of reform: drinking, swearing, ignoring the Sabbath, and consorting with evil women. With reckless living came reckless spending. All of this seemed to violate the very essence of middle-class values. And yet this behavior, placed in the context of the story of the prodigal son, could pull on the heartstrings of the middle class. A captain reported that before members of his crew became true Christians, they "had neglected their parents and friends for a long time." Once converted, "they felt very anxious to return to them" and, he believed, "they did return like the prodigal son to his father's house."[33] Reform publications were packed with stories of the return of the prodigal to the patient, loving, and forgiving arms of both mother and father, or sentimental portraits of mothers dying and lamenting the separation of the sailor son.[34] The sailor could thus be both an example of the shattering of the bonds of familial affection for the middle class, and an example of reconciliation with the family thereby affirming middle-class values.

While sometimes romanticizing the sailor's life and using him as a vehicle to express middle-class sentimentalized values, reformers recognized the waterfront as an alien environment. "Large portions of society," as one reform publication put it, considered sailors "as a distinct caste or order of beings."[35] Edward Dorr Griffin told his New York congregation, as he was trying to raise money for the Mariner's Church, that they had not made sailors welcome in their religious services. He did not really blame them for this lack of charity because "the vast republic of men who have their dwellings on the sea, constitutes in many respects a world by itself." These men had their own laws, and were "connected by a different language." Their "peculiar dress" also set them apart. They therefore needed their own religious establishment where they could feel welcome.[36] To be a missionary on the waterfront, then, was almost like traveling to Africa to minister to the Hottentots, or sail to the South Seas and work with the natives of Oahu. The difference was that the waterfront was just around the block, almost next door. And the object of reform might well be transformed by middle-class values and religion into a more recognizable entity.

Cleaning up the people of the waterfront would improve urban society in general. As one reform advocate put it, the sailor's "profaneness, debauchery, drunkenness, and contempt of the Sabbath, vices to which they are much addicted, have a most ruinous effect on the morals of our cities, and principal seaport towns."[37] From this perspective, preaching the gospel to seamen would "purify our cities" because "in every sea-port there is a large class of people of the most degraded character, whose support depended almost entirely upon the vicious habits of Seamen."[38] Without waterfront customers, some reformers believed, prostitution itself might go away. Convince Jack Tar to observe the Sabbath, and the holy day would be kept sacred throughout the city. Purge the seaman of his oaths, and the young would not have the most egregious examples of taking the name of the Lord in vain.[39] By the mid-1840s, after more than two decades of proselytizing, the *Sailor's Magazine* credited a decline in crime among sailors to the missionary efforts.[40]

Seamen's reform also had global implications. Placing the Bible in the hands of seamen would mean that "you have nailed the banner of the cross to every mast—you have erected the altar of devotion in every cabin," which then could be taken across oceans to foreign countries.[41] By the early nineteenth century Americans were trading around the world, contacting peoples who might be ripe for missionary activity. Without seamen, would-be missionaries could not travel to exotic places in the Pacific or to Africa and Asia. And as reports from foreign parts made clear, the unchristian behavior of Jack Tar easily corrupted natives and counteracted the work of the missionaries. Christian sailors, in contrast—men who did not drink, or swear, or misbehave on shore—could serve as role models for any native convert.[42] A circular report from the New-York Bethel Union explained, "No body of men, from the nature of their employment, are so well calculated to carry the glad tidings of salvation to distant lands, and to the isles of the sea, as christian seamen."[43]

On a pragmatic level, there was a certain calculating and self-serving rationale behind the middle-class concern for the sailor. Convert the waterfront to middle-class values, including sobriety and the work ethic, and you have a more compliant labor force. The author of one article on the salvation of seamen declared that "the morality of the Gospel" makes men "honest and happy in the present world," and argued that "the Gospel forbids every vice, and commands every virtue." Converting sailors would make them honest and truly happy. The author continued, "Now, it can never be a matter of indifference with commercial men, whether they commit a valuable cargo to the hands of honest men or to the hands of rogues and swindlers."[44] As W. P. Grinnell put it, "orders have been broken and voyages ruined" by intemperance.[45] The Marine Bible Society of New-York reminded merchants and captains of "the ships which have been wrecked, . . . the property which has been wasted, and . . . the lives which have been lost, through the superstition, the intemperance, the insubordination, and other misconduct of Seamen."[46] Captain Moses Hillard cast the same point in a more positive light. On a voyage in 1833 he served no liquor, distributed tracts and copies of the *Sailor's Magazine*, and held religious services. He reported that there was no swearing and that no one left the ship while visiting foreign ports. In fact, he declared that his men "have been a healthy, able, and peaceable crew, and they have done more work and done it better than I ever had a rum crew do."[47] By the 1830s a relationship emerged between temperance reformers and the insurance industry. The merchants and whaleship owners of New Bedford met in the Merchants Insurance Office in May 1830 to organize the New-Bedford Port Society, hoping to reform their workforce and reduce insurance rates.[48] In 1845 the American Seamen's Friend Society recognized this connection and collected $2,000 in contributions from four insurance companies. Zebedee Cook, Jr., president of the Mutual Safety Insurance Company, saw this donation as "the best investment" the company had made. He observed, "if it does not yield to the Company an annual interest, it does better, it reinsures the risks that the Company has assumed and adds greatly to their security."[49] In short, reform was good business.

Whatever the reasoning, reformers developed a specific program to transform the waterfront and make it in their own image with a middle-class definition of liberty. Central to this endeavor was bringing Christianity to the waterfront. Conversion would lead to a change in behavior, wiping away the sin that seemed to permeate maritime society. Reformers launched attacks on a variety of cultural practices like drinking and swearing and sought to destroy institutions like the boardinghouse, which they maintained helped to keep seaman in a state of virtual bondage. In turn, reformers supported ministers like Henry Chase, built mariner's churches in port after port, and created institutions like seaman's homes and savings banks to replace boardinghouses. Reaching beyond the waterfront, reformers also supported removing the grog ration and elimination of corporal punishment aboard ships. In all, this sweeping program sought to utterly alter the landscape and seascape of the American maritime world.

Everything hinged on religious revival. At first, reformers thought that all that they had to do was get the Bible into the hands of seamen, and once the word of God was revealed to the sailors, they would be converted. For this reason Henry Chase reported if a family had a Bible in his visits along the waterfront. The early efforts at reform began with Bible societies. But Bibles proved expensive. The Marine Bible Society of New-York, for example, could provide only a few hundred Bibles a year.[50] Reformers therefore concentrated on printed tracts with shorter religious stories. Chase distributed 166 tracts in one month.[51] Some waterfront ministers kept records of the number of tracts compared to Bibles they distributed. The Reverend William Yates of Charleston's Mariner's Church reported in 1837 that he handed out fifty thousand pages of tracts, and only thirty Bibles and ten testaments.[52] Moses How of New Bedford claimed that in one year in the 1840s he gave out 383 Bibles, 1,148 testaments, and about 10,000 newspapers, tracts, and pamphlets.[53] The American Tract Society asserted that in 1830 it had distributed 20,000 tracts in the frigate *Brandywine*, 30,000 in the sloop of war *Falmouth*, 28,000 in the sloop *Erie*, 20,000 in the sloop *Peacock*, and 14,500 in the *Shark*.[54] Some of the tracts, like *The Shipmates* by Richard Marks, originally published in Great Britain, strove to echo the sailor's language to reach its audience.[55] Others used the story line to catch Jack's attention. In *A Sailor's*

Tribute of Gratitude to Two Virtuous Women, Jack Carleton, the hero, willingly defended a young woman in the clutches of an ill-spirited tar, and despite an affinity for rum and bad company obtained redemption by reading the Bible. He became a Christian only as his poverty-stricken sweetheart dies. This tale played to the sympathies of the sailor, while revealing a familiarity with life and death on the waterfront.[56] Richard Henry Dana, Jr., held that "there is nothing which will gain a sailor's attention sooner, and interest him more deeply, than a tract, especially one which contains a story."[57] Occasionally the *Sailor's Magazine* commented on the effectiveness of a particular tract.[58] Many of the people visited by Chase and other mariner preachers responded positively to the tracts he distributed. At one point Chase noted in his diary that one widow he visited liked the last tract that he had given her so much that she lent it to her friends.[59]

Handing out religious literature was not enough to convert the waterfront. By the 1840s reformers were supporting ministers like Chase and How in almost every seaport. The annual report of the ASFS in 1850 included information about activities in Hawaii, China, Brazil, France, Sweden, the West Indies, and Chile overseas, and domestic operations in New Orleans, Mobile, Savannah, Charleston, Norfolk, Baltimore, Philadelphia, New York, Boston, Portland, and several inland locations.[60] The men who served as missionaries in these and other ports often expanded their activities. How kept a record of seven thousand seamen who sailed from New Bedford in 1846, and received and sent more than five hundred letters from almost every corner of the earth.[61] Equally important was the building of mariner's churches like the one on Roosevelt Street. These institutions were geared specifically for a maritime audience. The New Bedford pulpit, immortalized by Herman Melville and which can still be visited today, was shaped in the form of a ship's bow to reinforce the maritime connection. Sermons like the one preached by Melville's Father Mapple were often packed with nautical metaphors, the most common of which identified the Bible as a pilot to guide seamen through life's stormy seas. Occasionally a minister unknowingly misapplied the sailor's language, like the preacher "who exhorted his hearers to splice the main-brace," which meant for Jack Tar that the minister was recommending a glass of grog. Men such as Father Taylor in Boston, who like Melville's Mapple had served some time afloat and used nautical language, could be very effective. The *Sailor's Magazine* would sometimes reprint such sermons and reported on efforts to convert sailors worldwide.[62]

As reformers created their own institutions, they began to look around them and see what maritime institutions stood in their way. In the earliest phases of their activity Henry Chase and others tried to work with boardinghouse keepers. After attending prayer meetings at several boardinghouses, Chase reported that some landlords were willing to operate on temperance principles, distribute tracts, and even encourage attendance at the Mariner's Church.[63] One of the first things that the New-Bedford Port Society did was to create a committee to visit the city's boardinghouses to check on conditions there and to determine if any would be responsive to a temperance appeal.[64] However, reformers quickly came to believe that these key waterfront institutions were the fountainhead from which all evil flowed. When one boardinghouse keeper approached Chase after a prayer meeting during the 1822 yellow fever epidemic and told him that "he brought all of his boarders with him and wished he was a Christian," Chase responded that he should "be more solicitous to save their souls than to empty their pockets."[65] One reformer declared that boardinghouses "to an alarming extent" were "houses of almost every species of low and vulgar dissipation." The writer cautioned that "If the sailor would otherwise be a sober and moral man, here he is allured and hurried from one vice to another." He is taken "from gambling to profaneness, from profaneness to drunkenness, and from drunkenness to lewdness, till he has neither morals, property, nor reputation remaining." The grasping landsharks who ran the boardinghouses "are often made the depositaries of the sailor's wages when he comes on shore." The landlord "give promises, and inspire confidence, that the money deposited shall be faithfully preserved; but these promises are often most wickedly violated, and this confidence most basely betrayed."[66] Reformers portrayed the complicated symbiotic relationship between the sailor and the landlord in the darkest of colors. They also attacked the system of advancing a month's wages to a sailor who had just signed the articles for his next voyage. The idea of receiving money for work not yet performed irked middle-class reformers and, so they argued, allowed the landlord to take advantage of the sailor. As described by the reformers, what was often a mutually beneficial arrangement became a form of bondage that limited the sailor's freedom. In 1829 the *Sailor's Magazine* reported, "The landlord first encourages, or at least permits" the mariner to run up a little debt. "Then he lets him go deeper and deeper, until it will do to strike." With little choice now that he was in the clutches of the landlord, "poor Jack must ship, just how and where Mr. Landlord chooses to send him." To recover his loan, the landlord collected the advance. The sailor thus had to work his first month aboard ship for nothing.

Reformers believed that this power of the landlord left the sailor "in a condition akin to slavery." This connection was often made explicit and reflected a middle-class understanding of liberty that emphasized free labor and the right of each individual to negotiate his own work contract. Through the boardinghouse system of recruitment the sailor "thereby parts with his liberty, and becomes a slave to his creditor. In fact, the whole business of shipping a crew is often a good deal like a bargain and sale, where the landlord brings his slaves to market, and sells them to the highest bidder."[67] As another article concluded, "It is manifest therefore, that the seaman will never be a freeman, until the whole system is broken up," and sailors were paid, as are others, only after they have earned it.[68] Similar charges were repeated by others. With the landlord identified as the devil incarnate and his boardinghouse a hell on earth, regardless of how these characterizations reflected reality, reformers had their target.[69]

To counter the effects of boardinghouses reformers began to create institutions that could replace them. Since sailors had ordinarily placed their wages with boarding housekeepers, who then allowed them to run up a tab until they were in debt, and since sailors were renowned for their wastefulness, reformers advocated frugality and supported the establishment of seamen's savings banks as a safe depository for a sailor's wages. Repeatedly, reform publications reminded readers of the benefits of saving. One article quoted Benjamin Franklin's Poor Richard stating, "Six pounds a year is but a groat a day: and small sums are the constituent parts of greater." To save, however, meant that the sailor had to avoid the theater, lottery, superfluous dress, dram drinking, and "needless vicious pleasures."[70] The Reverend M'cartee argued that "One of the great causes of immorality among sailors is the sudden influx of means to indulge in every vicious propensity" when sailors return from a voyage. He believed that if seamen had a savings bank, "you will not only withdraw the temptation, and the means of its gratification, but you will also give a strong inducement to prudence in their expenditures, and self-denial in their desires."[71] Inspired by ideas like these, a group of merchants, captains, and other businessmen organized the New York Seaman's Savings Bank in 1829. The bank paid either 5 or 6 percent interest, depending on the size of the account, and was limited to conservative investments like government bonds. The directors were prevented by its charter of incorporation from borrowing its money for their own financial schemes. At first the bank was ridiculed for being devoted to a class of society not noted for frugality, but its deposits steadily grew. By 1841 it held $200,000 and by 1850 that figure had grown to $1 million. Stories about the bank emphasized the benefits a sailor would gain by saving. By making regular deposits, a seaman would have funds for old age or to carry him through a disability. Perhaps of even more importance were the moral implications of saving: "a handsome sum in the bank" not only served as "an antidote against the despair which a sailor feels when destitute of cash and friends," but it also "prompts to self-respect, to industrious habits, and is both a motive and a pledge for his moral improvement." The hope was that a savings account would free the sailor from the round of debt bondage dictated by the boardinghouse and be a path to middle-class values.[72]

A more direct effort at replacing the boardinghouse was by building seamen's homes that would provide a temperance haven for the sailor. As early as 1824 reformers began calling for Christian boardinghouses where morality would reign and where there would be libraries with the proper literature for the entertainment and edification of the seaman.[73] Reformers thereafter began to take notice of the regular boardinghouses that did not serve liquor and provided a godly and upright atmosphere for the sailor.[74] Such establishments seldom lasted long. Reformers opened temperance boardinghouses in the 1830s in several ports including Charleston (the first), Portland, Boston, Providence, and Baltimore.[75] As a temporary measure the ASFS rented a boardinghouse at 140 Cherry Street in New York, which opened in October 1837. To accommodate more than the thirty to fifty sailors ordinarily lodged in this building the ASFS leased a second boardinghouse in 1838. These measures, while making some inroads, were meant as a stopgap during the financially depressed late 1830s.[76] In October 1841 the ASFS laid the cornerstone of a new Sailor's Home that would act as a permanent bastion of Christianity and a boardinghouse for seamen "along one of the thoroughfares of profligacy which has hitherto been upon the right hand and the left, a trap to ensnare" the seaman. Amid what middle-class New Yorkers considered "the very depths of wickedness, a temple of virtue and of honesty" was to be built "as a monument not only to the liberality of New-York, but of the reformation of the age." Reformers had great hopes for this "noble enterprise," believing that it would bring "sobriety . . . where drunkenness was before, and where the words of profanity and desecration have oftenest been heard, they will be spoken no more."[77] The completed building was five stories high with 150 rooms, enough for three hundred seamen, but had difficulty in sustaining itself. The ASFS therefore continued to subsidize its operations in the belief that it was not simply a moneymaking operation, like other boardinghouses—it was an instrument of reform. Oddly, because the Sailor's Home took in destitute seamen it often loaned money against the advance of future wages. It was thereby guilty of the very practice reformers had condemned in other boarding houses. Again, the rationale was charity: a shipwrecked or homeless sailor could not be turned away. If work was scarce, as it was the winter after

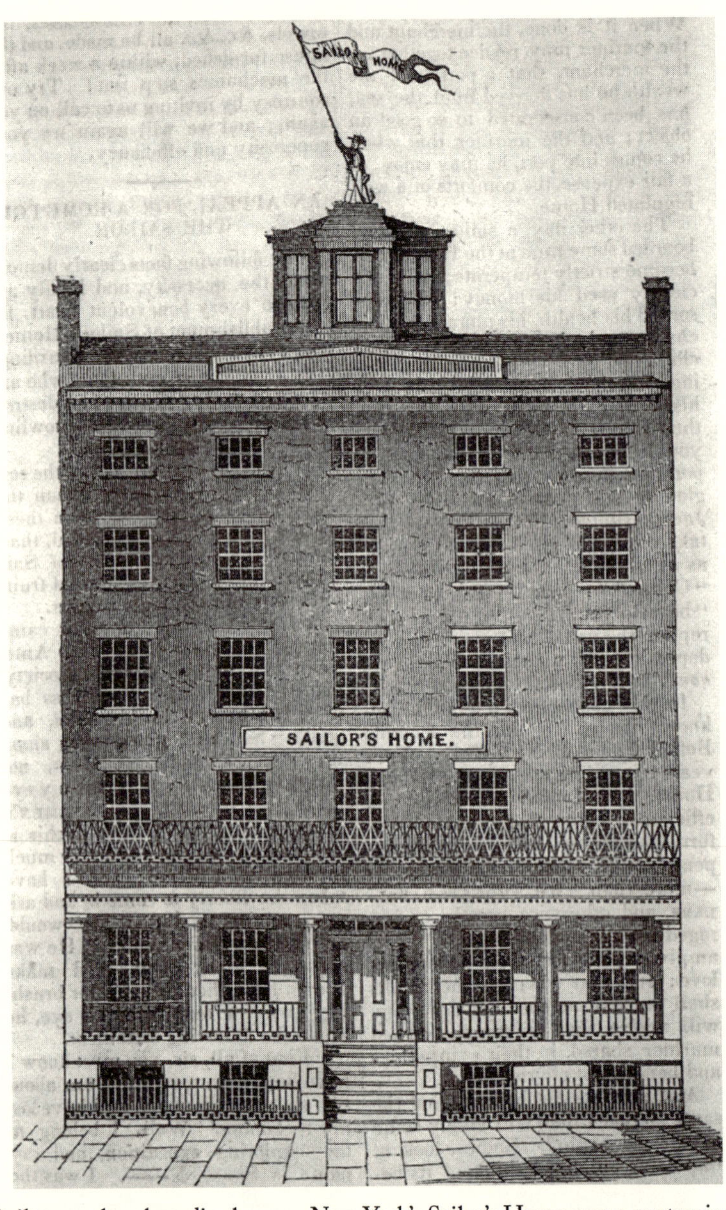

34. Built to replace boardinghouses, New York's Sailor's Home was a centerpiece of the effort to reform sailors. *Sailor's Magazine* (Sept. 1836). Kendall Whaling Museum.

the home opened, the Sailor's Home extended several thousand dollars and established an account with each sailor "to be paid out of future earnings."[78] The benefits, as far as the ASFS was concerned, outweighed other considerations. In fact, within a few years the Sailor's Home could report that it was holding prayer meetings and that as many as one-third of the boarders signed temperance pledges. Equally important, a large number of the boarders dressed neatly and husbanded "both their time and their money," maintained the Sabbath, and commenced "a life of prayer."[79]

This idea of having a Sailor's Home continued to spread. Within New York, the ASFS sponsored a smaller "Coloured Sailor's Home" in 1839. The only temperance house for African Americans during the 1840s, it struggled to meet its bills. Efforts to put it on an independent footing were not successful. As the "Coloured Sailor's Home" provided a Christian shelter with "moral and religious advantages" for several hundred African Americans each year, the ASFS provided a subsidy.[80] The Boston Seamen's Friend Society built a new Sailor's Home in 1845 that had ninety-one rooms and could accommodate one hundred and fifty sailors at a time.[81] By 1849 additional Sailor's Homes were established in Buffalo, Providence, Philadelphia, Alexandria, Washington, D.C., and Mobile. The *Sailor's Magazine* also identified eleven temperance and Christian private boardinghouses in New York and others in Bath, Maine, Portsmouth, New Hampshire, Salem, Massachusetts, Bristol, Rhode Island, New Bedford (including the only other such house dedicated to African Americans), New Haven, Charleston, Savannah, and New Orleans.[82]

Reformers did not forget the waterfront families. In 1832, following a pattern established in the 1790s, New York middle-class women organized the Female Bethel Association dedicated to providing charity for widows and the immediate relief of poor sailor families. In 1844 the society reorganized itself into the Mariner's Family Industrial Society with a slightly broader mission. Now the women reformers hoped not only to offer charity, but also to provide employment for the destitute women of the maritime community. They intended to relieve "poverty and its attendant evils by *appropriately rewarding honest industry*" by having women sew and provide bags and clothing for seamen to purchase before a voyage. They would thus "encourage the industrious poor" and "make the hearth cheerful and the heart glad of the sick and infirm." In its first annual report the society described several of the women they helped. Mrs. R was the perfect object of their benevolence, demonstrating "*habits of industry*, and a feeling of *self-dependence*." She had to provide for four children, and her husband had been out to sea almost a year and was feared lost. She came to the store to obtain some work. While waiting she saw other women leave with money and no work. She then "burst into tears and rose to depart," determined to go home and tell her children "that they must *starve*, for their mother could not beg." One of the representatives of the society stopped her, and, after discovering that she was too proud to take charity, promised to bring her work the next day. She sewed for the society all that winter; then her husband miraculously returned. At that point, and thanks to the Mariner's Family Industrial Society, she declared, "Oh, I could look my husband in the face and say, I have not disgraced you by asking alms." The organization struggled throughout the 1840s, however, because it paid wages that made its products more expensive than what could be purchased in other dockside slop shops. As a report in 1846 made clear, "the universal propensity to patronize the cheapest market," a concept that every middle-class businessman depended on, prevented the society from becoming self-sustaining and forced it to rely on donations. Repeatedly the society appealed for money from merchants and those who could afford it. The society also asked sailors to remember the women in their own lives and patronize the society's shop despite the higher prices.[83]

All of these efforts at reform sought to transform life and the concept of liberty on the waterfront. Through the distribution of Bibles and tracts, religious services, visits by ministers, creation of savings banks, opening Sailor Homes, and offering work and aid to women, evangelical reformers hoped not only to spread the gospel, but to change life in seaports. Temperance, observing the Sabbath, and wholesome living would go hand in hand with industry and thrift. Reformers, however, did not limit themselves to the land; they also strove to reach into the forecastle and alter the work environment at sea. They wanted the sailor to espouse the same middle-class values taught in the Mariner's Church and Sailor's Home while manning the capstain or bending the sails. To pursue these ends reformers supplied ships with Bibles, testaments, and other reading matter, opposed swearing and profanation of the Sabbath, and attacked the traditional grog ration. Although in many ways reformers sought to alter maritime culture and impose their own conception of liberty at sea, the belief in the perfectibility of man and the concern with the individual—both legacies of the revolution—led to an attack on the use of the lash and ultimately to a call for the protection of sailors' rights.

The Bible, along with other appropriate reading material, was supposed to work the same magic at sea that it did on land. The ASFS included in one of its annual reports a story of a seaman who took a "Bible, a hymn book, and

Baxter's Saint's Rest" with him to sea. These works changed his life, and also had an impact on others in the crew. "One night as he sat reading the Saint's Rest, he was so afflicted with a sense of his sins as to cry aloud for mercy." Once he found peace for his own soul, "he communicated his new views and feelings to two or three others who met with him in the dogwatch, from six to eight, for prayer." The tide of religion did not stop there. "Soon the mate became interested, then the captain, and before the voyage closed, the cabin was their house of prayer, and all on board apparently the subjects of renewing grace."[84] It was to this end that evangelical reformers gave Bibles and tracts to families on the waterfront and to seamen aboard ships. The New-Bedford Port Society believed that reading was so important that it set up a committee in 1833 to determine how many books were being sent on the whalers that left port.[85] Just bringing books was not enough. The type of reading material also mattered. Along the waterfront book hawkers sold "trash made for seamen," comprised of "song books, dream books, extravagant romances, licentious stories and pictures." The books were "usually of the worst description," including works like *Tales of the Ocean*, *Horrible Murders*, *Mysteries of Paris*, and *The Pirates Own Book*.[86] "Almost every sea-chest is supplied with some of this scum of the 'polite literature'" that was intended to "fill the imagination with scenes of debauchery and blood." Good books, like those written by John Bunyan, Richard Baxter, and John Flavel, despite their age, offered guidance for the sailor.[87] Creating libraries and providing opportunities for educating seamen would have a great impact: "Instead of a mere *brute animal* which many foremast hands now are[,] you will be able to point with generous pride to seeing citizens feeling that they are *men*." Ultimately, there was always the Bible itself. Few things could have warmed the heart of an evangelical reformer more than the sailor who reported putting away his novels and romances and reading his Bible on his path to a conversion experience.[88]

Evangelicals believed that religion at sea would be impossible to sustain as long as sailors took the name of the Lord in vain. Middle-class reformers therefore urged seaman to abandon swearing. "Where the name of God is constantly used with lightness and irreverence," argued one tract writer, "it is impossible that men should feel as they ought towards this greatest and best of all beings." This author continued, "the habit of profane swearing is a constant insult offered to God, and it makes the heart hard and wholly indifferent to religion." Worse, since seamen were susceptible to the elements, which were after all at God's disposal, it was "horrible" that sailors swore.[89] A Christian seaman advised his shipmates that to swear was no better "than if in a dreadful storm, when the red lightening was flashing and hissing along the

35. Evangelicals hoped to reach sailors on board ship as well as along the waterfront. "The Bethel Meeting." *Sailor's Magazine* (Dec. 1841). Kendall Whaling Museum.

deep, ye should dare the Almighty to strike you with his thunderbolt."[90] An evangelical reformer asserted that "the swearer is in a lost state . . . a state of condemnation." He also believed that "the swearer is forgetful of God" and the interests of his own soul. There could not be stronger proof of a sinner's alienation of heart from God than "profaning His name."[91] Sailors who experienced religion almost uniformly pointed to their blasphemous language before conversion as a signpost of their own depravity. In a world in which language was usually punctuated with curses, there was no surer evidence of evangelical Christianity for middle-class reformers or converted seamen than refusing to swear.

Reformers wanted seamen to keep the Sabbath holy and avoid all work. Obviously a ship at sea had to have some adjustments to rigging made, depending upon wind and water. Short of the absolute basics, however, reformers wanted to free Sundays for reflections on the Almighty. They believed that there was no reason to sail from port on Sunday, and even urged that whaleships should not lower boats to catch whales on the Sabbath. If there was some loss of work for the captain, it was more than compensated by both spiritual and material gain. Religious services would benefit the crew and add to the "comfort and happiness" of the master by promoting "a spirit of *subordination* and *obedience*," because "in proportion as men are brought to regard God, they are inclined to perform their duties to one another." Reformers saw a connection between respecting "a Master in heaven" and cheerfully yielding "obedience to their earthly superiors."[92]

Evangelicals also called for temperance aboard ships. For reformers the grog ration stood as the sailor's "daily sin—his prevailing temper—his flattering, false friend—his associate in joy—his refuge in grief—and the prime source of all the errors and evils that befall him."[93] The idea that men who worked the nation's ships, who were trusted with the nation's defense and commerce, daily imbibed spirits violated middle-class sensibilities. Repeatedly mutiny and disobedience were blamed on grog. In fact, naval records suggest that drunkenness aboard ship, which in the reformer's mind was connected to the official policy of doling out grog, often led to punishment at sea. As one letter to the *Sailor's Magazine* explained, "it is the judgement of the great majority of naval officers, that *intemperance alone* is the cause of nine-tenths of the degradation and wretchedness that occur on board our national vessels and at our different stations."[94] That men had to face storms while under the influence, that they had to climb high into the rigging of a rolling vessel, and that they navigated across the trackless sea with their head abuzz with alcohol struck terror into middle-class hearts. Shipwrecks and death at sea were often attributed to grog.[95] It also whetted the appetite for binge drinking on shore. As one article attacking the grog ration in the navy explained: "Twice a day for three years," the normal period of enlistment in the 1840s, "forms a habit which, in the long run, will not be satisfied with anything short of inebriation, at almost every opportunity." Finally, and most important for evangelicals, grog jeopardized a sailor's immortal soul.[96]

Starting in the late 1820s reformers began to pressure ship captains and merchants to abandon the grog ration. By the early 1830s many vessels sailed without the accustomed alcohol provision. Merchants quickly realized that this would be a nice cost-cutting measure, although sailor advocates hoped either that the grog would be replaced by coffee and sugar or that money would be added to wages. In May 1830 the *Sailor's Magazine* reported that over thirty vessels had left Boston pledged to temperance and the same journal declared that seventy-five of ninety-seven vessels that had left New Bedford had no alcohol in their holds.[97] Reformers recognized that getting captains and merchants to comply with a temperance platform was only half the battle. They also urged sailors to renounce the grog ration themselves. In 1831 Secretary of the Navy Levi Woodbury ordered that any sailor who did not line up by the grog tub was to be compensated six cents per serving.[98] In the spirit of middle-class frugality "The Cabin Boy's Locker," a section in the *Sailor's Magazine* devoted to young seamen, pointed out that this practice after forty years at sea would amount to savings with interest of $3,500. Such a princely sum for any common seaman would be enough to retire on.[99] By the 1840s, reflecting decades of evangelical effort, some common seamen in the navy had begun to organize temperance societies, signing abstinence pledges by the hundreds, and even participating in public processions where the sailors marched through the streets with a grog tub turned upside down.[100] Simultaneously, the campaign against grog worked its way through official channels sponsored by high-ranking naval officers and members of Congress. Reformers were outraged by the idea that the government first "mingled and mixed" and then placed the "cup of insidious poison" on the sailor's lips. Despite the vehemence of this language, despite memorials and petitions, and despite debates in Congress itself, the grog ration was not abolished until the Civil War.[101]

Connected to the "evil" of the grog ration was the "evil" of flogging. Both degraded the sailor in government service and aboard the merchant marine. For reformers the two practices were related, even if many sailors found solace in one and nothing good in the other. The grog ration was believed to be the "cause of a large amount of insubordination on ship board." Once "the *grog tub*" was set aside, "the occasion for flogging will be diminished if not entirely done away." Both were "illy sorted . . . for intellectual and moral improvement," and somehow seemed un-American and not representative of a republic that cherished liberty. Banishing flogging and grog, however, would mean that "the *person* of an American citizen" was protected "and his *proper manhood* rendered inviolate."[102] Both customs treated the sailor as an animal and denied his humanity. Flogging, especially, ran counter to the belief in the perfectibility of mankind so central to middle-class reformers. The process of dehumanization was simple and had the character of a self-fulfilling prophecy—"after being flogged" the sailor "feels degraded below the recovering point: he feels that he has been treated like a brute, and now appears to forget that he is a man, or that he is entitled to the consideration of a man." The result was that "his subsequent conduct is very like to correspond with his *assumed* position." At the end of this process, the flogged sailor is scarred for life and his health is injured. He does not correct his behavior because, as one officer explained, "a fear of the *cats* never deters a sailor from intoxication." Moreover, it leads to hatred "and even rebellious feelings which rankle in the breasts of sailors toward their officers," causing more insubordination and even mutiny.[103]

Flogging had been an accepted practice in the American navy since the Revolutionary War.[104] By 1831 reformer criticism, however, began to take its toll, and Navy Secretary Levi Woodbury mandated some restrictions on flogging. He ordered that captains were not to exceed the legal number of lashes, even if the punishment was for more than one offense, and, to prevent abuse by junior officers, he insisted that all punishment must be under the supervision of the commanding officer. Finally, he recommended that captains substitute "pecuniary fines, badges of disgrace, and other mild correction" for flogging. In 1840 President Martin Van Buren sought even more regulation by ordering officers to keep track of the use of the lash and report the nature of the offense, extent of the punishment, and provide an explanation for the commanding officer's judgment. In short, officers no longer had total discretionary power since they now had to explain their actions to a higher authority.[105] In a further step limiting corporal punishment, in 1845 Secretary of the Navy George Bancroft directed that there could be no flogging without written orders of the commanding officer.[106] These official actions divided the officer corps between those committed to continuing use of the lash and those who sided with the reformers. At times this division led to some awkward situations. During the cruise of the USS *Congress* in 1845–46, Captain Samuel Francis Du Pont and Commodore Robert F. Stockton found themselves at cross purposes. Du Pont believed that the cat-o'-nine-tails was the best road to discipline, whereas his superior officer was a navy innovator and advocated other forms of punishment.[107]

Debate also arose in Washington in 1848–50 and 1852 along sectional lines. Northern reformers, led by New Hampshire Senator John Parker Hale, pushed for ending flogging altogether. Hale, and many of his supporters, espoused middle-class ideals of liberty and viewed society as composed of free individuals (a position that would become the cornerstone of the Republican political party by the late 1850s). This free labor ideology compelled them to oppose flogging in the navy and African American slavery in the South, holding that both prevented individuals from fulfilling their potential. They believed that, given the choice, man would improve himself. Southerners had a more pessimistic understanding of human nature and saw the antiflogging campaign as part of the antislavery crusade, and an example of the "hyper-philanthropy" that contaminated the North. They believed that since sailors were "vicious and wicked" in nature, and were often foreigners or immigrants, nothing but the lash would keep them under control. Flooded with 271 petitions and memorials, and supported by public meetings in several northern cities, Congress abolished flogging in the U.S. Navy in 1850.[108]

This act also abolished flogging on vessels of commerce. By that time, many of the same pressures that had begun to limit the practice of flogging in the navy had some impact on private shipping as well. At the beginning of the nineteenth century flogging was a part of the repertoire of discipline available to any captain of a merchant ship. Most masters used it intermittently, as it was a sure way to alienate a crew and guarantee the loss of seamen upon arriving at the next port. The assault on flogging by reformers in the 1820s and 1830s made it even more difficult for captains to resort to flogging. "A Sailor's Friend" in 1829 blamed most problems at sea on overbearing officers. This author thought "the officers are most culpable, because they are prone to abuse their power, which is the most absolute of any known in civilized society." If a sailor was treated with kindness and taught religion, the author believed, he would naturally respond.[109] Dana's *Two Years Before the Mast* only intensified opposition to corporal punishment. Dana showed how an abusive captain's sadistic tendencies were whetted by asserting his authority with the end of a rope. In this stirring portrait both the captain and the sailor were dehumanized—when the sailor objected to being punished like a slave, the captain angrily retorted, "then I'll make you one," and compared himself to a slave driver. Dana also made it clear that there was no justice in this system, and little recourse for Jack Tar. He asked, "what is there for sailors to do?" His answer: not much. "If they resist, it is mutiny; and if they succeed, and take the vessel, it is piracy. If they ever yield again, their punishment must come; and if they do not yield, they are pirates for life." Resisting the captain was resisting the law, "and piracy or submission, are his only alternatives."[110] Dana, however, was a little disingenuous, or was at least taking some poetic license. By the 1830s and 1840s captains became increasingly constrained by the fact that sailors were becoming more aware of their rights and seeking legal recourse once they reached port. In fact, Dana gained a reputation among seamen in the 1840s as a lawyer who frequently defended sailors who had suffered physical abuse from a captain on a voyage.[111]

There were several reasons for the increased awareness of sailors' rights in the nineteenth century. Certainly the experience of political involvement before the War of 1812 and the national cry for "Free Trade and Sailors' Rights" had a big impact on the waterfront world. In the years after the Treaty of Ghent, middle-class reformers, including Dana, also helped to spread the word that Jack Tar was a citizen and had rights that needed to be protected. Evangelicals reformers made the connection between religion and liberty explicit. One reformer declared, "Thanks be to God, the happy day is very near when '*Holiness to the Lord*' shall be inscribed on every vessel, and the Bethel flag shall be the best protection of '*free trade and sailors' rights*.'"[112] At times the evangelicals merely talked about rights in relationship to reform. "A Short Sermon," appearing in the *Sailor's Magazine*, took as its text "Free Trade and Sailors' Rights," proclaiming that the sailor had the right to refuse grog, to stay in a boardinghouse of his own choosing, and "to cease to do evil and learn to do well." The "sermon" closed with an assertion that the sailor's true rights "should be respected and secured," since they are "guaranteed by Him who made the sea and the dry land."[113] At times the reformers combined legal and religious rights, pointing out that sailors had a legal right, and a moral obligation, not to work on Sundays in a port in the State of New York.[114]

The evangelicals were also concerned with rights not directly connected to religion. One of the first issues of the *Sailor's Magazine* reported a case from the United States District Court in New York in which the mate of the *William Tell* was charged with assault and battery for hitting a sailor with a piece of wood to enforce his commands. The judge regretted that the man had not been charged with manslaughter, since the sailor subsequently died, and sentenced the mate to ten days' hard labor and a fifty-dollar fine. During the sentencing the judge asserted that "sailors have their rights, and it is only by supporting them that those in authority over them can be maintained in the exercise of their power."[115] In another case in the same court, the judge expressed similar sentiments. He admitted that the law allowed corporal punishment, while asserting that it should be avoided and that the sailor should have his pay docked instead. In the case under consideration a ship's carpenter had refused to do some menial work demanded by an officer. The judge agreed that the carpenter aboard ship was just like any other seaman and had to obey commands. If he was ordered to clean the decks, he had to do it. His only recourse was to sue later if it violated his contract. The judge also determined, however, that the punishment had been too severe and therefore fined the mate and captain.[116]

Concern with Jack Tar's rights went beyond the issue of punishment to include the various claims a seaman had on his wages.[117] "A Friend 'To Sailors' Rights'" even argued that sailors were not only "poorly paid in proportion to the amount of labor performed," but were often taken advantage by their employers. If a sailor technically ended a voyage in debt to the ship owner, "A Friend" urged that the merchant should "make out the account as conscience would dictate" and ensure that the sailor get the appropriate reward for his labor.[118] Ultimately, evangelical reform led to a recognition of the sailor as an individual and to a concern with his rights.

How did Jack Tar respond to this effort of helping him from above? How did he feel about being the "proper object of Christian compassion"? The reformers who built Mariner's Church after Mariner's Church and who repeated scores of conversion narratives would suggest that the Second Great Awakening broke over the waterfront like a huge tidal wave engulfing everything in its path. Such an impression would be misplaced. Evangelical religion did make a difference in many maritime lives and transformed liberty for some people on the waterfront. Many more were untouched by revival and remained committed to traditional notions of a sailor's liberty. If Christian reformers swept ashore like great breakers pounding against the beach, their waters quickly receded, leaving only isolated pools of converted Christians along an otherwise barren coast.

While logically it would seem that few sailors would argue with efforts to do away with flogging, that was not always the case. Richard Henry Dana, Jr., paused at the idea of a complete abolition of flogging. Yes, he detested the lash. But he declared, "I should not wish to take command of a ship to-morrow," knowing and having the crew know, "that I could not, under any circumstances inflict even moderate chastisement."[119] This, of course, was imagining what it must be like standing on the quarterdeck. It was also possible to support corporal punishment from the forecastle. One sailor reportedly objected more to being admonished by an officer than to being flogged. As the tar put it: "Talk'n is sometimes more punishment than flogg'n."[120] Some sailors viewed flogging as a manly punishment, especially compared with serving time in the brig, or humiliating measures like being forced to wear a sign or some other token of general derision.[121]

Nor did every sailor eagerly embrace sabbatarianism, even though it had the potential to ease the work week. A superstitious salt preferred to sail on a Sunday than a Friday because the latter was seen as bringing bad luck to the voyage. Fishermen and whalers might object to not dropping lines or lowering boats on Sunday, knowing that they had to take advantage of their quarry whenever it appeared. As they were paid by shares, the vessel's loss was their loss. Finally, Sunday had long been delegated as a special day for the sailor. Although he had to work the ship as needed, he was also allowed to overhaul his sea-chest and have some extra time to himself. Religious service or Bible study could well detract from a tar's own pursuits.

Other reforms more directly threatened practices many seamen considered as a part of a sailor's liberty. Cursing was such an intimate part of the seaman's argot that any effort to purge the well-placed oath would be taken as sacrilege by most Jack Tars. Many likewise opposed the elimination of grog. Dana praised the efforts of the ASFS and even supported the general notion of temperance, considering it "the best thing that ever was undertaken for the sailor." He also wrote, however, that "sailors will never be convinced that rum is a dangerous thing" if it is taken away from them and still allowed for officers. That many vessels sailed under temperance articles as "a mere saving to the owners," without substituting something in its place, only alienated the tars more, leading many to "look upon the change as a new instrument of tyranny."[122] One of the seamen aboard the USS *Independence* watched his shipmates affix their signatures to a temperance pledge. When invited to add his name to the list, he responded, "Oh no! . . . I won't sign away my liberty."[123]

One measure of evangelical efforts is the number of seamen reached by the sailor homes and mariner's churches. During the 1840s the Sailor Home in New York served about 3,500 to 4,000 seamen a year. By the mid-1840s, as many as half signed a temperance pledge, a significant number. We must remember that more than 50,000 seamen probably shipped out of New York in any given year of that decade. While some of these resided at private temperance boardinghouses or with family, the vast majority continued to patronize boardinghouses that served alcohol. Similarly, the "Coloured Sailor's Home" was lucky if it was able to provide for four hundred African American sailors, a small percentage of the almost 3,000 African Americans that called New York their home port. Reverend Henry Chase got excited if a prayer meeting included a score of seamen. A few hundred may have attended the Mariner's Church. Yet these numbers are small compared to the polyglot mixture of mankind that crowded the waterfront. By the 1840s ASFS might claim hundreds of converts on a navy receiving ship, or describe religion sweeping through any given whaling crew. Compared to the tens of thousands that shipped in the merchant service, in the whale fishery, and in the navy, the numbers appear less significant.

Some sailors, even if they agreed with the aims of the evangelicals, were hostile to the reformers. Although Nathaniel Ames admitted that the moral condition of the sailor needed improvement, he thought that the members of the tract society and other evangelicals did not know how to appeal to Jack Tar. Ames even believed that temperance should be encouraged and, since sailors were such voracious readers, Bibles distributed. He found the *Sailor's Magazine* horrid, however, calling it "an exceedingly silly periodical." The essays written for seamen were "in a style too puerile for children of five years old." He then asked: "Why will not these self-constituted reformers of morals reflect, if only for one moment, that if sailors are babes in grace, they are by no means babes in common sense?"[124] Hugh Calhoun hoped "that seamen in general would turn their thoughts to heavenward, that at the last trumpet to muster around God's throne, none may be found wanting." But he thought the sermons of the navy chaplain aboard the USS *Ohio*, 1847–48, had little impact on the crew. The minister just could not communicate with the sailors. Calhoun believed that "should any of my shipmates become converted it will be recorded as a Miracle." Calhoun concluded that "it requires something more than Rhetoric to touch Jack's feelings" and that sailors were sensitive to "language emanating from the heart of the speaker."[125]

A few sailors were more callous in their approach. Jacob Hazen resented the missionary ladies who clambered aboard a vessel in port. He described one exchange between himself and "a little missionary" while he had been placed in irons. She was distressed that he was reading a novel and tried to give him a religious tract instead. He wanted no part of such propaganda. She pursued her quarry with Christian determination. She asked him, "But you are conscious of having a soul; do you care nothing for the welfare of your immortal soul?" Having suffered many injustices as a seaman, Hazen retorted, "No, for I fear it has been damned long ago," drawing his feet off the cable, creating "a clank of the irons that made the young lady recoil." Amazed, the woman exclaimed "You astonish me . . . surely you do not mean—." Hazen then launched into his morality lesson; the morality of a hardened seaman. He said, "I *do* mean just what I say, madam, and nothing else. I am cursed daily, up and down, alow and aloft, from larboard to starboard and back again." He went on, declaring that he had been cursed a dozen times that morning by the gentleman officer so politely escorting the missionary ladies and placed in irons by his order. "Could damning have sent me to the devil, it would have been all up with me long ago, and I really question whether my situation there would be much more intolerable than it is in this ship."[126]

Beyond the problem of open hostility was the fact that so much of seafaring culture revolved around values and practices and an understanding of liberty antithetical to evangelical goals. The result was that even the good-hearted could be led astray, either as youths or as backsliding adults. Simeon Crowell went to sea in 1795, before he was twenty. Aboard a fishing vessel off the Grand Banks he described his shipmates as including "The Thief—lyar—Drunkard—Profane Swearer and Fornicator." Crowell had been a religious youth, spending time reading the Bible and John Bunyan's *Pilgrim's Progress*. Now "this wicked crew" derided him for his sobriety, and "profane swearing, Idle talk, foolish jesting, and drunkenness surrounded" him "like a flood of iniquity." Crowell "was poisoned before the voyage ended" and became "less serious" and "did not pray so constantly as formerly." Soon

1843] SAILOR'S MAGAZINE. 22

EXTRACTS FROM THE TENTH ANNUAL REPORT OF THE FEMAL
SEAMEN'S FRIEND SOCIETY, OF PHILADELPHIA.

" The conversion of the world is secured by the promise of God. Every year, as it brings us nearer the consumation of this glorious purpose, furnishes clearer evidence of its approach, in denominated a season of ingather. At no period of ten years, since the gin of this Society, have we witnes such manifestations of the power of vine grace, in bringing in so many shea

36. Middle-class women organized their own societies to raise money and help sailors and their families. "Ladies' Seamen's Friend Society." *Sailor's Magazine* (Mar. 1843). Kendall Whaling Museum.

enough, after a few more cruises, Crowell himself had become a sinner, swearing and enjoying bawdy stories. Even working his way to becoming a captain and marrying a converted Baptist did not immediately change Crowell. At times he would have religious visions and even pray, only to return to his "old trade of foolish jesting," swearing, card playing, theatergoing—all of which he later counted as sins. Crowell kept up this round of flirting with religion and then abandoning it for years, experiencing a conversion only after he had quitted the sea.[127] Others had similar experiences. James Fenimore Cooper's Ned Myers became a temperance man once he retired. After he had narrated his story to Cooper he began drinking again, hastening his own death.[128] Evangelicals like Henry Chase were fully aware of the problem of backsliding. When Peter Smith opened his soul to Chase, the minister "plainly told him of the temptations to which he would be exposed, and exhorted him to perseverance and to set a good example before his shipmates, and do all the good he can in the world."[129]

Many seamen remained serious about religion, with and without the efforts of evangelical reformers. Fisherman Joshua Gott turned to religion shortly after the Revolutionary War, long before evangelical reformers sent missionaries to the waterfront. Similarly, despite losing his arm in battle and experiencing repeated financial setbacks, John Hoxse determined to place "A firm reliance upon an all-wise Providence" before the War of 1812. American prisoners of war in Cape Town experienced a revival of religion in 1814–15, forswearing gambling and other vices.[130] After evangelical efforts began in the 1820s some sailors had clearly inculcated the reform message and made it their own. Whaleman William Alfred Allen wrote a letter to his parents and brother that reflected how much he had internalized Christian morals. To his parents he wrote, "May He who in his unspeakable goodness, has seen fit to wrest me from the broad road that leads to destruction, also touch your hearts, and lead you to cry out with the poor penitent 'What shall I do to be saved!!'" He also addressed some advice to his younger brother who was just starting out in the world, declaring, "Oh, my Brother, may you never go the lengths in sin that I have," and urged him to "seek the Lord early, while he may be found." Speaking for himself, he thanked God for saving "so vile a sinner" and giving him "strength to overcome his passion for strong drink." Recognizing the reformers' concerns, Allen wrote, "Tell those who are interested for seamen to *pray* for us to *strive* for us continually for we need it," and reported that "Temperance is advancing and there is cheering news from all quarters."[131] James Webb expressed his religious sentiments in a poem he wrote for his mother during a storm at sea that lasted thirteen days. He began:

37. This fanciful illustration shows New York's Sailor's Home and Mariner's Church facing the docks. Both institutions were a few blocks from the wharves. In the foreground a group of respectably dressed seamen are greeted as they come ashore and pointed toward the Sailor's Home. "American Seamen's Friend Society Certificate." Mystic Seaport.

Awake, my fearful trembling heart
And in the Lord Jehovah trust.
Bid every anxious thought depart
For he is holy kind and just.

Webb continued by placing himself and all nature in the hands of God.

Defend me, by thy mighty hand
As on the Ocean's breast I go.
For waves are under thy command
And all the howling winds that blow.

The poem concluded with Webb asking that "when the closing scenes prevail" that the Lord's grace would support him and bear his "soul to the realms above."[132]

Reformers took advantage of religious tars by publishing their accounts of conversion. These stories portrayed the sailor as a dreadful sinner who was somehow touched by the hand of God. At times it was the majesty of the deep that transformed the sailor. At a prayer meeting in New York in 1822 a tar told of his religious experience that occurred in 1811. He described how one night he was at the helm of a brig sailing from Lisbon to London. He looked about him and "contemplated on the wonderful works of God in the firmament above." Then he cast his "eyes on the ocean below" and thought about how amazing God was for creating the earth. He also realized he had failed to love and worship God. Distressed, he prayed and read the Bible for four days, after which he committed his life to God.[133] Sometimes conversion occurred after the intercession of a reformer. One sailor had repeatedly injured himself by becoming falling down drunk on shore. After he was sent to the hospital with a broken leg, his thoughts began to turn to religion. One day as he dozed in bed a Methodist missionary made the rounds in the ward. Rather than disturbing the injured sailor, the Methodist left a tract, "Conversion of the Infidel," on his chest. When the tar awoke, "the title fixed his attention." He started reading and yielded his opposition to religion. He became "quite desirous to know the saving virtue of the word of God, and very soon in answer to prayer he found peace with God through our Lord Jesus Christ."[134] At other times it was a relative who intervened. "A Prodigal Sailor Boy" declared that although brought up religious, he went to sea and was "a follower of Satan—living in as debauched and sinful manner as any of the Sons of Neptune." Then he received a chest from his mother with clothing, books, and tracts. One of the tracts "made me feel uneasy in mind," so he reread it. "*That struck the blow*—I found I must be born again, or I could not enter the Kingdom of heaven." At sea at the time, he began praying and reading "other good books," wondering if it was too late to be saved. He was in a miserable condition because he could hardly eat or sleep, and "grew poor, and was fairly emaciated with pain and distress of mind, for my long sinning against so glorious a God." One night, after praying "for forgiveness of my long rebellion against heaven" till nearly midnight, he fell asleep "sick of life, and fearful of hell." About an hour later he awoke "and the glory of God shone bright around me." From that moment on he became a good Christian.[135]

The bottom line in these narratives was that each sailor had the potential for a transforming experience. Ultimately whole books of autobiography appeared that fed into an emerging literature of the common man. Writers like Horace Lane, who was both a sailor and a crook, could tell their life stories as instructional tales.[136] The reader might experience some voyeuristic pleasure from the detailed portrait of the dens of iniquity, while simultaneously knowing that ultimately God triumphed and redeemed the lost soul. The description of the depraved world of the sailor also unwittingly demonstrated the limits of evangelical reform. Try as they might, reformers could not fully transform life and liberty on the waterfront. They could not stop sailors from drinking, cursing, and profaning the Sabbath. Landlords continued to play a vital role in the shoreside lives of seamen. Both the men and the women of the waterfront continued to struggle for survival. Sin, in the eyes of the evangelical, remained deeply embedded in maritime culture. Yet, the conversion narratives also attest to the fact that middle-class reformers had some impact on their "proper objects of Christian compassion."

8

The Ark of the Liberties of the World

Herman Melville was a sailor. His reasons for seeking work at sea were complex: part necessity, part tradition, and part wanderlust. Born the scion of two distinguished families, he grew up in affluence. After he reached adolescence the family's fortunes took a turn for the worse. His father, Allan Melville, had made one poor investment after another, having borrowed against his own and his wife's inheritance. Allan died when Herman was twelve, leaving little but debts to his wife and children. This poverty limited young Herman's education. For the next seven years he held a variety of jobs as a clerk and as a teacher. The depression that struck the United States in the late 1830s narrowed his opportunities further. With the example of several family members before him, Herman began to think about going to sea. His father had traveled extensively in his failed effort to build an import and export business. Others in the Melville home talked of exploration and visiting foreign lands. Members of his extended family had already taken to the sea. Cousins Thomas W. Melvill and Leonard Gansevoort had even served on whalers, while another cousin, Guert Gansevoort, was promoted from midshipman to lieutenant in the U.S. Navy in 1837. Faced with tough choices, and perhaps hoping to escape his mother's shadow, Melville saw that a maritime career held out possibilities.[1]

Melville's experience at sea fit the profile of many of his generation. At age nineteen he signed on as a green hand—a boy—on the *St. Lawrence*, a merchant ship sailing out of New York to Liverpool. The voyage, including a brief stay in England, lasted almost four months. Melville decided to pursue a land career upon his return, but opportunities remained limited. Another effort at schoolteaching ended in failure, and a quick trip to Illinois revealed that the west would not bring any great rewards, either. Again Melville thought of the ocean. This time he convinced himself that he should sign aboard a whaler. January 1841 found the young Melville, still listed as a green hand, sailing out

38. Herman Melville spent some time aboard the whaleship *Lucy Ann*. John F. Martin, Log of the Ship *Lucy Ann*, 1841–1844. Kendall Whaling Museum.

of New Bedford on the whaleship *Acushnet*. What he expected to gain from this voyage, we can only guess. We do know that he was excited about heading for the Pacific. For a twenty-year-old with a wild imagination, that may have been enough.[2]

Over the next few years the young tar's life took many twists and turns. Whaling was grueling work. After a year and a half aboard the *Acushnet* with meager success in Atlantic and Pacific waters, Melville did what many young men did aboard unhappy ships—he ran. On July 9, 1842, he and another sailor named Richard Tobias Greene struck out for the interior of Nukuvia, one of the Marquesas Islands. They wandered for several days in the jungle before they reached the valley of the Typees, reputed cannibals who were almost untouched by contact with Euro-Americans. For these two young men this was high adventure. They had stumbled upon paradise, but neither wanted to stay very long. Greene escaped first, joining another whaling crew. Melville escaped a few weeks later, signing aboard the whaleship *Lucy Ann*. This vessel was fraught with tension between the officers and the crew. Within months Melville found himself stranded on Tahiti and charged with mutiny. Melville lived the beachcomber life for a few weeks and then escaped to a nearby island. Shortly thereafter he signed aboard another vessel, the *Charles and Henry*. This type of ship switching was not uncommon. Melville left his third whaling ship on the Hawaiian Islands. Again he was a beachcomber, then signed on as a clerk. As if to prove he had no settled direction, he joined the American navy aboard the frigate *United States* as an ordinary seaman on August 17, 1843. Either because it was more difficult and more risky to leave the American navy, or because his meandering course was eventually to return him to the United States, Melville remained in the navy until October 1844 when he obtained a discharge at the Charlestown naval yard in Boston.[3]

Thus ended Herman Melville's maritime career. For the better part of five years he lived as a common sailor either before the mast on merchant ships and whalers, or as one of the "people" on the gundeck of a great warship. Tens of thousands of other young Americans had followed this path before him. Tens of thousands would go after him. On each, the sea had left an indelible mark. Somewhere along the way, perhaps it was in the drowsy hours of a late night on deck or the leisure of a dogwatch, Melville had developed a knack for spinning a yarn. Better yet, he had gained experiences in the most of exotic of worlds; he had seen with his own eyes naked maidens swimming out to meet his whaleship and to greet his shipmates with an orgy that surpassed their wildest dreams; and he had shared a quiet moment of solitude with an

Eve-like Fayaway as she unwrapped her "robe of tapa" and used her undressed form as a mast and her raiment as a sail filled with wind to propel a canoe across a secluded lake.[4] Such tales aboard the *Lucy Ann*, the *Charles and Henry*, and the *United States* could easily gather a crowd of gawking tars waiting and hoping for the same opportunities. By the time Melville had reached Boston he had refined his story, embellished it, and could recite it with ease.[5]

Although he had served his time before the mast, Melville was no ordinary spinner of yarns. He had had a scintilla of education and had been brought up in a family that expected extraordinary things of the children. When that family heard his account of the South Pacific, they urged him to put his yarn into print. With few other opportunities before him, Herman Melville became an author and wrote a series of books based on his experience as a common seaman. First he wrote *Typee*, a book that told of his Edenic visit and extolled the virtues of the lovely Fayaway. Melville followed this work with *Omoo*, which traced his course after leaving the valley of the Typees and showed the life of the beachcomber stranded in the outposts of the South Pacific. His more fictional *Mardi* was less of a success and convinced him to rattle off two books, each written in the space of a couple of months, that recaptured his life as a green hand aboard a merchantman, *Redburn*, and discussed life aboard a man of war, *White Jacket*. Writing these five books within the space of four years was a staggering achievement that would have taxed the literary abilities of most men. Melville then sat down and wrote *Moby Dick*.[6]

While Melville's mastery stands out in the annals of American literature, many of his books also had a more practical purpose by describing the harsh conditions faced by every Jack Tar and calling for reform. Melville's first book had just touched the surface of the plight of the sailor in an effort to explain the author's running from the ship to the paradise of Typee. Implicit in the lyrical descriptions of a pristine society unspoiled by western civilization is a criticism of the world Melville had left for his sojourn with "cannibals."[7] *Omoo* was more explicit in describing the effects of European contact upon the South Sea Islanders and in detailing the conditions of the common seamen. Although Melville recognized that many of his shipmates had their faults, he portrayed their life aboard ship with a droll sense of humor that could only elicit sympathy. The forecastle, for instance, "was dungeon-like and dingy in the extreme." If these dark, sooty, smelly, cramped, and often wet accommodations were bad, Melville told his readers, the seamen did not have "undisputed possession of them." As Melville explained, "Myriads of cockroaches, and regiments of rats disputed the place with us." Crews might battle these

39. The imaginations of many sailors, including Herman Melville, were fired by the almost naked bodies of Pacific Island women. "Exotic South Sea Scrimshaw" (ca. 1840–1850). Kendall Whaling Museum.

legions, but "after a hard fight" they sometimes gave "themselves up, as it were, for lost, the vermin seem to take actual possession, the sailors being mere tenants by sufferance." As for the rats, so tame and brazen were they that "they darted in upon us at meal-times, and nibbled our food."[8] In *Redburn* Melville spent even more time describing living and working conditions of the common seaman. Without the South Pacific setting we get a better sense of the labor of the sailor. Melville emphasized the value of Jack Tar to society and proclaimed that "The business of a thorough-bred sailor is a special calling, as much of a regular trade as a carpenter's or lock-smith's." He believed that "Indeed, it requires considerably more adroitness, and far more versatility of talent" than land-based trades. Almost in the same breath he could mock his own meager skills as a green hand for whenever "any embroidery was going on in the rigging," a task only for the "able sailors," as a "boy" Melville "was set to the most inglorious avocations: as in the merchant service it is a religious maxim to keep the hands always employed at something or other, never mind what, during their watch on deck." Resistance to this maxim was futile. Given a hammer and slung over the side of the bow to chip away at the rust on the anchor, a monotonous and "a most uncongenial and irksome business," Melville noted, "There was a most remarkable fatality attending the various hammers I carried over with me." Yet no matter how many hammers he dropped into the sea, "the supply of reserved hammers seemed unlimited" as were "the blessings and benedictions I received from the chief mate for my clumsiness."[9] Melville's lighthearted style could also be bittersweet. Shortly after falling into a reverie on the wonders of ship, sky, and ocean, and declaring, "Yes! Yes! Give me this glorious ocean life, this salt-sea life, this briny, foamy life, when the sea neighs and snorts, and you breathe the very breath that the great whales respire!" Melville was called to clean chicken coops and prepare beds for pigs. With this rude awakening he quickly changed his tune: "Miserable dog's life is this of the sea!" and launched into a tirade that would strike a responsive chord in any reformer's heart, lamenting that he was "commanded like a slave, and set to work like an ass! vulgar and brutal men lording it over me, as I were an African in Alabama."[10] Melville was most outspoken in his call for reform in *White Jacket*. Again we see a varied portrait of sailors, some of whom are thieves, liars, and sodomites; others are trumpeted as seamen, storytellers, and high-spirited comrades. Melville also offered a critical portrait of the American navy, calling for an abolition of flogging. Indeed, he devoted four chapters to the subject.[11] Because of flogging, for the sailor "our Revolution was in vain; to him our Declaration of Independence is a lie." Melville pronounced the practice a moral wrong that needed to be purged. He considered this cause crucial for the United States because "we Americans are the peculiar, chosen people—the Israel of our time; we bear the ark of the liberties of the world" and "must lead in causes that are right and just."[12]

Melville's literary achievement and call for reform did not occur in a vacuum. His *Typee* quickly drew comparisons with Daniel Defoe's *Robinson Crusoe,* and the genre of the great sea tale reached back to the age of Homer.[13] Before Melville wrote a word, James Fenimore Cooper and Richard Henry Dana, Jr., had helped to create an audience for tales of the sea. Stories of shipwrecks, pirates, and maritime adventure had long found their way toward publication. The nineteenth century brought with it a steady stream of books about Jack Tar beyond the work of Cooper and Dana. With the rise of the common man, suddenly there emerged a new concern for the experience of Everyman, including those who dwelt in the forecastle. Melville's success went beyond the exotic; it was the placing of the sailor, just an average man, in the exotic setting that attracted readers. One review of *Typee* commented that the book itself was interesting, and then asserted, as if the statement were enough on its own to make the book worthwhile, "besides, it is by an American sailor."[14] Melville had to defend himself from charges that he had made up his visit to Typee and that he was not a real sailor. Only after his companion Toby identified himself and vouched for the authenticity of the experience did doubters disappear.[15] Melville used his personal experiences and his identity as a sailor to hype the democratic man in the age of democracy and to praise the individual in the age of individualism. He also placed that democratic man and that individual in an arena that so well suited the maritime experience—in conflict with nature.

Melville was fully aware of this larger literature of the sea when he wrote. He had read Cooper's sea novels and Dana's *Two Years Before the Mast.* Literary scholars have examined the lists of the libraries of some of the ships Melville sailed on to find them packed with an even broader array of sea literature. And when Melville set out to write he surrounded himself with books as reference material and to help fill in the detail. Without the article on "Mocha Dick"—a white whale—that appeared in the *Knickerbocker* magazine in 1839, and without Owen Chase's narrative of the wreck of the whaleship *Essex*—stove by a whale—there could have been no *Moby Dick.*[16]

The popularity and variety of maritime writing reflected an important development in the early nineteenth century—the idea that the common seaman represented the democratic man. The literature of the sea was written by some of the great authors of the day, especially Cooper and Dana. Books about the common seaman by the common seaman documented the memory of what Jack Tar had sacrificed for the United States and served as a call for equal rights that emerged from the forecastle. If there was such a call and if there was such a representation, it had limitations. Seamen did make efforts to take control of their own lives, but the harsh conditions of life and labor aboard ship and on the waterfront prevented such efforts from going very far. Economic and social reality kept many on the waterfront clinging to their own peculiar notions of liberty while trapped in a form of bondage.

Both Dana and Cooper shared with Melville maritime experience that informed their writing about the sea. Seventeen-year-old Cooper had sailed on a merchantman to Europe in 1806 and 1807, after which he received a commission as a midshipman. Dissatisfied with naval service in a period of peace, and eager to get married and live the life of a country gentleman, Cooper returned to the civilian world in 1811. In his years at sea Cooper had caught a nautical bug that would later surface in more than a dozen novels and a massive history of the American navy. Dana's experience was a little more limited. He took one voyage to the Pacific and the coast of California. Dana had been a student at Harvard, but trouble with his eyes compelled him to take time off from school. Afraid that he was a burden at home, and with some expectation of adventure and the hope that a rigorous life would help restore his health, Dana signed aboard the *Pilgrim* to sail before the mast. Although Dana was away only two years, he admitted that had he stayed longer at sea it might have been impossible for him to have resumed his studies. As it was he wrote a classic of American literature about his experiences, remained deeply interested in the world of the waterfront the rest of his life, and became a sailor advocate as a reformer and as a lawyer.[17]

Cooper is probably most responsible for the spread of interest in novels about the sea. *The Pilot*, which he published in 1823, became the bellwether by which all subsequent novels about the sea would be measured. Cooper wrote the book in the belief that he could capture the experience of the sea better than a landsman like Sir Walter Scott in *The Pirate*. Cooper was determined to get the ropes right. But he did more than that. He melded together a romance in a historical setting. Putting aside the well-heeled heroes of his work, who are forever pursuing and eventually wooing a high-born woman, Cooper offered some fascinating portraits of common seamen as secondary characters. In most of Cooper's sea novels there were two basic types of seamen: the hard-nosed and capable sailor, and, for comic relief, the red-nosed, ignorant, irresponsible, superstitious, and loyal stereotypical tar. "Long Tom" Coffin, who appeared in *The Pilot*, represented the first type. Tall, lean, and from New England, Coffin was "the seaman as democratic hero," according to Thomas Philbrick. Coffin was even born on board a boat and had little use for land, other "than now and then a small island, to raise a few vegetables, and to dry your fish." On first meeting this paragon Cooper had Coffin declare that even the sight of land "always makes me uncomfortable, unless we have the wind dead off shore." Whenever there is a crisis at sea, when the elements come most into play, there you will find Coffin demonstrating his full capabilities as a seaman.[18] This portrait was exaggerated—Nathaniel Ames commented that Coffin was "a *caricature* (and not a very good one) of an old salt"—but it did bring the common seaman before the public in a positive light.[19] Cooper's other stock seaman character was also a stereotype and mixed some admirable with less than admirable traits. The clown-like Scipio Africanus and Dick Fid in *The Red Rover* were short, thickset, powerful in their appearance, and "furnished the strongest proofs of long exposure to the severity of many climates, and numberless tempests." Their clothes, too, gave away their occupation for they wore "plain, weather-soiled, and tarred habiliments of common seamen," and they bore "about their persons the unerring evidences of their peculiar profession." Loyal to their teeth, they could also be led astray, at least temporarily, by drink, their belief in the supernatural, or some immediate reward. Whatever their faults, even these characters would invariably show their true colors and do what was clearly right.[20]

Although Cooper's depiction of common seamen was stultifying, and his novels really revolved around the lead characters from higher up in society, his books caught the public's imagination. Not only had Melville and Dana read Cooper before they went before the mast, but countless other young men did so as well. For example, shoemaker turned sailor Jacob Hazen read *The Red Rover* before he signed aboard a whaler. J. S. Henshaw, a teacher of mathematics for midshipmen on an American warship in the 1830s, wrote an account of his voyage heavily influenced by Cooper, imitating Cooper's florid prose and quoting extensive passages from Cooper's works, including statements made by Dick Fid.[21]

Cooper's books also had a patriotic message. This nationalism was most obvious in his *History of the Navy* which chronicled the many triumphs of American warships from before the American Revolutionary War to the last action against the Barbary pirates in 1815 led by Stephen Decatur.[22] It also appeared in most of his novels as well. *The Pilot* was a poorly disguised story about John Paul Jones's exploits off the coast of England. Even books like *The Red Rover*, which supposedly took place in 1759, emphasized the distinction between America and the old world. Similarly, Cooper's *Wing-and-Wing*, which centered on a French privateer battling the English on the Mediterranean coast of Italy, included an American character, Ithuel Boit, cut much from the same cloth as "Long Tom" Coffin. Like Coffin, Boit was a crackerjack seaman from New England. He also had a deep hatred of the English because of years of forced service he experienced as an impressed American.[23]

Ultimately Cooper was concerned with the common seaman. He invited an ex-shipmate of his, Ned Myers, to his estate at Cooperstown, New York. There he listened to the saga of Myers's life, which he then wrote down and published as a book tracing thirty-six years of suffering and strife at sea. Cooper presented Myers's tale almost unadulterated, with stories of floggings, alcohol abuse, shipwreck, prisons, disease, and death. He also relied heavily on Myers's own words, excluding the curses while keeping plenty of salty language. The common seamen in Cooper's later sea novels retained enough of Myers to be somewhat more believable than Cooper's earlier efforts.[24] Cooper's interest in the *Somers* mutiny, which occurred in 1842, also reflected a curiosity about things beyond the quarterdeck. The *Somers* case emerged as a cause celebre in the early 1840s and became part of the debate over naval reform. The *Somers* was an American training vessel packed with young men who apparently had vivid imaginations, fed in part by reading books like *The Red Rover*. In this case a group of young men aboard the *Somers* supposedly plotted a mutiny to overthrow the captain and turn pirate. No action was ever taken by the men to follow through on this plot. The captain, however, reacted quickly and severely by holding a court-martial at sea which convicted and executed three of the accused mutineers. With no war and no pressing threat of weather, Commander Mackenzie could easily have held off a week or two until the vessel reached a port in the United States before pressing the case. He opted instead for summary justice. This act brought controversy and criticism, especially since one of the executed was also the son of the Secretary of War. Cooper believed that the trial and execution were unwarranted and declared that "nowhere is tyranny so much out of place as in the government of a ship." Although ruthless in his personal attack on Mackenzie (he called the execution "a flagrant act of injustice and inhumanity"), Cooper also included some general comments about the nature of naval discipline. He claimed that "It is important . . . that the naval code be not too much at variance with the genius and spirit of the national mind," and asserted that "The right to *flog* is thought to be not in harmony with the spirit of the age, and with the true theory of punishment."[25]

James Fenimore Cooper, having served before the mast and as a midshipman, may have always had some general sympathy for common seamen, although his increased sensitivity to Jack Tar evident after 1840 might have also been influenced by the work of Richard Henry Dana, Jr. In the words of Thomas Philbrick, Dana's *Two Years Before the Mast* "changed the face of maritime fiction."[26] Dana provided the first popular portrait of life from the forecastle. Here was the sailor eagerly looking forward to his grog ration, working at picking oakum, as well as climbing into the rigging during storms to take in sail. Although Dana claimed "that the sailor has no romance in his everyday life to sustain him" and that it was "very much the same plain, matter-of-fact drudgery and hardship," his writings romanticized the sea, while revealing the harsh realities. Like Cooper, Dana wanted to see some reform, describing flogging and the abuse of seamen by officers on a merchant ship in stirring and unforgettable language. After Dana it became impossible to write about the sea without including life-like sailors.[27]

Dana gave up the sea after only two years, returned to his studies at Harvard and "all of the social and intellectual enjoyments of life," and became a Boston lawyer. He did not forget "that body of men, of whose common life" *Two Years Before the Mast* was "intended to be a picture." He had "yet borne them constantly in mind during" the book's preparation, and made aiding the common sailor a part of his career.[28] In 1839, before his fame as an author, he wrote an article decrying the leniency of Justice Joseph Story in a case where a merchant captain and mate had been convicted of killing a sailor at sea during a punishment. He also petitioned Congress in 1840 to allow for more speedy trials for cases based on incidents at sea, believing that the delays either kept the sailor ashore and out of work, or forced him to drop a suit when he went back to sea. Quick trials would give seamen "the equal distribution of justice." In an effort to standardize labor practices at sea Dana wrote the *Seamen's Friend,* which outlined the duties and obligations aboard a ship. Finally, Dana gained a reputation as a lawyer who would take seamen as clients in opposition to officers and the owners of merchant ships.[29]

Cooper, Dana, and Melville form a great triumvirate of American nineteenth-century sea literature. Other literary men, and other seamen, wrote stories about the sea. But the popularity and art of Cooper, Dana, and Melville set them apart. Although Cooper did not invent the genre, he took it to a new level. First he insisted on getting the details right. Second, he welded an American nationalism onto his characters, including those in the background like Long Tom Coffin. Dana, and then Cooper after him, moved those characters to the foreground, making the forecastle important in literature as it had been in the politics leading up to the War of 1812. Melville built on Cooper and Dana's success, adding a touch of the exotic and casting the democratic man in conflict with nature. Wherever their literature took them, all three kept Jack Tar in sight, called for reform without evangelical religion, and hoped to bring him to full participation in American citizenship. They were not alone in this endeavor.

During the first half of the nineteenth century an indigenous literature about sailors arose from several sources extraneous to the work of Cooper, Dana, and Melville. This literature built upon captivity narratives, tales of shipwreck and survival, and stories about mutiny and piracy that reached back centuries. It also had roots in eighteenth-century English literature and drama that had been adopted and adapted by Americans. More immediately, it was also the outgrowth of the rush of concern for the memory of the Revolution, of the experience of impressment, and of the War of 1812, as the generations that lived through this epic passed on. By the 1830s and 1840s the memory of any sailor as a representative of the common man became important. Evangelicals recited the lives of reformed drunkards and men who turned to God as a part of the religious revival of the Second Great Awakening. Some sailor tales, like those of Herman Melville, reflected the writing down of the oral tradition of the spun yarn from the forecastle and ended by asserting a call for sailors' rights in the age of Jacksonian democracy.

Survival against the elements and disaster has always piqued human curiosity. Whatever its moral message and ultimate yearning for civilization, Daniel Defoe's *Robinson Crusoe* was also a great adventure tale based loosely on the experience of Alexander Selkirk on the island of Juan Fernandez. Sailors could seldom pass that isolated mole in the Pacific without commenting on the four years Selkirk spent alone there.[30] While critics drew comparisons between Melville and Crusoe, other seamen had written their stories of survival on deserted islands and coasts before *Typee*. Captain Charles H. Barnard told of his being abandoned on the Falkland Islands during the War of 1812, and impressed seaman Joshua Penny described how he struggled to survive on Table Mountain after he escaped from the British navy at Cape Town.[31] Captivity could also come into play. Robert Adams's ship was wrecked off the coast of Senegal. He and most of the crew were taken by the Moors and forced into slavery for several years. Daniel Saunders experienced a slightly different fate when his ship wrecked off the southern coast of Arabia. Once the crew got ashore, they were robbed of most of their possessions and were compelled to march several days along the desert coast, with incredible suffering from hunger, thirst, and exposure, before reaching the safety of the city of Muscat.[32] The most famous of these tales was James Riley's *Authentic Narrative of the Loss of the American Brig "Commerce,"* which was reprinted countless times and sold more than a million copies in the nineteenth century. The book emphasized personal redemption in the face of shipwreck and captivity in the Sahara Desert. Embedded in this work was a strong antislavery message, as readers like Henry David Thoreau and Abraham Lincoln must have understood.[33] The demand for shipwreck stories of any type was so great that publishers printed huge compendiums of these tales. The title of one of these books, published at least nine times between 1835 and 1850, sums up its contents: *Interesting and Authentic Narratives of the Most Remarkable Shipwrecks, Fires, Famines, Calamities, Providential Deliveries, and Lamentable Disasters on the Seas in Most Parts of the World.* This tome had no other unifying theme. Eclectically organized, it rattled off one disaster after another. Some people survived despite themselves; others died regardless of their efforts. Some of the stories attested to the interposition of the hand of God; others suggested the fickleness of fate. Many shipwreck books, however, were more religious in tone and centered on role of providence in saving the survivors from the brink of death.[34]

Two other popular subjects in early maritime literature carried over to the nineteenth century were mutiny and piracy. Again, Daniel Defoe's influence reached far and wide. His *The Life and Adventure, and Piracies of Captain Singleton* was republished many times on both sides of the Atlantic, including editions in the first half of the nineteenth century. Perhaps even more influential was the collection of pirate stories by Charles Johnson, who some scholars believe was really Defoe.[35] Collections like *The History of Pirates . . .* published in 1825 and *The Pirates Own Book . . .*, first published in 1837, lifted whole chapters from Johnson/Defoe and added a host of tales printed as dying confessions of convicted pirates and other accounts.[36] Mutiny was directly related to piracy because any crime at sea was technically an act of piracy, and many mutineers turned to robbing at sea once they seized a vessel. The most famous mutineers of the period were the ones who took over the *Bounty* in the South Pacific. The disappearance of Fletcher Christian, and then the later discovery of the one survivor of the mutiny on Pitcairn Island, was a story that almost every sailor knew. The significance of this literature was not that it was new in the nineteenth century. Rather, it was that sailors read this literature and that increasingly the centerpiece of these tales became the common seaman.[37]

In the eighteenth century a few English authors and dramatists wrote about seamen. Theirs was not a very lifelike portrait. Thomas Philbrick called these sailors something of "a sea monster, a rough hearty creature" that was meant to be comical and had little depth. In the second half of the eighteenth century, perhaps in response to the role of the navy in the many wars for empire, a more sentimental image emerged. Sailors, while still crudely hewn, could have feelings and were seen with sweethearts, mothers, and sisters. These were the sailors who crowded the stage in Isaac Bickerstaff's operetta *Thomas and Sally; or the Sailor's Return* and who were celebrated in the popular ballads of Charles Dibden. This view not only gained ground during the Revolutionary and Napoleonic struggles, it was also borrowed and built upon on the American stage and in song during the 1790s and early 1800s. In other words, Americans made the sentimental seaman their own and transformed him into an important symbol for the new nation.[38]

As a result, Jack Tar became significant in conjuring the memory of the founding of the American republic. A few common seamen, like John Blatchford, managed to publish their story in the years immediately after the Revolutionary War. And before 1820, others like Nathaniel Fanning and Joshua Davis got their yarns in print.[39] It was only during the jubilee celebration of American Revolution in the mid-1820s that the interest in such stories led to the publication of a number of books about the experience of common men in the revolution. This change occurred for several reasons. First, there was the recognition that the days of the revolutionary generation were numbered. On July 4, 1826, both John Adams and Thomas Jefferson died, signaling the waning of the revolutionary leadership. It was also at this time that the Marquis de Lafayette made his grand tour of the United States, recalling memories of the war and Lafayette's relationship with George Washington. By the fiftieth anniversary of the Declaration of Independence only a few old soldiers and sailors were left in most communities, and local officials celebrating the national holiday would trudge out the old heroes of whatever rank, often bedecked in their aged uniforms, as the centerpiece of a parade and a symbol of the great national struggle. The memory of their experience, however humble their origins, now became the last thin threads tying the present to the past. Knots of youths and other hangers-on found listening to some old grandfather—it didn't matter whose—retell tales of John Paul Jones, or the adventure of privateering, an intrinsic part of the annual celebration. Year after year fewer old gentlemen appeared, making those that remained even more important. Ebenezer Fox explained in 1838 that he decided to publish his memoirs because his grandchildren wanted him to repeat his stories. Finding that his cough prevented him from speaking clearly, he wrote his narrative down. Fox offered an apology, as much form as substance, that revealed his thinking about his small part in the War for Independence: "Should it be thought that my simple narrative does not contain matter of importance sufficient to interest the reader, I can only say, that the partial judgement of friends, and my belief that any circumstances relating to the most interesting period of our history, would prove entertaining for the young, must be my excuse for presenting it to the public."[40] Veterans like Fox had become practiced in telling their story. Not only did they have the annual audience, but laws in 1818 and 1832 granting pensions to the soldiers and sailors of the revolution compelled thousands to recall the nature of their service. These laws represented both guilt over the treatment of aged veterans and a recognition that those who fought in the ranks had contributed mightily to the founding of the nation. This second point was connected to political developments. While there remained some individuals who clung to older notions of hierarchy, they faced an increasingly egalitarian world around them. In short, the politics of the age helped to make the veterans' tales more meaningful. The era of Jacksonian democracy was an age of common men. There should be little surprise that common men now felt that their own contribution to "the most interesting period in our history" was noteworthy.[41]

As the sailor became such an important symbol of the United States during the early republic, the memory of the sacrifice of common seamen as victims of impressment and in fighting the enemies of the nation also became worth writing down. This literature came in two waves. Some was published shortly after the experience reported and was used in part as political propaganda. Accounts of several sailors held as slaves by the Barbary potentates had a distinct ring of the captivity narrative that had become central to American literature. Men like John Willcock, Thomas Nicholson, and William Ray described their falling into the hands of infidels who then physically and emotionally abused them, treating them like abject slaves. These narratives highlighted the importance of the sailor and often provided a moral lesson on the evils of slavery.[42] Impressment narratives also served as a standard for the travails of seamen. A few stories of the suffering impressed American sailor were published during the opening decade of the nineteenth century. Many more appeared in part as propaganda around the War of 1812.[43] America's second war with Great Britain brought with it new stories of atrocities that American sailors were anxious to tell. In particular, the tragedy of the Dartmoor Massacre was detailed in several reminiscences published after the war. Within a few years the suffering of American seamen during the war quickly receded.[44] It was only a couple of decades later, just as the memory of the American Revolution became increasingly important, that the memory of all of the experiences of the interwar years and of the War of 1812 itself seemed to gain in interest with the American public.

The second wave of stories of common seamen after the Revolutionary War thus appeared at about the same time or shortly after the reminiscences of those who fought for independence. It was as if the whole ordeal from 1775 to 1815 had become one story celebrating the creation of the nation as those who had lived through the experience slipped away. As one sailor author put it, his story should be of interest to "every true hearted American" because it touched upon so much that was crucial to the new republic.[45] John Hoxse had been born in 1774, a year before the outbreak of hostilities with Great Britain. He had lost an arm in the Quasi War against the French and wrote *The Yankee Tar* in an effort to support himself in old age. Elijah Shaw, whose father had been a prisoner on the *Jersey*, picked up his pen for the same reason a few years later and could recount at least five wars: against France, Tripoli, Great Britain, Algiers, and West Indies pirates. Others wrote of impressment. Elias Hutchins fought for the British at Trafalgar and served twelve years in His Majesty's service. Dartmoor, too, was often mentioned. Nathaniel Hawthorne edited the diary of one ex-prisoner of war that described in detail life in the British prison and the May 6, 1815, massacre of Americans and published it in a magazine. Samuel Leech offered a vivid portrait comparing life in the British and American navies during the war that made serving under the Stars and Stripes appear infinitely preferable to sailing under the Union Jack. So important had the sailor become that it was possible to publish a book that skirted issues of patriotism; Moses Smith wrote a rollicking sailor's tale of his experiences in the navy from 1811 to 1815 that may have described battles, but seemed more consumed with detailing his drinking, fighting, and devising pranks than any sacrifice for the nation.[46]

In the 1830s and 1840s interest in Jack Tar expanded beyond the past and began to encompass the present. The success of Dana's *Two Years Before the Mast* both grew out of and enhanced that interest. Calls for reform since the 1810s and 1820s had made many Americans aware of the plight of the sailor. C. S. Stewart, a naval chaplain, had written in 1831, for example, that he loved the sailor "not the vulgarity and low vice . . ., but the nobler traits which belong more distinctly to him than to any order of men," including the "warm heart and generous soul, the clan-like tie which leads him to hail every round jacket and tarpaulin hat."[47] The same egalitarianism that increased interest in the experience of common seamen during the founding of the nation now made for an interest in his current condition. In the early 1830s Nathaniel Ames published two books about his experiences at sea that rejected a sentimentalized portrait of Jack Tar. Ames's irreverent tone embraced some aspects of the stereotypical sailor that in its own way emphasized the seaman as a breed apart.[48] After Dana's book appeared in 1840 there were a host of similar stories printed by men who claimed more authentic nautical roots than the Brahmin Dana. Books like George Little's *Life on the Ocean; or Twenty Years at Sea*, Leech's *Thirty Years from Home*, Nicholas Peter Isaacs's *Twenty Years Before the Mast*, and Henry Mercier's *Life in a Man-of-War* all suggest authorship by men who were at sea longer than Dana's short two years.[49] Some books were an odd mixture of genres. William Torrey combined an exotic tale with the reminiscence of the hard life of a sailor. Torrey ran away from a New England factory at age sixteen and went to sea. Shipwrecked in the South Pacific, he survived by living among the natives on an island for a year and a half. This was no brief flirtation like Melville's. He joined the war bands of his tribe, had his body extensively tattooed to demonstrate his commitment to the South Sea islanders, and married a young woman during his eighteen-month stay. This adventure formed only one section of his narrative. He told of many other voyages in the Pacific and the Atlantic. Eventually he attempted to settle in Newfoundland and married there. Life ashore was boring and it was difficult to find consistent work as a rigger, so he continued to sail off and on until, after a fourteen-year absence, he returned to New England.[50] Other sailors simply recounted the colorful life of the jolly tar. Mercier wrote comically of the common seaman in the American navy in the late 1830s. Recognizing the importance of sailors to the country, he caricatured the sailor's dialect and played upon his foibles. Mercier wrote, for example, that sailors looked at the loss of grog with "sorrowful faces betokening that they were bewailing the absence of a beloved and much valued friend."[51]

Several books and articles written by seamen sought to deflate romanticized notions of going to sea. Like Dana, they often sent mixed messages. While decrying the ordeal of the sea, they frequently made it appear as an adventure. An anonymous story entitled "The Fortunes of an Amateur Ragamuffin" contained an unambiguous lesson that tells of how a young man ran away to sea from an impoverished family. All he found was hard work, misery, bad company, and little excitement. At the end of his voyage he eagerly rejoined his family, vowing never to return to the sea.[52] Charles Nordhoff's signals were less clear. Retelling his experiences explicitly to convince young people that the romantic vision of the navy was overplayed, Nordhoff explained that "The sailor sees nothing of the world really worth seeing." Nordhoff's sailor was almost always confined to visiting seaports and, if lucky, had a few days' liberty which were spent in grog shops, with little money and less time to take in the sights. In short, Nordhoff declared, "While you belong to ship, you will see nothing." Yet he often described his life at sea in stirring terms. Moreover, a later edition of the book included dozens of illustrations of the many places he visited, including sights that a sailor would never take in, that "would increase its interest for young people."[53] J. Ross Browne's *Etchings of a Whaling Cruise*, consciously modeled after Dana's famous book, similarly warned the landlubber of the error of idealized notions of life at sea. On the very first page Browne admitted that a man who sails on a whaler "abandons all the enjoyments of civilized life, signs away his freedom, and voluntarily brings trouble upon his own head." Despite this cautionary language, Browne wrote many stirring passages describing the drama of the whale hunt and of his experiences in exotic lands.[54]

Stories of common seamen often found their way into print in this period because they also carried with them the message of temperance and evangelical reform. Owen Chase's story of survival after the whale attacked the *Essex* may have been a standard shipwreck tale that included a bit of cannibalism, but Thomas Chapple's version was meant to emphasize the role of providence and the call for reform. Horace Lane saw his own story of a debauched and criminal life as a great morality tale to show the evils of drink.[55] John Elliott published his memoirs, *The Reformed: An Old Sailor's Legacy*, in the hope that it would "help forward the great TEMPERANCE ENTERPRISE" by showing the evils of drunkenness. He called rum the "greatest pirate" and believed that "the evils which accrue to sailors in consequence of rum drinking" were the root of most of the sailor's problems. He asked: "How infinitely would their condition be improved were rum to come to total disuse on board all classes of vessels."[56] George Lightcraft also wrote a book that was as much a temperance tract as it was an adventure tale of whaling in the Pacific. Modeling himself after Melville and *Typee*, Lightcraft described the exotic Matea in Hawaii as an "unsophisticated child of nature." Unlike Melville, he praised the work of missionaries in the Pacific and attacked drinking liquor throughout. Many of the authors who related their life at sea, including George Little, Samuel Leech, and Nicholas Peter Isaacs, told how after years at sea they had turned to evangelical religion and had been saved.[57]

Ultimately out of this interest in the sailor and the rise of a literature centered on Jack Tar, some common seamen began to demand the rights of man. In other words, the ideas of liberty that emerged from the Age of Revolution worked their way into the forecastle. William Ray, who had suffered imprisonment in Tripoli after the capture of the *Philadelphia*, offered some of the earliest expressions of rights from a common seaman. His narrative is both an appeal to patriotism and a complaint about the navy. He drew comparisons between slavery and serving in the navy, declaring that it was distressing to see a shipmate who "himself had suffered, fought and bled in the achievement or the defense of freedom," punished "for a very trifling offense." That punishment included being "manacled, stripped, castigated, flayed, and mangled worse than the vilest Virginian's slave, or the most atrocious felon."[58]

Other seamen criticized the navy. James Durand complained of floggings for minor crimes, and viewed them as a violation of natural rights. He felt that "The situation of a sailor, exposed as he is to the vicissitudes of life, to the inclemencies of the seasons, to the fury of storms and tempests, is sufficiently arduous without its being rendered more so by the cruelties of his fellow beings."[59] William McNally also highlighted the unfair treatment of sailors aboard naval vessels. Referring to the navy as "purely aristocratic," he criticized Commodore Isaac Chauncey for trampling on inferiors and reminded him, "You must have forgotten the principle features in the declaration of independence and constitution of our country: 'All men are born equal.'" He pointed out that Chauncey "would prevent the toe of the plebeian from grazing the kibe of the patrician."[60] In 1841 Solomon H. Sanborn, who served in the navy as a petty officer, published *An Exposition of Official Tyranny in the United States* in which he complained that justice was seldom meted out fairly on American naval vessels. He quoted Thomas Jefferson's statement on the title page: "I have sworn upon the altar of God, eternal hostility to every invasion of the rights of man." Having offered this testimony from the author of the Declaration of Independence, Sanborn wrote: "If the Rights of Man for which our fathers bared their breasts to the bayonets of the oppressor be worth preserving, they are worth preserving well; and every citizen, from the proudest to the most humble, is *equally* entitled to the protection of the laws of the land." Like other seamen, he compared sailors to southern slaves by stating, "The cruelties practiced toward the crews of our ships of war far exceed any thing I have ever witnessed where slavery exists in its most odious form."[61] Tiphys Aegyptus complained of the treatment of sailors in the navy in 1843. Believing it was the "duty of a citizen" to bring the abuse of American navy men before the public, he called the use of the colt—a type of whip—as treating men "worse than the slave on the plantation."[62] F. P. Torrey, who was born in Vermont where he "inhaled her principles of freedom," had a "hatred to oppression and cruelty." He found naval justice arbitrary and described how one man had been given thirty lashes for being in a fight and tearing out the eye of his opponent. A second man who had merely used a little profanity when spoken to by an officer was given sixty lashes.[63] Roland Gould, who repeated the story in his own reminisces of the same voyage, wondered: "Is this giving impartial justice between man and man?" Gould believed that "some of the officers make their own laws to suit their own malicious purposes." From his perspective flogging was "a species of torture which would disgrace the Spanish Inquisition."[64]

Several of these seamen authors concluded that the difficulty in getting Americans to join the navy stemmed in part from the harsh treatment of common seamen. Gould asked, in a passage he lifted largely from Torrey, "What American, who feels the noble impulse of freedom throbbing in his bosom, would ever consent to rivet the chains of slavery upon himself?"[65] Gould's answer was that "The clanking of the chains which have been riveted on the few native [American-born] seamen, who are found in Naval service, has served to deter others from selling their birthright for a mess of pottage."[66] Jacob Hazen shared these sentiments: "American sailors, as well as citizens, are peculiarly jealous of their personal rights." He observed, "If the government refuse or neglect to redress the wrongs and injuries, wilfully, and often maliciously, inflicted upon them by their captains and commandants, they have little cause to murmur at any apathy or reluctance shown on the part of humble sailors towards entering the service."[67]

Sailor authors also objected to the treatment they received in merchant and whaling vessels. Like Dana, they attacked the practice of flogging on civilian ships. J. Ross Browne felt deep resentment toward his tyrannical captain and hoped that the time would come "when I would have it in my power to show him that even a foremast hand may have feeling, and is not to be abused with impunity." He viewed his life on a whaler as little better than slavery and declared, "I would gladly have exchanged my place with that of the most abject slave in Mississippi." Browne saw flogging as "a disgrace to the American flag," sarcastically noting, "What a spectacle of Republican perfection we present to the world!"[68] Several sailors shared these views. McNally criticized northeastern shipowners who were also abolitionists, reminding them, "Those who rail at negro slavery should take care that none of their own servants are receiving the treatment of slaves." Speaking for his fellow tars, he asserted, "Seamen know that they are born free, and freemen will never submit to the lash of slavery." He also asked why the articles of agreement signed by every sailor before he takes on a voyage do not mention flogging explicitly. His answer: "no American worthy of the name would ever affix his name to an agreement that would vest another with the power to flog him."[69] Nathaniel Ames believed that corporal punishment might be necessary in a man-of-war with its hundreds of seamen and military discipline, but he thought that it was inappropriate on a merchant ship and open to abuse. He mockingly described the merchant captain as strutting "across the eight-by-ten feet quarter deck . . . with six men, a great dog and a black cook under his despotic sway." Despite the size of this realm and the pathetic number of his subjects, "*he* can seize up or at least put in irons, handspike or shoot, stab or rope's end as he pleases."[70]

Long before 1850 some American seamen were willing and able to articulate ideas about equal rights that seemed to challenge the dictatorship of the quarterdeck. These men held out the hope that changes could be wrought not only in freeing seamen from the lash, but in also making seamen the equal of

40. Seamen often practiced handwriting in their journals and doodled interesting sketches. The ribbon in this American eagle beak reads "William A. Allen's" in the longer strand, and "liberty" in the shorter strand. Journal of William Alfred Allen (ca. 1840). New Bedford Whaling Museum.

all men. Joseph G. Clark wrote that some of this change depended on what sailors did themselves. "When seamen shall feel their relative importance in the great operations of the country, and indeed of the world, when they recover in a measure from the effects of their former degradation, it will be clearly seen that there are freemen alike in the forecastle and the cabin, each having their appropriate duties and spheres of action." He also argued that a sailor's "rights as a social and accountable being" had been wrested away from him," and he advocated an association of seamen, "inspired by a love of republicanism, enlightened, and acting in harmonious concert," that would "effect a revolution" that would transform the treatment of seamen.[71] In the first half of the nineteenth century, as the common man became more important in all areas of American life, as old soldiers and sailors called upon their memories to tell the story of their contribution in creating the nation, as the clarion for the reform of Jack Tar issued from evangelicals and sailors alike, and as more and more sailors spun their yarns into print, it just seemed possible that "a man should be secured the rights of a citizen, as well on the *planks* as the *soil* of his country."[72]

Where did all this talk lead? Did sailors act on their own to protect their rights? Did the call for sailors' rights lead to any great change in the world of the waterfront? And, perhaps most important, was there any relationship between the actions of the waterfront and the emergence of a larger labor movement in the first half of the nineteenth century? These are difficult questions that have no one answer. Yes, at times the people of the waterfront took the rhetoric to heart and banded together in labor actions. There were even some successes. Skilled workers like shipwrights often had some control over their work and lives. Sailors and dock workers could organize for only shorter periods of time. However, both groups had an impact on the larger developments within labor in the period. Skilled workers participated in some of the earliest labor organizations. Sailors and dockworkers may have been responsible for developing the "strike" as an effective tool of labor negotiation. Whatever was achieved was short-lived—a system of exploitation of the waterfront work force and limited political rights remained in place regardless of the reach of the rhetoric. Liberty retained its ambiguous and conflicted meaning.

A few skilled maritime workers sustained trade societies over several years, helping to create the foundation of the American labor movement. Artisans in most port cities created mutual benefit societies in the years after the Revolutionary War. These groups, whose main purpose was to provide assistance in case of sickness and to support widows and families of deceased members, were the forerunners of unions. The maritime trades were active in forming these societies and combined support for republican ideals with pride in the "mysteries"—skill—of their trade. In parades celebrating the ratification of the Constitution, tradesmen of all ranks, including masters, journeymen, and apprentices, had marched together to demonstrate their republicanism, their unity, and their craft. Several trades had floats with workmen displaying their skills. In the New York City parade the sailmakers completed all the sails for a 250–ton ship on their float.[73] The iconography of the certificates of membership to each society also reveals much about their purposes. A master sailmaker's certificate from New York in 1793 contains seven illustrations depicting the nature of the work process, aid being provided to a bereaved widow, and Lady Liberty offering freedom to a slave. Combined here is pride in craft, assurance of mutual support, and commitment to higher ideals of liberty and free labor.[74] Similar themes appeared in the shipwright's and caulker's certificate, where a female Liberty and a Neptune emerging from the sea stand next to an eagle and an American flag on one side and a shipyard on the other.[75] These first trade groups downplayed conflict between masters—owners of the means of production—and journeymen. The ropemaker's emblem from the celebration of the opening of the Erie Canal in 1825 repeated the republican themes of the certificates, and showed a master wearing a jacket and a journeyman in shirt sleeves bound together around images of work, patriotism, and justice.[76]

Unity in the maritime trades, as with nonmaritime artisans, did not last. The shipwright society of the 1790s was dominated by master craftsmen. In 1804 the journeymen formed their own organization as a mutual benefit society and to help regulate the workplace. Building on the republican principles of the American Revolution, they sought to prevent new investors in the shipbuilding business from hiring unskilled labor and driving down wages. By the 1820s the original society had disappeared. A new organization emerged in 1833 focused more on working conditions. The New York City shipyard workers not only sought to raise wages, they also were one of the first groups to limit the length of the workday. After years of conflict, including intermittent strikes, they successfully convinced their employers and the city government to allow them to build a bell tower that would guarantee only ten hours of labor by tolling the beginning and end of the workday.[77] Boston shipyard workers also struggled for the ten-hour day, striking at least three times in the 1820s and 1830s. Although the evidence is unclear, they must have sustained a labor organization for several years that had masters and journeymen standing together to improve their living and working conditions. The Boston association did not last beyond the 1830s; content with their relatively higher wages, masters separated from journeymen, ending any future possibility of united action.[78] Sometime in the 1830s African American ship caulkers in Baltimore organized themselves and used the threat of a strike for leverage to raise wages. They were able to maintain their favored position until the 1850s when white competitors violently drove them from the waterfront.[79]

41. Ropemakers were an important trade for the waterfront. This banner made for the celebration of the opening of the Erie Canal shows master and journeymen surrounding liberty, with an eagle and American flag in the background. It also depicts a ropemaker at work, a ropewalk, and a ship on the waterfront. "Ropemaker's Arms, Grand Canal Parade, 1825." I. N. Stokes Collection, Miriam and Ira D. Wallach Division of Art, Prints, and Photographs. New York Public Library.

Sailors and less skilled maritime workers could not sustain similar organizations over long periods of time, but participated in early worker agitation. Some scholars believe that the word "strike" as applied to a labor action began in Great Britain and came from a practice of sailors who would "strike" the sails of a ship to prevent it from sailing during a labor stoppage.[80] Whatever the origins of the term, American maritime workers struck several times in the early nineteenth century, drawing on the British precedent, long-standing practice at sea, and the revolutionary experience.

British sailors occasionally struck over working conditions and for wages during the eighteenth century. The most famous of these strikes were the great mutinies in the British navy at Spithead and the Nore in 1797.[81] There were other less noted examples of waterfront strikes among civilians. Dockside workers were the shock troops in the labor unrest in London in 1768. Shipwrights in Portsmouth refused to work at the beginning of the American Revolution in opposition to a new piecework system of payment.[82] During a dispute over wages in Liverpool, one crew unrigged a ship on August 25, 1775. Officials arrested some of these men, only to find themselves overwhelmed by a crowd of three thousand sailors who rescued the prisoners. The strike quickly spread as sailors marched behind a red flag—a symbol of piracy—along the waterfront, forcing others to join them and beating those who did not. Under the leadership of two men, one of whom called himself "General Gage," a racially mixed crowd of strikers then turned their wrath upon shipowners, attacking the houses of several Guinea merchants and the Exchange. Hired thugs defended these buildings, killed several strikers, and eventually drove them back. The next day the strikers appeared again, and this time they were armed. Several more deaths occurred and the military had to be called in to quell the disturbance.[83] More permanent labor associations emerged among some British maritime workers, such as the men who worked the coasters and coalers in the River Tyne region. With strong leadership, a united front, and a workforce recruited from the same community, they engaged in two successful strikes, raising wages in 1792 and protecting wages in 1815.[84]

At sea, Anglo-American sailors occasionally opposed their conditions of labor through collective action. Marcus Rediker included sixty incidents in his partial list of Anglo-American mutinies in the first half of the eighteenth century. Only one-third of these led to piracy. We can assume that the other two-thirds were in reaction to conditions aboard ship and reflected some attempt on the part of the crew to negotiate, however forcefully, their labor relationship with the officers. No doubt even some mutineers who turned pirate were merely responding to working conditions aboard ship.[85] Although mutiny could have dire consequences, including the hangman's noose, seamen resorted to this option throughout the period from 1750 to 1850. An informal network of communication kept knowledge of the techniques of mutiny alive in almost every forecastle. Herman Melville had signed a round-robin aboard the *Lucy Ann* in 1842. When Melville told his story in *Omoo* he included a copy of the sacred document, which he pointed out had been written upon leaves torn from "a damp, musty volume, entitled 'A History of the most Atrocious and Bloody Piracies.'"[86]

American waterfront workers also gained years of experience in collective action along the docks in the eighteenth century and in the American Revolution. Anti-impressment riots were a form of labor agitation. Participation in the popular disturbances against British imperial regulation after 1765 further taught waterfront workers the effectiveness of collective action. Demonstrating how well they learned this lesson as early as January 1779, Philadelphia sailors struck against payment of wages in depreciated currency. They repeated this action in May 1781, leading to the final collapse of the paper currencies in Philadelphia and the surrounding region. As Levi Hollingsworth explained to a Virginia friend, "Our seamen have been Collected these three days last in a tumultuous manner & have broken off all labour in consequence of the Money." The sailors continued their demonstrations and at times threatened violence. Elizabeth Drinker confided to her diary on May 8 that "the sailors getting together by hundreds with Clubbs, cursing the Continental Money, and declaring against it."[87] As we have seen, American maritime workers showed continued ability to mobilize themselves in the politics and popular disorder after the Revolutionary War.

American maritime strikes at sea and on land in the nineteenth century took on new forms more directly related to labor relations. By the time that Melville wrote *Omoo*, some aspects of mutiny seem to have been shifting. Jeff Bolster has argued that between 1820 and 1920 the nature of maritime insurrection changed from mutiny bordering on piracy to labor negotiation. He traces this development to three factors. First, the rise of the democratic man undercut the authoritarian nature of earlier shipboard relations. Second, the rise of steam made the work less onerous and voyages shorter. And third, alterations in the legal structure provided the sailor with more rights.[88] Although steam power had not yet had a significant impact before 1850, changing shipboard relations and increased sailors' rights were already affecting ideas about work stoppages at sea in the first half of the nineteenth century. Melville's attitude toward his mutiny reflected this change. He described the deliberations among the sailors as a "forecastle parliament" and wrote about the round-robin half in jest, while making sure the reader understood that it was the harsh treatment of the contemptible mate and the poor food that compelled the men to resist authority and affix their names to a statement of grievances.[89] Other sources from the period confirm this attitude. F. P. Torrey reported that because the captain had provided "lousy" provisions aboard an American merchantman in Smyrna, American seamen had stopped work when the USS *Ohio* entered port. In defense of the rights of the seamen the captain of the *Ohio* threatened to seize the vessel and send it back to the United States if the merchant captain did not provide better fare for the men. Jacob Hazen described an incident on a whaler led by "Old black Sam," who convinced his shipmates to "strike" in the South Atlantic after the captain had ordered a man flogged for a disagreement with the mate. Persuaded that the mate was abusive, the captain promised better treatment if the men returned to work. It was even possible for men in the navy to rely on such actions. While he was serving in the Mediterranean William McNally wrote that four to five hundred men refused to do duty because the captain had not granted any liberty at Port Mahon.[90]

Once ashore, on terra firma, a sailor's notions of rights could lead to labor action as well. Roland Gould determined that after his ship reached Boston, and because his term of service in the navy had expired, "that according to the laws of the United States" he was "a citizen." As soon as he could, he started to leave the ship. In response to an officer's attempt to stop him, Gould proclaimed he was a civilian citizen and threatened to defend his rights with his life. The captain interceded and let him go. A few days later, on July 26, 1841, between two and three hundred of the crew whose time had expired met at the Mariner's Inn to discuss their not being paid. They marched en masse to the commodore's lodging and presented him a reasoned list of grievances over the lack of pay, the debts they were accruing to landlords, and the desire of many who lived at a distance to quit Boston with what was rightfully theirs—their pay. The commodore politely thanked the men for their good order and promised to help them as quickly as possible. Although these actions can be seen as a form of labor agitation, they reflected, despite Gould's assertion of citizenship, a more traditional relationship between the people of the ship and those who presided over the quarterdeck. Even Gould's departure from the vessel was under the paternalistic eye of the captain. The list of grievances drawn up at the Mariner's Inn and the procession to the commodore's residence represented a forceful action by the people, but their goal was to petition their superior—and petitioning had long been a method whereby the powerless gave voice to grievances. It was not a demand of rights. These seamen operated within the hierarchy of the ship, deferring to their betters, while the commodore reciprocated by promising to provide relief.[91]

There were also moments when sailors and dockside workers became more aggressive. In these instances labor could stand opposed to capital and insist on higher wages or change in the conditions of employment. In October 1802, a seamen's strike in New York City was remarkably similar to the Liverpool strike of 1775, only without the extremes of violence. The "combination of seamen" was well organized. The white sailors followed two "commodores," who wore hats "decorated with ribbons and feathers." Black seamen were arrayed under two black "commodores" and acted in concert with the whites. The white commodores had sent a letter to the landlords along the waterfront "enjoining them to ship no seamen for less than fourteen dollars a month" instead of the ten dollars offered on some vessels. For several days "effectually to support this combination" the sailors "traversed the docks with drums and colors." After it appeared that some vessels might sail against their injunction, the strikers boarded a schooner about to depart, and "with great coolness and order . . . proceeded to dismantle her of her sails and rigging, which," showing a respect for property absent in the Liverpool strike, "they carefully stowed away in the hold." New York officials could not tolerate such an affront to the sanctity of property and arrested the ringleaders at "a rendezvous house hard by, where they [the strikers] were regaling themselves after their exploits."[92] Seamen, however, struck for wages only rarely. Baltimore sailors turned out for wages in 1800, marching along the wharves with "drums and fife, and colours flying," attacking a vessel with underpaid seamen.[93] A similar strike occurred in Boston in September 1827. About two to three hundred seamen paraded through the streets with a flag, drums and a bugle. They stopped several times to hear speeches and collected money from those who passed by. It remains unclear as to how successful they were.[94]

Other waterfront workers occasionally turned to labor action. Again, their efforts were more episodic than prolonged. In March 1825 a wave of strikes swept through New York City. The stevedores, riggers, and day laborers along the docks decided to stand out for higher wages as well. Like their predecessors in 1802, they paraded up and down the docks. Discovering that their demonstration was not enough to convince some of their fellow workers to join them, they boarded vessels chanting, "Leave off work! Leave off work!" and threatened physical violence against any men who continued to work. The police interceded for the shipowners and arrested the ringleaders, dispersing the rest of the strikers.[95] Three years later the stevedores and riggers of New York became even more militant. On the morning of March 14, 1828, two to three hundred white and black workers gathered on the north end of the East River docks and headed south, sweeping all before them. They boarded ships and coerced others to join them. Having stopped work along the East River, they crossed the city to the Hudson River and continued their efforts. No one attempted to stop them until they reached the ship *Sully* unloading ballast. The captain refused to let the strikers come on board. This opposition was not to be taken lightly. The strikers picked up the ballast stones and started heaving them at the vessel and its defenders. Peace could be established only by a troop of cavalry that drove the strikers from the docks.[96] A similar strike began on February 22, 1836. A crowd of riggers and stevedores forced hundreds of workers from the docks, and severely manhandled two policemen. Nine strikers were arrested and the men returned to work after the mayor called out the militia.[97]

Although this labor activity pulled on traditions indigenous to the waterfront, it must also be seen in the larger context of the labor movement. There were few strikes among any workers before 1800. After that date American workers began to rely increasingly on work stoppages to negotiate wages and control the workplace. That sailors and dockside workers were among the first to use the "turn out" suggests that this group of workers helped to develop the strike as a labor tactic—and here the supposed etymology of the word *strike* is instructive. The relationship of the waterfront to the beginnings of the American labor movement remains complex. Starting in the 1820s seldom did the maritime workers operate in isolation. In New York City the 1825, 1828, and 1836 strikes all came in the midst of activities by other groups of workers. Shipwrights struggled for a ten-hour day in Boston and New York just as other workers sought the same goal. The waterfront and the larger labor movement often acted in tandem. When the coal heavers on the Schuylkill waterfront demonstrated along the Philadelphia docks in late May and early June 1835, they triggered a general strike for the ten-hour day.[98] By the late 1830s, with the collapse of the economy, the labor movement lost its momentum for more than a decade. Throughout the 1840s most workers, whether on or off the waterfront, struggled just to gain employment. A more concerted labor movement would wait until after the Civil War.[99]

The particular problems of the waterfront in the American labor movement, and the difficulty in applying the ideals of the rights of man to their lives, can be seen in a brief effort by sailors to organize themselves in New York City in 1834. Sometime before the big spring hiring season sailors organized a union to set and protect their wages. In typical sailor fashion they assumed a name with tongue in cheek by appropriating from the middle-class reformers the title Seamen's Friend Society. Boardinghouse keepers played a leading role in this organization; after all, they were the ones who usually negotiated the individual tar's contract, with one boardinghouse keeper, John

42. This picture by a common sailor shows typical maritime outfits and reflects something of sailor values. One sailor is emptying a tankard in the background. In the foreground are the words "This what ye call comfort Jack—and I'll be d—d if ta[i]nt. I am." "Sketch of three sailors, one drinking, two smoking." Unsigned, ca. 1840. Peabody Essex Museum.

Munson of Cherry Street, being elected president. As early as mid-February the union seems to have run into trouble. For some reason, Munson and his supporters attacked Michael Farrel's boardinghouse at 350 Water Street, breaking furniture and taking money from him. April brought more problems as several merchants attempted to lower wages from $15 to $12 a month. Munson called a meeting at Harmony Hall, where he stirred up a crowd which then left for the waterfront. Unfortunately for Munson, he lingered behind. The crowd of sailors was intercepted by another boarding house keeper (the accounts identify him as a rival of Munson's), who managed to convince the angry sailors that it was Munson who was signing sailors up for less than the going wage. Quickly the wrath of the crowd shifted to their erstwhile leader, and they proceeded to Cherry Street where they broke into

Munson's establishment, shattering doors, windows, and furniture. They also helped themselves to liquor from the bar and beat the barkeeper.[100]

The 1834 waterfront Seamen's Friend Society quickly disappeared from the historical record. We have limited knowledge about the nature of this group. We do not know the rhetoric that Munson used in his speech to the crowd in April that year, nor do we have a record of the other two boarding-house keepers who spoke that evening. We also do not know how Munson's rival managed to redirect the sailor crowd. We do know that by this era many sailors had become aware of the ideals of the Age of Revolution and clung to phrases like "Free Trade and Sailors' Rights" long after the War of 1812 and impressment had ended. We also know that some sailors recognized the need to claim their rights as American citizens and that their cause was trumpeted by the memory of sacrifice and the emergence of American literary greatness. Collectively, however, sailors acted together only briefly to protect their wages. Almost in spite of themselves, sailors could not take the slogans or the ideals to the next level. Organization, at least for the common seamen and the less skilled along the waterfront, was short lived. Given the varied meaning of liberty on the waterfront, it should not come as a surprise that, whatever their intentions, efforts by sailors to protect wages could end in mistakenly tearing apart the barroom of their own elected president.

43. The sailors' mixed attitude toward liberty is suggested by this comical scrimshaw where Jack's motto, "Free Trade and Sailors Rights," reflected his commitment to the nation, represented by the eagle, and his grog. Hinsdale Collection, New Bedford Whaling Museum.

Epilogue

Perhaps Herman Melville best captured the spirit of the ambiguity and contradictions of Jack Tar in the portrayal of the heroes in two of his shorter novels: *Israel Potter* and *Billy Budd.* The one was a patriot of the American Revolution; the other, although English, was the epitome of the skilled seaman. One suffered grievously for his commitment to liberty and his country; the other suffered the ultimate penalty for his stutter, an apt metaphor for the sailor's inability to express himself when confronted with the powers of civilization. In both characters we can see that the ideals of the Age of Revolution touched Jack Tar, but did not dramatically alter his world. And yet the fact that Melville wrote both stories about humble seamen suggests how important Jack Tar had become to the democratic ideal.

Melville took the broad outlines of *Israel Potter* from the published life of one of those revolutionary sailors who put their story into print as Americans prepared to celebrate the fiftieth anniversary of independence. Potter had been captured at sea during the war but escaped in Great Britain. He journeyed to France, perhaps as an agent for the British government, and returned to England to melt into the general population. He lived a life of obscurity and poverty, traveling to the United States to seek a pension in his old age. Unsuccessful in his bid to get government support, he published a little book in 1824 proclaiming himself "one of the few survivors who fought and bled for American independence."[1] Melville embellished Potter's yarn, portraying him not only as a crackerjack seaman, but also as a true hero of the people. Melville's Potter first goes to sea before the Revolutionary War, abandoning the Berkshire Hills (the real Potter was from Cranston, Rhode Island) because he fails to win a fair maid. Potter then takes several voyages, but 1775 finds him, Cincinnatus-like, working behind a plow when the call arrives to fight the British at Boston. But unlike Cincinnatus and Israel Putnam, who at the time Melville wrote was immortalized for leaving the plowfield for the battlefield, Israel Potter decided that with only a half acre left to till he would finish one job before commencing another. Having finished plowing, off he went to fight at Bunker Hill, "mingling his blood with his sweat." For

Melville, Potter's experience was a lesson in how much we owe to the common man who fought the revolution. He reminded the reader: "while we revel in broadcloth, let us not forget what we owe to linsey-woolsey."[2]

The real saga, and the place where Melville added greatly to the story, begins after Potter returns to the sea. As an experienced seaman, Potter volunteers for Washington's little navy created to harass British shipping in and out of Boston harbor. Unfortunately, Potter's ship is captured three days out. After Potter's escape, and a visit to France where he meets both Benjamin Franklin and John Paul Jones, he is pressed into the British navy. Melville played to American resentment of this British practice by having Potter protest his being impressed, "I'm no Englishman." The British officer replies, "Oh! that's the old story . . . Come along. There's no Englishmen in the English fleet. All foreigners. You may take their own word for it." Melville understood the dilemma faced by many sailors who found themselves powerless to control their lives. Placed aboard a large British warship, Potter was confronted with the real possibility of fighting against his own country. But fate, and Melville's pen, would twist things around again. As Melville explained, summing up the experience of many sailors in the Age of Revolution, "Thus repeatedly and rapidly were the fortunes of our wanderer planted, torn up, transplanted, and dropped again, hither and thither, according as the Supreme Disposer of sailors and soldiers saw fit."[3] Potter is assigned to a boat crew, which, in turn, is captured by none other than John Paul Jones. Our sailor hero becomes the right-hand man to the great naval hero, fights in the battle against the *Serapis*, and sails for the United States several months later aboard the *Ariel*. But again fate intervenes. The *Ariel* runs into a British privateer. As the Americans start to board the vessel, the British veer off. Potter had taken hold of the privateer's spanker boom and finds himself separated from his own ship.

The accident that left Potter on a British ship allowed Melville to have great fun and play on the adaptability of the common sailor and the anonymity of a warship. Potter determines to try to avoid prison and pretends to be one of the two hundred men on the privateer. Using his head, and by asserting a familiarity with all, Potter tries to worm his way into every mess in the ship. But Potter's warm-hearted overtures cannot pierce the camaraderie of each mess. The size of the vessel allows him to go undetected for a time, since each mess insists that he belongs to another, but sooner or later he was left alone and isolated. Melville sustained this comedy by having Potter singled out by the officer of the deck. Potter confounds the officer by claiming to be Peter Perkins of the maintop. Distressed, the officer orders Potter to be taken away. But there is really no place to take him. When the captain noticed this, leading Israel hither and thither in "indefinite style," he, too, interviews the intrepid sailor with similar lack of success. In the end, Potter becomes one of the crew, serves with alacrity, and because of his good qualities as a sailor, is assigned to the maintop. Melville's final words on this part of the story are sheer irony:

> One pleasant afternoon, the last of the passage, when the ship was nearing the Lizard, within a few hours' sail of her port, the officer of the deck, happening to glance upwards towards the main-top, descried Israel there, leaning leisurely over the rail, looking mildly down where the officer stood.
>
> "Well, Peter Perkins, you seem to belong to the main-top, after all."
>
> "I always told you so, sir," smiled Israel, benevolently down upon him, "though, at first, you remember, sir, you would not believe it."[4]

The aplomb and good humor with which Potter confronted adversity was typical of the sailor. Melville knew this, and used this knowledge to demonstrate that every man's life, however much a shift of wind or a shift of fate may have affected it, was important. That Potter lived the rest of his life in obscurity, and died without recognition with "his scars . . . his only medals," only amplified this point.[5] Melville commented that "the gloomiest and truthfulest dramatist seldom chooses for his theme the calamities, however, extraordinary, of inferior and private persons; least of all, the paupers" because they are fully aware "that to the craped palace of the king lying in state, thousands of stares shall throng; but few feel enticed to the shanty, where, like a pealed knuckle-bone, grins the unupholstered corpse of the beggar."[6] Potter, the sailor, thus represented the unheralded heroes of the American Revolution.

Billy Budd, another inferior, faced a different set of calamities that speak to the adversities confronted by all too many common seamen in the Age of Revolution. It almost did not matter that Billy Budd was not American. His personality and experience with impressment in the Age of Revolution represented the essence of the American sailor that Melville knew from his own years at sea. After all, Melville dedicated the tale to Jack Chase, the English-born captain of the maintop that Melville had met in 1843 aboard the American frigate *United States*. In many ways Jack Chase, Billy Budd, and Jack Tar were one. All were thorough seamen, who had "no perceptible trace of the vainglorious" and had "the offhand unaffectedness of natural regality" about them that instantly earned the respect of shipmates. Billy—the epitome of the common seaman—was "invariably a proficient in his perilous calling" who was equally adroit with his fists in a waterfront brawl. Handsome enough to be described as almost feminine, he was still a manly sailor. His shipmates relished telling tales of his exploits ashore and aloft. Wherever there was danger and need for a skilled hand, Billy was sure to be foremost. "Close reefing topsails in a gale," the Handsome Sailor would be "astride the weather yardarm-end, foot in the Flemish horse [a foothold in the topsail] as stirrup, both hands tugging at the earing as at a bridle, in very much the attitude of young Alexander curbing the fiery Bucephalus. A superb figure, tossed up as by the horns of Taurus against the thunderous sky, cheerily hallooing the strenuous file along the spar."[7]

Melville made Billy Budd a foundling, in part to indicate that a seaman had few ties ashore. Although we know that this stereotype did not hold true in most cases, it works as a metaphor to suggest that while at sea many a sailor was cast loose from his shoreside ties and left to drift where the winds took him. Surely this was the experience of the Jack Chase so much admired by the young Melville, and of the future author himself when he was in the Pacific, jumping from ship to shore to ship again. Billy's obscure origins also worked to Melville's poetic advantage by allowing him to suggest "noble descent." But unlike James Fenimore Cooper, who might use a similar birth as a ruse for some later social ascent, Melville merely implies that this genesis helped to explain the nobility of Billy's character.[8]

That nobility, however, was at least equally due to Billy Budd's maritime career. With almost all of his short life spent at sea, Billy had not been corrupted by civilization. He could not read. Yet he could sing, "and like the illiterate nightingale was sometimes the composer of his own song." He was honest and giving, with no pretension or self-consciousness. He knew little of life on land, and as a result Billy's "simple nature remained unsophisticated by those moral obliquities which are not in every case incompatible with that manufacturable thing known as respectability." While the sailor participated in behavior ashore that the good middle class might decry, Melville found little to blame in this liberty. He could hardly call it vice because it lacked "the crookedness of heart" and seemed "less to proceed from viciousness than exuberance of vitality after long constraint." These "frank manifestations in accordance with natural law," along with his ability as a seaman on his natural element, made the sailor "little more than a sort of upright barbarian, much such perhaps as Adam presumably might have been ere the urbane Serpent wriggled himself into his company."[9] From this perspective the common seaman was a "child-man" with natural grace and intelligence, but with little experience in the wily ways of the world. He was thus different from the landsman—"the sailor is frankness, the landsman is finesse." Landsmen were forever playing games, plotting, and making wars. Melville could only conclude: "Yes, as a class, sailors are in character a juvenile race." But it was that very character which suited them for their profession, and, as primitive beings, to navigate successfully upon "the ocean, which is inviolate Nature primeval."[10]

If Billy Budd's character can stand for the sailor in general, his fate, too, had symbolic significance. Melville placed his story at the very center of the Age of Revolution, in the late 1790s and shortly after the great mutinies of Spithead and the Nore. For Melville, writing at the end of his life, as sail gave way to steam, this was a distant era. Yet, by drawing comparisons to the *Somers* mutiny, he also tied it directly to the 1840s when he had served before the mast. Billy may have been a victim of impressment, but he was also the victim of a changing world and the intrusion of civilization upon the natural element—the sea.[11]

A ship itself was not the problem. Aboard the aptly named *Rights of Man,* anarchy had ruled before the Handsome Sailor's arrival. This state of nature gave way to a society of mutuality under a beneficent captain with the added catalyst of the natural man—Billy Budd. We can only imagine what awaited the ship once Billy Budd bade farewell to the *Rights of Man*. On the floating symbol of civilization—the warship *Bellipotent*—the impressed "child-man" could not work all of his magic. There were too many landsmen on board, and one of these, Clagget, the master-at-arms, became jealous of the Handsome Sailor and took a disliking to him. This unnatural situation sealed Billy Budd's fate. Clagget plotted Billy's downfall; childlike Billy refused to take heed and in his natural innocence found himself sacrificed before the altar of civilization.

Religion could not save Billy Budd. Awaiting his execution, Billy "was wholly without irrational fear" of death. As such, the chaplain from civilized Christianity failed to impress "the young barbarian with ideas of death akin to those conveyed in the skull, dial and crossbones of old tombstones" and found it "equally futile . . . to bring home to him the thought of salvation and a Savior." Melville generalizes Billy's response as typical to all sailors. He commented that Billy listened to the chaplain "less out of awe or reverence" and more "from a certain natural politeness, doubtless at bottom regarding all that much in the same way that most mariners of his class take any discourse abstract or out of the common tone of the workaday world." For Melville, the chaplain represented the evangelical efforts of the middle-class reformers of the nineteenth century to impose their understanding of liberty on sailors.

Although the evangelicals did have some impact on the waterfront, Melville dismissed their efforts by pushing the uncivilized analogy and stating that "this sailor way of taking clerical discourse is not wholly unlike the way in which the primer of Christianity, full of transcendent miracles, was received long ago on tropic isles by any superior *savage*, so called." The sailor and the savage "out of natural courtesy . . . received, but did not appropriate" the religious message. Melville wrote: "It was like a gift placed in the palm of an outreached hand upon which the fingers do not close."[12]

Without delving too deeply into the complex symbolism of Melville's art, we see in Billy Budd the vision of the common seaman in an age of turmoil. Aware of the currents of change churning in a world swept by ideas of liberty and equality—seamen aboard the *Bellipotent* knew of the great mutinies of 1797 and could chuckle at the reference to Tom Paine's work in the name of Billy's merchant vessel—they remained powerless in the face of the forces of the standing order. No ideology could save Billy Budd when Clagget accused him of treason. His stutter and his inarticulateness spoke volumes about the plight of the common seaman. When Billy struck his mortal blow against Clagget in front of the captain, the inexorable machinery of civilization was set in motion. Convicted by a drumhead court, with officers aware of the revolution smoldering beneath the surface, Billy, an obedient and good sailor to the end, found himself strung up from a yardarm. All his shipmates could do was to repeat his last words of loyalty to the captain and revere the lethal spar as if it were the Cross of Christ.[13]

Glossary

ARTICLES OF THE SHIP: the formal agreement or contract stipulating conditions of labor aboard a ship and usually outlining the nature and extent of the voyage.

BACKSTAY: the rope running from the back of a mast to the side of a ship, slanting aft (to the back).

BARK (ALSO BARQUE): a three-masted vessel with foremast and mainmast rigged with square sails and mizzenmast rigged fore and aft.

BEAM-ENDS: condition of a ship when it is over on its side, almost capsized, and the beams are nearly vertical.

BEFORE THE MAST: phrase to indicate a common seaman's place on a ship. Because the forecastle was located before (in front of) the foremast, and sailors slept in the forecastle, they sailed "before the mast."

BENDING: to attach a sail or a rope with a knot. Bending sails was to tie the knots that held the sail to a yardarm.

BETHEL: a place of religious meetings for sailors. The idea of designating a nonchurch location as a Bethel—a holy place for religious meetings—was developed by eighteenth-century English Methodists. English waterfront missionaries adopted the practice and used a special Bethel flag flown over a building or ship to denote the location of Bethel services. The London Bethel Union presented New York evangelicals with a Bethel flag to use in their mission efforts on the waterfront. This flag was raised for the first time on March 11, 1821. The practice of using the Bethel flag spread rapidly to other American ports.

BRIG: a two-masted vessel that was square-rigged.

CABLE TIER: the place in a ship between decks where the cable was stowed. This location on a warship was often where prisoners were kept. Although often uncomfortable with little head room, it was not packed with stores since it had to have some space for access to the cable when arriving in port.

CAPSTAN: the mechanism or crank used to wind up rope or cables, especially to lift an anchor or move heavy objects aboard ship. In the age of sail the capstan was cranked by several sailors who inserted long poles into the stationary crank and pushed the poles in unison.

CHANTEY: shipboard work songs to accompany specific tasks and coordinate physical activity. Often sung in a call-and-response format.

CHANTEYMAN: the lead singer in a chantey issued the call that the rest of the sailors responded to.

DOGWATCH: short evening watch of two hours (between four and six o'clock) when all the crew was on deck. The dogwatch enabled the vessel to shift times in the watch schedule. Technically, it was a work period, but it was often a time of extra leisure since the entire crew was on deck. The dogwatch was marked by songs and the telling of tales.

DUFF PUDDING: common shipboard food that was a flour-based pudding usually boiled or steamed in a cloth bag.

DUNNAGE: small pieces of wood and other matter often used to protect the cargo when packed. Also used to describe the sailor's baggage.

FORE AND AFT RIGGING: the organization of the principal sails aboard a vessel where the sails ran the length of the ship and were directly attached to the masts.

FORECASTLE (ALSO FO'C'SLE USUALLY PRONOUNCED FŌKSL): originally the raised part of a ship in front of a vessel (the forward castle). It became the name for the common seamen's quarters under the front part of a vessel, whether the deck was raised or not.

FOREMAST: the mast nearest the bow, or front, of a ship.

FURL: to roll up a sail.

GREEN HAND: an inexperienced sailor. Also a landsman.

GROG: mixture of rum and water served aboard many ships at least once a day.

HALYARDS: ropes or tackle used to raise or lower sails, spars, yards into the rigging aboard a ship.

JACK TAR: a generic name for the sailor. It is derived from the popular nickname for John—suggesting the common origins of every sailor—and the word tarpaulin. Tarpaulin was canvas covered in tar to make it waterproof. A sailor was therefore covered in tar both figuratively and literally to make him waterproof.

KID: the common pot in which a sailor's meal was served aboard ship.

LAND SHARK: refers to any person on shore who took advantage of seamen. Often applied to crooked boardinghouse keepers and tavern keepers.

LANDSMAN: a specific status on ship of a person without much sea experience. This individual would be paid less than more experienced seamen and would often be referred to as a "boy," regardless of age. The term could also be applied to any person who lived and worked on the land.

LEE: the side away from the wind. A lee shore was having the land in the direction that the wind was blowing, a potentially dangerous situation.

LOBSCOUSE: type of shipboard stewlike food which was a mixture of meat and vegetables, often with potatoes as most prominent, mushed together.

LOG: the journal that was the official record of a ship's voyage. Kept daily, usually by the first mate, it noted distance traveled, longitude, latitude, and weather conditions. Sometimes it described work done aboard ship. Occasionally it had more personal comments about life at sea.

MAINMAST: the principal mast of a vessel, usually the second mast on a three-masted ship.

MAINTOP: the high platform of the main mast and a location reserved for skilled seamen on a warship.

MARLINSPIKE: a pointed tool used by sailors to separate rope strands while splicing.

MESSMATE: Sailors aboard warships were divided into messes of four to six men who would share cooking and eating and thereby form strong bonds with each other. To refer to a person as a messmate indicated a powerful fraternal bond.

MIZZENMAST: the last mast in a three-masted ship.

OAKUM: the loose fibers obtained by untwisting old rope that would be then used to caulk a vessel. Picking oakum was the tedious and unskilled job of obtaining oakum from old rope. This menial task was usually performed by landsmen in moments when there was no more demanding work necessary during a watch.

PROTECTION: the official document issued by an American magistrate asserting citizenship for seamen. These easily forged documents were meant to protect Americans from impressment by foreign navies, especially the British navy.

QUARTERDECK: originally the term referred to the upper deck in the rear of the ship, which was an area reserved for officers and the steersmen on duty. The quarterdeck was applied to the deck area at the rear of the vessel whether it was raised or not and to the officers of a ship in general.

RATLINE: the series of small ropes run between the shrouds (ropes running from the ship's side to hold the mast) of a ship used to climb into the rigging.

REEFING: using reefs, which were the strips across the sail that could be rolled up or taken in, to reduce the area of the sail.

ROUNDHOUSE: small shed built on the deck of a ship.

SCHOONER: a sailing ship usually with two masts with fore and aft rigging and the rear sail larger than the forward sail.

SEIZINGS: the fastening of ropes together with smaller strands of thread.

SHEETS: a rope attached to the bottom of a sail that helps to control the direction of the sail.

SHIP: This term can be used in two ways. It may refer to any vessel that is larger than a boat that transports people and goods on the sea. More specifically, it was a three-masted square-rigged vessel.

SLOOP: a one-masted vessel with fore and aft rigging.

SPANKER BOOM: the piece of wood that hold the spanker—a fore and aft sail set on the after side of a mast.

SPAR: strong wooden pole used for a mast or yard.

SPLICE THE MAIN BRACE: technically the splicing of the main rope holding a mainmast; but generally a sailor's term for having a drink of alcohol.

SQUARE RIGGING: the organization of the principal sails aboard a vessel where the sails extended from horizontal yards.

STEWARD: the individual aboard a ship whose duties included serving the captain and the officers. The steward would also often do the regular work on a ship, but would not stand a watch with the rest of the crew.

SUPERCARGO: an agent of the shipowner in charge of the commercial aspects of the voyage.

TACK: to turn the vessel to change the direction the wind strikes the sails. Tacking was necessary in order to sail in directions where the wind was coming toward the front of the vessel.

TON: the standard unit for measuring ships for registration. A ton is the equivalent of one hundred cubic feet. This form of measurement allowed for comparison in vessels of different dimensions.

VENTURE: the investment in goods that sailors were often allowed as merchant seamen.

WINDLASS: a winch used to haul objects on a ship. It was used sometimes used to lift an anchor or to bring equipment aloft into the rigging.

YARD: the tapered spar, or piece of wood, from which a square-rigged sail hung. A yardarm was the outer portion of a yard.

Notes

The following abbreviations appear in the notes:

AAS	American Antiquarian Society, Worcester, Massachusetts
AN	*American Neptune*
CHSM	*Christian Herald and Sailors Magazine*
EIHC	*Essex Institute Historical Collections*
GWBWL	G. W. Blunt White Library, Mystic Seaport, Mystic, Connecticut
HSP	Historical Society of Pennsylvania, Philadelphia
JAH	*Journal of American History*
JER	*Journal of the Early Republic*
JSH	*Journal of Social History*
MdHS	Maryland Historical Society, Baltimore
MeHS	Center for Maine History, Portland
MHS	Massachusetts Historical Society, Boston
NA	National Archives, Washington, D.C.
NA-NY	National Archives, New York Branch, New York, New York
NBFPL	New Bedford Free Public Library, New Bedford, Massachusetts
NEHGR	*New England Historical and Genealogical Review*
NEQ	*New England Quarterly*
NHA	Nantucket Historical Association, Nantucket, Massachusetts
NHHS	New Hampshire Historical Society, Concord
NMM	National Maritime Museum, Greenwich, London
NYHS	New-York Historical Society, New York
ODHS	Old Dartmouth Historical Society, New Bedford Whaling Museum, New Bedford, Massachusetts
PEM	Phillips Library, Peabody Essex Museum, Salem, Massachusetts
PH	*Pennsylvania History*
PMHB	*Pennsylvania Magazine of History and Biography*
PRO	Public Records Office, Kew, United Kingdom
RCPA	Records of the Pennsylvania Court of Admiralty
RIHS	Rhode Island Historical Society, Providence, Rhode Island
SM	*Sailor's Magazine*
WMQ	*William and Mary Quarterly*
Yale	Yale Collection of Western Americana, Beinecke Rare Book and Manuscript Library, Yale University, New Haven, Connecticut

Chapter 1. The Sweets of Liberty

1. Horace Lane, *The Wandering Boy, Careless Sailor, and Result of Inconsideration: A True Narrative* (Skaneateles, N.Y., 1839), 69–70.

2. Ibid., 103–4.

3. Richard Henry Dana, Jr., *Two Years Before the Mast: A Personal Narrative of Life at Sea*, Thomas Philbrick, ed. (New York, 1981; orig. pub. 1840), 168.

4. Herman Melville, *White Jacket: or The World in a Man-of-War*, Harrison Hayford et al., eds. (Evanston, Ill., 1970; orig. pub. 1850), 226.

5. Andrew Brown, *A Sermon on the Dangers of the Seafaring Life; Preached Before the Protestant Dissenting Congregation at Halifax and Published at the Desire of the Marine Society in that Place* (Boston, 1793), 39.

6. New-Bedford Port Society, *First Annual Report* (New Bedford, 1831), 7–10.

7. "The Diary of Mr. Ebenezer Townsend, Jr., the Supercargo of the Sealing Ship 'Neptune,' on her Voyage to the South Pacific and Canton," Thomas R. Trowbridge, Jr., ed., *Papers of the New Haven Colony Historical Society*, 4 (New Haven, 1888), 102–3.

8. John C. Purse, *Songs in the Purse; or, Benevolent Tar, A Musical Drama in One Act. As Performed at the New Theatre, Philadelphia* (Philadelphia, 1794), 6–7. Much of the following analysis in this and subsequent chapters depends heavily on songs and chanteys relating to sailors and the waterfront community. These songs and chanteys have been taken from a variety of manuscript and printed sources. The terms are not synonymous; chanteys were used to help coordinate group work like tugging on a rope or raising an anchor, whereas songs were sung for entertainment. Two other points are important for understanding chanteys and songs. American and British maritime culture shared the same music. And there is little difference between the printed sources and in seamen's journals. Some manuscript songs were a bit more ribald. See also Frederick J. Davis and Ferris Tozer, *Sailors' Songs or "Chanties,"* 3rd ed. (London, [1906]); William Main Doerflinger, *Songs of the Sailor and Lumberman*, rev. ed. (New York, 1972); Frank M. Stuart, "Ballads and Songs of the Whale-Hunters, 1825–1895: From the Manuscripts in the Kendall Museum" (Ph.D. diss., Brown University, 1985); Frederick Pease Harlow, *Chanteying Aboard American Ships* (Barre, Mass., 1962); Gale Huntington, *Songs the Whalemen Sang* (Barre, Mass., 1964).

9. *The Festival of Mirth, and American Tar's Delight: A Fund of the Newest Humorous, Patriotic, Hunting, and Sea Songs . . .* (New York, 1800), 6–7, 18, 34.

10. Harlow, *Chanteying*, 21–23.

11. Ibid., 25–27.

12. Samuel Leech, *A Voice from the Main Deck: Being a Record of the Thirty Years' Adventures of Samuel Leech*, introduction and notes by Michael J. Crawford (Annapolis, 1999; orig. pub. 1843), 36.

13. James Fenimore Cooper, *Red Rover* (New York, n.d.; orig. pub., 1850), 21–24, 36–42, 57–58, 61–67, 282–87, 344–55.

14. Leech, *A Voice from the Main Deck*, 36.

15. Joseph Emerson, *A Chart for Seamen: Exhibited in a Sermon Preached in Beverly, March 18th, 1804. Particularly Addressed to Seamen* (Salem, Mass., 1804).

16. Simeon Crowell, "Commonplace Book of Simeon Crowell," 1818–46, 6, 54–56, MHS. See also Margaret Baker, *Folklore of the Sea* (Newton Abbot, 1979), 164–84; Frederick Elkin, "The Soldier's Language," *American Journal of Sociology*, 51 (1946), 414–22; J. H. Parry, "Sailors' English," *Cambridge Journal* (1948–49), 660–70.

17. J. Ross Browne, *Etchings of a Whaling Cruise*, John Seelye, ed. (Cambridge, 1968; orig. pub. 1846), 151–53.

18. Ibid., 275.

19. George Jones, *Sketches of a Naval Life, With Notes of Men, Manners and Scenery . . . By a Civilian* (New Haven, 1829), 1:76.

20. Paul A. Gilje, *The Road to Mobocracy: Popular Disorder in New York City, 1763–1834* (Chapel Hill, N.C., 1987), 236.

21. Ibid., 123–24.

22. Gerry to Helen Gerry, Sept. 26, 1816, Gerry-Knight Papers II, 1768–1853, MHS.

23. Ebenezer Fox, *The Adventures of Ebenezer Fox, in the Revolutionary War* (Boston, 1847; orig. pub. 1838), 219.

24. J. Fenimore Cooper, ed., *Ned Myers; or, A Life Before the Mast*, introduction and notes by William S. Dudley (Annapolis, 1989; orig. pub. 1843), 206.

25. Christopher Hawkins, *The Adventures of Christopher Hawkins. . .*, introduction and notes by Charles I. Bushnell (New York, 1864), 37.

26. Joshua Penny, *The Life and Adventures of Joshua Penny . . .* (New York, 1815), 39.

27. *SM*, 2 (Dec. 1829), 112.

28. Mathew Carey, *Sailor's Medley: A Collection of the Most Admired Sea and Other Songs* (Philadelphia, 1800), 4.

29. Thomas Farel Heffernan, *Stove by a Whale: Owen Chase and the Essex* (Hanover, N.H., 1981), 100.

30. Charles Nordhoff, *A Man-of-War Life: A Boy's Experience in the United States Navy, During a Voyage Around the World in a Ship-of-the-line*, introduction and notes by John B. Hattendorf (Annapolis, 1985; orig. pub. 1855), 244.

31. William Ray, *Horrors of Slavery: or the American Tars in Tripoli* (Troy, N.Y., 1808), 36.

32. For a further discussion of these themes not connected to the sailor's liberty see Jesse Lemisch, "Jack Tar in the Streets: Merchant Seamen in the Politics of Revolutionary America, *WMQ*, 3rd ser., 25 (1968), 371–407; Marcus Rediker, *Between the Devil and the Deep Blue Sea: Merchant Seamen, Pirates, and the Anglo-American Maritime World, 1700–1750* (Cambridge, 1987); Peter Linebaugh and Marcus Rediker, "The Many-Headed Hydra: Sailors, Slaves and the Atlantic Working Class in the Eighteenth Century," in Colin Howell and Richard Twomey, eds., *Jack Tar in History: Essays in the History of Maritime Life and Labour* (Fredericton, New Brunswick, 1991), 11–36; and Linebaugh and Rediker, *The Many-Headed Hydra: Sailors, Slaves, Commoners, and the Hidden History of the Revolutionary Atlantic* (Boston, 2000).

33. Alfred M. Lorrain, *The Helm, the Sword, and the Cross: A Life Narrative* (Cincinnati, 1862), 93.

34. Leech, *A Voice From the Main Deck*, 154–55.

35. John Elliott, *The Reformed: An Old Sailor's Legacy* (Boston, 1841), 200–213.

36. William Torrey, *Torrey's Narrative . . .* (Boston, 1848), 274–76.

37. Herman Melville, *Moby Dick, or the Whale* (New York, 1982; orig. pub. 1851), 2.

38. Henry James Mercier, *Life in a Man-of-War, or Scenes in "Old Ironsides" During Her Cruise in the Pacific* (Boston, 1927; orig. pub. 1841), 87–88.

39. Penny, *Life and Adventures*, 39. See also George Edward Clark, *Seven Years of a Sailor's Life* (Boston, 1867), 107.

40. Lane, *The Wandering Boy*, 27.

41. Philip Greggs v. Charles Jimmison, July 16, 1788, Box 7, RPCA, HSP.

42. Ruth Wallis Herndon, "The Domestic Cost of Seafaring: Town Leaders and Seamen's Families in Eighteenth-Century Rhode Island," in Margaret S. Creighton and Lisa Norling, eds., *Iron Men and Wooden Women: Gender and Seafaring in the Atlantic World, 1700–1920* (Baltimore, 1996), 55–69; Charles P. Kindleberger, *Mariners and Markets* (New York, 1992).

43. Charles Abbot, *A Treatise of the Laws Relative to Merchant Ships and Seamen . . .* (Philadelphia, 1802); [United States], *An Act for the Government and Regulation of Seamen in the Merchant Service* (Warren, R.I., 1792).

44. *Enterprise* v. *Catherine*, Sept. 10, 1762, Box 1, Records of the Vice Admiralty Courts of the Province and State of New York (hereafter cited as NY Vice Admiralty Courts), RG 21, NA-NY.

45. Memorandum of Wm. Peterson, Dec. 17, 1809, Box 19/20, David Gelston Papers, Coll. 170, GWBWL.

46. John Willcock, *The Voyages and Adventures of John Willcock, Mariner: Interspersed With Remarks . . .* (Philadelphia, 1798), 66–67.

47. For sample fishing contracts see "Eighteenth-Century Fishing Information," Marblehead Historical Society, Marblehead, Mass. Daniel Vickers, *Farmers and Fishermen: Two Centuries of Work in Essex County, Massachusetts, 1630–1850* (Chapel Hill, N.C., 1994), 165.

48. The King v. *Prosperous Polly* (1762), Box 3, NY Vice Admiralty Courts, RG 21, NA-NY.

49. Nicholas Peter Isaacs, *Twenty Years Before the Mast, or Life in the Forecastle . . .* (New York, 1845), 57 and passim.

50. John Allen, "Voyage to Cuba, 1809," Jacob Reeves Papers, 1809–1835, MHS.

51. Crowell, "Commonplace Book," 54–58, MHS.

52. The King v. William Wood (1774), Box A, NY Vice Admiralty Courts, RG 21, NA-NY.

53. John Fillmore, *A Narration of the Captivity of John Fillmore and His Escape From the Pirates* (Suffield, [Conn.], 1802).

54. Deposition of John Stanford, Brigantine *Ocean*, Thomas Roach, Master, 1803, Box 1/27, Marine Jurisprudence Papers, Coll. 98, GWBWL.

55. Alan Taylor, *William Cooper's Town: Power and Persuasion on the Frontier of the Early American Republic* (New York, 1995), 343–45.

56. Judith Fingard, *Jack in Port: Sailortowns of Eastern Canada* (Toronto, 1982), 192–241; W. Jeffrey Bolster, *Black Jacks: African American Seamen in the Age of Sail* (Cambridge, Mass., 1997), 182–89.

57. *Enterprise* v. *Catherine*, Sept. 10, 1762, Box 1, NY Vice Admiralty Courts, RG 21, NA-NY.

58. John Lury v. Sloop *Sally*, June 28, 1770, Box 6, NY Vice Admiralty Courts, RG 21, NA-NY; McNaughton et al. v Sloop *Sally*, Nov. 7, 1771, Box 6, NY Vice Admiralty Courts, RG 21, NA-NY; Norsworthy and Taylor v. Brigantine *Claudia*, May 1786, Box 2, NY Vice Admiralty Courts, RG 21, NA-NY.

59. Isaacs, *Twenty Years Before the Mast*, 35–37.

60. Case of the Ship *Union*, 1809–10, Box 19/26, David Gelston Papers, Coll. 170, GWBWL.

61. See the discussion in Chapter 7.

62. Elijah Cobb, *A Cape Cod Skipper (1768–1848)* (New Haven, 1925), 65–66.

63. James Walthen to William Bowers, n.d., William R. Bowers Papers, RIHS; New-Bedford Port Society, *First Annual Report*; Judith Downey, "List of Mariners, including their residence, plus list of Boarding Houses, Compiled from the New Bedford City Directory," 1845, MS, ODHS, 1996.

64. Nathaniel G. Robinson to Mary Francis Robinson, July 4, 1843, *Nantasket*, 1842–43, Misc. MS, M-N, PEM.

65. Susan Gardner (Harose) to her mother, Jan. 3, 1827, Gardner Family Papers NHA.

66. B. S. Hammond to Timothy Hammond, Apr. 10, 1830, Hammond Family Papers, ODHS; Andrew Craige Hammond to Timothy Hammond, Mar. 18, 1830, ibid.

67. Cooper, ed., *Ned Myers*, 149. See also ibid., 141–51, 214–19, 225, 246, 251.

68. Marine Hospital Books, vol. 1, 1840–42, Marine Hospital Records, U.S. Customs House Papers, Providence, RIHS.

69. *CHSM*, 11 (Apr. 17, 1824), 248–53; *SM*, 2 (December 1829), 111–13; Joseph G. Clark, *Lights and Shadows of Sailor Life. As Exemplified in Fifteen Years Experience* (Boston, 1848), 253–64.

70. George Gardner to Susan Gardner (Harose), Aug. 13, Oct. 24, 1825, Gardner Family Papers, NHA.

71. While the costs listed here were incurred in a foreign port, they suggest the outlines of expenses elsewhere. Susan planned to move to New York City and establish a boardinghouse there with whatever capital she could take from her Le Havre investment. Susan Gardner (Harose) to her mother, Jan.5, 1827, Gardner Family Papers, NHA. For further discussion of boardinghouse keepers see Paul A. Gilje, "On the Waterfront: Maritime Workers in New York City, 1800–1850," *New York History*, 77 (1996), 395–426. See also Fingard, *Jack in Port*; Fingard, "'Those Crimps of Hell and Goblins Damned': The Image and Reality of Quebec's Sailortown Bosses," in Rosemary Ommer and Gerald Panting, eds., *Working Men Who Got Wet* (St. Johns, Newfoundland, 1980), 321–33; Sarah B. Palmer, "Seamen Ashore in Late Nineteenth Century London: Protection from the Crimps," in Paul Adams, ed., *Seamen in Society* (Bucharest, 1980), Part III, 54–62. For an anecdotal account see Stan Hugill, *Sailortown* (London, 1967).

72. Lane, *Wandering Boy*, 75.

73. John Remington Congdon, Oct. 25–26, 1840, Journal, Congdon Family Papers, RIHS.

74. Jacob A. Hazen, *Five Years Before the Mast, or Life in the Forecastle Aboard a Whaler and Man-of-War*, 2nd ed. (Philadelphia, 1854), 19–58.

75. Baker v. Howland, 1847, Box 1, Dana Legal Papers, AAS.

76. Browne, *Etchings of a Whaling Cruise*, 11. See also Elmo Paul Hohman, *The American Whaleman: A Study of Life and Labor in the Whaling Industry* (London, 1928), 89–113.

77. For examples of recruitment during the American Revolutionary War see William James Morgan, ed., *Naval Documents of the American Revolution* (Washington, D.C., 1976), 7:220–21, 521–22, 532, 574; [Nathaniel Fanning], *Narrative of the Adventures of an American Naval Officer . . .* (New York, 1806), 45, 102; John Kilby, "Narrative of John Kilby: Quarter-Gunner of the U.S. Ship 'Bon Homme Richard' Under Paul Jones," *Scribner's Magazine* (July 1905), 28. For rendezvous houses after the Revolutionary War see John Hoxse, *The Yankee Tar: An Authentic Narrative of the Voyages and Hardships of John Hoxse . . .* (Northampton, Mass., 1840), 46–47. For examples of bills paid during recruitment see Boxes 353–55 (1750–1841), Naval Records Collection, RG 45, NA.

78. Ray, *Horrors of Slavery*, 25.

79. Ira Dye, *The Fatal Cruise of the "Argus": Two Captains in the War of 1812* (Annapolis, 1994), 45.

80. William Fairgreve to Wm. B. Preston, Sec. of U.S. Navy, Apr. 20, 1850, Box 353, Naval Records Collection, RG 45, NA. See also Gilje, *Road to Mobocracy*, 180.

81. Hoxse, *Yankee Tar*, 56.

82. Gary B. Nash, *The Urban Crucible: Social Change, Political Consciousness, and the Origins of the American Revolution* (Cambridge, Mass., 1979), 322–23.

83. John Brice v. *Nancy*, Nov. 8, 1783, Box 5, RPCA, HSP.

84. Billy G. Smith, *The "Lower Sort": Philadelphia's Laboring People, 1750–1800* (Ithaca, N.Y., 1990), 111.

85. J. Smith v. *Hannah* (1761), Dec. 23, 1761, Box 11, NY Vice Admiralty Courts, RG 21, NA-NY; Ship's Papers, Box 1, Joshua Burnham Papers, PEM.

86. An examination of the articles of agreement of any voyage reveals these differentials. For examples of a long run of such articles from the 1790s through the 1820s ee Boxes 1–5, Hale Shipping Collection Papers, NHHS.

87. Jacob C. Treadwell v. Zebulon York and Daniel Evans, June 10, 1804, Box 1, Hale Shipping Collection Papers, NHHS.

88. Ledger, Payments to Officers and Crews, 1823–25, Edward Carrington Papers, RIHS. See Greenhoo et al. v. *Mentor*, Nov. 28, 1798, Box B, NY Vice Admiralty Courts, RG 21, NA-NY. For a discussion of the different ratings of seamen see Chapter 3.

89. Lane, *The Wandering Boy*, 105; William McNally, *Evils and Abuses in the Naval and Merchant Service, Exposed; With Proposals for their Remedy and Redress* (Boston, 1839), 71–72, 76–77.

90. *Enterprize* v. *Susanna and Ann* (1762), Box 5, NY Vice Admiralty Courts, RG 21, NA-NY.

91. *Enterprise* v. *Catherine*, Sept. 10, 1762, Box 1, NY Vice Admiralty Courts, RG 21, NA-NY.

92. Articles of the Ship *Borneo*, Dec. 2, 1831, Ship's Papers, Box 1, Gillis Papers, PEM.

93. James Durand, *James Durand: An Able Seaman of 1812: His Adventures on "Old Ironsides" and as an Impressed Sailor in the British Navy*, George S. Brooks, ed. (New Haven, 1926; orig. pub. 1820), 12.

94. Hammond Family Papers, ODHS. See also Allan A. Arnold, "Merchants in the Forecastle: The Private Ventures of New England Mariners," *AN*, 41 (1981), 165–87.

95. *Dolphin*, Dec. 5, 1764, Ship's Papers, Box 1, Joshua Burnham Papers, PEM.

96. *Enterprize* v. *York Castle*, May 8, 1762, Box 5, NY Vice Admiralty Courts, RG 21, NA-NY.

97. *Abigail*, Dec. 1761, Joshua Burnham Papers, PEM; *Rose in Bloom*, 1807, Samuel Herrick Papers, 1800–1823, MHS; [Shipping Articles], *It is Agreed Between the Master, Seamen, and Mariners . . .* ([Providence, 1796]).

98. Vickers, *Farmers and Fisherman*, 143–203, 264–89; Fishing Agreement for the Schooner *Polly*, Mar. 14, 1793,; Fishing Agreement for the Schooner *Sally*, Mar. 17, 1793, and Apr. 5, 1795,and Record of the Fishing Schooner, *Two Friends*, Mar. 18, 1795, Eighteenth-Century Fishing Information, Marblehead Historical Society.

99. List of Crew, Aug. 3–5, 1846, Ship *Columbia*, Charles G. and Henry Coffin Collection, 1829–62, NHA. Additional crew members might have been signed when the vessel visited the Azores.

100. Hohman, *American Whalemen*, 217–71. See also Briton Cooper Busch, *"Whaling Will Never Do for Me": The American Whaleman in the Nineteenth Century* (Lexington, Ky., 1994); Lance E. Davis, Robert E. Gallman, and Karin Gleiter, *In Pursuit of Leviathan: Technology, Institutions, Productivity, and Profits in American Whaling, 1816–1906* (Chicago, 1997); Lisa Norling, *Captain Ahab Had a Wife: New England Women and the Whalefishery, 1720–1870* (Chapel Hill, N.C., 2000); Edouard A. Stackpole, *The Sea Hunters: The New England Whalemen During Two Centuries, 1635–1835* (Philadelphia, 1953); Alexander Starbuck, *A History of the American Whale Fishery from Its Earliest Inception to the Year 1876* (New York, 1964; orig. pub. 1878).

101. "Return of the Crew of the Privateer Sloop *Comet*," Mar. 29, 1780, Box 3, RPCA, HSP.

102. Wilfred Harold Munro, "The Most Successful American Privateer: An Episode of

the War of 1812," American Antiquarian Society, *Proceedings*, 23 (1913), 12–62. See also the information on shares from the privateer *Diomede* in Box 1, Crowinshield Family Papers, PEM.

103. Elijah Shaw, *A Short Sketch, of the Life of Elijah Shaw who Served for Twenty-two Years in the United States Navy*... (Rochester, 1843), 14.

104. Accounts of the Ship *Franklin*, Ledger, Payments to Officers and Crews, 1823–25, Edward Carrington Papers, RIHS.

105. Seamen's Accounts, vol. 1 (1844–51), Box 14, Swift and Allen Collection, ODHS. See also *Harbinger* (ship) Records, 1842–61, Box 63, Cory Family Papers, ODHS.

106. James Webb to his mother, Oct. 4, 1845, Box 84, Business Records Collection, ODHS; same to same, May 16, 1848, ibid. For examples of typical deductions see Bark *Hind's* Receipt Book, 1809–11, Box 2, Crowinshield Family Papers, MS 54, PEM; and Bark *Mars* Accounts, 1842–45, NBFPL.

107. See Privateering Agent Papers, 1812–13, Shipping Papers, Box 2, Gregory Family Papers, PEM.

108. Abbot, *A Treatise of the Law*; Richard Henry Dana, Jr., *The Seaman's Friend* (New York, 1979; orig. pub. 1851), 222; *SM*, 1 (Apr. 1829), 245–48.

109. Their total profit may have been higher since several seamen were advanced large sums in the East Indies which might represent the money they invested in goods that they shipped as private ventures on the return voyage. Accounts of the Ship *Franklin*, Ledger, Payments to Officers and Crews, 1823–25, Edward Carrington Papers, RIHS.

110. Daniel Vickers, "Nantucket Whalemen in the Deep-Sea Fishery: The Changing Anatomy of an Early American Labor Force," *JAH*, 72 (1985), 277–96; W. Jeffrey Bolster, "'To Feel like a Man': Black Seamen in the Northern States, 1800–1860," *JAH*, 76 (1990), 1173–99.

111. "Jefferson's Notes on Sheffield's *Observations on the Commerce of the American States*," in Julian P. Boyd, ed., *The Papers of Thomas Jefferson* (Princeton, N.J., 1974), 19:131.

112. *Mariners' Church* [New York, 1818], 5.

113. "Seamen in the United States," *Army and Navy Chronicle*, 1 (Nov. 26, 1835), 382.

114. NY Vice Admiralty Courts, RG 21, NA-NY.

115. Paul A. Gilje, "Loyalty and Liberty: The Ambiguous Patriotism of Jack Tar in the American Revolution," *PH*, 67 (2000), 165–93.

116. Crew Lists and Shipping Articles, 1789–1900, Box 1, U.S. Customs House Papers, Providence, RIHS.

117. Smith, *"Lower Sort,"* 153; Christopher McKee, "Foreign Seamen in the United States Navy: A Census of 1808," *WMQ*, 3rd ser., 42 (1985), 383–93. See also F. S. Harrod, "Americanization of the United States Navy Enlisted Force," Adam, ed., *Seamen in Society*, Part II, 196–201.

118. Melville, *Moby Dick*, 45–46.

119. New-Bedford Port Society, *Seventh Annual Report* (New Bedford, 1836), 6. Whaling crews were less diverse before 1830, but had long had some mixture of races and peoples. Hohman, *The American Whaleman*, 48–83; Vickers, "Nantucket Whalemen."

120. Gary B. Nash, *Forging Freedom: The Formation of Philadelphia's Black Community, 1720–1840* (Cambridge, Mass., 1988), 148–49; Bolster, *Black Jacks*; Michael Cohn and Michael K. H. Platzer, *Black Men of the Sea* (New York, 1978); James Farr, "A Slow Boat to Nowhere: The Multi-Racial Crews of the American Whaling Industry," *Journal of Negro History*, 68 (1983), 159–70. Harold D. Langley, "The Negro in the Navy and the Merchant Service, 1798–1860," *Journal of Negro History*, 52 (1967), 273–86.

121. Frederick Douglass, *The Narrative and Selected Writings*, Michael Meyer, ed. (New York, 1984), 51–56, 99–110.

122. Bolster, *Black Jacks*; Nash, *Forging Freedom*, 146.

123. For tables showing the percentage of black seamen in crews in Providence, New York, Philadelphia, Baltimore, Savannah, and New Orleans see Bolster, *Black Jacks*, 235–37.

124. Vickers, *Farmers and Fishermen*, 143–203.

125. Vickers, "Nantucket Whalemen."

126. NY Vice Admiralty Courts, RG 21, NA-NY.

127. Smith, *"Lower Sort,"* 153.

128. Daniel Vickers and Vince Walsh, "Young Men and the Sea: The Sociology of Seafaring in Eighteenth-Century Salem, Massachusetts," *Social History*, 24 (1999), 17–38. Crew list of the schooner *Alert*, 1805, 1806, Samuel Herrick Papers, MHS.

129. Samuel Smith to Rebecca Smith, Oct. 25, 1841, Box 73, Business Records Collection, ODHS.

130. Dec. 30, 1849, Log of the *Sheffield*, Log #351, GWBWL. For a sociological discussion of different types of sailors see Knut Weibust, *Deep Sea Sailors: A Study of Maritime Ethnology*, 2nd ed. (Stockholm, 1976).

131. The average age of prisoners during these wars was probably higher than the average age of the peacetime seafaring population. During wars, privateers recruited many landsmen who might be older than the average sailor. Also, at least during the American Revolution, the British tended to simply impress boys in their young teens into His Majesty's Service. Ira Dye, "Physical and Social Profiles of Early American Seafarers, 1812–1815," in Howell and Twomey, eds., *Jack Tar in History*, 222. The ages of the revolutionary seamen was determined by examining the descriptions of escaped prisoners of war held in Mill and Forton prisons in England. See the reports on escaped prisoners of war found in the letters of the Commissioners of Hurt and Sick Seamen, in Adm/M/404–05, microfilm, NMM.

132. Bolster, *Black Jacks*, table 3, 239. See also Ira Dye, "Early American Merchant Seafarers," *Proceedings of the American Philosophical Society*, 120 (1976), 331–60.

133. See Vickers and Walsh, "Young Men and the Sea." To verify age cohorts for seamen I used a sample derived from crew lists from Providence in 1803, 1806, 1823, 1826, 1843, 1846 and Baltimore in 1843. I also took a sample from prisoner-of-war records during the American Revolution in 1781. The findings of my sample showed that except during the war the average age of seamen signing on ships ranged from 25.16 to 27.99. The age cohorts ranged from about 10–20 percent under age twenty (with most older than seventeen), with about 55–60 percent in the twenties, 15 to 25 percent in the thirties, and from about 3 percent to 12 percent forty or over. The prisoners-of-war average was 29.32, with more men in their thirties (34.28 percent). But the majority were still young men: over 46 percent were in their twenties and about 18 percent under twenty. Boxes 1, 5, 6, 11, U.S. Customs House Papers, RIHS; Box 7, Bureau of Customs, Baltimore, Maryland, RG 36, NA; Adm 98/13, microfilm, PRO.

134. *Mariner's Church*, 5.

135. F. A. De Peyster, Memoirs, Bound Typescript, 163, PEM.

136. *CHSM*, 8 (Aug. 18, 1821), 218.

137. Melville, *Moby Dick*, 1.

138. Lane, *Wandering Boy*, 58.

139. Leech, *A Voice from the Main Deck*, 156.

140. Henry Chase, Diary, (1821–22), NYHS.

141. Gregory Family Papers, PEM.

142. Joseph Baker, *The Confessions of Joseph Baker, A Canadian by Birth* . . . [Philadelphia, 1800].

143. Isaacs, *Twenty Years Before the Mast*, 37.

144. Stephen D. Gray, "Diary and Account Book, 1836–1843," Misc. Vol. 390, GWBWL. Daniel Vickers and Vince Walsh have demonstrated the flexibility of employment between shore and sea and across ranks in mid eighteenth-century Salem. Vickers and Walsh, "Young Men and the Sea."

145. Philip Chadwick Smith, ed., *The Journals of Ashley Bowen (1728–1813) of Marblehead* in *Publications of the Colonial Society of Massachusetts, Collections*, 44 (Boston, 1973); Daniel Vickers, "An Honest Tar: Ashley Bowen of Marblehead," *NEQ*, 69 (1996), 531–53; Vickers, "Ashley Bowen of Marblehead: Revolutionary Neutral," in Nancy L. Rhoden and Ian K. Steele, eds., *The Human Tradition in the American Revolution* (Wilmington, 2000), 99–115.

146. Crowell, "Commonplace Book," MHS.

147. Hammond Family Papers, ODHS.

148. Isaacs, *Twenty Years Before the Mast.*

149. Hoxse, *The Yankee Tar.*

150. Case of the *Halifax Packet* (1760), Box 2, NY Vice Admiralty Courts, RG 21, NA-NY; Ship *Charlotte*, May 20, 1803, Crew Lists, Box 1, U.S. Customs House Papers, Providence, RIHS; Schooner *Rival of Calais*, Feb. 7, 1843, Crew Lists, Box 11, U.S. Customs House Papers, Providence, RIHS.

151. Bolster, *Black Jacks*, 219, 292, n.11.

152. Vickers and Walsh, "Young Men and the Sea," 17–33.

Chapter 2. The Maid I Left Behind Me

1. "Diary of William Widger of Marblehead, Kept at Mill Prison, England, 1781," *EIHC*, 73 (1937), 347. Jesse Lemisch uses this dream to highlight the importance of the history of the "inarticulate." See Lemisch, "Listening to the 'Inarticulate': William Widger's Dream and the Loyalties of the American Revolutionary Seamen in British Prisons," *JSH*, 3 (1969), 1–29.

2. The Age of Revolution was not a period of great political or social transformation for most women. Some scholars have emphasized the emergence of a republican motherhood centered on the home as a breeding ground for a virtuous citizenry among the middle class. In the early nineteenth century, republican motherhood led to a sentimentalized ideal that included a belief that women occupied a separate sphere limited to the household. More recently, some historians have suggested that this separate sphere did not create an inseparable barrier between the male and female worlds. Poor women, like many of those found on the waterfront, were often too busy with work to fulfill either a republican or domestic ideal. Nor did they have much time to create a separate sphere. Rather than experiencing an enhanced role as the special repositories of virtue, most women found that democratization of male society, which centered on the role of independent men in the polity, left them increasingly dismissed as dependent persons with little or no political identity. See Ruth H. Bloch, "The Gendered Meanings of Virtue in Revolutionary America," *Signs*, 13 (1987), 37–58; Jeanne Boydston, *Home and Work: Housework, Wages, and the Ideology of Labor in the Early Republic* (New York, 1990); Boydston, "The Woman Who Wasn't There: Women's Market Labor and the Transition to Capitalism in the United States," in Paul A. Gilje, ed., *Wages of Independence: Capitalism in the Early American Republic* (Madison, Wis., 1997), 23–47; Joan R. Gundersen, "Independence, Citizenship, and the American Revolution," *Signs*, 13 (1987), 59–77; Ronald Hoffman and Peter J. Albert, eds., *Women in the Age of the American Revolution* (Charlottesville, Va., 1989); Susan Juster, *Disorderly Women: Sexual Politics and Evangelicalism in Revolutionary New*

England (Ithaca, N.Y., 1994); Catherine E. Kelly, *In the New England Fashion: Reshaping Women's Lives in the Nineteenth Century* (Ithaca, N.Y., 1999); Linda K. Kerber, *Women of the Republic: Intellect and Ideology in Revolutionary America* (Chapel Hill, N.C., 1980); Kerber, "Separate Spheres, Female Worlds, Woman's Place: The Rhetoric of Women's History," *JAH*, 75 (1988), 9–39. Kerber et al. "Beyond Roles, Beyond Spheres: Thinking About Gender in the Early Republic," *WMQ*, 3rd ser., 46 (1989), 565–85; Jan Lewis, "The Republican Wife: Virtue and Seduction in the Early Republic," *WMQ*, 3rd ser., 44 (1987), 689–722; Mary Beth Norton, *Liberty's Daughters: The Revolutionary Experience of American Women, 1750–1800* (Boston, 1980); Jacqueline Reimer, "Rearing the Republican Child," *WMQ*, 3rd ser., 39 (1982), 150–63; Christine Stansell, *City of Women: Sex and Class in New York, 1789–1860* (New York, 1986); Joan Hoff Wilson, "The Illusion of Change: Women and the American Revolution," in Alfred F. Young, ed., *The American Revolution: Exploration in the History of American Radicalism* (DeKalb, Ill., 1976), 383–445.

3. For other discussions of women on the waterfront see David Cordingly, *Women Sailors and Sailors' Women: An Untold Maritime History* (New York, 2001); Elaine Forman Crane, *Ebb Tide in New England: Women, Seaports, and Social Change, 1630–1800* (Boston, 1998); Lisa Norling, *Captain Ahab Had a Wife: New England Women and the Whalefishery, 1720–1870* (Chapel Hill, N.C., 2000); Linda M. Maloney, "Women in Maritime America: The Nineteenth Century," in Paul Adam, ed., *Seamen in Society* (Bucharest, 1980), Part III, 113–21; Suzanne J. Stark, *Female Tars: Women Aboard Ship in the Age of Sail* (Annapolis, 1996); and the essays in Margaret S. Creighton and Lisa Norling, *Iron Men, Wooden Women: Gender and Seafaring in the Atlantic World, 1700–1920* (Baltimore, 1996). For a general discussion of gender see Thomas Laqueur, *Making Sex: Body and Gender from the Greeks to Freud* (Cambridge, Mass., 1990); Michel Foucault, *The History of Sexuality*, Robert Hurley, trans. (New York, 1978).

4. For a discussion of ideas on manhood within the working class and antebellum youth culture see Richard B. Stott, *Workers in the Metropolis: Class, Ethnicity, and Youth in Antebellum New York City* (Ithaca, N.Y., 1990), and Amy S. Greenberg, *Cause for Alarm: The Volunteer Fire Department in the Nineteenth Century City* (Princeton, 1998). For a general discussion of manhood in this period see E. Anthony Rotundo, "Boy Culture: Middle-Class Boyhood in Nineteenth-Century America," in Mark C. Carnes and Clyde Griffen, eds., *Meanings for Manhood: Constructions of Masculinity in Victorian America* (Chicago, 1990), 15–36; Rotundo, *American Manhood: Transformations in Masculinity from the Revolution to the Modern Era* (New York, 1993); Elliot J. Gorn, *The Manly Art: Bare-Knuckle Prize Fighting in America* (Ithaca, N.Y., 1986); Michael Kimmel, *Manhood in America: A Cultural History* (New York, 1996).

5. Richard Henry Dana, Jr., *Two Years Before the Mast: A Personal Narrative of Life at Sea*, Thomas Philbrick, ed. (New York 1981; orig. pub. 1840), 242, 249, 330.

6. A Brother Cruiser, "The Boatswain's Mate," *Naval Magazine*, 1 (1836), 516–521.

7. J. Ross Browne, *Etchings of a Whaling Cruise*, John Seelye, ed. (Cambridge, 1968; orig. pub., 1846), 166.

8. *The Festival of Mirth and America Tar's Delight: A Fund of the Newest Humorous, Patriotic, Hunting, and Sea Songs . . .* (New York, 1800), 30–31.

9. George G. Carey, ed., *A Sailor's Songbag: An American Rebel in an English Prison, 1777–1779* (Amherst, Mass., 1976), 30–31.

10. *Festival of Mirth*, 50–51.

11. Carey, ed., *A Sailor's Songbag*, 54–55.

12. William Main Doerflinger, *Songs of the Sailor and Lumberman*, rev. ed. (New York, 1972), 305–6.

13. Division of labor modified these strains to some degree. Youths and blacks often

were relegated to the supposedly least masculine tasks of cooking and serving. For a fuller discussion of these issues see Margaret S. Creighton, "American Mariners and the Rites of Manhood, 1830–1870," in Colin Howell and Richard J. Twomey, eds., *Jack Tar in History: Essays in the History of Maritime Life and Labour* (Fredericton, New Brunswick, 1991), 143–63; Creighton, "Fraternity in the American Forecastle, 1830–1870," *NEQ*, 63 (1990), 531–57; Creighton, *Rites and Passages: The Experience of American Whaling, 1830–1870* (Cambridge, 1995); Creighton, *Dogwatch and Liberty Days: Seafaring Life in the Nineteenth Century* (Worcester, Mass., 1982).

14. Herman Melville, *Billy Budd, Sailor, and Other Stories*, Harold Beaver, ed., (New York, 1967), 328–31.

15. Herman Melville, *White Jacket, or the World in a Man-of-War*, Harrison Hayford et al., eds. (Evanston, Ill., 1970; orig. pub. 1849), 376; Melville, *Moby Dick, or the Whale* (New York, 1930; orig. pub. 1851), 74–76. See also the discussion in Robert K. Martin, *Hero, Captain, and Stranger: Male Friendship, Social Critique, and Literary Form in the Sea Novels of Herman Melville* (Chapel Hill, N.C., 1986); Martin, "Knights-Errant and Gothic Seducers: The Representation of Male Friendship in Mid-Nineteenth-Century America," in Martin Bauml Duberman et al., eds., *Hidden from History: Reclaiming the Gay and Lesbian Past* (New York, 1989), 169–82; B. R. Burg, *An American Seafarer in the Age of Sail: The Erotic Diaries of Philip C. Van Buskirk, 1851–1870* (New Haven, 1994), 89–90.

16. There are no studies for the American navy comparable to Arthur N. Gilbert, "Buggery and the British Navy, 1700–1861," *JSH*, 10 (1976), 72–98.

17. There was a fourth case in which only one individual was charged in early December 1845. "Discipline and Minor Delinquencies: Record of Punishments, U.S. Frigate *Congress*, 1845–1848," Box 283, Naval Records Collection, RG 45, NA. Christopher McKee mentions a case of homosexuality concerning an officer. He also asserts that other officers considered this behavior as unusual. Christopher McKee, *A Gentlemanly and Honorable Profession: The Creation of the U.S. Naval Officer Corps, 1794–1815* (Annapolis, 1991), 438–39.

18. Josiah Cobb, *A Green Hand's First Cruise, Roughed Out From the Log-Book of Memory, of Twenty-Five Years Standing* . . ., 2 vols. (Boston, 1841), 2:246.

19. H. Baily to [Charles G. Coffin and Henry Coffin], Sept. 15, 1844, Charles G. and Henry Coffin Collection, 1829–62, NHA.

20. In addition to this case and two others, one from 1838 and the other from 1835, Creighton describes an 1861 sodomy trial of a whaleship captain. Although convicted, the captain continued to protest his innocence. Creighton, *Rites and Passages*, 190–92.

21. Burg's book is a fascinating exploration of Van Buskirk's sexuality, but he pushes the evidence too far. For example, Burg writes that Samuel Leech, a nineteenth-century sailor who wrote a book of his experiences, "claimed sodomy hardly merited serious attention." What Leech really said was that a Portuguese lad had been sent ashore at Madeira "for attempting a crime unfit to be mentioned in these pages, but quite common among the Spaniards and the Portuguese." My reading of this passage is that the practice, which we are left to presume was a homosexual act, was common among a despised group like the Hispanics. By implication, it was not common among American sailors. Burg, *An American Seafarer in the Age of Sail*, 74. For the Leech passage see Samuel Leech, *A Voice from the Main Deck: Being a Record of the Thirty Years' Adventures of Samuel Leech*, introduction and notes by Michael J. Crawford (Annapolis, 1999; orig. pub. 1843), 56. See also Burg's discussion in *Sodomy and the Pirate Tradition: English Sea Rovers in the Seventeenth-Century Caribbean* (New York, 1983).

22. For similar conclusions see Cordingly, *Women Sailors and Sailors' Women*, 138–46; Eric W. Sager, *Seafaring Labour: The Merchant Marine of Atlantic Canada, 1820–1914* (Montreal, 1989), 239.

23. Quoted in Margaret S. Creighton, "Davy Jones' Locker Room: Gender and the American Whaleman, 1830–1870," in Creighton and Norling, eds., *Iron Men and Wooden Women*, 126.

24. Cited in Ira Dye, *The Fatal Cruise of the "Argus": Two Captains in the War of 1812* (Annapolis, 1994), 11.

25. "Letters of Samuel Dalton of Salem, An Impressed American Seaman, 1803–1814," *EIHC*, 68 (1932), 323–24.

26. Joseph Valpey, Jr., *Journal of Joseph Valpey, Jr. of Salem, November 1813–April 1815: With Other Papers Relating to His Experience in Dartmoor Prison* (n.p., 1922), 42.

27. *CHSM*, 9 (Oct. 5, 1822), 319–20.

28. Paul A. Gilje, ed., "A Sailor Prisoner of War During the War of 1812," *Maryland Historical Magazine*, 85 (1990), 67–69.

29. *A Circumstantial Narrative of the Loss of the Halewell, East Indiaman* . . . (Springfield, Mass., 1786), 70.

30. Cobb, *A Green Hand's First Cruise*, 2:74–83.

31. Valpey, *Journal of Joseph Valpey, Jr.*, 15, 38, 45, 46.

32. Caroline Moseley, "Images of Young Women in Nineteenth-Century Songs of the Sea," *Log of Mystic Seaport*, 35 (1984), 132–39; Stuart M. Frank, *Oooh, You New York Girls! The Urban Pastorale in Ballads and Songs about Sailors Ashore in the Big City* (Sharon, Mass., 1996), 3–4.

33. Carey, ed., *A Sailor's Songbag*, 150–51.

34. *The Cabin-Boy and Forecastle Sailor's Delight: A Collection of Choice Songs* (New York, 1817); "Dibden's Sea Songs," *New World*, 3 (Sept. 4, 1841), 145–46; *Festival of Mirth*; *Patriotic Melody: Being a Collection of Patriotic, Sentimental, Hunting, and Sea Songs* . . . (New York, 1800); *The Sailor's Medley: A Collection of the Most Admired Sea and Other Songs* (Philadelphia, 1800); *The Syren; A Choice Collection of Sea, Hunting, and Other Songs* (Philadelphia, 1800); [James Cobb], *A Sailor Lov'd a Lass Composed by S. Storace for the Cherokee* (Philadelphia, [1796]); John C. Cross, *Songs in the Purse; or, a Benevolent Tar, A Musical Drama in One Act. As Performed at the New Theatre, Philadelphia* (Philadelphia, 1794). See also the songs from whalemen's journals in Gale Huntington, *Songs the Whalemen Sang* (Barre, Mass., 1964), 90–100.

35. Charles Dibden, *The Taken* (Philadelphia, [1794].

36. Henry James Mercier, *Life in a Man-of-War, Or Scenes in "Old Ironsides" During Her Cruise in the Pacific* (Boston, 1927; orig. pub. 1841), 221–22.

37. See for example "Nancy or Sailor's Journal," in Charles P. Clinton, "His Journal Book, 1802–1806," Yale.

38. J. C. Cross, *The Purse; or, Benevolent Tar. A Musical Drama in One Act as Performed at the Boston Theatre, Federal Street* (Boston, 1797).

39. Isaac Bickerstaff, *Thomas and Sally; or, The Sailor's Return. A Musical Entertainment* . . . (Philadelphia, 1791).

40. Huntington, *Songs the Whalemen Sang*, 121–22.

41. On scrimshaw see E. Norman Flayderman, *Scrimshaw and Scrimshanders: Whales and Whalemen* (New Milford, Conn., 1972); Nina Hellman and Norman Brouwer, *A Mariner's Fancy: The Whaleman's Art of Scrimshaw* (Seattle, 1992); Martha Lawrence, *Scrimshaw: The Whaler's Legacy* (Atglen, Pa., 1993); Richard C. Malley, *Graven by the Fishermen Themselves: Scrimshaw in Mystic Seaport Museum* (Mystic, Conn., 1983); Charles R. Meyer, *Whaling and the Art of Scrimshaw* (New York, 1976).

42. John Baker, Logbook, *Polly*, 1804–5, PEM.

43. Prince Hoare, *The Sailor Boy* [Philadelphia, 1793].

44. Logbook, *General Wolfe*, 1767–69, PEM.

45. Frances Boardman, Logbook, *Vaughan*, 1767, PEM.

46. *Patriotic Medley*, 143–44.

47. Carey, ed., *A Sailor's Songbag*, 98, 24.

48. Frederick Pease Harlow, *Chanteying Aboard American Ships* (Barre, Mass., 1962), 51.

49. A picture of this scrimshaw whale tooth can be found in Lawrence, *Scrimshaw*, 74. For similar examples of scrimshaw see pp. 73, 81, 130.

50. For illustrations from after 1850 see Creighton, *Dogwatch and Liberty Days*, 64; Creighton, *Rites and Passages*, 151, 171.

51. Alfred Terry, front page, Logbook, *Vesper*, 1846–48, Log 955, GWBWL.

52. Frank, *Oooh, You New York Girls!* 12, 14.

53. Joseph G. Clark, *Lights and Shadows of Sailor Life, As Exemplified in Fifteen Years' Experience* . . . (Boston, 1847), 260–61.

54. Frank, *Oooh, You New York Girls!* See also Karen Halttunen, *Confidence Men and Painted Women: A Study of Middle-Class Culture in America, 1830–1870* (New Haven, 1982).

55. Ezra Goodnough, Mar. 1, 3, 7, June 6, 10, July 8, 24, 1847, Logbook, *Ann Perry*, PEM.

56. *The Cabin-Boy and Forecastle Sailor's Delight*, 18–19.

57. Frank, *Oooh, You New York Girls!* 19.

58. Horace Lane, *The Wandering Boy, Careless Sailor, and Result of Inconsideration. A True Narrative* (Skaneateles, N.Y., 1839), 106–7.

59. *The Syren*, 5–6.

60. Stan Hugill, *Sailortown* (London, 1967), 76.

61. *New-York Journal*, Oct. 16, 1793. Mother Carey's, however, was not on the waterfront. See also Paul A. Gilje, *The Road to Mobocracy: Popular Disorder in New York City, 1763–1834* (Chapel Hill, N.C., 1987), 87–91.

62. John Palmer Cipher Book, 1775, John Palmer Papers, Coll. 53, GWBWL.

63. Charles to Henry Babock, Sept. 28, 1841, Box 73, Cory Family Papers, ODHS.

64. Clinton wrote this on the cover of his brother's journal. Clinton, "His Journal, 1802–1806," Yale.

65. Nathaniel Ames, *Nautical Reminiscences* (Providence, 1832), 17, 38.

66. Dana, *Two Years Before the Mast*, 331–32.

67. Joshua Penny, *The Life and Adventures of Joshua Penny* . . . (New York, 1815), 39.

68. John Blatchford, *Narrative of the Remarkable Occurrences, In the Life of John Blatchford of Cape Ann* . . . (New London, 1788), 16–19.

69. Robert Adams, *The Narrative of Robert Adams, An American Sailor, Who Was Wrecked on the Western Coast of Africa, in the Year 1810* . . . (Boston, 1817), 59–77.

70. *The Cabin-Boy and Forecastle Sailor's Delight*, 5–7.

71. See William Bligh, *A Narrative of the Mutiny, on Board His Britannic Majesty's Ship "Bounty"* . . . (Philadelphia, 1790). See also Greg Dening, *Mr. Bligh's Bad Language: Passion, Power and Theatre on the "Bounty"* (Cambridge, 1992).

72. Terry, Feb. [?], 1847, Logbook, *Vesper*, Log 955, GWBWL.

73. William Clarke, Sept. 3, 1838, Logbook, USS *Relief*, PEM.

74. Frank, *Oooh, You New York Girls!* 4–5.

75. Herman Melville, *Typee: A Peep at Polynesian Life During a Four Months' Residence in A Valley of the Marquesas* (New York, 1964; orig. pub., 1846), 94–95, 104–5. See also Joan Druett, "More Decency and Order: Women and Whalemen in the Pacific," *Log of Mystic Seaport*, 39 (1987), 65–74.

76. Valerie Burton, "The Myth of Bachelor Jack: Masculinity, Patriarchy, and Seafaring Labour," in Howell and Twomey, eds., *Jack Tar in History*, 79–98.

77. Nov. 8, 1781, Typescript, William Russell Journal, PEM. See also William Russell, "Journal of William Russell (1776–1782)," in Ralph D. Payne, *The Ships and Sailors of Old Salem: The Record of a Brilliant Era of American Achievement* (New York, 1908), 152–53.

78. Jonathan Deakins to his wife, Mill Prison, Dec. 8, 1782, Continental Army and Navy Letters, Marblehead Historical Society, Marblehead, Mass. The Marblehead Historical Society has five such letters written by prisoners of war during the Revolutionary War. Ibid.

79. See, for example, Richard Waters to John Mitchell, July 3, 1814, and John Walpole to John Mitchell, July 1, 1814, John Mitchell Papers, HSP.

80. Most of the letters discussed below come from relationships where the men were working their way to the command of a ship. Such individuals and their wives were not only likely to have stable relationships, but were also likely to save letters so that their descendants could donate them to a library. While these circumstances create a bias, they also suggest one end of a range of possible interactions between men and women on the waterfront.

81. Letters between Jacob W. Ball and Mary Timbrell Ball, 1822–1831, Ball Family Papers, NYHS.

82. Nathan J. Coleman to Elizabeth Hodgdon, May 17, May 23, Nov. 4, 1842; Feb. 4, Nov. 12, 1843; Elizabeth H. Coleman (née Hodgdon) to Coleman, Sept. 8, 1844; Sanborn Family Papers, 1785–1875, MHS.

83. These journals can be found in the Congdon Family Papers, RIHS.

84. E. H. Hodgdon to Sarah Hodgdon, Apr. 22, 1842; [Elizabeth Hodgdon] to cousin, May 1842; S. Hodgdon to E. Hodgdon, June 4, 1842; Elizabeth H. Hodgdon to Mr. and Mrs. Coleman, April 26, 1842; E. H. Hodgdon to Mr. and Mrs. Coleman, Dec. 29, 1842, Sanborn Family Papers, 1785–1875, MHS.

85. Elizabeth Rogers Hammond to parents, n.d., Hammond Family Papers, ODHS.

86. Lisa Norling, "Contrary Dependedencies: Whaling Agents and Whalemen's Families, 1830–1870," *Log of Mystic Seaport*, 42 (1990), 3–12; Norling, *Captain Ahab Had a Wife*.

87. See, for example, Boston Marine Society, *The Constitution and Laws of the Boston Marine Society* . . . (Boston, 1802); Marblehead, Mass., Marine Society, *Laws and Regulations of the Marine Society at Marblehead* . . . (Boston, 1798); Marine Society of the City of New York . . ., *Charter of the Marine Society of the City of New-York* . . . (New York, 1796); Marine Society of Portland, *Laws of the Marine Society, Instituted at Portland* . . . (Portland, 1798); Newburyport Marine Society, *Acts and Laws of the Newburyport Marine Society* . . . ([Newburyport, 1804]); Newport, R.I., Marine Society, *Laws of the Marine Society* . . . (Newport, 1799); Society for the Relief of Poor and Distressed Masters of Ships, Their Widows and Children, *An Act for Incorporating the Society* . . . (Philadelphia, 1800).

88. Ruth Wallis Herndon, "The Domestic Cost of Seafaring: Town Leaders and Seamen's Families in Eighteenth-Century Rhode Island," in Creighton and Norling, eds., *Iron Men, Wooden Women*, 55–69.

89. W. Jeffrey Bolster, *Black Jacks: African American Seamen in the Age of Sail* (Cambridge, Mass., 1997), 158–89.

90. Joseph Tuckerman, "Diary, 1826–27 and 1829," 10–27, Tuckerman Papers, MHS.

91. *The Journals of Ashley Bowen (1728–1813) of Marblehead*, Philip Chadwick Foster Smith, ed., *Publications of the Colonial Society of Massachusetts, Collections*, 44 (1973), 46–51, 149, 280–90.

92. For a full exploration of this concept see Laurel Thatcher Ulrich, *Good Wives: Image and Reality in the Lives of Women in Northern New England, 1650–1750* (New York, 1980).

93. Lydia Hill Almy, Aug. 29, 1797–June 20, 1799, Journal, PEM.

94. For examples see William Bugin to John H. Gregory, et al., Feb. 20, 1813, Privateering Agent Papers, 1812–13, Shipping Papers, Box 2, Gregory Family Papers, PEM; William Caswell to Gregory, Sept. 1, 1812, ibid.

95. Power of Attorney to Betsy Pedrick, Aug. 9, 1810, Richard Pedrick Papers, Marblehead Historical Society.

96. The agreement is stated as between two men, but the signatures are by a woman (Mary Veails) and an "x" that probably represents Mary Powers' mark. The end result was that Mary Powers was paid $35.58. Charles Veail to John H. Gregory, Feb. 17, 1813, Privateering Agent Papers, 1812–13, Shipping Papers, Box 2, Gregory Family Papers, PEM.

97. Joseph C. Hart, *Miriam Coffin or the Whale-Fishermen* (New York, 1969; orig. pub. 1834).

98. Kerber, "Separate Spheres, Female Worlds, Woman's Place," 9–39.

99. Lisa Norling, "Ahab's Wife: Women and the American Whaling Industry, 1820–1870," in Creighton and Norling, eds., *Iron Men, Wooden Women*, 70–91; and Norling, *Captain Ahab Had a Wife.*

100. Cynthia S. Congdon (nee Sprague), Mar. 1, 2, 3, 5, 8, May 26, and June 1, 1841, Journal, Congdon Family Papers, RIHS.

101. *A Full and Particular Account of the Trial of Francisco Dos Santos for the Murder of Archibald Graham . . .* (New York, 1806), 6–7.

102. Commonwealth v. William Johnson, 1848, Box 2, Dana Legal Papers, AAS. See also the examples in Billy G. Smith, *The "Lower Sort": Philadelphia's Laboring People, 1750–1800* (Ithaca, N.Y., 1990), 113–15.

103. Thomas Gregory to John H. Gregory, Mar. 22, 1817, Thomas Gregory to Joseph Gregory, Oct. 2, 1817, Thomas Gregory to John H. Gregory, June 24, 1821, Family Corespondence, Box 1, Gregory Family Papers, PEM.

104. Pension Petition of June Hammond of Marblehead, 1846, Pensions, Box 3, Gregory Family Papers, PEM.

105. Elizabeth R. H. to Harriet (sister), Oct. 16, 1840, Hammond Family Papers, ODHS.

106. In a sample of 120 people who signed sailors into the Marine Hospital, Providence, Rhode Island in 1840–42, 32 women are listed. Twenty-eight of these have the same last name as the individual listed, indicating a relationship to the sailor. U.S. Customs House Papers, Marine Hospital Books, vol. 1, 1840–42, Marine Hospital Records, Providence, RIHS.

107. Lisa Norling offers an extended discussion of this companionship for whaling officer wives. see Norling, "Ahab's Wife," in Creighton and Norling, eds., *Iron Men, Wooden Women*, 82–85; and Norling, *Captain Ahab Had a Wife*, 165–270. See also Stansell, *City of Women*, 41–62; and Carroll Smith-Rosenberg, "The Female World of Love and Ritual: Relations Between Women in Nineteenth-Century America," *Signs*, 1 (1975), 1–29.

108. Cynthia S. Congdon, Jan. 8, 11, Aug. 10, 1841, Journal, Congdon Family Papers, RIHS.

109. Henry Chase, Diary, 1821–22, 1822–23, NYHS.

110. Ibid.

111. See Privateering Agent Papers, 1812–13, Shipping Papers, Box 2, Gregory Family Papers, PEM.

112. John Moffat Howe, June 30, 1837, Diary, John Moffat Howe Papers, 1827–45, NYHS.

113. The document does not even name the sister. William Alfred Allen, 1840–49, Business Records Collection, Box 5, ODHS.

114. Gilje, *Road to Mobocracy*, 86–92; Stansell, *City of Women*, 23–26.

115. *A Full and Particular Account of the Trial of Francisco Dos Santos*, 3–6.

116. Timothy J. Gilfoyle, *City of Eros: New York City, Prostitution, and the Commercialization of Sex, 1790–1920* (New York, 1992), 66. See also Cordingly, *Women Sailors and Sailors' Women*, 8–22.

117. Gilfoyle, *City of Eros*, 55–74; Stansell, *City of Women*, 171–92; Patricia Cline Cohen, *The Murder of Helen Jewett: The Life and Death of a Prostitute in NineteenthCentury New York* (New York, 1999); Linda M. Maloney, "Doxies at Dockside: Prostitution and American Maritime Society, 1800–1900," in Timothy J. Runyon, ed., *Ships, Seafaring and Society: Essays in Maritime History* (Detroit, 1987), 217–25; Marilynn Hill Wood, *Their Sister's Keepers: Prostitution in New York City, 1830–1870* (Berkeley, Calif., 1993).

118. Gilfoyle, *City of Eros*, 49–53.

119. Lane, *The Wandering Boy*, 69–70.

120. Gilfoyle, *City of Eros*, 41–43, 48–53.

121. Dana, *Two Years Before the Mast*, 237.

122. William McNally, *Evils and Abuses in the Naval and Merchant Service, Exposed; With Proposals For Their Remedy and Redress* (Boston, 1839), 23–24.

123. Lawrence, *Scrimshaw*, 62, 79.

124. Lisa Norling, "The Sentimentalization of American Seafaring: The Case of the New England Whalefishery, 1790–1870," in Howell and Twomey, eds., *Jack Tar in History*, 164–78; Norling, *Captain Ahab Had a Wife*, 83–116.

125. Emiline Fish to Nathan G. Fish, April 19, [1835?], and Nathan G. Fish to Emiline Fish, April 9, 1839, Box 1, Nathan Gallup Fish Collection, Coll. 252, GWBWL. For a larger context discussing sentimentalization and love in correspondence in the Victorian Era see Karen Lystra, *Searching the Heart: Women, Men, and Romantic Love in Nineteenth-Century America* (New York, 1989).

126. Julia C. Bonham, "Feminist and Victorian: The Paradox of the American Seafaring Woman of the Nineteenth Century," *AN*, 37 (1977), 203–18; Joan Druett, *Hen Frigates: Wives of Merchant Captains Under Sail* (New York, 1998); Druett, "Those Female Journals," *Log of Mystic Seaport*, 40 (1989), 115–25; and Haskell Springer, "The Captain's Wife at Sea," in Creighton and Norling, eds., *Iron Men and Wooden Women*, 92–117. For examples see Stanton Garner, ed., *The Captain's Best Mate: The Journal of Mary Chipman Lawrence on the Whaler "Addison," 1856–1860* (Hanover, N.H., 1966); L. Tracy Girdler, ed., *An Antebellum Life at Sea* (Montgomery, Ala., 1997).

127. Cynthia Congdon, May 22, 1841, Journal, Congdon Family Papers, RIHS.

128. Cynthia Congdon, Oct. 27, 1844, Journal, Congdon Family Papers, RIHS. Lydia Hill Almy had had similar dreams almost fifty years earlier. Almy, Journal, Jan. 11, Feb. 24, Sept. 21, 1798, Jan. 10, 1799, PEM.

Chapter 3. A Sailor Ever Loves to Be in Motion

1. J. Ross Browne, *Etchings of a Whaling Cruise*, John Seelye, ed. (Cambridge, Mass., 1968; orig. pub. 1846), 24.

2. Ibid., 22–31.

3. Herman Melville, *Moby Dick, or the Whale* (New York, 1982; orig. pub. 1851), 1–8.

4. Richard Henry Dana, Jr., *Two Years Before the Mast: A Personal Narrative of Life at Sea*, Thomas Philbrick, ed. (New York, 1981; orig. pub. 1840), 44–49, 426.

5. Horace Lane, *The Wandering Boy, Careless Sailor, and Result of Inconsideration. A True Narrative* (Skaneateles, N.Y., 1839), 58.

6. "Traits of the Sailors Character," in Hugh Calhoun, "Journal, 1847–1848," MHS.

7. William Wilson, Dec. 31, 1849, Logbook, *Cavalier*, Log 18, GWBWL.

8. David Bryant, Feb. 7, 1816, Logbook, *Tartar*, PEM.

9. Benjamin Morrell, Jr., *A Narrative of Four Voyages*... (New York, 1832), xi.

10. George Little, *Life on the Ocean; or Twenty Years at Sea*... (New York, 1843), 31–39.

11. For some descriptions of this relentless work see John Richard Child, Logbook, *Hunter*, 1810–15, John Richard Child Papers, MHS; Dana, *Two Years Before the Mast*, 50–65; Jan. 13, 1789, Logbook, *Three Sisters*, Box 1, Derby Peabody Papers, MHS; Logbook, *Liberty*, 1774–76, MHS; F. A. DePeyster, Memoirs, 52–56, 110–28, Typescript, PEM.

12. Melville based *Moby Dick* on his experience as a whaler, *Billy Budd* and *Redburn* on his experience in the merchant marine, and *White-Jacket* on his time aboard an American warship. Melville, *Moby Dick*; Melville, *Billy Budd, Sailor, and Other Stories*, Harold Beaver, ed. (New York, 1967); Melville, *Redburn: His First Voyage, Being the Sailor-boy Confessions and Reminiscences of the Son-of-a-Gentleman in the Merchant Service*, Harold Beaver, ed. (New York, 1976; orig. pub. 1849); Melville, *White-Jacket, or The World in a Man-of-War*, Harrison Hayford et al., eds. (Evanston, Ill., 1970; orig. pub. 1850).

13. Philip Chadwick Smith, ed., *The Journals of Ashley Bowen (1728–1813) of Marblehead* in *Publications of the Colonial Society of Massachusetts, Collections*, 44 (Boston, 1973); Daniel Vickers, "An Honest Tar: Ashley Bowen of Marblehead," *NEQ*, 69 (1996), 531–53.

14. Simeon Crowell, "Commonplace Book of Simeon Crowell, 1818–46," MHS.

15. Gurdon L. Allyn, *The Old Sailor's Story, or, a Short Account of the Life and Adventures of Capt. Gurdon L. Allyn*... (Norwich, Conn., 1879).

16. James Fenimore Cooper, ed., *Ned Meyers; or, A Life Before the Mast*, introduction and notes by William S. Dudley (Annapolis, 1989; orig. pub. 1843).

17. For examples of others who sailed in more than one type of service see Barnaby Childs to John D. Childs, May 11, 1848, Box 73, Cory Family Papers, ODHS; Charles Babcock to Henry Babcock, Sept. 28, 1841, Box 73, Cory Family Papers, ODHS; Samuel L. Wood to George T. Baily, Sept. 10, 1841, Box 94, Business Records Collection, ODHS; Wilson, Oct. 2, 1848, Logbook, *Cavalier*, Log 18, GWBWL.

18. Gary M. Walton, "Sources of Productivity Change in American Colonial Shipping, 1675–1775," *Economic History Review*, 2nd ser., 20 (1967), 67–78; Douglass C. North, "Sources of Productivity Change in Ocean Shipping, 1600–1850," *Journal of Political Economy*, 76 (1968), 953–70.

19. Dana, *Two Years Before the Mast*, 193–94, 297–98.

20. These numbers include one ship of 568 tons and an abnormally large crew of fifty-eight bound for the East Indies. If this vessel is deducted from the sample then the average ship in 1806 leaving from Baltimore was 254.45 tons with an average crew of about fourteen. The per-crew tonnage thereby increases to about 17.6 tons per man.

21. The sample was taken from Baltimore Entrances and Clearances, vols. 1–4 (1782–88), 15–21 (1802–6), 32 (1816), 57–58 (1837–44), Bureau of Customs, United States, RG 36, NA; and Baltimore Crew Lists, Boxes 1–2 (1806–16), 4–5, 7–8 (1835–43), Bureau of Customs, United States, RG 36, NA. A similar trend appears in a sample taken from Crew Lists and Shipping Articles, 1792–1884, ser. 13, U.S. Customs House Papers, Providence, RIHS. On changes in vessel design see Howard I. Chapelle, *The Search for Speed Under Sail, 1700–1855* (New York, 1967).

22. The variations of the rigging on both sloops and schooners was great. Toward the end of the period under study here, some schooners had more than two masts. Customs House records, however, simply list the vessel by this generic type. For a good description with illustrations of different vessel types see Graham Blackburn, *The Illustrated Encyclopedia of Ships, Boats, Vessels and other Water-borne Craft*... (Woodstock, N.Y., 1978).

23. A sense of the size of coasters can be gleaned from Baltimore Entrances and Clearances, vols. 1–4 (1782–88), Bureau of Customs, United States, RG 36, NA.

24. This conclusion is based on the sample taken from Baltimore and Providence customs records. See Baltimore Entrances and Clearances, vols. 1–4 (1782–88), 15–21 (1802–6), 32 (1816), 57–58 (1837–44), Bureau of Customs, United States, RG 36, NA; and Baltimore Crew Lists, Boxes 1–2 (1806–16), 4–5, 7–8 (1835–43), Bureau of Customs, United States, RG 36, NA; Crew Lists and Shipping Articles, 1792–1884, U.S. Customs House Papers, Providence, RIHS.

25. Carl C. Cutler, *Greyhounds of the Sea: The Story of the American Clipper Ship*, 3rd ed. (Annapolis, 1984; orig. pub., 1930), 65–66.

26. The U.S. Congress codified the law on the seaman's contract in 1790. Congress based the legislation on the English law passed in 1729. See [United States], *An Act for the Government and Regulation of Seamen in the Merchants Service: Passed, at New York, By the Honourable The First Congress of the United States, at their Second Session* (Warren, R.I., 1792); and Walter Macarthur, *The Seaman's Contract, 1790–1918: A Complete Reprint of the Laws Relating to American Seamen* . . . (San Francisco, 1919).

27. Baltimore Vessel Entrances, vol. 57 (1837–44), Bureau of Customs, United States, RG 36, NA.

28. Nathaniel Ames, *Nautical Reminiscences* (Providence, 1832), 38.

29. Richard Henry Dana, Jr., *The Seaman's Friend* (Delmar, N.Y., 1979; orig. pub. 1851), 158–67. For a good descriptions with illustrations of the work aboard ship see John Harland, *Seamanship in the Age of Sail: An Account of the Shiphandling of the Sailing Man-of-War 1600–1860, Based on Contemporary Sources* (Annapolis, 1985); and Stan Hugill, *Shanties and Sailors' Songs* (New York, 1969), 67–110.

30. See, for example, Sargent S. Day, Mar. 18, Apr. 16, 28, 30, Dec. 15, 1846, Logbook, *Chilo*, PEM; Logbook, *Agnes*, 1808, PEM. Dana, *Seaman's Friend*, 138–46.

31. N.d., p. 5, Logbook, *William Shroder*, 1848, PEM.

32. Dana, *Seaman's Friend*, 131–58; Daniel Vickers, "Nantucket Whalemen in the Deep-Sea Fishery: The Changing Anatomy of an Early American Labor Force," *JAH*, 72 (1985), 277–96; W. Jeffrey Bolster, *Black Jacks: African American Seamen in the Age of Sail* (Cambridge, Mass., 1997), 170.

33. Crowell, "Commonplace Book," 45–55, MHS.

34. Daniel Vickers, *Farmers and Fishermen: Two Centuries of Work in Essex County, Massachusetts, 1630–1850* (Chapel Hill, N.C., 1994).

35. Both Herman Melville and J. Ross Browne provide wonderful descriptions of whaling. See *Moby Dick* and *Sketchings of A Whaling Cruise*. See also Margaret S. Creighton, *Rites and Passages: The Experience of American Whaling, 1830–1870* (Cambridge, 1995); Elmo Paul Hohman, *The American Whaleman: A Study of Life and Labor in the Whaling Industry* (London, 1928); Briton Cooper Busch, *"Whaling Will Never Do for Me": The American Whaleman in the Nineteenth Century* (Lexington, Ky., 1994); Lance E. Davis, Robert E. Gallman, and Karin Gleiter, *In Pursuit of Leviathan: Technology, Institutions, Productivity, and Profits in American Whaling, 1816–1906* (Chicago, 1997); Lisa Norling, *Captain Ahab Had a Wife: New England Women and the Whalefishery, 1720–1870* (Chapel Hill, N.C., 2000); Edouard A. Stackpole, *The Sea Hunters: The New England Whalemen During Two Centuries, 1635–1835* (Philadelphia, 1935); Alexander Starbuck, *History of the American Whale Fishery from Its Earliest Inception to the Year 1876* (New York, 1964; orig. pub. 1878).

36. Theodore Lewis, Nov. 21, 1836, Logbook, *Atlantic*, Log 822, GWBWL.

37. For a description of the work day aboard a navy vessel see George Jones, *Sketches of*

Naval Life, With Notices of Men, Manners and Scenery . . . By a "Civilian," 2 vols. (New Haven, 1829), 1:96–105.

38. Some sense of life aboard a privateer can be gleaned in Dr. Josiah Bartlett, Logbook, *Pilgrim*, 1781–82, MHS; Logbook, *Alfred*, 1812, PEM; Logbook, *America*, 1812–13, PEM; Logbook, *John*, 1812–13, PEM.

39. Little, *Life on the Ocean*, 371–72; Calhoun, Sept. 3, 1847, "Journal," MHS.

40. Joseph Ward, May 9, 1809, Logbook, *President Adams*, AAS.

41. Apr. 14, 1789, Logbook, *William and Henry*, PEM; July 18, 1792, Logbook, *Grand Turk*, PEM.

42. June 9, 1833, Logbook, *Talma*, Log 968, GWBWL.

43. Browne, *Sketchings of A Whaling Cruise*, 110.

44. Almost any journal of sea life will mention these dangers. W. Fitch Taylor describes two such incidents back to back in *The Broad Pennant: or a Cruise in the United States Flag Ship of the Gulf Squadron . . .* (New York, 1848), 238–39. See also Dec. 1, 1849, Logbook, *Sheffield*, Log 351, GWBWL; Ebenezer Clinton, Aug. 24, 1804, Logbook, *Vancouver*, Yale; Samuel Furgerson, July 15, 1809, Logbook, *Otter*, Yale; Calhoun, Aug. 25, 1847, "Journal," MHS.

45. Vickers, *Farmers and Fishermen*, 285–86.

46. William M. Fowler, Jr., *Jack Tar and Commodores: The American Navy, 1783–1815* (Boston, 1984), 250.

47. Edward Norris, Logbook, 1820–21, typescript, Norris MS, *Dispatch*, MHA.

48. See for example of the collection of stories in R. Thomas, *Interesting and Authentic Narratives of the Most Remarkable Shipwrecks, Fires, Famines, Calamities, Providential Deliveries, and Lamentable Disasters on the Sea in Most Parts of the World* (Boston, 1835) and *God's Wonders in the Great Deep, Recorded in Several Wonderful and Amazing Accounts . . .* (Newburyport, Mass., 1805). For an example of a fictionalized depiction of shipwreck for the stage see Samuel James Arnold, *The Shipwreck: A Comic Opera in Two Acts* (New York, 1785).

49. Thomas, *Interesting and Authentic Narratives*, 175–79.

50. Nathaniel Philbrick, *In the Heart of the Sea: The Tragedy of the Whaleship "Essex"* (New York, 2000); Thomas Farel Heffernan, *Stove by a Whale: Owen Chase and the "Essex"* (Hanover, N.H., 1981).

51. The origin of yellow fever was hotly debated at the time. For a good statement connecting the disease to trade with the West Indies see [Mathew Carey], *Occasional Essays on the Yellow Fever* (Philadelphia, 1800). For an opposite view see Benjamin Rush, *Observations Upon the Origin of the Malignant Bilious, or Yellow Fever in Philadelphia . . .* (Philadelphia, 1799). The best general account remains J. H. Powell, *Bring out Your Dead: The Great Plague of Yellow Fever in Philadelphia in 1793* (New York, 1949).

52. David Lewis, Logbook [no vessel named], 1802, Lewis Family Collection, Falmouth Historical Society, Falmouth, Mass.

53. Francis M. Gardner to Frederick S. Allen, Feb. 2, 1839, Box 41, Swift and Allen Collection, ODHS.

54. William Meachum Murrell, *Cruise of the Frigate "Columbia" Around the World, Under the Command of Commodore George C. Read, 1838, 1839, and 1840* (Boston, 1840); W. Fitch Taylor, *A Voyage Around the World, and Visits to Various Foreign Countries in the United States Frigate "Columbia"* . . ., 5th ed. (New Haven, 1856).

55. Dana, *Two Years Before The Mast*, 95.

56. Ward, Logbook, *President Adams*, 1809, AAS.

57. For a discussion of seasickness among green hands see Creighton, *Rites of Passage*,

59–60. For experienced salts getting seasick see Samuel Leech, *A Voice from the Main Deck: Being a Record of Thirty Years' Adventures of Samuel Leech*, introduction and notes by Michael J. Crawford (Annapolis, 1999; orig. pub. 1843), 169–70; Nathaniel Sexton Morgan, Sept. 7, 8, 17, 1849, Logbook, *Hannibal*, Log 862, GWBWL; Wilson, Sept. 30, 1849, Logbook, *Cavalier*, Log 18, GWBWL.

58. Scholars of these work songs disagree over when, or how often tars used chanteys. Some believe that they only became prominent on American and English merchant ships in the nineteenth century. Others suggest that they were also used earlier. On chanteys, see Frederick J. Davis and Ferris Tozer, *Sailors' Songs or "Chanteys,"* 3rd ed. (London, [1906]); William Main Doerflinger, *Songs of the Sailor and Lumberman*, rev. ed. (New York, 1972); Stuart M. Frank, "Ballads and Songs of the Whale-Hunters, 1825–1895: From the Manuscripts in the Kendall Museum" (Ph.D. diss., Brown University, 1985); Hugill, *Shanties and Sailors' Songs*; Hugill, *Shanties from the Seven Seas: Shipboard Work-Songs Used as Work-Songs from the Great Days of Sail* (Mystic, Conn., 1994).

59. Leech, *A Voice from the Main Deck*, 41–42.

60. Melville, *Redburn*, 106–14, 162–63, 328.

61. Wm. French to Chs. G. and H. Coffin, Mar. 11, 1845, Ship *Zenas Coffin*, 1840–43, Letters, Charles G. and Henry Coffin Collection, 1829–62, NHA.

62. Benjamin Carter, Sept. 15, 1798, Logbook, *Ann and Hope*, RIHS.

63. Oct. 3, 1847, Logbook, *Charlotte*, Coll. 228, GWBWL.

64. Alfred Terry, July 30, 1847, Logbook, *Vesper*, Log 955, GWBWL.

65. William Silver, Oct. 21, 1834, Logbook, *Bengal*, PEM.

66. Furgerson, May 9 and Sept. 5, 1809, Logbook, *Otter*, Yale.

67. Henry James Mercier, *Life in a Man-of-War, or Scenes in "Old Ironsides" During Her Cruise in the Pacific* (Boston, 1927; orig. pub. 1841), 207–10.

68. Samuel Tucker to Amer. Commissioners, July 12, 1778, Samuel Tucker Papers, Peter Force Papers, Series VII E, Reel 54, LC.

69. Last v. Porter, 1847, Box 1, Dana Legal Papers, AAS.

70. Browne, *Etchings of a Whaling Cruise*, 24, 305–16.

71. Silas Fitch, Jan. 6, 1843, Logbook, *Charles Phelps*, Log 142, GWBWL. See also his entry on Jan. 31, 1843.

72. Ames, *Nautical Reminiscences*, 73–74.

73. Browne, *Etchings of a Whale Cruise*, 315, 356; Leech, *A Voice from the Main Deck*, 41–42; William McNally, *Evils and Abuses in the Naval and Merchant Service, Exposed; With Proposals for Their Remedy and Redress* (Boston, 1839), 121; Melville, *Redburn*, 119; Moses Smith, *Naval Scenes in the Last War . . .* (Boston, 1846), 42.

74. The normal punishment was twelve lashes. Sometimes the punishment was less; occasionally it was more. "Record of Punishments, U.S. Frigate *Congress*, 1845–48," Box 283, Naval Records Collection, RG 45, NA.

75. Flogging was not outlawed until 1850. Dana, *The Seaman's Friend*, 192–95.

76. Morgan, Oct. 20, 1849, Logbook, *Hannibal*, Log 862, GWBWL. See also Wilson, Logbook, *Cavalier*, Log 18, GWBWL.

77. McNally, *Evils and Abuses*, 71.

78. Knut Weibust, *Deep Sea Sailors: A Study in Maritime Ethnology*, 2nd ed. (Stockholm, 1976), 372.

79. *Enterprise* v. *Catherine*, Sept. 10, 1762, Box 1, NY Vice Admiralty Courts, RG 21, NA-NY.

80. Samuel Curson, Logbook, *Thomas Russell*, 1798–99, MHS.

81. Day, Mar. 18, Apr. 28, 30, 1847, Logbook, *Chilo*, PEM.

82. Arthur to Coffins, Apr. 18, 1849, Arthur to Coffins, Oct. 25, 1851, Charles G. and Henry Coffin Collection, 1829–62, NHA.

83. [William Leeds], June 13–15, 1844, Logbook, *Catherine*, Log 940, GWBWL.

84. Robert J. Taylor et al., eds., *Papers of John Adams*, 8 vols. (Cambridge, Mass., 1977–), 6:182; Samuel Eliot Morison, *John Paul Jones: A Sailor's Biography* (Boston, 1959), 167–72.

85. Day, Oct. 18, 1846, Logbook, *Chilo*, PEM.

86. Samuel W. Chase, Aug. 18, 19, 1843, Logbook, *Arab*, Maritime Records, MeHS.

87. Morgan, July 24, 1850, Logbook, *Hannibal*, Log 862, GWBWL.

88. For good discussion of relationships and conditions aboard ship see Marcus Rediker, *Between the Devil and the Deep Blue Sea: Merchant Seamen, Pirates, and the Anglo-American Maritime World, 1700–1750* (Cambridge, 1987); and Creighton, *Rites and Passages*. See also N. A. M. Rodgers, *The Wooden World: An Anatomy of the Georgian Navy* (Annapolis, 1984), 205–51.

89. James Durand, *James Durand: An Able Seaman of 1812: His Adventures on "Old Ironsides" and as an Impressed Sailor in the British Navy*, George S. Brooks, ed. (New Haven, 1926; orig. pub. 1820), 38.

90. Caleb Foote, ed., "Reminiscences of the Revolution: Prison Letters and Sea Journal of Caleb Foot: Born, 1750; Died 1787," *EIHC*, 26 (1889), 90–122.

91. Dana, *Two Years Before the Mast*, 120–21.

92. Last v. Porter, 1847, Box 1, Dana Legal Papers, AAS. For examples of grumbling and resistance, see Mar. 20, June 20, 28, July 10, Sept. 3, 1846, Logbook, *Santiago*, William Goddard Papers, GWBWL.

93. Capt. John Manly to Hector McNeill, Boston, May 6, 1777, Boston Marine Society, MS, MHS.

94. Robert Wilden Neeser, ed., *Letters and Papers Relating to the Cruises of Gustavus Conyngham, A Captain of the Continental Navy, 1777–1779* (New York, 1915), 6.

95. Thomas Handsayd Cabot, Journal, May 19, 1834, Lee Family Papers, MHS.

96. *Brooklyn* (ship), Manuscript Legal Documents, 1846–48, relating to the case of John C. Dunford, Cooper v. Samuel Jeffrey, Master of the *Brooklyn*, GWBWL.

97. Day, Mar. 7, 8, 10, 1848, Logbook, *Chilo*, PEM.

98. Knowlton v. Boles, 1848, Box 1, Dana Legal Papers, AAS.

99. Aug, 29–31, 1841, Logbook, *Israel*, Log 90, GWBWL.

100. Amos A. Evans, *Journal Kept on Board the Frigate "Constitution," 1812* (Lincoln, Mass., 1967; orig pub. 1895), 382, 472–73.

101. Richard J. Cleveland, "Fur Trading Voyage," Yale.

102. William James Morgan, ed., *Naval Documents of the American Revolution*, 7 (Washington, D.C., 1976), 1004–5. This document is taken from the log of the *Tyrannicide*, AAS.

103. Sir John Barrow, *The Eventful History of the Mutiny and Piratical Seizure of HMS "Bounty": Its Causes and Consequences* (London, 1831); Little, *Life on the Ocean*, 132.

104. For examples of this popular literature from the late eighteenth and early nineteenth centuries see *The History of the Pirates, Containing the Lives of Those Noted Pirate Captains . . . To Which is Added A Correct Account of the Late Piracies Committed in the West Indies; and the Expedition of Com. Porter* (Haverhill, Mass., 1825); James Cobb, *The Capture. A Favorite Song in the Pirates. Composed by S. Storace* (Philadelphia, [1793]); Charles Johnson, *The History of Black-Beard & Roche, Two Noted Pyrates* (Salem, 1802).

105. Josiah Cobb, *A Green Hand's First Cruise, Roughed Out from the Log-Book of Memory, of Twenty-Five Years Standing* . . . 2 vols. (Boston, 1841), 1: 15.

106. The King v. William Wood (1774), Box A, NY Vice Admiralty Courts, RG 21, NA-NY. For other examples of this type of piracy see *An Interesting Trial of Edward Jordan, and Margaret His Wife, Who Were Tried at Halifax, N.S. Nov. 15th, 1809, for the Hor-*

rid Crime of Piracy and Murder... (Boston, [1809]); *The Interesting Trials of the Pirates for the Murder of William Little, Captain of the Ship American "Eagle"* (Newburyport, Mass. [1797]); *The Last Words and Dying Confession of the Three Pirates, Who were Executed This Day (May 9th, 1800)* (Philadelphia, [1800]); *A Report of the Trial of Samuel Tulley, and John Dalton, on an Indictment for Piracy, Committed January 21st, 1812* . . . (Boston, 1812); Joseph Baker, *The Confession of Joseph Baker, A Canadian by Birth, Who, For Murder and Piracy* . . . ([Philadelphia, 1800]); A. Solis, *Dying Confession [of] Pirates* . . . ([Boston, 1794]).

107. Marcus Rediker and Robert Ritchie have studied the piracy that developed in the postwar period of the late seventeenth and early eighteenth centuries. Rediker, *Between the Devil and the Deep Blue Sea*, 254–87; Rediker, "'Under the Banner of King Death': The Social World of Anglo-American Pirates, 1716 to 1726," *WMQ*, 3rd ser., 38 (1981), 203–27; Robert C. Ritchie, *Captain Kidd and the War Against the Pirates* (Cambridge, Mass., 1986).

108. James Fenimore Cooper, *The Red Rover* (New York, n.d.; orig. pub. 1828).

109. *Dying Declaration of Nicholas Fernandez, Who with Nine others were Executed in front of Cadiz Harbour, December 29, 1829 for Piracy and Murder on the High Seas*, Ferdinand Bayer, trans. ([New York], 1830).

110. Rediker, *Between the Devil and the Deep Blue Sea*, 254–87; Rediker, "'Under the Banner of King Death,'"

111. Little, *Life on the Ocean*, 172.

112. Calhoun, Nov. 20, 1847, "Journal," MHS.

113. McNally, *Evils and Abuses*, 71–72; William Lay and Cyrus M. Hussey, *A Narrative of the Mutiny on Board the Whaleship "Globe,"* introduction by Edouard A. Stackpole (New York, 1963; orig. pub. 1828).

114. Jones, *Sketches of Naval Life*, 1: 218.

115. William Clarke, Nov. 30, 1841, Logbook, USS *Relief*, PEM.

116. Dana, *Two Years Before the Mast*, 393.

117. Mercier, *Life in a Man-of-War*, 58.

118. Joseph Valpey, Jr., *Journal of Joseph Valpey, Jr. of Salem, November, 1813–April, 1815: With Other Papers Relating to His Experience in Dartmoor Prison* (n.p., 1922), 7, 9, 10.

119. Cobb, *A Green Hand's First Cruise*, 1:104–17, 175; Ebenezer Fox, *The Adventures of Ebenezer Fox in the Revolutionary War* . . . (Boston, 1838), 87; Valpey, *Journal*, 9; Benjamin Waterhouse, *A Journal of a Young Man of Massachusetts* . . . (Lexington, 1816), 9.

120. Little, *Life on the Ocean*, 125.

121. Edward Cutbush, *Observations on the Means of Preserving the Health of Soldiers and Sailors* . . . (Philadelphia, 1808), 127–28.

122. James Minor, Apr. 30, 1849, "Journal of James Minor, March 24–June 5, 1849," GWBWL.

123. Child, Oct. 19, 1810, Logbook, *Hunter*, MHS.

124. Curson, Logbook, *Thomas Russell*, 1798–99, MHS. For a discussion of the Neptune ritual, see Weibust, *Deep Sea Sailors*, 169–82; Henning Henningsen, *Crossing the Equator: Sailor's Baptism and Other Initiation Rites* (Copenhagen, 1961); Creighton, *Rites and Passages*, 116–38. For other examples see Calhoun, July 27, 1847, "Journal," 35–37, MHS; Goodnough, Dec. 13, 1845, Logbook, *Ann Parry*, PEM. For examples crossing a tropic line see William Hodges, Jr., May 4, 1769, Logbook, *General Wolfe*, PEM; Jan. 1, 1813, Logbook, *John*, PEM.

Chapter 4. The Sons of Neptune

1. Blatchford states that he was acquitted in his narrative, but given his subsequent experience he may have had a sentence that was commuted to transportation to the East Indies. John Blatchford, *Narrative of Remarkable Occurrences in the Life of John Blatchford . . .* (New London, 1788).

2. Ibid., 10.

3. Ibid. Blatchford, despite the testaments attached to his short book, may have made the whole story up. Personally, I take him at his word because his story differs from others only in the varied nature of his experience. Regardless of the truth of each detail, his tale of suffering and woe represents an important type of literature that emerges out of the revolution emphasizing the experience of common men like Blatchford. For a discussion of this type of reminiscence from the American Revolution see Sarah J. Purcell, "Sealed with Blood: National Identity and Public Memory of the Revolutionary War, 1775–1825" (Ph.D. diss., Brown University, 1997); Alfred F. Young, *The Shoemaker and the Tea Party: Memory and the American Revolution* (Boston, 1999), esp. 132–42.

4. Dirk Hoerder, *Crowd Action in Revolutionary Massachusetts, 1765–1780* (New York, 1977), 230, n. 44.

5. James H. Hutson, "An Investigation of the Inarticulate: Philadelphia's White Oaks," *WMQ*, 3rd ser., 28 (1971), 3–25. Jesse Lemisch and John K. Alexander argue that the White Oaks should not be confused with common seamen. One of the premises of this study is that the boundary between those on board ship and on the docks was not that clear cut. See Lemisch and Alexander, "The White Oaks, Jack Tar and the Concept of the Inarticulate," *WMQ*, 3rd ser., 29 (1972), 109–34. See also the comments and rebuttal of Simeon J. Crowther and James H. Hutson, ibid., 34–42.

6. *The Journals of Ashley Bowen (1728–1813) of Marblehead*, Philip Chadwick Foster Smith, ed., *Publications of the Colonial Society of Massachusetts, Collections*, 45 (Boston, 1973), 422–550. See also Daniel Vickers, "An Honest Tar: Ashley Bowen of Marblehead," *NEQ*, 69 (1996), 531–53; Vickers, "Ashley Bowen of Marblehead: Revolutionary Neutral," in Nancy L. Rhoden and Ian K. Steele, eds., *The Human Tradition in the American Revolution* (Wilmington, 2000), 99–115.

7. Carl Bridenbaugh, *Cities in the Wilderness: The First Century of Urban Life in America, 1625–1742* (New York, 1938), 223–24; *New York Gazette and Weekly Post-Boy*, Mar. 2, 1752.

8. Norman S. Cohen, "The Philadelphia Election Riot of 1742," *PMHB*, 92 (1968), 306–19; William T. Parsons, "The Bloody Election of 1742," *PH*, 36 (1969), 290–306.

9. Thomas C. Barrow, *Trade and Empire: The British Customs Service in Colonial America, 1660–1775* (Cambridge, Mass., 1967), 91; Hoerder, *Crowd Action*, 63.

10. Jesse Lemisch, "Jack Tar in the Streets: Merchant Seamen in the Politics of Revolutionary America," *WMQ*, 3rd ser., 25 (1968), 371–407.

11. John Lax and William Pencak, "The Knowles Riot and the Crisis of the 1740s in Massachusetts," *Perspectives in American History*, 10 (1976), 167–214; Hoerder, *Crowd Action*, 62; Gary B. Nash, *The Urban Crucible: Social Change, Political Consciousness, and the Origins of the American Revolution* (Cambridge, Mass., 1979), 221–24.

12. Paul A. Gilje, *Rioting in America* (Bloomington, Ind., 1996), 22–24. For Pope Day in Marblehead see *Journals of Ashley Bowen*, I, 225–26.

13. Gilje, *Rioting in America*, 22–24; Paul A. Gilje, *The Road to Mobocracy: Popular Disorder in New York City, 1763–1834* (Chapel Hill, N.C., 1987), 25–30; Francis D. Cogliano, *No King, No Popery* (Westport, Conn., 1995), 30; Brendan McConville, "Pope's Day Revisited, 'Popular' Culture Reconsidered," *Explorations in Early American Culture*, 4 (2000), 258–80.

14. R. R. Livingston to [former Gov. Monckton], Nov. 8, 1765, Box 3, Transcripts, Livingston Family Papers, New York Public Library; Gilje, *Road to Mobocracy*, 44–52.

15. Edmund S. Morgan and Helen M. Morgan, *The Stamp Act Crisis: Prologue to Revolution* (Chapel Hill, N.C., 1953); Nash, *Urban Crucible*, 292–311.

16. Hoerder, *Crowd Action*, 144–70.

17. Wm. Shappard to Board of Commissioners, April 1769, "The Aspinwall Papers," *Collections of the Massachusetts Historical Society*, 4th ser., 10 (1871), 611–17.

18. *Boston Gazette*, Oct. 16, 1769; [New York] *Post Boy* (Holt's), Dec. 26, 1765; *New York Journal*, June 23, 1768, Feb. 16, July 6, Oct. 19, 1769; *New York Mercury*, Apr. 7, 1766; G. D. Scull, ed., *The Montressor Journals* (New-York Historical Society, *Collections*, 14 [New York, 1881]), 342–44, 346, 361; Edward Countryman, *A People in Revolution: The American Revolution and Political Society in New York, 1760–1790* (Baltimore, 1981), 37–45; Hoerder, *Crowd Action*, 125, 130, 144, 165, 183, 189, 209–23; Benjamin W. Labaree, *Patriots and Partisans: The Merchants of Newburyport, 1764–1815* (New York, 1962), 19; Pauline Maier, *From Resistance to Revolution: Colonial Radicals and the Development of American Opposition to Britain, 1765–1776* (New York, 1972), 7–12, 20; Morgan and Morgan, *Stamp Act Crisis*, 212–33, 252, 321; Steven Rosswurm, *Arms, Country, and Class: The Philadelphia Militia and the "Lower Sort" During the American Revolution, 1775–1783* (New Brunswick, N.J., 1987), 30–31; Donna J. Spindel, "Law and Disorder: The North Carolina Stamp Act Crisis," *North Carolina Historical Review*, 57 (1980), 11–13.

19. Isaac Q. Leake, *Memoir of the Life and Times John Lamb, an Officer of the Revolution, Who Commanded the Post at West Point at the Time of Arnold's Defection* . . . (Albany, N.Y., 1857), 46–47; *Boston Gazette*, Oct. 16, 1769. Tarring and feathering may have been used on occasion before 1768, but references are scarce.

20. *New York Journal*, Oct. 19, 1769; Rosswurm, *Arms, Country, and Class*, 31–33.

21. Gilje, *Rioting in America*, 47–48.

22. *The Trial of the British Soldiers, of the 29th Regiment of Foot* . . . (Miami, 1969; orig. pub. 1807). See also Hoerder, *Crowd Action*, 223–34; Hiller B. Zobel, *The Boston Massacre* (New York, 1970).

23. The following analysis builds upon my work on riots published elsewhere. See Gilje, *Rioting in America*.

24. *New York Gazette and Weekly Post Boy*, July 12, 1764; *Newport Mercury*, July 16, 1764; Hoerder, *Crowd Action*, 164–70.

25. Gordon S. Wood, *The Creation of the American Republic, 1776–1787* (Chapel Hill, N.C., 1969), 18–28, 319–28.

26. Nash, *Urban Crucible*; Jesse Lemisch, *Jack Tar vs. John Bull: The Role of New York's Seamen in Precipitating the Revolution* (New York, 1997); Marcus Rediker, "A Motley Crew of Rebels: Sailors, Slaves, and the Coming of the American Revolution," in Ronald Hoffman and Peter J. Albert, eds., *The Transforming Hand of Revolution: Reconsidering the American Revolution as a Social Movement* (Charlottesville, Va., 1995), 155–98.

27. Obviously some men served aboard more than one vessel. A frigate would have more than 300 men, but even relatively small schooners would have 75 to 125 men as privateers.

28. For the naval war see Jack Coggins, *Ships and Seamen of the American Revolution: Vessels, Crews, Weapons, Gear, Naval Tactics, and Actions of the War for Independence* (Harrisburg, Pa., 1969); Robert Gardiner, ed., *Navies and the American Revolution, 1775–1783* (Annapolis, 1996); Nathan Miller, *Sea of Glory: A Naval History of the American Revolution* (Annapolis, 1974); William James Morgan, "American Privateering in America's War for Independence, 1775–1783," in Commission Internationale d'Histoire Maritime, *Course et*

Piraterie: Etudes Présentées à la Commission Internationale d'Histoire Maritime (Paris, 1975), 556–71; William James Morgan, *Captains to the Northward: The New England Captains in the Continental Navy* (Barre, Mass., 1959). See also Richard Buel, Jr., *In Irons: Britain's Naval Supremacy and the American Revolutionary Economy* (New Haven, 1998); Barbara W. Tuchman, *The First Salute* (New York, 1988).

29. Ebenezer Fox, *The Adventures of Ebenezer Fox in the Revolutionary War Illustrated By Elegant Engravings From Original Designs* (Boston, 1838), 60–70.

30. John Kilby, "Narrative of John Kilby: Quarter-Gunner of the U.S. Ship 'Bon Homme Richard' Under Paul Jones," *Scribner's Magazine* (July 1905), 31–33.

31. Nathaniel Fanning, *Narrative of the Adventures of an American Naval Officer Who Served During Part of the American Revolution Under the Command of Com. John Paul Jones, Esq.* (New York, 1806), 58.

32. For the perspective of one American common seaman aboard a British man-of-war during a fleet action see Joshua Davis, *A Narrative of Joshua Davis, An American Citizen, Who Was Pressed and Served on Board Six Ships of the British Navy* (Baltimore, 1811), 40–46.

33. Christopher Vail, "Christopher Vail's Journal, 1775–1783," Peter Force Papers, Ser. VII E, Reel 54, LC; "Personal Reminiscences of the Revolutionary War, by the Late Thomas Painter, of West Haven," Henry Howe, ed., *Papers of the New Haven Colony Historical Society*, 4 (New Haven, 1888), 232–44.

34. John Fairbanks, Logbook, *Wasp*, 1782, MeHS.

35. For a good example of the privateering experience see Samuel Eliot Morison, ed., "Log of the *Pilgrim*, 1781–1782," Colonial Society of Massachusetts, *Transactions*, 25 (1924), 94–124.

36. Caleb Foote, ed., "Reminiscences of the Revolution. Prison Letters and Sea Journal of Caleb Foot: Born, 1750; Died, 1787," *EIHC*, 26 (1889), 113, 118.

37. Gary B. Nash, *Forging Freedom: The Formation of Philadelphia's Black Community, 1720–1840* (Cambridge, Mass., 1988), 51–52; W. Jeffrey Bolster, *Black Jacks: African American Seamen in the Age of Sail* (Cambridge, Mass., 1997), 3, 94, 153–54, 157.

38. Francis Boardman, ca. Mar. 6, 1776, Logbook, *Adventure*, PEM.

39. For a discussion of the ethnic diversity of the Continental Army see Charles Patrick Neimeyer, *America Goes to War: A Social History of the Continental Army* (New York, 1996).

40. Ebenezer Putnam, comp., "American Prisoners at Quebec During the Revolution," *Genealogical Quarterly Magazine*, 3rd ser., 3 (April 1902), 43–44. Similar variety of nationalities appear in the crew lists provided by Charles Herbert for prisoners held in Mill Prison, 1777–1779. See Charles Herbert, *A Relic of the Revolution, Containing a Full and Particular Account of the Sufferings and Privations of All the American Prisoners Captured on the High Seas . . .* (Boston, 1847), 243–58.

41. Leonard W. Labaree et al., eds., *The Papers of Benjamin Franklin*, 36 vols. to date (New Haven, 1959–), 30:203–4, 390; William Bell Clark, *Ben Franklin's Privateers: A Naval Epic of the American Revolution* (Baton Rouge, 1956), 33–92. See also Henri Malo, "American Privateers at Dunkerque," *United States Naval Institute Proceedings*, 37 (1911), 933–93.

42. Lords Admiralty (henceforth Adm.) to Commissioners of Sick and Hurt Seamen (henceforth CSHS), Mar. 8, 1783, Adm./M/405, microfilm, NMM.

43. Labaree et al., eds. *Papers of Benjamin Franklin*, 28:486–89; James Fenimore Cooper, *History of the Navy of the United States of America*, 2nd ed., 2 vols. (Philadelphia, 1840), 1:146–49.

44. Fanning, *Narrative*, 35; Kilby, "Narrative," 29–30; Samuel Eliot Morison, *John Paul Jones: A Sailor's Biography* (Boston, 1959), 208; Cooper, *History*, 1:175.

45. Foote, ed., "Reminiscences of the Revolution," 112, 115. On the history of the *South*

Carolina see Richard G. Stone, Jr., "'The *South Carolina* We've Lost': The Bizarre Saga of Alexander Gillon and His Frigate," *AN*, 39 (1979), 159–72.

46. Samuel Tucker, July 8, 10, 11, 1778, Logbook, *Boston*, PEM.

47. Herbert, *A Relic of the Revolution*, 116–18.

48. Nash, *Forging Freedom*, 66–67. Fighting for the American cause did not guarantee freedom for African Americans, either. In 1777 slaveowners attempted to sell their slaves even after they had served aboard the brigantine *Freedom*. See R. T. Paine to ——, May 8, 1777, R. T. Paine Papers, MHS.

49. The men also believed that Jones had altered the *Ranger*'s articles to extend their enlistment and that he had stalled payment of prize money. Robert J. Taylor et al., eds., *Papers of John Adams*, 8 vols. (Cambridge, Mass. 1977–), 6:182; Morison, *John Paul Jones*, 167–72.

50. Kilby, "Narrative," 35–37; Morison, *John Paul Jones*, 293–301; Fanning, *Narrative*, 83–88.

51. Andrew Sherburne, *Memoirs of Andrew Sherburne: A Pensioner of the Navy of the Revolution* (Utica, N.Y., 1828), 80; William Widger, "The Diary of William Widger of Marblehead, Kept at Mill Prison, England, 1781," *EIHC*, 73 (1937), 329; Widger, "Diary," *EIHC* 74 (1938), 24, 43; Mary S. Coan, ed., "A Revolutionary Prison Diary: The Journal of Dr. Jonathan Haskins," *NEQ*, 17 (1944), 298.

52. Foote, ed., "Reminiscences of the Revolution," 90–101.

53. Silvester Stevens to Mrs. Stevens (his wife), May 23, 1780, prison ship *Hunter*, Continental Army and Navy Letters, Marblehead Historical Society, Marblehead, Mass.; Peter Smothers to his wife, prison ship *Jersey*, Jan. 21, 1781, ibid.; Peter Smothers to his wife, prison ship, Halifax Harbor, June 29, 1782, ibid.; Jonathan Deakins to wife, Mill Prison, Dec. 8, 1782, ibid.

54. Widger, "Diary," *EIHC*, 73 (1937), 340.

55. For a discussion of a mixture of motives for going to sea during the Revolutionary War see Francis D. Cogliano, *American Maritime Prisoners in the Revolutionary War: The Captivity of William Russell* (Annapolis, 2001), 1–29.

56. For assessments of the impact of the Revolutionary War on seafaring see Samuel Eliot Morison, *The Maritime History of Massachusetts, 1783–1860* (Boston, 1979; orig. pub. 1921), 29–30; Daniel Vickers, *Farmers and Fisherman: Two Centuries of Work in Essex County, Massachusetts, 1630–1850* (Chapel Hill, N.C., 1994), 264–66.

57. Fox, *Adventures*.

58. William Bell Clark, ed., *Naval Documents of the American Revolution* (Washington, D.C., 1968), 3:110–11. While comparing discipline in the British and American navies, Greg Dening writes, "There was a strong privateering spirit abroad [on American ships during the revolution] against which the rhetoric of loyalty and sacrifice faltered." Greg Dening, *Mr. Bligh's Bad Language: Passion, Power and Theatre on the Bounty* (Cambridge, 1992), 149–50.

59. Thomas Andros, *The Old "Jersey" Captive or a Narrative of the Captivity of Thomas Andros . . .* (Boston, 1833), 5–6.

60. Fred Anderson, *A People's Army: Massachusetts Soldiers and Society in the Seven Years' War* (Chapel Hill, N.C., 1984), 185–95.

61. John S. Barnes, ed., *The Logs of the "Serapis," "Alliance," "Ariel" Under the Command of John Paul Jones, 1779–1780: With Extracts from Public Documents, Unpublished Letters, and Illustrated with Reproductions of Scarce Prints* (New York, 1911), 32, 36, 37, 39, 45.

62. Louis F. Middlebrook, *History of Maritime Connecticut During the American Revolution, 1775–1783*, 2 vols. (Salem, Mass., 1925), 1:105–11.

63. Christopher Hawkins, *The Adventures of Christopher Hawkins . . .* (New York, 1864),

16–18; Clark, *Naval Documents*, 3:1177–788; Papers in Connection with Alleged Mutiny on Board Mass. Brigantine *Hazard*, Apr. 22, 1778, NJ—Individual Cases, 1779–1827, Box 280, Naval Records Collection, RG 45, NA.

64. Clark, ed., *Naval Documents*, 3:47.

65. Fox, *Adventures*, 57.

66. Sherburne, *Memoirs*, 33–34.

67. Ibid., 34–36.

68. Fanning, *Narrative*, 44, 102; Kilby, "Narrative," 28; William James Morgan, ed., *Naval Documents of the American Revolution* (Washington, D.C., 1976), 7:220–21, 299–300, 521–22, 532.

69. Noyes Palmer to John Palmer, Apil 17, 1776, John Palmer Papers, Coll. 53, GWBWL.

70. Joshua Gott, "Commonplace Book, 1781–1807," PEM. For a similar career path see "James Gray's Memorandum, Aug.?, 1783?," Nathan-Dane Papers, MHS.

71. Quotation from Morgan, ed., *Naval Documents*, 7:543. See also pp. 11, 17, 30, 31, 56–57, 83, 85, 205, 208, 301, 357, 374, 510, 543–44, 983, 1006–7, 1062–63, 1255.

72. Labaree et al., eds., *Papers of Benjamin Franklin*, 29:238, 276–78, 448–49; Morison, *John Paul Jones*, 196–97.

73. Fanning, *Narrative*, 182–97.

74. Labaree et al., eds., *Papers of Benjamin Franklin*, 32:616–17.

75. John C. Dann, ed., *The Revolution Remembered: Eyewitness Accounts of the War for Independence* (Chicago, 1980), 321.

76. Petition of Thomas Haley, Sept. 21, 1777, Adm./M/404, microfilm, NMM.

77. Sherburne, *Memoirs*, 75.

78. Deakens to his wife, Mill Prison, Dec. 8, 1782. Even men with strong local connections might join the British navy. Admiral Peter Parker refused to exchange five New Englanders who "have been volunteers for many months" even though their friends had sent five captured British sailors to the fleet off Rhode Island for a specific exchange. Admiral Peter Parker to Richard Cooke, June 7, 1777, Norcross Collection, 1751–1791, MHS.

79. Vail later ran from the vessel in Portugal, joined a French privateer, and returned to the United States to serve again under the American flag. Vail, "Journal," Peter Force Papers, Ser. VII E, Reel 54, LC.

80. Joseph Bartlett Reminiscences, 1778–1782, MHS.

81. On the general British policy toward prisoners see Francis Abell, *Prisoners of War in Britain, 1756 to 1815: A Record of Their Lives, Their Romance and Their Sufferings* (London, 1914); Richard H. Amerman, "Treatment of American Prisoners During the Revolution," *New Jersey Historical Society Proceedings*, 78 (1960), 257–75; Olive Anderson, "The Treatment of Prisoners of War in Britain During the American War of Independence," *Bulletin of the Institute of Historical Research*, 28 (1955), 63–83; Larry G. Bowman, *Captive Americans: Prisoners During the American Revolution* (Athens, Ga., 1976); Danske Dandridge, *American Prisoners of the Revolution* (Baltimore, 1967; orig. pub. 1911); Charles H. Metzger, *The Prisoner in the American Revolution* (Chicago, 1971).

Besides the relevant works by individual prisoners, conditions in the English prisons are discussed in Howard Lewis Applegate, "American Privateersmen in the Mill Prison During 1777–1782," *EIHC*, 97 (1961), 303–20; John K. Alexander, "'American Privateersmen in the Mill Prison During 1777–1782': An Evaluation," *EIHC*, 102 (1966), 318–40; Alexander, "Forton Prison During the American Revolution: A Case Study of British Prisoner of War Policy and the American Prisoner Response to that Policy," *EIHC*, 103 (1967), 365–89; Cogliano, *American Maritime Prisoners*; Sheldon S. Cohen, *Yankee Sailors in British Gaols: Prisoners of War at Forton and Mill, 1777–1783* (Newark, Del., 1995); and

Jesse Lemisch, "Listening to the 'Inarticulate': William Widger's Dream and the Loyalties of American Revolutionary Seamen in British Prisons," *JSH*, 3 (1969), 1–29. For conditions in the British navy see Peter Kemp, *The British Sailor: A Social History of the Lower Deck* (London, 1970); Christopher Lloyd, *The British Seaman, 1200–1860: A Social Survey* (London, 1968); Dudley Pope, *Life in Nelson's Navy* (Annapolis, 1981); N. A. M. Rodger, *The Wooden World: An Anatomy of the Georgian Navy* (Annapolis, 1986). Conditions on the New York prison ships are discussed in Eugene L. Armbruster, *The Wallabout Prison-Ships, 1776–1783* (New York, 1920); James Lenox Banks, *David Sproat and Naval Prisoners in the War of the Revolution* ([New York], 1909); Henry Onderdonk, Jr., *Revolutionary Incidents of Suffolk and Kings Counties; With an Account of the Battle of Long Island, and the British Prisons and Prison-Ships at New-York* (New York, 1849), 207–50; Louis H. Roddis, "The New York Prison Ships in the American Revolution," *United States Naval Institute Proceedings*, 61 (1935), 331–36. Similar conditions existed in other American ports occupied by the British. See John Chandler, "Autobiography," original in MeHS, copy in MHS; CSHS to Adm., Jan. 6, 1779, Adm. 98/11/406, microfilm, PRO.

82. These numbers are only the roughest estimates. For commentary at the end of the war on the number of prisoners to die on New York prison ships see *Pennsylvania Packet* (Philadelphia), Apr. 29, 1783; *Connecticut Gazette* (New London), Apr. 25, 1783. For the list of prisoners in England see Marion Kaminkow and Jack Kaminkow, *Mariners of the American Revolution* (Baltimore, 1967). See also *Boston Gazette*, June 24, July 1, 8, 1782.

83. Albert Greene, *Recollections of the "Jersey" Prison Ship: From the Manuscripts of Capt. Thomas Dring . . .* (New York, 1961; orig. pub. 1829), 14–20.

84. Vail, "Journal," Peter Force Papers, Ser. VII E, Reel 54, #146, LC.

85. CSHS to Adm., June 25, 1781, Adm. 98/13/372, microfilm, PRO. In 1779, when there were supposed to be 70,000 men in the British navy (there were probably fewer), 1,658 died and 28,592 were sick. For conditions in the British navy see Lloyd, *British Seamen*, 258–64.

86. William Russell to Mrs. William Russell, Mar. 4, 1781, insert in William Russell Journal, typescript, PEM. Also quoted in Cogliano, *American Maritime Prisoners*, 56.

87. Cogliano, *American Maritime Prisoners*, 56–86.

88. Lemisch, "Listening to the 'Inarticulate'," 1–29.

89. For statements linking the refusal to desert to patriotism see ibid., 16; and Cohen, *Yankee Sailors*, 102–5, 142–44.

90. Kaminkow and Kaminkow, *Mariners of the American Revolution*, 107. See also Widger, "Diary," *EIHC*, 74 (1938), 148, 155.

91. Fox, *Adventures*, 135–53.

92. Based on Kaminkow and Kaminkow, *Mariners of the American Revolution*. Herbert indicates that thirty of sixty-one volunteers for the British navy came from the British Isles during his time at Mill Prison. Herbert, *Relic of the Revolution*, 243–58.

93. Herbert, *Relic of the Revolution*, 107, 155, 157, 159, 169–72, 183, 216.

94. Ibid., 201–2.

95. This torment was not universal. On at least one occasion the "volunteers" and remaining prisoners parted on friendly terms cheering for each other on separation. Thomas Pye to Adm., May 30, 1781, in Adm. to CSHS, June 5, 1781, Adm./M/405, microfilm, NMM; Herbert, *Relic of the Revolution*, 172.

96. Kemp, *British Sailor*; Lloyd, *British Seaman*; Pope, *Life in Nelson's Navy*; Rodger, *Wooden World*.

97. Lemisch, "Jack Tar in the Streets," 381–95; Gilje, *Road to Mobocracy*, 12–13, 23–24.

98. Betsy Knight, "Prisoner Exchange and Parole in the American Revolution," *WMQ*, 3rd ser., 48 (1991), 201–22. For an example of a state-arranged cartel see Massachusetts

Council's instructions to Captain Greely about the cartel ship *Happy Release*, Nov. 28, 1778, Revere Family Papers, MHS.

99. Foote, ed., "Reminiscences of the Revolution," 110. For rumors of exchange see Fanning, *Narrative*, 23; Russell, Mar. 23, 24, June 2, 1781, "Journal," typescript, PEM; Widger, "Diary," *EIHC*, 73 (1937), 317, 320; Widger, "Diary," *EIHC*, 74 (1938), 36 47. See also Catherine M. Prelinger, "Benjamin Franklin and the American Prisoners of War in England During the American Revolution," *WMQ*, 3rd. ser., 32 (1975), 260–94.

100. For examples of escape in these areas see Andros, *Old "Jersey" Captive*, 21–80; Fox, *Adventures*, 116–30, 159–204; Greene, *Recollections*, 5–6; William Lambert Letterbook, 1740–1820, 127–54, Caleb Snow Papers, MHS; Deposition of Arthur Mclellan, July 1781, Snow Papers, MHS; Deposition of Captain William Keith, July 9, 1781, Snow Papers, MHS; Vail, "Journal," Peter Force Papers, Ser. VII E, Reel 54, LC.

101. For a statement of this position see Lemisch, "Listening to the 'Inarticulate,'" 18–20; and Cohen, *Yankee Sailors*, 105–8, 144–47. For a contrasting view see Olive Anderson, "American Escapes from British Naval Prisons During the War of Independence," *Mariner's Mirror*, 41 (1955), 238–40. See also Francis D. Cogliano, "'We Fled from the Valley of Destruction': American Escapes From Mill and Forton Prisoners, 1777–1782," *AN*, 58 (1998), 125–43; Cogliano, *American Maritime Prisoners*, 94–112.

102. Marcus Rediker, *Between the Devil and the Deep Blue Sea: Merchant Seamen, Pirates, and the Anglo-American Maritime World, 1700–1750* (Cambridge, 1987), 116–52; Knut Weibust, *Deep Sea Sailors: A Study in Maritime Ethnology*, 2nd ed. (Stockholm, 1976), 437–45.

103. Gerald O. Haffner, "The Treatment of Prisoners of War by the Americans During the War of Independence" (Ph.D. diss., Indiana University, 1952), 47–48, 82, 92–93, 136–37, 147–48, 225, 234, 239; Abell, *Prisoners of War in Britain*, 146–47, 160–61, 230–31, 363; Morgan, ed., *Naval Documents*, 7:195, 241–42, 324, 1171.

104. For cartel agreements between European powers see CSHS to Adm., Nov. 12, 1779, Adm. 98/12/264, 316–34, microfilm, PRO; CSHS to Adm., Feb. 23, 1781, Adm. 98/13/237–47, microfilm, PRO. For examples of French prisoners escaping see CSHS to Adm., July 16, Aug. 10, 30, 1779, Adm. 98/12/102–3, 127–28, 155, microfilm, PRO; see also William Richard Cutter, ed., "A Yankee Privateersman in Prison in England, 1777–1779," *NEHGR*, 32 (1878), 70, 166–68, 282, 284. For a general discussion see Olive Anderson, "The Establishment of British Supremacy at Sea and the Exchange of Naval Prisoners of War, 1689–1783," *English Historical Review*, 55 (1960), 77–89.

105. CSHS to Adm., Jan. 14, 30, 1778, Adm. 98/11/154–55, 165–66, microfilm, PRO; Labaree et al., eds., *Papers of Benjamin Franklin*, 25:414–19.

106. Fanning, *Narrative*, 25.

107. Cutter, "A Yankee Privateersman," *NEHGR*, 30 (1876), 174–77, 343–52; Cutter, "A Yankee Privateersman," 31 (1877), 18–20, 212–13, 284–88; Cutter, "A Yankee Privateersman," 32 (1878), 70–73, 165–68, 280–86.

108. A survey of the escapes listed in Kaminkow and Kaminkow, eds., *Mariners of the American Revolution*, shows that there were 30 successful escapes out of 54 captains listed; 43 out of 127 other officers were successful; 19 out of 86 petty officers were successful, and 108 out of 2,235 seamen were successful. While these numbers may not be fully accurate, the trend is apparent and supported by other evidence discussed in the text. For CSHS reports on escapes and recaptures see CSHS to Adm., Oct. 27, 1779, Adm. 98/12/240–41 microfilm, PRO; CSHS to Adm., Nov. 22, 1780, Adm. 98/13/136–41 microfilm, PRO.

109. Foote, ed., "Reminiscences of the Revolution," 97–100.

110. Herbert, *Relic of the Revolution*, 199.

111. Anonymous to Adm., July 28, 1778, Adm./M/404, microfilm, NMM.

112. Samuel Cutler, "Prison Ships, and the 'Old Mill Prison,' Plymouth, England, 1777," *NEHGR*, 32 (1878), 397. See also George Thompson, "Diary of George Thompson of Newburyport, Kept at Forton Prison, England, 1777–1781," *EIHC*, 76 (1940), 232–36; and Taylor et al., eds., *John Adams Papers*, 6:407.

113. Nathaniel Harrington, "Letter of Nathaniel Harrington, Jr., in 1781, to His Father," *NEHGR*, 51 (1897), 322–23.

114. Except for Samuel Cutler and Israel Potter, every sailor who escaped and left a personal record sooner or later signed aboard a warship. This included Joshua Barney, John Blatchford, Thomas Dring, Ebenezer Fox, Caleb Foot, Christopher Hawkins, and Luke Mathewman.

115. Deposition of John Long, Sept. 29, 1781, in [Thos.] Fitzwilliams to Adm., Nov. 3, 1781, Adm./M/405, microfilm, NMM.

116. Cohen reports only fifteen recaptures and declares, "Kinsey's efforts exemplify many of the Yankee captives' undaunted desires to get clear of their incarceration by any available means." We have no direct evidence of Kinsey's motives beyond the suggestions of the British officials. Cohen, *Yankee Sailors*, 180; CSHS to Adm., Dec. 11, 1781, Jan. 7, Feb. 5, Mar. 5, 19, 1782, Adm. 98/14/29, 59–60, 79, 97–98, 112, microfilm, PRO.

117. Adm. to CSHS, July 10, 1777, Adm./M/404, microfilm, NMM.

118. Fitzwilliams to Adm., Sept. 28, 1781, Adm./M/405, microfilm, NMM.

119. Fitzwilliams to Adm., Oct. 17, 1781, Adm./M/405, microfilm, NMM.

120. Many sailors used the money for a spree. It is possible some sailor with an acquisitive instinc saved the money for the future. Timothy Connor identified the "five pounder" as the bounty hunter eager to capture the escaped American prisoner. Luke Mathewman identifies the "five pounder" as the escaped American prisoner out on a lark. In all likelihood, sailors in prison used the term both ways. Lemisch and Cohen refer to five-pounders only as English bounty hunters. See Lemisch, "Listening to the 'Inarticulate'," 19; and Cohen, *Yankee Sailors*, 77, 108, 146–47, 186, 220, 221. For Connor's references see Cutter, "A Yankee Privateersman," *NEHGR*, 30 (1876), 347; Cutter, "A Yankee Privateersman," *NEHGR* 31 (1877), 19; Cutter, "A Yankee Privateersman," *NEHGR* 32 (1878), 165. For a definition of a "five pounder" as escaped prisoner of war see Luke Mathewman, "Narrative of Lieut. Luke Mathewman of the Revolutionary Navy," *Magazine of American History*, 2 (1878), 182. The CSHS often discussed the problem of the reward. See CSHS to Adm., May 7, Oct. 27, 1779, Adm. 98/12/10–11, 240–41, microfilm, PRO; CSHS to Adm., Mar. 5, Apr. 12, 1782, Adm. 98/14/99–100, 141, microfilm, PRO. See also Adm. to CSHS, Oct. 15, 1779, Adm./M/404, microfilm, NMM; Gen Smith to Adm., Feb. 14, 1782 in Adm. to CSHS, Mar. 2, 1782, Adm./M/405, microfilm, NMM. For the order reducing the reward see Adm. to CSHS, May 1, 1782, microfilm, NMM.

121. Herman Melville, *Israel Potter: His Fifty Years of Exile*, Harrison Hayford et al., eds. (Evanston, Ill., 1982; orig. pub. 1855). Potter's full story remains a mystery. He claimed that he served as a courier to France after his escape, but he may have been a British spy. He lived in obscurity in England for most of the rest of his life. David Chacko and Alexander Kulcsar, "Israel Potter: Genesis of a Legend," *WMQ*, 3rd ser., 41 (1984), 365–89.

122. Herbert, *Relic of the Revolution*, 169; Adm. to CSHS, Oct. 20, 1780, Adm./M/404, microfilm, NMM; CSHS to Adm., Apr. 25, 1777, Adm. 98/11/95, microfilm, PRO; CSHS to Adm., Oct. 17, 23, 1780, Adm. 98/13/108, 114, microfilm, PRO; Labaree et al., eds., *Papers of Benjamin Franklin*, 24:402, 26:12–13, 179, 382–83, 28:553–54; 29:646–48.

123. Hafner, "Treatment of Prisoners of War," 82, 90, 145–48.

124. Abell, *Prisoners of War in Britain*, 56, 58–59, 80, 141, 182, 202–4, 229–32, 280. For an American sailor's description of the French during the War of 1812 see Charles

Andrews, *The Prisoners' Memoirs, or Dartmoor Prison; Containing a Complete and Impartial History of the Entire Captivity of the Americans in England*... (New York, 1815), 24, 43–54, 72–75, 86.

125. Greene, *Recollections*, 25, 84–88.

126. For a contrasting argument see Lemisch, "Listening to the 'Inarticulate,'" 26; and Cohen, *Yankee Sailors*, 113–14, 137–38.

127. George Ralls, "Narrative of His Capture, May 1777 . . ," NYHS; Fanning, *Narrative*, 25; Cutler, "Prison Ships, and the 'Old Mill Prison,'" 395; Coan, ed., "Revolutionary Prison Diary," 294, 303; Herbert, *Relic of the Revolution*, 97; CSHS to Adm., Jan. 14, 1778, Adm. 98/11/154–55, microfilm, PRO.

128. Thornton is a shadowy figure; the name may be an alias. He later became an agent for the British. Labaree et al., eds., *Papers of Benjamin Franklin*, 25:26–27, 414–19; Herbert, *Relic of the Revolution*, 219.

129. Labaree et al., eds., *Papers of Benjamin Franklin*, 26:165.

130. Sherburne, *Memoirs*, 86.

131. Cutter, "A Yankee Privateersman," *NEHGR*, 30 (1876), 350.

132. Petition of Prisoners at Mill Prison, in Adm. to CSHS, June 23, 1781, Adm./M/405, microfilm, NMM.

133. Petition of Fourteen Persons confined in the inner Prison at Forton, in Adm. to CSHS, Mar. 25, 1778, Adm./M/404, microfilm, NMM.

134. For examples of other petitions from prisoners see Labaree et al., eds., *Papers of Benjamin Franklin*, 31:442–43; "Petition of American Prisoners on the *Diligente*," July 4, 1782, Adm./M/405, microfilm, NMM; Petition of John Dagon . . ., Oct. 20, 1777, Adm./M/404, microfilm, NMM. See also CSHS to Adm., June 1, 25, 1781, Adm. 98/13/353, 371–73, microfilm, PRO; CSHS to Adm., Oct. 4, 1782, Adm. 98/14/254, microfilm, PRO.

135. Herbert, *Relic of the Revolution*, 145–48; Coan, ed., Revolutionary Prison Diary," 427–28; Sherburne, *Memoirs*, 83. See also CSHS to Adm., Jan. 27, 1779, Adm. 98/11/442–44, microfilm, PRO.

136. Hawkins, *Adventures*, 24, 62–63. See also Francis D. Cogliano, "'We All Hoisted the American Flag': National Identity Among American Prisoners in Britain During the American Revolution," *Journal of American Studies*, 32 (1998), 19–37.

137. George G. Carey, ed., *A Sailor's Songbag: An American Rebel in an English Prison, 1777–1779* (Amherst, Mass., 1976). Connor also included several clearly British patriotic and antiwar songs.

138. Herbert, *Relic of the Revolution*, 142.

139. Russell, July 3, 4, 1781, "Journal," typescript, PEM.

140. Sherburne, *Memoirs*, 86.

141. Herbert, *Relic of the Revolution*, 79.

142. Sherburne, *Memoirs*, 99–100.

143. Foote, ed., "Reminiscences of the Revolution," 107.

144. Widger, "Diary," *EIHC*, 74 (1938), 156.

145. Cutler, "Prison Ships and the 'Old Mill Prison,'" 185, 187, 306.

146. See examples in Fox, *Adventures*, 85–90; and Ralph D. Paine, *Joshua Barney: A Forgotten Hero of Blue Water* (New York, 1924), 80–81.

147. Foote, ed., "Reminiscences of the Revolution," 112, 119.

148. Davis, *Narrative*, 35–39.

Chapter 5. Brave Republicans of the Ocean

1. James Durand, *James Durand: An Able Seaman of 1812: His Adventures on "Old Ironsides" and as an Impressed Sailor in the British Navy*, George S. Brooks, ed. (New Haven, 1926; orig. pub. 1820), 18–19.

2. Ibid., 32–37. Campbell claimed that he confined seven men, see United States, Office of Naval Records and Libray, *Naval Documents Related to the United States Wars with the Barbary Powers*, 6 vols. (Washington, D.C., 1944), 6:556–57.

3. Durand, *An Able Seaman*, 3–17.

4. Ibid., 38.

5. Ibid., 50–86. Quotations on 61–62, 65.

6. For a different argument examining the ferment in the Atlantic world at this time, and tracing the roots of radicalism to the seventeenth century, see Peter Linebaugh and Marcus Rediker, *The Many-Headed Hydra: Sailors, Slaves, Commoners, and the Hidden History of the Revolutionary Atlantic* (Boston, 2000). This book expands upon the authors' arguments as expressed in earlier essays. See Linebaugh, "All the Atlantic Mountains Shook," *Labour/Le Travailleur*, 10 (1982), 87–121; and Linebaugh and Rediker, "The Many Headed Hydra: Sailors, Slaves and the Atlantic Working Class in the Eighteenth Century," in Colin Howell and Richard J. Twomey, eds., *Jack Tar in History: Essays in the History of Maritime Life and Labour* (Fredericton, New Brunswick, 1991), 11–36.

7. Elijah Cobb, *A Cape Cod Skipper (1768–1848)* (New Haven, 1925), 27–40.

8. Simon P. Newman, *Parades and the Politics of the Street: Festive Culture in the Early Republic* (Philadelphia, 1997), 65–66, 150.

9. Meade Minnigerode, *Jefferson Friend of France, 1793: The Career of Edmond Charles Genet* (New York, 1928), 184–97; Stanley Elkins and Eric McKitrick, *The Age of Federalism: The Early American Republic, 1788–1800* (New York, 1993), 330–54; *General Advertiser* (Philadelphia), May 17, 18, 1793.

10. Paul A. Gilje, *The Road to Mobocracy: Popular Disorder in New York City, 1763–1834* (Chapel Hill, N.C., 1987), 100–101.

11. Alfred F. Young, *The Democratic Republicans of New York: The Origins, 1763–1797* (Chapel Hill, N.C., 1967), 354–55.

12. Newman, *Parades and the Politics of the Street*, 65–66, 150. Quoted on 66.

13. *New York Journal*, Mar. 12, 1794; John Anderson, Mar. 7, 10, 1794, "Diary," NYHS; Alexander Anderson, Mar. 10, 1794, "Diarium," Columbia University Library.

14. *New York Journal*, July 18, 1792, June 15, July 3, 10, 17, 1793. Newman, *Parades and the Politics of the Street*, 120–51, 170.

15. France, Consulate, Philadelphia, *They Steer to Liberty's Shores* (Philadelphia, 1793), broadside.

16. United States, *American State Papers: Documents, Legislative and Executive, of the Congress of the United States . . .* (Washington, D.C., 1832), 1:151, 167–71.

17. *The Last Words and Dying Confession of the Three Pirates Who Were Executed This Day (May 9, 1800)* (Philadelphia, 1800); William Wheland, *A Narrative of the Horrid Murder and Piracy Committed on Board the Schooner "Eliza," of Philadelphia, On the High Sea, By Three Foreigners* ([Philadelphia, 1800]).

18. Minnigerode, *Jefferson Friend of France, 1793*, 289–316.

19. Frances Sergeant Childs, *French Refugee Life in the United States, 1790–1800: An American Chapter of the French Revolution* (Baltimore, 1940).

20. Christopher McKee, ed., "*Constitution* in the Quasi-War with France: The Letters of John Roche, Jr., 1798–1801," *AN* (1967), 145.

21. Horace Lane, *The Wandering Boy, Careless Sailor, and Result of Inconsideration, A True Narrative* (Skaneateles, N.Y., 1839), 59–68.

22. Julius S. Scott, "Afro-American Sailors and the International Communication Network: The Case of Newport Bowers," in Howell and Twomey, eds., *Jack Tar in History*, 37–52.

23. Gilje, *Road to Mobocracy*, 147–50; Gary B. Nash, *Forging Freedom: The Formation of Philadelphia's Black Community, 1720–1840* (Cambridge, Mass., 1988), 176.

24. W. Jeffrey Bolster, *Black Jacks: African American Seamen in the Age of Sail* (Cambridge, Mass., 1997), 144–53.

25. Scott, "Afro-American Sailors and the International Communication Network," in Howell and Twomey, eds., *Jack Tar in History*, 37–52; Douglas R. Egerton, *He Shall Go Out Free: The Lives of Denmark Vesey* (Madison, Wis., 1999).

26. James Dugan, *The Great Mutiny* (New York, 1965); Dudley Pope, *The Black Ship* (New York, 1998; orig. pub. 1963); Joseph P. Moore, III, "'The Greatest Enormity that Prevails': Direct Democracy and Workers' Self-Management in the British Naval Mutinies of 1797," in Howell and Twomey, eds., *Jack Tar in History*, 76–104.

27. Dugan, *The Great Mutiny*, 80, 120, 393; Pope, *The Black Ship*, 280–92.

28. Job Sibly, *The Trial of Richard Parker, Complete; President of the Delegates, for Mutiny, &c* . . . (Boston, 1797).

29. For newspaper coverage see *Philadelphia Gazette*, June 13, 15, 16, 27, Aug. 1, 2, 3, 10, 11, 19, 21, 22, 26, 28, 30, 1797.

30. Marshall's comments can be found in his speech on Mar. 7, 1800, in *Annals of the Congress of the United States, Sixth Congress* (Washington, D.C., 1851), 596–618. Quotations are from pp. 617 and 600. See also the copy of the speech in Charles T. Cullen, ed., *The Papers of John Marshall* (Chapel Hill, N.C., 1984), 4:82–109.

31. Pope, *The Black Ship*, 280–92; James Monroe to John Adams, Feb 9, 1801, Box 611, Naval Records Collection, RG 45, NA; United States, *American State Papers: Documents. Legislative and Executive, of the Congress of the United States* . . . (Washington, D.C., 1832), 2:763; *Annals of Congress, Sixth Congress*, 511, 515–18, 526, 532–33, 541–78, 583–623. See also Alexander DeConde, *The Quasi-War: The Politics and Diplomacy of the Undeclared War with France, 1797–1801* (New York, 1966), 204–5.

32. Gilje, *Road to Mobocracy*. See also Newman, *Parades and the Politics of the Street*; David Waldstreicher, *In the Midst of Perpetual Fetes: The Making of American Nationalism, 1776–1820* (Chapel Hill, N.C., 1997).

33. Newman, *Parades and the Politics of the Street*, 40–42.

34. Paul A. Gilje, "The Common People and the Constitution: Popular Culture in New York City in the Late Eighteenth Century," in Gilje and William Pencak, eds., *New York in the Age of the Constitution, 1775–1800* (Rutherford, N.J., 1992), 48–73.

35. Fisher Ames to Thomas Dwight, May 6, 1794, in Seth Ames, ed., *Works of Fisher Ames: With a Selection from His Speeches and Correspondence,* 2 vols. (Boston, 1854), 1:144. See also *New York Journal*, Mar. 1, 1794; J. Thomas Scharf, *History of Baltimore City and County, From the Earliest Period to the Present Day* (Philadelphia, 1881), 780–81; Mathew Page Andrews, *History of Maryland: Province and State* (Garden City, N.Y., 1929), 412–14; Moreau de St. Méry, *Moreau de St. Mery's American Journey (1793–1798)*, trans. and ed. Kenneth Roberts and Anna M. Roberts (Garden City, N.Y., 1947), 44, 59; Childs, *French Refugee Life in the United States,* 82.

36. *New York Journal*, July 1, 1795.

37. *New York Journal*, July 8, 11, 15, 1795.

38. Stephen Higginson to Thomas Pickering, Sept. 21, 1795, in John Franklin Jameson, ed., "Letters of Stephen Higginson," *Report of the American Historical Association for 1896*, 1: 795; William Bruce Wheeler, "Urban Politics in Nature's Republic: The Development of Political Parties in the Seaport Cities in the Federalist Era" (Ph.D. diss., Uni-

versity of Virginia, 1967), 97–99; Gilje, *Road to Mobocracy*, 103–4; Rachel N. Klein, *Unification of a Slave State: The Rise of the Planter Class in the South Carolina Backcountry, 1760–1808* (Chapel Hill, N.C., 1990), 219–20; George R. Lamplugh, "'Oh the Colossus! The Colossus!': James Jackson and the Jeffersonian Republican Party in Georgia, 1796–1806," *JER*, 9 (1989), 329.

39. Delbert Harold Gilpatrick, *Jeffersonian Democracy in North Carolina, 1789–1816* (New York, 1967; orig. pub. 1931), 83.

40. *New York Time Piece*, Aug. 30, 1798. See also DeConde, *Quasi-War*; Howard P. Nash, Jr., *The Forgotten Wars: The Role of the U.S. Navy in the Quasi War with France and the Barbary Wars, 1798–1805* (South Brunswick, N.J., 1968).

41. Gilje, *Road to Mobocracy*, 107–11.

42. Lynn Warren Turner, *The Ninth State: New Hampshire's Formative Years* (Chapel Hill, N.C., 1983), 177.

43. July 27, 1800, Logbook, *Ann and Hope*, RIHS.

44. *The Festival of Mirth and American Tar's Delight . . .* (New York, 1800), 12–13. See also *The Sailor's Medley: A Collection of the Most Admired Sea and Other Songs* (Philadelphia, 1800); *Patriotic Medley: Being a Choice Collection of Patriotic, Sentimental, Hunting, and Sea Songs . . .* (New York, 1800); and *The Syren; A Choice Collection of Sea, Hunting, and Other Songs* (Philadelphia, 1800).

45. Charles P. Clinton, Apr. 24, 1805, "His Journal Book," 1802–6, Yale.

46. *New York American Citizen*, April 28, 29, 1806; De Witt Clinton to captain of *Leander*, May 1, 1806, Clinton to James Madison, May 3, 1806, Clinton to Mr. Barclay, May 3, 1806, Clinton to Madison, May 6, 1806, Clinton Letterbook, Columbia University Library.

47. Henry Adams, *History of the United States . . .* (New York, 1909), 4:27; *American Register*, 2 (1808), 190–207; *American Register*, 3 (1808), 3–93; *New York Evening Post*, July 6, 1807. See also Spenser C. Tucker and Frank T. Reuter, *Injured Honor: The "Chesapeake"-"Leopard" Affair, June 22, 1807* (Annapolis, 1996).

48. Robert E. Cray, Jr., "Commemorating the Prison Ship Dead: Revolutionary Memory and the Politics of Sepulture in the Early Republic, 1776–1808," *WMQ*, 3rd. ser., 56 (1999), 565–90. Quotation found on pp. 584–85.

49. *New York Public Advertiser*, Oct. 7, 1808.

50. Quoted in John Bach McMaster, *A History of the People of the United States, From the Revolution to the Civil War* (New York, 1891), 3:292n.

51. Gilje, *Road to Mobocracy*, 182–83.

52. J. Thomas Scharf and Thompson Wescott, *History of Philadelphia, 1609–1884* (Philadelphia, 1884), 1:530.

53. *New York Evening Post*, Feb. 8, 1808.

54. *New York Public Advertiser*, Sept. 2, 1808.

55. *New York Evening Post*, Jan. 27, 30, 1809.

56. *American Register*, 5, 241; *New York Evening Post*, Feb. 4, 1809.

57. *New York Public Advertiser*, Dec. 5, 1808.

58. *New York American Citizen*, May 1, 1806.

59. Scharf and Wescott, *History of Philadelphia*, 1:538–39.

60. *New York American Citizen*, Apr. 27, 1808.

61. *New York Evening Post*, Aug. 23, Sept. 30, Oct. 11, 1814.

62. Paul Liecester Ford, ed., *The Works of Thomas Jefferson*, 12 vols. (New York, 1904), 4:85–86, 449–50.

63. William T. Hutchinson, ed., *The Papers of James Madison*, 17 vols. (Chicago, 1962–92), 14:168, 244–46.

64. Quoted in David Hackett Fischer, *The Revolution in American Conservatism: The Federalist Party in the Era of Jeffersonian Democracy* (New York, 1965), 183.

65. Ames, ed., *Works of Fisher Ames*, 2:111–12.

66. Gilje, *Road to Mobocracy*, 78–92; Gilje, "The Baltimore Riots of 1812 and the Breakdown of the Anglo-American Mob Tradition," *JSH*, 13 (1980), 547–64; Gilje, "'Le Menu Peuple' in America: Identifying the Mob in the Baltimore Riots of 1812," *Maryland Historical Magazine*, 81 (1986), 50–66.

67. *New York Argus*, Aug. 27, 1799.

68. Scharf and Wescott, *History of Philadelphia*, 1:519.

69. *New York Evening Post*, Apr. 9, 1802, Mar. 18, 1811, Dec. 16, 1811, Jan. 13, 1812; *Niles' Weekly Register*, 1 (Nov. 30, 1811), 237–38; *New York Gazette*, Jan. 22, 1811; *New York Columbian Centinel*, Sept. 12, 1807; Scharf and Wescott, *History of Philadelphia*, I, 519; *American Register*, 5: 242–43; Irving Brant, *James Madison*, 6 vols. (New York, 1941–61), 5:315; Gilje, *Road to Mobocracy*, 123–25.

70. June 24, July 4, 1809, Logbook, *President Adams*, AAS; *New York Commercial Advertiser*, Sept. 19, 22, 1809; *New York Evening Post*, Sept. 22, 1809; Reginald Horsman, *The Causes of the War of 1812* (New York, 1962), 195.

71. In part this symbolic significance was simply the result of a British legacy lionizing the common seaman that harkened to the days of the defeat of the Spanish Armada and reached a new height during the period under consideration here.

72. Mathew Carey, *A Short Account of Algiers . . . and of Their Several Wars . . .*, 2nd ed. (Philadelphia, 1794); James Wilson Stevens, *An Historical and Geographical Account of Algiers . . .* (Philadelphia, 1797); [Royall Tyler], *The Algerine Captive; or the Life and Adventures of Doctor Updike Underhill . . .* (Walpole, N.H., 1797); Susanna Rowson, *Slaves in Algiers, or, Struggle for Freedom* (Philadelphia, 1794). See also John Willcock, *The Voyages and Adventures of John Willcock, Mariner . . .* (Philadelphia, 1798); *Humanity in Algiers: Or the Slave of Azem, By an American, Late a Slave of Algiers* (Troy, N.Y., 1801); Thomas Nicholson, *An Affecting Narrative of the Captivity and Sufferings of Thomas Nicholson [A Native of New Jersey] Who Has Been Six Years a Prisoner Among the Algerines . . .* (Boston, 1816). See also Robert J. Allison, *The Crescent Obscured: The United States and the Muslim World, 1776–1815* (New York, 1995).

73. Carey, *Short Account of Algiers*, 44. Allison suggests that the American sailors who were slaves in North Africa were not as poorly treated as black slaves in North America. Allison, *Crescent Obscured*, 110–13.

74. Stevens, *Historical and Geographical Account*, 93. For general accounts of the Barbary Wars see Allison, *Crescent Obscured*; Nash, *Forgotten Wars*, 177–291.

75. John Foss, *A Journal of the Captivity and Sufferings of John Foss . . .* (Newburyport, Mass., [1798]), 64–65.

76. The best account is William Ray, *Horrors of Slavery: or the American Tars in Tripoli* (Troy, N.Y., 1808). For an officer's perspective see Jonathan Cowdry, *American Captives in Tripoli . . .*, 2nd ed. (Boston, 1806).

77. Ray, *Horrors of Slavery*, 151–52.

78. Ibid. Ray's view of conditions is supported by a reminiscence published much later. That author, Elijah Shaw, a ship's carpenter, never called himself a slave, but described the brutal treatment he received, including being struck for not working hard enough, and painful corporal punishment for acts of resistance. Elijah Shaw, *A Short Sketch of the Life of Elijah Shaw Who Served for Twenty-two Years in the United States Navy* (Rochester, 1843), 21–28.

79. Ray, *Horrors of Slavery*, 149.

80. Ibid., 18.

81. Raynor Taylor, *The American Captives Emancipation. Written by a Tar* (Philadelphia, 1805).

82. Shaw, *Short Sketch*, 53. For accounts of the campaign against the Barbary Pirates see William Eaton, *Interesting Detail of the Operations of the American Fleet in the Mediterranean . . .* (Springfield, 1805); Eaton, *To the Honorable Secretary of the Navy of the United States* (1805); United States, 8th Cong., 1803–5, *Documents Accompanying the Bill for the Relief of the Captors of the Moorish Armed Ships, Meshouda & Mirboha . . .* (Washington, D.C., 1804); U.S. President, *Message from the President of the United States, Transmitting a Letter from Commodore Preble . . .* (Washington, D.C., 1805).

83. Allison, *Crescent Obscured*, 187–88, 192–206.

84. Foss, *Journal of the Captivity*, 67–70. For the *Fortune* see Allison, *Crescent Obscured*, 159.

85. John Hoxse, *The Yankee Tar: An Authentic Narrative of the Voyages and Hardships of John Hoxse, and the Cruises of the U. S. Frigate Constellation . . .* (Northampton, Mass., 1840), 36–47.

86. See William Fairfield to American Council at Naples, Aug. 18, 1809, claim sent to Mr. Clay for ship *Margaret* on France, Sept. 20, 1826, A. Huntington to John Crowinshield, Aug. 9, 1836, J. Hardy Price to Crowinshield, Jan. 17, 1837, Box 2, Crowinshield Papers, PEM. For other examples of seized and searched vessels see Daniel Arnold, Aug. 8–11, 1799, Logbook, *Ann and Hope*, RIHS; and Samuel Winchester, Logbook, *Dolly*, 1809–10, MdHS.

87. *American State Papers*, 1:82.

88. *American State Papers*, 2:489.

89. *New York Evening Post*, Feb. 8, 1808.

90. For examples see *Festival of Mirth . . .*; and *Sailor's Medley . . .* (Philadelphia, 1800).

91. *Patriotic Medley*, 34–35.

92. "Come All Ye Yankee Sailors," ballad, 1799, Misc. Bound MS, 1799, MHS.

93. *Festival of Mirth*, 5.

94. See *American State Papers:* 1:763–64; 2:129–36, 269–80, 361–62, 471–74, 776–98; United States, *American State Papers: Documents, Legislative and Executive of the Congress of the United States . . .* (Washington, D.C., 1832), 3:36–80, 348. During the Nootka Sound controversy in 1790, John Cutting claimed that two thousand Americans had been pressed by the British navy. John Browne Cutting, *Facts and Observations, Justifying the Claims of John Browne Cutting . . .* ([Philadelphia, 1795]); *American State Papers*, 1:123.

95. [Illegible] to James Monroe, Apr. 26, 1816, Box 611, Naval Records Collection, RG 45, NA; United States, *American State Papers: Documents Legislative and Executive of the Congress of the United States . . .* (Washington, D.C., 1834), 4:56–95.

96. For a general discussion of impressment see J. R. Hutchinson, *The Press-Gang: Afloat and Ashore* (New York, 1914); Clement Cleveland Sawtell, "Impressment of American Seamen by the British," *EIHC*, 76 (1940), 314–44; George Selement, "Impressment and the American Merchant Marine, 1782–1812," *Mariner's Mirror*, 59 (1973), 409–18; James Fulton Zimmerman, *Impressment of American Seamen* (Port Washington, N.Y., 1966; orig. pub. 1925). See also U.S. Eighth Congress, *A Bill Further to Protect the Seamen of the United States* (Washington, D.C., 1804); U.S. Department of State, *Letter from the Secretary of State, Accompanying Statements and Abstracts Relative to the Number of American Seamen Who Have Been Impressed . . .* ([Washington, D.C., 1805]).

97. Joshua Penny, *The Life and Adventures of Joshua Penny, A Native of Southold, Long Island . . .* (New York, 1815), 9.

98. John Bateman to David Gelston, Sept. 5, 1807, Captain Cochrane to Gelston, Sept. 6, 1807, Box 23, David Gelston Papers, GWBWL. See also Cutting, *Facts and Observa-*

tions; Undated Remarks of Captain Balch of Ship *Stratford*, Box 4, Hale Shipping Papers, NHHS.

99. *American State Papers*, 2:731; 3:347–48. See also 1:761–66; 2:126–50, 292–94; 3:36–79.

100. Wm. Fairfield to Crowinshield, Feb. 20, 1811, Box 2, Crowinshield Papers, PEM.

101. Nov. 23–24, 1805, Logbook, *Susanna*, PEM.

102. *American State Papers*, 2:272–73.

103. Ibid., 2:593–95.

104. Nov. 21, 22, 1805, Jan. 25, 1806, Logbook, *Prudent*, PEM.

105. *American State Papers*, 2:784–85.

106. Ibid., 2:795–97.

107. Penny, *Life and Adventures*, 11.

108. James M'Lean, *Seventeen Years' History, of the Life and Sufferings of James M'Lean. An Impressed American Seaman* . . . (Hartford, 1814). For other experiences of impressed seamen see John Edgar to his mother, May 11, 1804, Dr. Arthur C. Bining Collection, HSP; John Briggs, "An Impressed American Seaman, John Briggs of Windham, Maine, 1811–1812," *Moorsfield Antiquarian*, 1 (1937), 157–62; Samuel Dalton, "Letters of Samuel Dalton of Salem, an Impressed American Seaman, 1803–1814: From the Originals in the Possession of Caroline L. Martin," *EIHC*, 68 (1932), 321–29; William M. Byant, *The Old Sailor: A Thrilling Narrative of the Life and Adventures of Elias Hutchins, During Forty Years on the Ocean.—Related By Himself* (Biddeford, Me., 1853); Lane, *The Wandering Boy*; *Niles' Weekly Register*, 9 (Sept. 9, 1815), 30; Epes Sargent, "Epes Sargent's Account of a British Press Gang in 1803," *EIHC*, 88 (1952), 19–23; Christopher Backman to Joseph Sims, Mar. 1, 1814, Box 611, Naval Records Collection, RG 45, NA; Mathias Conkle to James Monroe, Jan. 14, 1814, Box 611, Naval Records Collection, RG 45, NA. Herman Melville captures the experience of being impressed in "Billy Budd, Sailor," in Harold Beaver, ed., *Billy Budd, Sailor and Other Stories* (New York, 1967), 317–409.

109. Penny, *Life and Adventures*.

Chapter 6. Free Trade and Sailors' Rights

1. Samuel Leech, *A Voice from the Main Deck: Being a Record of the Thirty Years' Adventures of Samuel Leech*, introduction and notes by Michael J. Crawford (Annapolis, 1999; orig. pub. 1843), viii. For general descriptions of the battle see James Fenimore Cooper, *The History of the Navy of the United States of America* (New York, 1988; orig. pub. 1841); William Fowler, *Jack Tar and Commodores: The United States Navy, 1783–1815* (Boston, 1984), 176–77.

2. Leech, *Voice from the Main Deck*, 80–90.

3. Ibid., 85–86.

4. Ibid., 91–95.

5. Ibid., 95–117.

6. Ibid., 129–31.

7. Ibid., 84–98.

8. Ibid., 108–9.

9. Ibid., 110–11.

10. Ibid., 118, 127–28.

11. Ibid., 134.

12. Ibid., 135–36.

13. Ibid., 140–41.

14. Ibid., 155–211.

15. Ibid., xxi-xxii, 194.

16. Ibid., 117–18.

17. United States, *American State Papers: Documents, Legislative and Executive, of the Congress of the United States* . . . (Washington, D.C., 1832), 3:405–8.

18. *The Inaugural Addresses of the Presidents of the United States, 1789–1985* (Atlantic City, N.J., 1985), 16.

19. Several vessels raised a pendant with that slogan from the masthead. See Fowler, *Jack Tar and Commodores*, 162–84; Donald R. Hickey, *The War of 1812: A Forgotten Conflict* (Urbana, Ill., 1989), 90–99.

20. Fowler, *Jack Tar and Commodores*, 205–6.

21. Amos A. Evans, *Journal Kept on Board the Frigate "Constitution," 1812* (Lincoln, Mass., 1967; orig. pub. 1895), 382, 472–73; Moses Smith, *Naval Scenes in the Last War* . . . (Boston, 1846), 38–39; Fowler, *Jack Tars and Commodores*, 177.

22. Hickey, *War of 1812*, 154–57. See also Ira Dye, *The Fatal Cruise of the "Argus": Two Captains in the War of 1812* (Annapolis, 1994).

23. James Fenimore Cooper, ed., *Ned Myers; or, a Life Before the Mast*, introduction and notes by William S. Dudley (Annapolis, 1989; orig. pub. 1843), 53–54.

24. Ibid., 63–64.

25. Ibid., 76–100.

26. Ibid., 132–33.

27. Ibid., 111.

28. Ibid., 117.

29. Leech, *Voice from the Main Deck*, 118, 121–23, 127–28; Smith, *Naval Scenes*, 6.

30. Smith, *Naval Scenes*, 41–42.

31. David S. Heidler and Jeanne T. Heidler, eds., *Encyclopedia of the War of 1812* (Santa Barbara, Calif., 1997), 429.

32. May 11–27, 1813, Logbook, *Young Teazer*, Maritime Records, MeHS.

33. Accounts of *Thomas* Privateer Schooner, 1813, GWBWL. For further discussion of privateers during the War of 1812 see Jerome R. Garitee, *The Republic's Private Navy: The American Privateering Business as Practiced by Baltimore During the War of 1812* (Middletown, Conn., 1977); Wilfred Harold Munro, "The Most Successful American Privateer: An Episode of the War of 1812," American Antiquarian Society, *Proceedings*, 23 (1913), 12–62.

34. Josiah Cobb, *A Green Hand's First Cruise: Roughed Out From the Log-Book of Memory, of Twenty-Five Years Standing* . . ., 2 vols. (Boston, 1841), 1:40–55.

35. George Little, *Life on the Ocean; or Twenty Years at Sea* . . . (New York, 1843), 197, 220.

36. *The Trial of John H. Jones, First Lieutenant of the Privateer Schooner "Revenge"* . . . (Philadelphia, 1813); B. J. Vernon, *Early Recollections of Jamaica, with the Particulars of an Eventful Passage Home Via New York and Halifax, at the Commencement of the American War in 1812* . . . (London, 1848), 81–82.

37. Joseph Valpey, Jr., *Journal of Joseph Valpey, Jr. of Salem, November 1813–April 1815: With Other Papers Relating to His Experience in Dartmoor Prison* (n.p., 1922), 5.

38. Benjamin Waterhouse, *A Journal of a Young Man of Massachusetts, Late a Surgeon on Board an American Privateer, Who Was Captured at Sea by the British* . . . (Lexington, Ky., 1816), 6–7. The author of this journal was not Benjamin Waterhouse, who was born in 1754. Instead the true author of the book was Amos G. Babcock who had served aboard the privateer *Enterprise*, was captured, and was a prisoner of war during the War of 1812. Babcock approached Waterhouse with his journal, and the older doctor agreed to edit it.

It was published under Waterhouse's name. Because it is listed in all bibliographic references under Waterhouse, to avoid confusion, references in the text simply refer to Waterhouse as the author and the person who lived through the imprisonment experience. See Henry R. Viets, "A Journal of a Young Man of Massachusetts . . . Written By Himself, Boston: 1816 and a Note on the Author," *Yale Journal of Biology and Science*, 12 (1940), 605–22.

39. For general discussion of the prisoner-of-war experience in the War of 1812 see Francis Abell, *Prisoners of War in Britain, 1756 to 1815: A Record of Their Lives, Their Romance and Their Sufferings* (London, 1914); Justin Atholl, *Prison on the Moor: The Story of Dartmoor Prison* (London, 1953); Anthony G. Dietz, "The Use of Cartel Vessels During the War of 1812," *AN*, 28 (1968), 165–94; Ira Dye, "American Maritime Prisoners of War, 1812–1815," in Timothy J. Runyan, ed., *Ships, Seafaring and Society: Essays in Maritime History* (Detroit, 1987), 293–320; Robin F. A. Fabel, "Self-Help in Dartmoor Prison: Black and White Prisoners in the War of 1812," *JER*, 9 (1989), 165–90; Reginald Horsman, "The Paradox of Dartmoor Prison," *American Heritage*, 26 (1975), 12–17, 85; Basil Thomson, *The Story of Dartmoor Prison* (London, 1907). For a contemporary description of Dartmoor see John Melish, *A Description of Dartmoor Prison, with an Account of the Massacre of the Prisoners . . .* (Philadelphia, 1816).

40. Cobb, *A Green Hand's First Cruise*, 1:104–17, 157–61. For similar behavior when captured see Waterhouse, *Journal of a Young Man*, 9.

41. Alden White, Daybook, 1813, volume 4, Box 74, Alden White Papers, Biographical Collection, ODHS.

42. Valpey, *Journal*, 43.

43. Robert Stevenson Coffin, *A Concise Narrative of the Barbarous Treatment Experienced by American Prisoners in England and the West Indies . . .* (Danville, Vt., 1816), 23–24.

44. Charles Andrews, *The Prisoner's Memoirs, or Dartmoor Prison, Containing a Complete and Impartial History of the Entire Captivity of the Americans in England . . .* (New York, 1815), 34–35. For celebrations in 1813 and 1814 in a prison ship see Waterhouse, *Journal of a Young Man*, 120–27; Francis G. Selman, "Extracts From the Journal of a Marblehead Privateersman Confined on Board British Prison Ships, 1813, 1814, 1815," in Samuel Roads, Jr., *The Marblehead Manual* (Marblehead, Mass., 1883), 61

45. Benjamin F. Palmer, *The Diary of Benjamin F. Palmer, Privateersman: While a Prisoner on Board English War Ships at Sea, in the Prison at Melville Island and at Dartmoor* (n.p., 1914), 79.

46. Waterhouse, *Journal of a Young Man*, 120–27. For a celebration of the Fourth of July in the West Indies see Nathaniel Hawthorne, ed., *The Yarn of a Yankee Privateer* (New York, 1926), 95–98.

47. Andrews, *The Prisoners' Memoirs*, 93–104.

48. Jeduthan Upton, Jr., April 8–9, 1813, Logbook, *Polly*, typescript, MHS.

49. Waterhouse, *Journal of a Young Man*, 93, 58.

50. Leech, *Voice from the Main Deck*, 134–37.

51. *A Narrative of the Capture of the United States Brig "Vixen" . . .* (New York, 1813), 17–19. For differences in prison governments see Waterhouse, *Journal of a Young Man*, 53–54, 137.

52. Palmer, *Diary*, 19–20, 22, 26, 28, 32, 74, 116–17, 127, 130; Reports Concerning American Prisoners of War of Melville Island prison, John Mitchell Papers, 1812–14, HSP.

53. John Allen, "Trip from the *Jason* prison ship to Dartmoor," 1813, Jacob Reeves Papers, 1809–1835, MHS.

54. Palmer, *Diary*, 24, 29; Upton, April 16, 1813, Logbook. *Polly*, typescript, MHS; Charles Calvert Egerton, *The Journal of an Unfortunate Prisoner, on Board the British Prison Ship "Loyalist," in Jamaica . . .* (Baltimore, 1813), 20–28.

55. Palmer, *Diary*, 117; Upton, April 16, 1813, Logbook, *Polly*, typescript, MHS; Waterhouse, *Journal of a Young Man*, 53–55, 145–46; Allen, "Trip from the *Jason* prison ship to Dartmoor," 1813, Jacob Reeves Papers, 1809–1835, MHS.

56. Andrews, *The Prisoners' Memoirs*, 44–45.

57. Cobb, *A Green Hand's First Cruise*, 2:137; Hawthorne, ed., *Yarn of a Yankee Privateer*, 177–81; Waterhouse, *Journal of a Young Man*, 53–55; Allen, "Trip from the *Jason* prison ship to Dartmoor," 1813, Jacob Reeves Papers, 1809–1835, MHS. For an example of articles of government passed by prisoners see Palmer, *Diary*, 244–46.

58. Andrews, *The Prisoner's Memoirs*, 35–36, 70, 112–17.

59. Even at 6 feet 3 inches, Craftus would have been eight or nine inches taller than the average sailor. See W. Jeffrey Bolster, *Black Jacks: African American Seamen in the Age of Sail* (Cambridge, Mass., 1997), 102–3.

60. Waterhouse, *Journal of a Young Man*, 174; Hawthorne, ed., *Yarn of a Yankee Privateer*, 181–87.

61. Bolster, *Black Jacks*, 108–9.

62. Perez Drinkwater, "Sailing Problems and Examples; Account of Imprisonment in Dartmoor Prison, Feb. 1815," Maritime Records, MeHS. See also *Narrative of the "Vixen,"* 26–28; Alden White, Daybook, 1813, Volume 4, Box 74, Alden White Papers, Biographical Collection, ODHS.

63. Andrews, *The Prisoners' Memoirs*, 72–74; Cobb, *A Green Hand's First Cruise*, 2:23–25; Hawthorne, ed., *Yarn of a Yankee Privateer*, 208–19; L. P. C., "Reminiscences of a Dartmoor Prisoner," *Knickerbocker*, 23 (1844), 517–20. See also Ewart C. Freeston, *Prisoner-of-War Ship Models, 1775–1825* (Annapolis, 1973). Prisoners in other locations also made money through their enterprise. See Coffin, *A Concise Narrative*, 9–10.

64. Cobb, *A Green Hand's First Cruise*, 2:40, 132–36; Hawthorne, ed., *Yarn of A Yankee Privateer*, 208; Waterhouse, *Journal of a Young Man*, 157.

65. Cooper, ed., *Ned Myers*, 119; Leech, *Voice from the Main Deck*, 137; *Narrative of the Vixen*, 18–19; Palmer, *Diary*, 8, 56, 70; Nathaniel Pierce, "Journal of Nathaniel Pierce of Newburyport, Kept at Dartmoor Prison, 1814–1815," *EIHC*, 73 (1937), 27; Waterhouse, *Journal of a Young Man*, 92–93, 157.

66. Cobb, *A Green Hand's First Cruise*, 2:167–70. See also Cooper, ed., *Ned Myers*, 119–20; Palmer, *Diary*, 104.

67. Pierce, "Journal," 53–55.

68. Cobb, *A Green Hand's First Cruise*, 2:172–73.

69. Andrews, *The Prisoners' Memoirs*, 69; Waterhouse, *Journal of a Young Man*, 90–94.

70. Valpey, *Journal*, 16–20; Pierce, "Journal," 33–34.

71. Waterhouse, *Journal of a Young Man*, 174–81; Hawthorne, ed., *Yarn of a Yankee Privateer*, 191–97, 237–40.

72. [Illegible] to James Monroe, April 26, 1816, Box 611, Naval Records Collection, RG 45, NA; Andrews, *The Prisoners' Memoirs*, 80, 91; Cobb, *A Green Hand's First Cruise*, 2:170–72; L. P. C., "Reminiscences," 521–22; John Baker, Jr. to Mr. John Baker, May 14, 1814, War of 1812, MdHS; George Dennison to Father, 1814, Misc. Box 94/16, MeHS; Hawthorne, ed., *Yarn of a Yankee Privateer*, 210–11.

73. Andrews, *The Prisoners' Memoirs*, 56, 252–80; Waterhouse, *Journal of a Young Man*, 97; Upton, April 16, 1813, Logbook, *Polly*, typescript, MHS.

74. Cooper, ed., *Ned Myers*, 106–12.

75. Andrews, *The Prisoners' Memoirs*, 59, 70, 86, 88.

76. Waterhouse, *Journal of a Young Man*, 105, 135–36.

77. Cobb, *A Green Hand's First Cruise*, 2:152–53; Hawthorne, ed., *Yarn of a Privateer*, 223–28; Waterhouse, *Journal of a Young Man*, 171, 183, 191.

78. Cobb, *A Green Hand's First Cruise*, 2:13, 43–53; Pierce, "Journal," 28–29; Waterhouse, *Journal of a Young Man*, 170–72, 183, 192.

79. Egerton, *Journal of an Unfortunate Prisoner*, 30–31, 41.

80. Andrews, *The Prisoners' Memoirs*, 126.

81. Andrews, *The Prisoners' Memoirs*, 33–36, 109; Egerton, *Journal of an Unfortunate Prisoner*, 79–80; Palmer, *Diary*, 17, 24, 39–40, 93, 155; Pierce, "Journal," 28–29; Waterhouse, *Journal of a Young Man*, 15–16, 84, 107, 112, 131–33, 159; Selman, "Extracts from the Journal of a Privateersman," 59, 68–69.

82. Hawthorne, ed., *Yarn of a Yankee Privateer*, 82.

83. Waterhouse, *Journal of a Young Man*, 239.

84. Waterhouse, *Journal of a Young Man*, 167; Andrews, *The Prisoners' Memoirs*, 136–38; Hawthorne, ed., *Yarn of a Yankee Privateer*, 261.

85. Andrews, *The Prisoners' Memoirs*, 61, 130–42, 151 161; Pierce, "Journal," 37; Waterhouse, *Journal of a Young Man*, 191–92; Selman, "Extracts from the Journal of a Privateersman," 71; Hawthorne, ed., *Yarn of a Yankee Privateer*, 244. For similar action in other prisons against volunteers for the British navy see Waterhouse, *Journal of a Young Man*, 97–98.

86. Waterhouse, *Journal of a Young Man*, 172–73.

87. Andrews, *The Prisoners' Memoirs*, 141–49. Cobb says that the British found the man and returned him to solitary confinement. Cobb, *A Green Hand's First Cruise*, 2:199–209.

88. Andrews, *The Prisoners' Memoirs*, 157–61; Cobb, *A Green Hand's First Cruise*, 2:187–91; L. P. C., "Reminiscences," 459–60; Waterhouse, *Journal of a Young Man*, 192–93. For information on Beasley's efforts to help prisoners see Box 566, Naval Records Collection, RG 45, NA.

89. Waterhouse, *Journal of a Young Man*, 75–85.

90. Andrews, *The Prisoners' Memoirs*, 165–70; Cobb, *A Green Hand's First Cruise*, 2:210–13; Hawthorne, ed., *Yarn of a Yankee Privateer*, 264–68; Palmer, *Diary*, 176–78; Pierce, "Journal," 39; Waterhouse, *Journal of a Young Man*, 195–97.

91. United States, *The Debates and Proceedings in the Congress of the United States . . . Fourteenth Congress (1815–1816)* (Washington, D.C., 1854), 1520–24; Cobb, *A Green Hand's First Cruise*, 2:214.

92. United States, *Debates and Proceedings* (1815–1816), 1524; *Niles' Weekly Register*, 8 (Aug. 5, 1815), 390; Palmer, *Diary*, 179–80; Hawthorne, ed., *Yarn of a Yankee Privateer*, 233–77.

93. United States, *Debates and Proceedings* (1815–1816), 1524, 1527, 1535, 1560, 1579.

94. Ibid., 1514.

95. Ibid., 1571–81.

96. Andrews, *The Prisoners' Memoirs*, 172–82; *Niles' Weekly Register*, 8 (July 8, 1815), 321–25.

97. United States, *Debates and Proceedings* (1815–1816), 1528, 1536, 1546, 1570.

98. Palmer, *Diary*, 182; *Niles' Weekly Register*, 8 (June 17, 1815), 267, 283; *Niles' Weekly Register*, 8 (July 8, 1815), 324. Andrews said that the man was stabbed to death on Shortland's order. Andrews, *The Prisoners' Memoirs*, 173–79.

99. United States, *Debates and Proceedings* (1815–1816), 1515, 1530–31, 1548, 1570, 1573, 1575–77.

100. Ibid., 1559–60.

101. Sorting out the narrative of events on April 6, 1815, in Dartmoor is a difficult if not impossible task based on the contradictory evidence that was collected at the time. For

descriptions by American sailors see Andrews, *The Prisoners' Memoirs*, 172–82; Cobb, *A Green Hand's First Cruise*, 2:214–21; Hawthorne, ed., *Yarn of a Yankee Privateer*, 271–79; L. P. C., "Reminiscences," 459–60; 460–63; Palmer, *Diary*, 179–95; Pierce, "Journal," 40–41; Valpey, *Journal*, 27; and *Niles' Weekly Register*, 8 (June 17, 1815), 267–71, 283; *Niles' Weekly Register, 8* (July 8), 321–28; *Niles' Weekly Register,* 8 (Aug. 5, 1815), 389–92. This view, which portrays the Americans as innocent victims, has to be balanced against the evidence collected by the joint Anglo-American commission that investigated the massacre. This testimony can be found in Box 605, RG 45, NA; United States, *Debates and Proceedings* (1815–1816), 1511–81; United States, *American State Papers*, 4:19–56; and *Dartmoor Massacre* [Pittsfield, Mass., 1815].

102. *Niles' Weekly Register*, 8 (July 8, 1815), 321–28; Palmer, *Diary*, 180.

103. Andrews, *The Prisoners' Memoirs*, 182–206; Cobb, *A Green Hand's First Cruise*, 2:221–23; Palmer, *Diary*, 195–98; Waterhouse, *Journal of a Young Man*, 196–233.

104. Andrews, *The Prisoners' Memoirs*, 211; Cobb, *A Green Hand's First Cruise*, 2:222–23.

105. Niles quoted several such stories. *Niles' Weekly Register*, 8 (June 17, 1815), 267–71, 283; *Niles' Weekly Register*, 8 (July 8, 1815), 321–24, 346–47; *Niles' Weekly Register*, 8 (Aug. 5, 1815), 389–92.

106. *Horrid Massacre at Dartmoor Prison, England . . .* (Boston, [1815]); Glover Broughton, *Dartmoor Prison* (n.p., 1815); *Massacre of the American Prisoners of War at Dartmoor Prison on the 6th of April 1815 by the Somersetshire Militia* (n.p., [1815]); John Hunter Waddell, *The Dartmoor Massacre* ([Boston, 1815]).

107. Copies of the King-Larpent Report can be found in United States, *Debates and Proceedings* (1815–1816), 1511–17; *American State Papers*, 4:20–23; and *Dartmoor Massacre*. For the reaction of the American prisoners to the report see *Niles' Weekly Register*, 8 (Aug. 5, 1815), 389–92.

Chapter 7. Proper Objects of Christian Compassion

1. *CHSM*, 9 (Feb. 15, 1823), 602.

2. Henry Chase, Diary (1821–1822) and (1822–1823), NYHS, are full of records of these visits. See also *CHSM*, 10 (Dec. 6, 1823), 445.

3. *CHSM*, 9 (Jan. 18, 1823), 537; *CHSM*, 9 (Feb. 15, 1823), 603.

4. For Chase's general comments on prayer meetings see *CHSM*, 8 (Aug. 18, 1821), 217–18. For other examples of prayer meetings see *CHSM*, 8 (Dec. 15, 1821), 475; *CHSM*, 8 (Mar. 2, 1822), 638–39; *CHSM*, 8 (Apr. 20, 1822), 732–34; *CHSM*, 9 (Dec. 21, 1822), 474–76; *CHSM*, 9 (Jan. 18, 1823), 535; *CHSM*, 9 (Mar. 15, 1823), 671–72; *CHSM*, 9 (Apr. 5, 1823), 701–4; *CHSM*, 9 (May 5, 1823), 785–86; *CHSM*, 10 (Dec. 20, 1823), 479–80; *CHSM*, 11 (Feb. 21, 1824), 126–28; *CHSM*, 11 (Mar. 20, 1824), 191.

5. *CHSM*, 9 (Feb. 15, 1823), 602–3.

6. Chase, "Diary," Jan. 2, 1823 (1822–1823), NYHS.

7. For Truair and his money raising efforts see *CHSM*, 8 (Jan. 19, 1822), 544; *CHSM*, 9 (June 15, 1822), 87–89; *CHSM*, 9 (Sept. 21, 1822), 287–88; *CHSM*, 9 (Jan. 18, 1823), 535; *CHSM*, 9 (Mar. 1, 1823), 671–72; *CHSM*, 9 (Nov. 16, 1822), 436; *CHSM*, 9 (Dec. 7, 1822), 443–48; *CHSM*, 10 (Nov. 15, 1823), 416; *CHSM*, 10 (Dec. 20, 1823), 480; *CHSM*, 11 (Mar. 20, 1824), 189–90. For problems with debt see *CHSM*, 9 (June 1, 1822), 64; *CHSM*, 10 (July 5, 1823), 123; *CHSM*, 10 (Aug. 2, 1823), 187; *CHSM*, 10 (Sept. 6, 1823), 255–56. For Chase's dismissal see *CHSM,* 11 (Nov. 20, 1824), 714. See also *CHSM*, 9 (June 15, 1822), 89.

8. Nathan O. Hatch, *The Democratization of American Christianity* (New Haven, 1989);

Christine Leigh Heyrman, *Southern Cross: The Beginnings of the Bible Belt* (New York, 1997); Paul E. Johnson, *A Shopkeeper's Millennium: Society and Revivals in Rochester, New York, 1815–1837* (New York, 1978).

9. Edward Dorr Griffin, *The Claims of Seamen: A Sermon Preached November 7, 1819, in the Brick Church, New-York; For the Benefit of the Mariner Missionary Society of that City* (New York, 1819), 7.

10. For surveys on reform see Alice Felt Tyler, *Freedom's Ferment: Phases of American Social History from the Colonial Period to the Outbreak of the Civil War* (New York, 1944); Ronald G. Walters, *American Reformers, 1815–1860* (New York, 1978). See also Roger E. Carp, "The Limits of Reform: Labor and Discipline on the Erie Canal," *JER*, 10 (1990), 191–219; Myra C. Glenn, *Campaigns Against Corporal Punishment: Prisoners, Sailors, Women and Children in Antebellum America* (Albany, 1984); Roald Kverndal, *Seamen's Missions: Their Origin and Early Growth: A Contribution to the History of the Church Maritime* (Pasadena, Calif., 1986); Harold D. Langley, *Social Reform in the United States Navy, 1798–1862* (Urbana, 1967).

11. Griffin, *The Claims of Seamen*, 17–18; *CHSM*, 8 (Jan. 5, 1822), 504; Langley, *Social Reform*, 45–50. For comprehensive coverage of British efforts see Kverndal, *Seamen's Missions*, 71–404.

12. *The Naval Chaplain, Exhibiting A View of American Efforts to Benefit Seamen* (Boston, 1831), 31–35; George Sidney Webster, *The Seaman's Friend: A Sketch of the American Seaman's Friend Society, By Its Secretary* (New York, 1932), 5. The Boston organization, formed in 1812 with the "support of the most distinguished commercial gentlemen" of the city, mainly distributed tracts and advocated prayer on ships. It struggled during the War of 1812. See Boston Society for the Religious and Moral Improvement of Seamen, *An Address to Masters of Vessels on the Objects of the Boston Society for the Moral and Religious Improvement of Seamen* (Boston, 1812), and *The First Annual Report of the Executive Committee of the Boston Society for the Religious and Moral Improvement of Seamen* (Boston, 1813). See also Langley, *Social Reform*, 50–51; and Kverndal, *Seamen's Missions*, 417–34.

13. Stafford described all of his missionary efforts in New York in *New Missionary Field: A Report to the Female Missionary Society for the Poor of the City of New-York and Its Vicinity, at Their Quarterly Prayer Meeting, March 1817* (New York, 1817). He then published separately extracts from that pamphlet that pertained to seamen in *Important to Seamen. Extracts From a report Entitled New Missionary Field* (New York, 1817). These publications became the clarion for action to reach out to the waterfront with missionary work. For Stafford's impact as a catalyst in forming auxiliary societies elsewhere see Samuel B. Ingersoll, *Address, Delivered Before the Marine Bible Society of New-Haven, Auxiliary to the Marine Bible Society of New-York: With a Particular Address to Seamen* (New Haven, 1819). See also *The Mariner's Church* ([New York, 1818]); and *The Naval Chaplain*, 35–37; *CHSM*, 8 (July 7, 1821), 22–24; *CHSM*, 8 (Jan. 5, 1822), 504–11; *SM*, 8 (Sept. 1835), 28–35.

14. For discussion of the middle class, reform, and religion in the nineteenth century see Stuart M. Blumin, *The Emergence of the Middle Class: Social Experience in the American City, 1760–1900* (Cambridge, 1989); Johnson, *A Shopkeeper's Millennium*; Mary P. Ryan, *Cradle of the Middle Class: The Family in Oneida County, New York, 1790–1865* (Cambridge, 1981); and Anthony F. C. Wallace, *Rockdale: The Growth of an American Village in the Early Industrial Revolution* (New York, 1972).

15. A list of the managers can be found in *CHSM*, 8 (Oct. 6, 1821), 315. Occupations were checked in a New York City directory. Only one was an artisan, listed as a house carpenter and joiner (he may well have been a builder given his home address on Broadway). The others who were not identified as merchants or captains were either not listed or their

names were too common to provide a clear identification. For example, there were too many Joseph Smiths and John Taylors to provide a positive identification. (Both names had a merchant listed among other occupations.) Jona Olmsted, *Longworth's American Almanac, New-York Register and City Directory* (New York, 1819).

16. The Graham connection was important enough that it was mentioned in Bethune's obituary. *CHSM*, 11 (Oct. 16, 1824), 626–32. For Graham see Paul A. Gilje and Howard B. Rock, eds., *Keepers of the Revolution: New Yorkers at Work in the Early Republic* (Ithaca, N.Y., 1992), 275–80.

17. Jack M. Seymour, *Ships, Sailors and Samaritans: The Woman's Seamen's Friend Society of Connecticut, 1859–1976* (New Haven, 1976).

18. *CHSM*, 9 (July 20, 1822), 155–60; *CHSM*, 9 (Jan. 18, 1823), 537–40; *CHSM*, 9 (Feb. 1, 1823), 574–76; *CHSM*, 11 (June 5, 1824), 345–50; *The Naval Chaplain*, 40–42, 71–74; *SM*, 8 (Oct. 1835), 48–55; *SM*, 8 (Nov. 1835), 73–80; *SM*, 8 (Dec. 1835), 111–13; *SM*, 8 (Feb. 1836), 176–79; *SM*, 8 (Mar. 1836), 209–11; *SM*, 8 (Apr. 1836), 231–35; *SM*, 8 (June 1836), 304–7; *SM*, 8 (July 1836), 345–48.

19. *SM*, 2 (June 1830), 311–12; *SM*, 2 (July 1830), 376; *SM*, 3 (Oct. 1830), 56–57; *SM*, 3 (June 1831), 300–321; *SM*, 4 (Feb. 1832), 195.

20. John Truair, *Call from the Ocean. Or an Appeal to the Patriot and Christian in Behalf of Seamen* (New York, 1826); Hugh H. Davis, "The American Seamen's Friend Society and the American Sailor, 1828–1838," *AN*, 39 (1979), 45–57; Langley, *Social Reform*, 51–67; Webster, *The Seamen's Friend*, 17–29; *The Naval Chaplain*, 85–87; *SM*, 9 (July 1828), 1; *SM*, 9 (Nov. 1836), 74–77.

21. Abiel Abbot, *The Mariner's Manual: A Sermon Preached in Beverly, on Lord's Day, March 4, 1804* (Salem, Mass., 1804).

22. *SM*, 4 (Apr. 1832), 241.

23. See Joseph Emerson, *A Chart for Seamen; Exhibited in a Sermon Preached in Beverly, March 18, 1804. Particularly Addressed to Seamen* (Salem, Mass., 1804); William Miltimore, *Seamen's Farewell: A Discourse, Preached in Falmouth, at the Meeting-House Erected by Seamen, Near the Water. February 22, 1811* (Portland, Me., 1811); *God's Wonders in the Great Deep, Recorded in Several Wonderful and Amazing Accounts of Sailors, Who Have Met with Unexpected Deliverance from Death . . .* (Newburyport, Mass., 1805); Barnabas Downs, Jr., *A Brief and Remarkable Narrative of the Life and Extreme Sufferings of Barnabas Downs, Jun.* ([Boston], 1786).

24. *SM*, 7 (Nov. 1834), 65.

25. *CHSM*, 10 (May 17, 1823), 31–32; *SM*, 10 (Apr. 1838), 233–41; *SM*, 10 (May 1838), 364–69; *SM*, 10 (July 1838), 437–40; *SM*, 10 (Aug. 1838), 468–72; *SM*, 11 (Sept. 1838), 15–19.

26. *The Naval Chaplain*, 43.

27. *SM*, 15 (July 1843), 331.

28. *SM*, 5 (Sept. 1832), 12–13.

29. Report of the Agent, Dec. 10, 1843, Box 1, Bible Society of Salem and Vicinity, PEM.

30. *The Naval Chaplain*, 43.

31. *CHSM*, 11 (Mar. 7, 1824), 153–54.

32. Chase, "Diary" Jan. 9, 1823 (1822–1823), NYHS.

33. *SM*, 3 (June 1831), 304.

34. For references to the prodigal son see *SM*, 2 (Jan. 1830), 159; *SM*, 4 (Mar. 1832), 224. For sentimental references to mothers see *CHSM*, 9 (Oct. 5, 1822), 319–20; *SM*, 7 (May 1835), 281–82; *SM*, 10 (May 1838), 388; *SM*, 13 (Sept. 1838), 28–29; *SM*, 14 (Jan. 1842), 155; *SM*, 15 (May 1843), 280; *SM*, 16 (Nov. 1843), 91–92, 96, 102–3; *SM*, 16

(July 1844), 336; *SM*, 17 (Jan. 1845), 145; *SM*, 18 (Nov. 1845), 72–73; *SM*, 19 (Apr. 1847), 234.

35. *First Annual Report of the Board of Managers of the New-Bedford Port Society For the Moral Improvement of Seamen* . . . (New Bedford, 1831), 4.

36. Griffen, *The Claims of Seamen*, 7–9.

37. *CHSM*, 10 (July 19, 1823), 153–54.

38. *Mariner's Church*, 7.

39. *SM*, 3 (Feb. 1831), 194; *SM*, 3 (July 1831), 359–60.

40. *SM*, 16 (June 1844), 303.

41. *SM*, 5 (Sept. 1832), 12.

42. *CHSM*, 10 (Aug. 16, 1823), 214–16; Marine Bible Society of New-York, *Constitution of the Marine Bible Society of New-York, Auxiliary of the American Bible Society* . . . (New York, 1817), 7–12.

43. *CHSM*, 8 (Oct. 6, 1821), 313. See also *CHSM*, 10 (July 19, 1823), 155–56; *CHSM*, 10 (Sept. 2, 1823), 281–85; *SM*, 7 (June 1835), 299–300; Truair, *Call from the Ocean*, 8–9.

44. *CHSM*, 10 (July 19, 1823), 153–54.

45. W. P. Grinnell to Samuel Rodman, Oct. 31, 1833, New-Bedford Port Society Misc. Papers, ODHS.

46. Marine Bible Society of New-York, *Constitution*, 5.

47. *SM*, 6 (Jan. 1834), 160.

48. Record of Meetings, May 17, 1830, New-Bedford Port Society, ODHS. See also *SM*, 7 (Jan. 1835), 144–45.

49. *SM*, 17 (Mar. 1845), 217–20.

50. *CHSM*, 8 (June 2, 1821), 60–62; Truair, *Call from the Ocean*, 3–6.

51. Chase, "Diary," Jan. 31, 1823 (1822–23), NYHS.

52. *SM*, 9 (July 1837), 343.

53. Moses How, "Diary," July 15, 1848, NBFPL.

54. *SM*, 3 (Dec. 1830), 114–16.

55. Richard Marks, *The Shipmates. An Evening Conversation; Being a Supplement to the Tract Intitled, Conversation in a Boat* (Hartford, 1818). See also Kverndal, *Seamen's Missions*, 167.

56. Boston Society for the Religious and Moral Improvement of Seamen, *A Sailor's Tribute of Gratitude to Two Virtuous Women* (Boston, 1812). For examples of other tracts see Gamaliel Bradford, *The Seaman's Friend* (Boston, 1817); *Dialogue Between Two Seamen After a Storm* ([Hartford], 1816); Hannah Mather Crocker, *The School of Reform, or Seaman's Safe Pilot to the Cape of Good Hope* (Boston, 1816).

57. Richard Henry Dana, Jr., *Two Years Before the Mast: A Personal Narrative of Life at Sea*, Thomas Philbrick, ed. (New York, 1986; orig. pub., 1840), 479.

58. *SM*, 9 (Sept. 1836), 34; *SM*, 10 (Jan. 1838), 147–48; *SM*, 11 (Dec. 1838), 125–26.

59. Unfortunately Chase did not provide any titles of tracts he distributed. Chase, "Diary" (1822–23), Jan. 7, 1823, NYHS.

60. *SM*, 22 (June, 1850), 290–300.

61. How, "Diary," July 15, 1846, NBFPL. See also Chase, "Diary" (1821–1822) (1822–1823), NYHS; Report of the Agent, Dec. 10, 1843–Dec. 22, 1844, Box 1, Bible Society of Salem and Vicinity, PEM; John Moffat Howe, "Diary," 1837, NYHS; Joseph Tuckerman, "Diary," 1826–1827, 1829, MHS.

62. On the proper and improper use of nautical language for sermons see *SM*, 19 (Apr. 1847), 225–27. For examples of sermons with nautical metaphors see *SM*, 1 (Mar. 1829), 201–5; *SM*, 6 (Sept. 1833), 31. For an example of the Reverend Taylor's sermon see *SM*, 6 (Nov. 1833), 68–73. See also Kverndal, *Seamen's Missions*, 493–99, 638–39.

63. Chase, "Visits to Families of Mariners, Nov. 18, 1821 to Dec. 18, 1821," NYHS; Jan. 5, Feb. 8, Mar. 8, Sept. 11, 1822, Jan. 10, 13, 21, Feb. 4, 12, 1823, "Diary" (1821–22), NYHS; *CHSM*, 8 (Aug. 18, 1821), 218; *CHSM*, 8 (Mar. 2, 1822), 638–39; *CHSM*, 8 (Apr. 20, 1822), 732–34; *CSHM*, 9 (Dec. 21, 1822), 473–75; *CSHM*, 9 (Jan. 18, 1823), 535–37; *CSHM*, 9 (Apr. 5, 1823), 701–3; *CSHM*, 10 (Nov. 1, 1823), 383; *CSHM*, 10 (Nov. 20, 1824), 706–13.

64. Record of Meetings, July 1, 1830, Oct. 28, 1831, New-Bedford Port Society, ODHS; *Second Annual Report of the Board of Management of the New-Bedford Port Society for the Improvement of Seamen* (New Bedford, 1832), 9; *Twelfth Annual Report of the Board of Management of the New-Bedford Port Society for the Improvement of Seamen*, 6–7.

65. Chase, Sept. 11, 1822, "Diary" (1822–23), NYHS.

66. *CHSM*, 11 (Apr. 17, 1824), 248. See also *First Annual Report of the Board of Directors of the Boston Seamen's Friend Society* (Boston, 1829), 6–8.

67. *SM*, 2 (Dec. 1829), 111–12.

68. *SM*, 3 (Sept. 1830), 12.

69. *SM*, 5 (Apr. 1833), 236; *SM*, 7 (June 1835), 301; *SM*, 7 (July 1835), 325–27; *SM*, 7 (Aug. 1835), 365–66; *SM*, 8 (Oct. 1835), 46–48; *SM*, 9 (Apr. 1837), 238–45; *SM*, 9 (May 1837), 271–72; *SM*, 10 (Nov. 1837), 78–80; *SM*, 10 (Dec. 1837), 105–10; *SM*, 11 (Feb. 1839), 185–87.

70. *SM*, 2 (July 1830), 357.

71. *CHSM*, 11 (Feb. 7, 1824), 93–96.

72. *SM*, 3 (Mar. 1831), 228; *SM*, 7 (June 1835), 210–11; *SM*, 12 (May 1840), 283; *SM*, 14 (Mar. 1842), 228–29; *SM*, 18 (July 1846), 349–50; *SM*, 22 (Aug. 1850), 373. See also [Seaman's Bank for Savings], *The Seaman's Bank for Savings in the City of New York: One Hundred Fifteen Years of Service, 1829–1944* ([New York], 1944). For other savings banks see *SM*, 7 (Oct. 1834), 47; *SM*, 12 (Sept. 1839), 13.

73. *CHSM*, 11 (Apr. 17, 1824), 250–51.

74. *CHSM*, 11 (Jan. 17, 1824), 59; *SM*, 2, (May 1830), 293; *SM*, 3 (June 1831), 303; *SM*, 6 (May 1834), 288.

75. *SM*, 10 (Apr. 1838), 357–58; *SM*, 11 (Sept. 1838), 13–14; *SM, 11* (June 1839), 308; *SM*, 11 (Aug. 1839), 375–76; *SM*, 12 (Apr. 1840), 259.

76. *SM*, 7 (Jan. 1835), 296–97; *SM*, 8 (Nov. 1835), 80–82; *SM*, 9 (Jan. 1837), 156–57; *SM*, 9 (Mar. 1837), 211–13; *SM*, 10 (Oct. 1837), 67; *SM*, 10 (Dec. 1837), 129; *SM*, 10 (Jan. 1838), 161; *SM*, 10 (Mar. 1838), 212–15; *SM*, 10 (June 1838), 409; *SM*, 11 (Oct. 1838), 70–71; *SM*, 11 (Dec. 1838), 125; *SM*, 12 (Dec. 1839), 131; *SM*, 12 (June 1840), 304; *SM*, 13 (Oct. 1840), 66–67; *SM*, 13 (June 1841), 308–10. For statements on the effectiveness of this early Sailor's Home in New York see R. Gelston to Executive Committee, July 31, 1838, Box 1, ASFS Papers, GWBWL; Report of the Sailor's Home for the year ending Oct. 31, 1838, Box 2, ASFS Papers, GWBWL.

77. *SM*, 14 (Nov. 1841), 89–90.

78. *SM*, 15 (Jan. 1843), 153; George Duncan Campbell, "The Sailors' Home," *AN*, 37 (1977), 179–84.

79. *SM*, 18 (June 1846), 291–93.

80. *SM*, 12 (Dec. 1839), 131; *SM*, 12 (Feb. 1840), 186; *SM*, 12 (June 1840), 325; SM, 14 (Feb. 1842), 197; *SM*, 15 (Jan. 1843), 157; *SM*, 18 (June 1846), 291, 382–86; *SM*, 19 (June 1847), 291; *SM*, 21 (Aug. 1849), 372; *SM*, 22 (May 1850), 286.

81. *SM*, 18 (June 1846), 292–93. For more on Boston reform efforts see William Sullivan, *Sea Life; or What May or May Not Be Done, and What Ought to be Done By Ship-Owners, Ship-Masters, Mates, and Seamen* (Boston, 1837).

82. *SM*, 21 (July 1849), 352.

83. *SM*, 16 (Mar. 1844), 228–29; *SM*, 17 (Apr. 1845), 228–29; *SM*, 19 (Feb. 1846), 185–86; *SM*, 21 (Aug. 1849), 372–73. See also Kverndal, *Seamen's Missions*, 519–21. For similar organizations in Boston and Salem see *Seamen's Widow and Orphan Association of Salem* (Salem, Mass., 1843); John Brazer, *The Duty and Privilege of an Active Benevolence* . . . (Salem, Mass., 1836); [Seamen's Aid Society], *Ninth Annual Report of the Seamen's Aid Society of the City of Boston* (Boston, 1842).

84. *SM*, 19 (June 1847), 298. Baxter's Saint's Rest refers to Richard Baxter, *The Saint's Everlasting Rest, or a Treatise of the Blessed State of the Saints in the Enjoyment of God in Heaven* . . . (London, 1649), a tract republished several times in the eighteenth and nineteenth centuries.

85. The committee was also trying to find out how many vessels had liquor aboard. "Letters from Ship Owners and Captains to a Committee that had Enquired about Shipping Liquor and Books on Board Their Ships," Request made Oct. 31, 1833, New-Bedford Port Society, Misc. Papers, ODHS.

86. All but *Horrible Murders* are easily identified. Martingale Hawser, *Tales of the Ocean, and Essays for the Forecastle Containing Matters and Incidents Humorous, Pathetic, Romantic and Sentimental* (Boston, 1841); Eugene Sue, *The Mysteries of Paris* (New York, n.d.); *Pirates Own Book or, Authentic Narratives of the Lives and Exploits, and Executions of the Most Celebrated Sea Robbers* . . . (Philadelphia, 1839). *Horrible Murders* may refer to *Four Great and Horrible Murders, or Bloody News from Islington* . . . (London, 1674).

87. These authors are identified by name. The reference is probably to John Bunyan's *Pilgrim's Progress*, which went through countless editions, and the often reprinted Baxter's *Saint's Rest* and John Flavel, *Navigation Spiritualized; or a New Compass for Seamen, Consisting of XXXII Points* . . . (Newburyport, 1796). See also *SM*, 11 (Feb. 1839), 194–95; *SM*, 13 (July 1841), 345.

88. *SM*, 3 (May 1831), 269; *SM*, 19 (May 1847), 262; *Twelfth Annual Report . . . of the New-Bedford Port Society* . . ., 7; Ch. Berry Wackford to Charles W. Morgan, July 9, 1848, Box 41, Swift and Allen Collection, ODHS. See also Marine Bible Society (Charleston), *First Annual Report of the Marine Bible Society. Charleston, South-Carolina, Auxiliary to the American Bible Society, Presented April 19, 1819* (Charleston, 1819); Marine Bible Society of New-York, *Report of the Marine Bible Society of New-York; at their First Anniversary Meeting, April 21, 1817* (New York, 1817), and *The Third Annual Report of the Marine Bible Society of New-York, Auxiliary to the American Bible Society* (New York, 1819).

89. Boston Society for the Religious and Moral Improvement of Seamen, *Address to a Master of a Vessel, Intended to Accompany a Book of Prayers Prepared for the Use of Seamen* (Boston, 1815), 4–5.

90. *SM*, 12 (Jan. 1840), 149.

91. *SM*, 19 (May 1847), 270–72.

92. Boston Society for the Religious and Moral Improvement of Seamen, *Address to a Master*, 9–10; *SM*, 1 (Dec. 1828), 126; *SM*, 2 (Oct. 1829), 43–44; *SM*, 2 (May 1830), 297–99; *SM*, 5 (Oct. 1832), 57–58; *SM*, 5 (Jan. 1833), 137–40; *SM*, 7 (Dec. 1834), 99–109; *SM*, 7 (Apr. 1835), 231–32; *SM*, 8 (Nov. 1835), 86; *SM*, 8 (May 1837), 293; *SM*, 11 (Mar. 1839), 208–15; *SM*, 11 (July 1839), 344.

93. *SM*, 12 (June 1840), 307–8; quote from *SM*, 14 (Jan. 1842), 156.

94. *SM*, 14 (Mar. 1842), 221.

95. *SM*, 9 (May 1837), 286.

96. *SM*, 14 (Mar. 1842), 221; *SM*, 18 (Apr. 1846), 242.

97. *SM*, 2 (May 1830), 277; *SM*, 4 (Dec. 1832), 123; *SM*, 7 (Dec. 1834), 99–109; *SM*, 7 (Apr. 1835), 250–52.

98. Langley, *Social Reform*, 227.

99. *SM*, 1 (Mar. 1829), 210.

100. *SM*, 14 (Mar. 1842), 220–21; *SM*, 15 (June 1843), 292.

101. *SM*, 2 (Feb. 1830), 190; *SM*, 2 (May 1830), 280–81; *SM*, 3 (Dec. 1830), 110–12; *SM*, 5 (Nov. 1832), 65–66; *SM*, 5 (Nov. 1849), 92; *SM*, 14 (Jan. 1842), 156; *SM*, 19 (May 1847), 273; *SM*, 22 (Nov. 1849), 92; *SM*, 22 (Dec. 1849), 119. For a general discussion see Langley, *Social Reform*, 207–69.

102. *SM*, 18 (Nov. 1845), 86–87.

103. *SM*, 22 (Feb. 1850), 177–79.

104. John Adams drew up the first regulations for the Continental navy. Although he hoped to limit excessive punishment, he accepted flogging as an instrument of discipline. The naval regulations of the 1790s and early 1800s were also modeled on British precedent and continued to allow the use of the lash. Robert J. Taylor, *Papers of John Adams*, 8 vols. (Cambridge, Mass., 1979–), 146–56; James E. Valle, *Rocks and Shoals: Order and Discipline in the Old Navy, 1800–1861* (Annapolis, 1980), 38–40, 77–83; Major Leo F. S. Horan, "Flogging in the United States Navy: Unfamiliar Fact Regarding Its Origin and Abolition," *United States Naval Institute Proceedings*, 76 (1950), 969–75.

105. Glenn, *Campaigns Against Corporal Punishment*, 9–12, 128–29; Langley, *Social Reform*, 148–69.

106. *SM*, 18 (Nov. 1845), 86–87.

107. Jane Litten, "Navy Flogging: Captain Samuel Francis Du Pont and Tradition," *AN*, 58 (1998), 145–65. See also Valle, *Rocks and Shoals*, 248–52.

108. Quotations are in Glenn, *Campaigns Against Corporal Punishment*, 112–30. See also Langley, *Social Reform*, 170–206.

109. *SM*, 1 (Mar. 1829), 195.

110. Dana, *Two Years Before the Mast*, 151–57.

111. J. G. Hodge to Dana, Oct. 15, 1842, Box 8, Dana Family Papers, I, 1841–1842, MHS.

112. In good middle-class style, the author added a concern for property by saying that it was also "one of the surest safeguards against piracy, plunder, and death." *CHSM*, 9 (Jan. 18, 1823), 535.

113. *SM*, 19 (Dec. 1846), 120–21.

114. *SM*, 19 (Mar. 1847), 208.

115. *SM*, 1 (Dec. 1828), 114–15.

116. *SM*, 6 (Mar. 1834), 223.

117. *SM*, 1 (Apr. 1829), 245–48.

118. *SM*, 7 (Sept. 1834), 15.

119. Dana, *Two Years Before the Mast*, 469–72.

120. Quoted in Langley, *Social Reform*, 147.

121. Valle, *Rocks and Shoals*, 81–82.

122. Dana, *Two Years Before the Mast*, 392–94, 477–83. The *Sailor's Magazine* admitted that Dana's criticism held true in some cases. *SM*, 13 (Feb. 1841), 180–81.

123. *SM*, 15 (Aug. 1843), 371–72.

124. Nathaniel Ames, *Nautical Reminiscences* (Providence, 1832), 47–48.

125. Hugh Calhoun, "Journal, 1847–1848," 33, MHS.

126. Jacob A. Hazen, *Five Years Before the Mast, or Life in the Forecastle Aboard of a Whaler and Man-of-War*, 2nd ed. (Philadelphia, 1854), 205–16.

127. Simeon Crowell, "Commonplace Book of Simeon Crowell," 1818–46, 1854–56, MHS.

128. James Fenimore Cooper, ed., *Ned Myers; or, a Life Before the Mast*, introduction and notes by William S. Dudley (Annapolis, 1989; orig. pub. 1843), xvii–xviii.

129. Chase, Jan. 2, 1823, "Diary" (1822–1823), NYHS.

130. John Hoxse, *The Yankee Tar. An Authentic Narrative of the Voyages and Hardships of John Hoxse* . . . (Northampton, [Mass.], 1840); Samuel Leech, *A Voice from the Main Deck: Being a Record of the Thirty Years' Adventures of Samuel Leech*, introduction and notes by Michael J. Crawford (Annapolis, 1999; orig. pub. 1843), 143–44.

131. William Alfred Allen to Parents and Brother, Mar. 1845, Box 5, Business Records Collection, ODHS.

132. James Webb to his Mother (1846–47), Box 84, Business Records Collection, ODHS.

133. *CHSM*, 9 (Dec. 21, 1822), 474–76.

134. *SM*, 18 (June 1846), 300.

135. *SM*, 4 (Mar. 1832), 224. See also *SM*, 10 (Feb. 1835), 191–92; *SM*, 13 (Mar. 1841), 208–12.

136. Horace Lane, *The Wandering Boy, Careless Sailor, and Result of Inconsiderateness. A True Narrative* (Skaneateles, N.Y., 1839).

Chapter 8. The Ark of the Liberties of the World

1. The biographical material in this and the subsequent paragraphs is drawn from Hershel Parker, *Herman Melville: A Biography, Volume I, 1819–1851* (Baltimore, 1996). On the sea experience of Melville's cousins see pp. 141–42.

2. Ibid., 143–86.

3. Ibid., 189–289.

4. Herman Melville, *Typee: A Peep at Polynesian Life During a Four Months' Residence in a Valley of the Marquesas* (New York, 1964; orig. pub. 1846).

5. Parker, *Melville*, I, 231, 264.

6. Parker, Melville, I, chapters 18–40. For further discussion of these works see William B. Dillingham, *An Artist in the Rigging: The Early Work of Herman Melville* (Athens, Ga., 1972); Robert K. Martin, *Hero, Captain, and Stranger: Male Friendship, Social Critique, and Literary Form in the Sea Novels of Herman Melville* (Chapel Hill, N.C., 1986).

7. Melville, *Typee*, 82–116.

8. Herman Melville, *Omoo: A Narrative of Adventures in the South Seas*, Harrison Hayford et al., eds. (Evanston, Ill., 1968; orig. pub. 1847), 38–40.

9. Herman Melville, *Redburn: His First Voyage. Being the Sailor-boy Confessions and Reminiscences of the Son-of-a Gentleman, in the Merchant Service*, Harold Beaver, ed. (New York, 1976; orig. pub. 1849), 181–83.

10. Melville, *Redburn*, 119.

11. Herman Melville, *White Jacket: or the World in a Man-of-War*, Harrison Hayford et al., eds. (Evanston, Ill., 1970; orig. pub. 1850), chapters 33–36.

12. Melville, *White Jacket*, 144, 151.

13. Parker, *Melville*, I, 276–77, 392, 460.

14. Ibid., 409, 418, 431–35.

15. Ibid., 214.

16. On Melville's reading and use of the literature of the sea see Parker, *Melville*, I, 231–33, 268–70, 454–56, 499, 659, 694–95, 698, 723. J. N. Reynolds, "Mocha Dick: or the White Whale of the Pacific: A Leaf from a Manuscript Journal," *Knickerbocker*, 13 (1839), 377–92; Owen Chase, "Narrative of the Most Extraordinary and Distressing

Shipwreck of the Whaleship *Essex*, of Nantucket . . .," in Thomas Farel Heffernan, *Stove by a Whale: Owen Chase and the "Essex"* (Hanover, N.H., 1981), 15–76.

17. Hugh McKeever Egan, "Gentlemen-Sailors: The First Person Narratives of Dana, Cooper, and Melville" (Ph.D. diss., University of Iowa, 1983); Thomas Philbrick, *James Fenimore Cooper and the Development of American Sea Fiction* (Cambridge, Mass., 1961); Philbrick, Introduction to Richard Henry Dana, Jr., *Two Years Before the Mast* (New York, 1959; orig. pub. 1840), 7–29.

18. James Fenimore Cooper, *The Pilot: A Tale of the Sea* (New York, n.d.; orig. pub. 1823), 12.

19. Quoted in Philbrick, *James Fenimore Cooper*, 116.

20. James Fenimore Cooper, *The Red Rover* (New York, n.d.; orig. pub. 1828), 19; Philbrick, *James Fenimore Cooper*, 79–83, 127–31.

21. Jacob A. Hazen, *Five Years Before the Mast, or, Life in the Forecastle Aboard of a Whaler and a Man-of-War*, 2nd ed. (Philadelphia, 1854); J. S. Henshaw, *Around the World: A Narrative of a Voyage in the East India Squadron, Under Commodore George C. Reed, By an Officer of the U.S. Navy*, 2 vols. (New York, 1840).

22. James Fenimore Cooper, ed., *History of the Navy of the United States of America*, 2nd ed., 2 vols. (Philadelphia, 1840).

23. James Fenimore Cooper, *The Wing-and Wing, or Le Feu-Follet. A Tale*, Thomas Philbrick, ed. (New York, 1998; orig. pub. 1842).

24. James Fenimore Cooper, *Ned Myers; or, A Life Before the Mast*, introduction and notes by William S. Dudley (Annapolis, 1989; orig. pub. 1843); Philbrick, *James Fenimore Cooper*, 129–31.

25. James Fenimore Cooper, *The Cruise of the "Somers": Illustrative of the Despotism of the Quarter Deck; and of the Unmanly Conduct of Commander Mackenzie* (New York, 1844), 5–8; Egan, "Gentlemen-Sailors."

26. Philbrick, introduction to Dana, *Two Years Before the Mast*, 22.

27. Dana, *Two Years Before the Mast*, 151–66, 392–94, 462–83.

28. Ibid., 28, 482.

29. Richard Henry Dana, Jr., *Cruelty to Seamen, Being the Case of Nichols and Couch* (Berkeley, 1937; orig. pub. 1839). Petition to Congress, Drawn by R. H. Dana, Jr., ca. 1840, Box 39, Dana Family Papers, I, MHS; *The Seaman's Friend* (Delmar, N.Y., 1979; orig. pub. 1851).

30. Daniel Defoe, *Life and Adventures of Robinson Crusoe*, Angus Ross, ed. (New York, 1965; orig. pub. 1719); Parker, *Melville*, I, 392, 460.

31. Charles H. Barnard, *A Narrative of the Sufferings and Adventures of Capt. Charles H. Barnard* . . . (New York, 1829); Joshua Penny, *The Life and Adventures of Joshua Penny, A Native of Southhold, Long Island* . . . (New York, 1815).

32. Robert Adams, *The Narrative of Robert Adams* (Boston, 1817); Daniel Saunders, Jr., *A Journal of the Travels and Sufferings of Daniel Saunders* . . . (Salem, Mass., 1794).

33. James Riley, *An Authentic Narrative of the Loss of the American Brig "Commerce"* (Hartford, 1817). See also Robert J. Allison, *The Crescent Obscured: The United States and the Muslim World, 1776–1815* (New York, 1995), 207–25.

34. R. Thomas, *Interesting and Authentic Narratives of the Most Remarkable Shipwrecks, Fires, Famines, Calamities, Providential Deliveries, and Lamentable Disasters on the Seas in Most Parts of the World* (Boston, 1835); *God's Wonders in the Great Deep, Recorded in Several Wonderful and Amazing Accounts of Sailors, Who Have Met with Unexpected Deliverances from Death* . . . (Newburyport, 1805); *Ben Boatswain's Yarns* (n.p., 1840); William Allen, *Accounts of Shipwreck and other Disasters at Sea, Designed to be Interesting and Useful to Mariners* . . . (Brunswick, Me., 1823).

35. Daniel Defoe, *The Life and Adventures, and Piracies of Captain Singleton*, Sir Walter Scott, ed. (reprint of the 1840 edition, New York, 1973; orig. pub. 1720); Maximillian E. Novak, *Daniel Defoe, Master of Fictions: His Life and Times* (Oxford, 2001), 642.

36. *The History of the Pirates, Containing the Lives of Those Most Noted Pirate Captains* . . . (Haverhill, Mass., 1825); *The Pirates Own Book, or Authentic Narratives of the Lives, Exploits, and Executions of the Most Celebrated Sea Robbers* (Salem, Mass., 1924; orig. pub. 1837).

37. Sir John Barrow, *The Eventful History of the Mutiny and Piratical Seizure of the HMS Bounty: Its Causes and Consequences* (London, 1831). One of the most famous mutinies in the early nineteenth century occurred on the whaleship *Globe*. See William Lay and Cyrus M. Hussey, *A Narrative of the Mutiny Aboard the Whaleship "Globe"* (New York, 1963; orig. pub. 1828).

38. Philbrick, *James Fenimore Cooper*, 10–12.

39. John Blatchford, *Narrative of Remarkable Occurrences in the Life of John Blatchford of Cape-Ann* . . . (New London, 1788); Fanning, *Narrative of the Adventures of an American Navy Officer, Who Served During Part of the American Revolution Under the Command of Com. John Paul Jones, Esq.* (New York, 1806); Joshua Davis, *A Narrative of Joshua Davis, An American Citizen, Who Was Pressed and Served on Board Six Ships in the British Navy* (Baltimore, 1811).

40. Ebenezer Fox, *The Adventures of Ebenezer Fox in the Revolutionary War* . . . (Boston, 1838), vi.

41. On the memory of the American Revolution see Michael Kammen, *A Season of Youth: The American Revolution and the Historical Imagination* (New York, 1978), esp. 41–49; Alfred F. Young, *The Shoemaker and the Tea Party: Memory and the American Revolution* (Boston, 1999), esp. 132–42.

42. John Willcock, *The Voyages and Adventures of John Willcock* . . . (Philadelphia, 1798); Thomas Nicholson, *An Affecting Narrative of the Captivity and Sufferings of Thomas Nicholson* . . . . (Boston, 1816); William Ray, *The Horrors of Slavery: Or the American Tars in Tripoli* (Troy, N.Y., 1808).

43. Davis, *A Narrative of Joshua Davis*; James M'Lean, *Seventeen Years' History, of the Life and Sufferings of James M'Lean. An Impressed American Citizen and Seaman* . . . (Hartford, 1814); Penny, *Life and Adventures*; James Durand, *James Durand: An Able Seaman of 1812: His Adventures on "Old Ironsides" and as an Impressed Sailor in the British Navy*, George S. Brooks, ed. (New Haven, 1926; orig. pub. 1820).

44. Charles Andrews, *The Prisoners' Memoirs, or Dartmoor Prison; Containing A Complete and Impartial History of the Entire Captivity of the Americans in England* . . . (New York, 1815); *A Narrative of the Capture of the United States Brig "Vixen"* . . . (New York, 1813); Robert Stevenson Coffin, *A Concise Narrative of the Barbarous Treatment Experienced by American Prisoners in England and the West Indies* . . . (Danville, Vt., 1816); John Hunter Wadell, *The Dartmoor Massacre* [Boston, 1815]; Benjamin Waterhouse, *A Journal of a Young Man of Massachusetts, Late a Surgeon on Board an American Privateer, Who Was Captured at Sea by the British* . . . (Boston, 1816).

45. Elijah Shaw, *A Short Sketch, of the Life of Elijah Shaw, Who Served for Twenty-Two Years in the Navy of the United States* . . . (Rochester, N.Y., 1843), iii-iv.

46. John Hoxse, *The Yankee Tar: An Authentic Narrative of the Voyages and Hardships of John Hoxse* . . . (Northampton, Mass., 1840); Shaw, *Short Sketch*; William M. Bryant, *The Old Sailor: A Thrilling Narrative of the Life and Adventures of Elias Hutchins, During Forty Years on the Ocean* (Biddleford, Me., 1853); Nathaniel Hawthorne, ed., *The Yarn of a Yankee Privateer* (New York, 1926; portions were originally published in *United States Magazine and Democratic Review*, 1846); Samuel Leech, *A Voice from the Main Deck: Being a Record of the Thirty Years' Adventures of Samuel Leech*, introduction and notes by

Michael J. Crawford (Annapolis, 1999; orig. pub. 1843); Moses Smith, *Naval Scenes in the Last War . . .* (Boston, 1846).

47. C. S. Stewart, *A Visit to the South Seas, in the U.S. Ship "Vincennes," During the Years 1829 and 1830 . . .* (New York, 1970; orig. pub. 1831), 19.

48. Ames, *A Mariner's Sketches* (Providence, 1830); *Nautical Reminiscences* (Providence, 1832).

49. The first edition of Leech's book was titled *Thirty Years at Home, or a Voice from the Main . . .* The twentieth-century edition reversed the title. George Little, *Life on the Ocean; or Twenty Years at Sea . . .* (New York, 1843); Leech, *A Voice from the Maindeck*; Nicholas Peter Isaacs, *Twenty Years Before the Mast, or Life in the Forecastle . . .* (New York, 1845); Henry James Mercier, *Life in a Man-of-War, or Scenes in "Old Ironsides" During Her Cruise in the Pacific . . .* (Boston, 1927; orig. pub. 1841).

50. William Torrey, *Torrey's Narrative . . .* (Boston, 1848).

51. Mercier, *Life in a Man-of-War*, 61. See also S. C. D., "Incidents in the Life of a Sailor," *American Penny*, 2 (Sept. 12, 1846), 499–500.

52. W. A. G., "Fortunes of an Amateur Ragmuffin," *New Yorker*, 8 (Nov. 30, 1839), 162–65.

53. Charles Nordhoff, *Man-of War Life: A Boy's Experience in the United States Navy, During a Voyage Around the World in a Ship-of-the-Line*, introduction and notes by John B. Hattendorf (Annapolis, 1985; orig. pub. 1853), 211, 5.

54. J. Ross Browne, *Etchings of a Whaling Cruise*, John Seelye, ed. (Cambridge, Mass., 1968; orig. pub. 1846), 1.

55. Chapple's account is in Haffernan, ed., *Stove by a Whale*, 219–24; Horace Lane, *The Wandering Boy, Careless Sailor, and Result of Inconsideration. A True Narrative* (Skaneateles, N.Y., 1839).

56. John Eliott, *The Reformed: An Old Sailor's Legacy* (Boston, 1841), iii-iv, 34–35.

57. George Lightcraft, *Scraps from the Log Book of George Lightcraft, Who Was More than Twenty Years a Sailor . . .* (Syracuse, 1847), 88–90; Little, *Life on the Ocean*; Leech, *A Voice from the Maindeck*; Isaacs, *Twenty Years Before the Mast.*

58. Ray, *Horrors of Slavery*, 18–20.

59. Durand, *An Able Seaman of 1812*, 18–19.

60. William McNally, *Evils and Abuses in the Naval and Merchant Service, Exposed; With Proposals For Their Remedy and Redress* (Boston, 1839), 95.

61. Solomon H. Sanborn, *An Exposition of Official Tyranny in the United States Navy* (New York, 1841), 5, 28.

62. Tiphys Aegypytus, *The Navy's Friend, or Reminiscences of the Navy, Containing Memoirs of a Cruise, in the U.S. "Enterprise"* (Baltimore, 1843), vi, 12, 43.

63. F. P. Torrey, *Journal of the Cruise of the United States Ship "Ohio," Commodore Isaac Hull, Commander, in the Mediterranean, In the Years 1839, '40, 41* (Boston, 1841), 23–24.

64. Roland Gould, *The Life of Gould, an Ex-Man-of-War's Man, with Incidents on Sea and Shore . . .* (Claremont, N.H., 1867), 78–79, 191.

65. Torrey, *Journal of the Cruise*, 111.

66. Gould, *Life of Gould*, 191.

67. Hazen, *Five Years Before the Mast*, 181.

68. Browne, *Etchings of a Whaling Cruise*, 50, 315, 495–96.

69. McNally, *Evils and Abuses*, 129–31.

70. Ames, *Nautical Reminiscences*, 73–74.

71. Joseph G. Clark, *Lights and Shadows of Sailor Life, As Exemplified in Fifteen Years' Experience . . .* (Boston, 1847), 311–12.

72. Leech, *A Voice from the Main Deck*, 161.

73. Paul A. Gilje, "The Common People and the Constitution: Popular Culture in New York City in the Late Eighteenth Century," in Gilje and William Pencak, eds., *New York in the Age of the Constitution, 1775–1800* (Rutherford, N.J., 1992), 48–73. Stephen Allen, "The Memoirs of Stephen Allen," typescript, 42, NYHS.

74. Certificate of Membership in the Society of Master Sail Makers of the City of New York, 1795, NYHS.

75. Certificate of Membership, Union Society of Shipwrights and Caulkers, New York, 1790, Museum of the City of New York.

76. Ropemakers Arms, Grand Canal Parade, 1825, New York Public Library. See also Howard B. Rock, "'All Her Sons Join as One Social Band': New York City's Artisanal Societies in the Early Republic," in Howard B. Rock, Paul A. Gilje, and Robert Asher, eds. *American Artisans: Crafting Social Identity, 1750–1850* (Baltimore, 1995), 155–75.

77. Paul A. Gilje and Howard B. Rock, *Keepers of the Revolution: New Yorkers at Work in the Early Republic* (Ithaca, N.Y., 1992), 87–97, 148–49; Sean Wilentz, *Chants Democratic: New York City and the Rise of the American Working Class, 1788–1850* (New York, 1984), 137–38; John H. Morrison, *History of New York Ship Yards* (New York, 1909), 54–91.

78. Bruce Laurie, "'Spavined Ministers, Lying Toothpullers, and Buggering Priests': Third Partyism and the Search for Security in the Antebellum North," in Rock et al., *American Artisans*, 104.

79. Christopher Philips, *Freedoms Port: The African American Community of Baltimore, 1790–1860* (Urbana, Ill., 1997), 78, 172.

80. Peter Linebaugh and Marcus Rediker, "The Many-Headed Hydra: Sailors, Slaves and the Atlantic Working Class in the Eighteenth Century," in Colin Howell and Richard J. Twomey, eds., *Jack Tar in History: Essays in the History of Maritime Life and Labour* (Fredericton, New Brunswick, 1991), 29–30.

81. James Dugan, *The Great Mutiny* (New York, 1965).

82. John Rule, *The Experience of Labour in Eighteenth-Century English Industry* (New York, 1981), 179; C. R. Dobson, *Masters and Journeymen: A Prehistory of Industrial Relations, 1717–1800* (Totowa, N.J., 1980).

83. R. Barrie Rose, "A Liverpool Sailors' Strike in the Eighteenth Century," *Transactions of the Lancashire and Cheshire Antiquarian Society*, 68 (1958), 85–92.

84. Norman McCord, "Early Seamen's Unions in North East England," in Paul Adam, ed., *Seamen in Society* (Bucharest, 1980), part III, 88–95.

85. Marcus Rediker, *Between the Devil and the Deep Blue Sea: Merchant Seamen, Pirates, and the Anglo-American Maritime World, 1700–1750* (Cambridge, 1987), 205–53, 308–9.

86. Melville, *Omoo*, 73–77.

87. Richard Buel, Jr., *In Irons: Britain's Naval Supremacy and the American Revolutionary Economy* (New Haven, 1998), 195; Steven Rosswurm, *Arms, Country, and Class: The Philadelphia Militia and "Lower Sort" During the American Revolution, 1775–1783* (New Brunswick, N.J., 1987), 166.

88. Wm. Jeffrey Bolster, "The Changing Nature of Maritime Insurrection," *Log of Mystic Seaport*, 31 (1979), 14–21. See also the discussion in Briton Cooper Busch, *"Whaling Will Never Do for Me": The American Whaleman in the Nineteenth Century* (Lexington, Ky., 1994), 51–61.

89. Melville, *Omoo*, 73–77.

90. Torrey, *Journal of a Cruise*, 75–76; Hazen, *Five Years Before the Mast*, 111–19; McNally, *Evils and Abuses*, 115.

91. Gould, *Life of Gould*, 198–99, 204–6.

92. *New York Spectator*, Oct. 23, 1802; *New York Evening Post*, Oct. 21, 1802; Paul A. Gilje, *The Road to Mobocracy: Popular Disorder in New York City, 1763–1834* (Chapel Hill, N.C., 1987), 182–83.

93. David J. Saposs says the strike occurred in New York, but the long quotation he includes says the strike took place in Fell's Point, which is in Baltimore. Saposs, "Colonial and Federal Beginnings (to 1827)," in John R. Commons et al., *History of Labour in the United States*, vol. 1 (New York, 1918), 110–11.

94. *New York Evening Post*, Sept. 24, 1827.

95. People v. Joseph Thompson et al., Apr. 11, 1825, Court of General Sessions, Municipal Archives and Records Center, New York City (henceforth CGS); *New York Evening Post*, Mar. 22, 1825; *New York American*, Mar. 22, 1825; *New York Gazette*, Mar. 22, 1825; *New York National Advocate*, Mar. 23, 1825; *New York Statesman*, Mar. 25, 1825; Gilje, *Road to Mobocracy*, 183–85.

96. People v. William Denwick et al., July 16, 1828, CGS; People v. James Perry et al., July 16, 1828, CGS ; People v. John Jackson, July 17, 1828, CGS; People v. Lewis Jackson et al., July 17, 1828, CGS; *New York Evening Post*, July 21, 1828; *New York Gazette*, July, 15, 16, 19, 1828; *New York Statesmen*, July 19, 30, 1828; Gilje, *Road to Mobocracy*, 185–86.

97. Wilentz, *Chants Democratic*, 288.

98. Bruce Laurie, *Working People of Philadelphia, 1800–1850* (Philadelphia, 1980), 21, 90–91.

99. Commons et al., *History of Labour in the United States*, vol. 1; Gilje and Rock, eds., *Keepers of the Revolution*; Bruce Laurie, *Artisans into Workers: Labor in Nineteenth-Century America* (New York, 1989); Laurie, *Working People of Philadelphia*; Rock et al., eds., *American Artisans*; Howard B. Rock, *Artisans of the New Republic: The Tradesmen of New York City in the Age of Jefferson* (New York, 1979); W. J. Rorabaugh, *The Craft Apprentice: From Franklin to the Machine Age in America* (New York, 1986); Ronald Schultz, *The Republic of Labor: Philadelphia Artisans and the Politics of Class, 1720–1830* (New York, 1993); Charles G. Steffen, *The Mechanics of Baltimore: Workers and Politics in the Age of Revolution, 1763–1812* (Urbana, Ill., 1984); Richard B. Stott, *Workers in the Metropolis: Class, Ethnicity, and Youth in Antebellum New York City* (Ithaca, N.Y., 1990); Wilentz, *Chants Democratic*.

100. Michael Farrel v. John Rockwood et al., Feb. 15, 1834, Box 7446 (1833–1834), Police Court Cases, Supreme Court, Municipal Archives and Records Center, New York City; *New York Courier and Enquirer*, Apr. 26, 28, 1834; Gilje, *Road to Mobocracy*, 186–87.

Epilogue

1. David Chacko and Alexander Kulcsar, "Israel Potter: Genesis of a Legend," *WMQ*, 3rd ser., 41 (1984), 365–89; Israel R. Potter, *Life and Remarkable Adventures of Israel R. Potter (A Native of Cranston, Rhode Island): Who Was a Soldier in the American Revolution* (Providence, 1824; facsimile reprint in Herman Melville, *Israel Potter His Fifty Years of Exile*, Harrison Hayford et al., ed.) Evanston, 1982), 286–394. Quote from p. 289.

2. Ibid., 13.

3. Ibid., 84.

4. Ibid., 132–41.

5. Ibid., 169.

6. Ibid., 161.

7. Herman Melville, *Billy Budd, Sailor and Other Stories*, Harold Beaver, ed. (New York, 1967), 321–22.

8. Ibid., 329–31.

9. Ibid., 330–31.

10. Ibid., 363–64, 387.

11. On the relevance of the period see ibid., 323, 332–34, 336–38, 381, 389. For the comparison to the *Somers* mutiny see pp. 390–91. Melville was personally connected to the *Somers* mutiny and defended the prosecution of the supposed mutineers. His cousin Guert Gansevoort was the first lieutenant aboard the *Somers* and played a leading role in the trial of the mutineers. See Hugh McKeever Egan, "Gentleman Sailors: The First-Person Narratives of Dana, Cooper, and Melville" (Ph.D. diss., University of Iowa, 1983).

12. Melville, *Billy Budd*, 397–98.

13. Ibid., 399–409.

Index

Acknowledgments

Over the years that I have worked on this project I have been repeatedly asked how I could write on a maritime subject while living in a land locked state. The answer is simple: with a lot of help from my friends—institutions, libraries, and people. I began research in earnest on this project as a Rockefeller Resident Fellow at the program of Atlantic History and Culture at Johns Hopkins University in 1987–88. I also held a fellowship in the spring of 1991 at the Center for the History of Freedom, Washington University, St. Louis, under the directorship of Richard Davis. My work has been enhanced by funding from the Massachusetts Historical Society, the Peabody Essex Museum, a Summer Stipend from the National Endowment for the Humanities, and two grants from the Oklahoma Humanities Council. The University of Oklahoma has been incredibly generous in its support of my research, providing at least eight separate grants for this project as well as time off and course releases. I would like to particularly thank Deans Paul Bell and Roland Lehr of the College of Arts and Sciences, and Vice Presidents for Research Lee Williams and Eddie Smith for their ongoing support. I am also grateful to the Samuel Roberts Noble Foundation and to President David Boren of the University of Oklahoma for a Samuel Roberts Noble Foundation Presidential Professorship.

I have had the opportunity to present some of my research and findings in publication and as papers. I have incorporated in this volume portions of "Liberty and Loyalty: The Ambiguous Patriotism of Jack Tar in the American Revolution," *Pennsylvania History*, 67 (2000), 165–93; "On the Waterfront: Maritime Workers in New York City in the Early Republic, 1800–1850," *New York History*, 77 (1996), 395–426; "The Extent of Freedom for American Waterfront Workers in the Age of Revolution," in David Konig, ed., *Possessing Liberty: The Conditions of Freedom in the New American Republic*, volume 5, *History of Freedom* (Stanford, Calif.: Stanford University Press and the Center for the History of Freedom, Washington University, St.

Louis, 1995), 109–40. I appreciate the willingness of these publishers to permit me to include material from these essays in this book. I offer a special thanks to Robyn McMillen who traced the ownership of the illustration on the frontpiece and the back cover and to Nick West for permission to use this picture.

I gratefully acknowledge all of the many comments I have received at the numerous institutions where I have presented papers on this subject, including the program of Atlantic History, Culture, and Society at Johns Hopkins University, the Philadelphia Center of Early American History and Culture, Center for the History of Freedom, Washington University, St. Louis, the Virginia Society of Cincinnati at Washington and Lee University, the Rothermere American Institute, Oxford University, Florida International University, University of Glasgow, University of Edinburgh, Peabody Essex Museum, and Massachusetts Historical Society. I presented some preliminary thoughts on the project at the Organization of American Historians meeting in New York City in 1986, and more developed ideas at the conference of the Omohundro Institute of Early American History and Culture at the University of Glasgow in 2001.

A quick look at the notes will indicate the many debts I owe to libraries. My greatest debt is to the University of Oklahoma Library, especially to its interlibrary loan staff, which managed to obtain more old books than I could have imagined. I also thank the libraries at Washington University and Johns Hopkins University during my sojourns at those institutions. The core of my research was in manuscripts at a number of libraries and historical societies. I am deeply indebted to the exceptional staffs of the following institutions: the Beinecke Rare Book and Manuscript Library at Yale University, Center for Maine History, Columbia University Library, Connecticut Historical Society, the G. W. Blunt White Library at Mystic Seaport, the Historical Society of Pennsylvania, the Kendall Whaling Museum, the Library of Congress, the Marblehead Historical Society, the Maryland Historical Society, the Massachusetts Historical Society, the Nantucket Historical Association, the National Archives in New York and Washington, D.C., the New Bedford Free Public Library, the New Hampshire Historical Society, the New-York Historical Society, the New York Public Library, the Old Dartmouth Historical Society at the New Bedford Whaling Museum (now the Kendall Institute, New Bedford Whaling Museum), the Peabody Essex Museum, and the Rhode Island Historical Society. I want to especially thank a few individuals whose guidance in their archives was invaluable, including Kelly Drake at Mystic Seaport, Peter Drummey at the MHS, Michael P. Dyer at the

Kendall, Betsy Lowenstein at Nantucket, Tina Furtado at the New Bedford Free Public Library, Candace B. McKinniss at the New Hampshire Historical Society, Judith Downey at the Old Dartmouth Historical Society, Rick Stattler at the Rhode Island Historical Society, and William T. La Moy, Kathy Flynn, Charity Galbreath, and Irene Axelrod at the Peabody Essex Museum.

The notes also only begin to suggest the debt I owe to the many historians who have gone before me. Although I disagree with their conclusions, and they with mine, without the work of Jesse Lemisch and Marcus Rediker, I might not have ever written this book. I also owe a tremendous debt to the published research of a talented group of maritime historians whose own work I relied on more than the notes suggest. Foremost among this group are Jeff Bolster, Margaret Creighton, Ira Dye, Christopher Mckee, and Daniel Vickers.

Several individuals have generously commented on various parts of this manuscript, including Betsy Blackmar, Cathy Brown, Elaine Foreman Crane, Cathy Kelly, John Larson, Simon Newman, and Lisa Norling. My friends Bill Pencak and Frank Cogliano read the entire manuscript and provided much needed advice. Since my semester in St. Louis I have obtained fellowship (not the money kind) and encouragement from my amigos Peter Onuf, Alan Taylor, Jan Lewis, and David Konig. I am grateful to Howard Rock, my sometime collaborator, whose continued friendship has been important to me for over twenty years. At the University of Oklahoma I have many supportive colleagues, none more so than Robert Griswold, who on the Great Plains has heard more about sailors than he thought possible and who as the chair of the history department has supported this project in more ways than I can recount. I must also acknowledge the staff of the Department of History—Barbara Million, Rhonda George, and Suzi Goerlach—for a thousand kindnesses that have made my life easier and have facilitated the writing of this book.

I owe a heartfelt thanks to Dan Richter for his comments on the manuscript, and to Bob Lockhart and the University of Pennsylvania Press for their enthusiasm for the book. I must also say thank you to Noreen O'Connor for her careful sharpening of my prose as my copyeditor.

Although I have never sailed upon the ocean, I grew up in Brooklyn less than a mile from the sea. The maritime world was all around me. When I was little we had boarders in our house who were Norwegian seamen. My father's best friends had all been to sea, and I remember visiting some of their ships as a young boy. I had an uncle who worked his way to become a captain on a tanker. I will never forget when another uncle, Gerry Rottingen, who served aboard a whaler as a young man and tried his hand in lobstering as he moved toward retirement, told my family of his youthful experience in the South Atlantic in the 1930s. My fondest memories of my father-in-law, Karl Liebermann, are of his relating stories about serving in the Norwegian navy and sailing the world over aboard an oil tanker. I suspect that I could not have written this book without this background, and I must acknowledge a debt to this vicarious exposure to a more recent maritime culture.

My family, as always, has been my mainstay. I began this book as my son, Erik, entered kindergarten. It is published shortly before he graduates college. My daughter, Karin, was not yet two during my sabbatical year at Johns Hopkins. Now she helps me check quotations and notes and will soon start her own college career. Most important of all has been the years of love and affection I have shared with my wife, Ann.